The Archaeology of Celtic Britain and Ireland

The image of the Celt is one of the most emotive in the European past, evoking pictures of warriors, feasts and gentle saints and scholars. This comprehensive and fully illustrated book re-appraises the archaeology of the Celtic-speaking areas of Britain and Ireland from the late fourth to the twelfth centuries AD, a period in which the Celts were a leading cultural force in northern Europe. Drawing on recent scientific advances, the book provides a new perspective on the economy, settlement, material culture, art and technological achievements of the early medieval Celts and re-examines their interaction with the Romans and Vikings. Including a full survey of artefacts and archaeological sites, from memorial stones to monasteries, this is essential reading for any student or scholar with an interest in Celtic archaeology, history or culture.

LLOYD LAING is Associate Professor of Archaeology at the University of Nottingham.

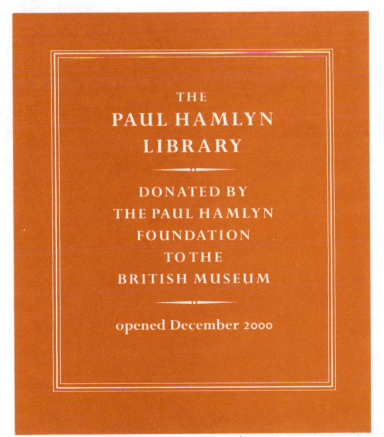

THE
PAUL HAMLYN
LIBRARY

DONATED BY
THE PAUL HAMLYN
FOUNDATION
TO THE
BRITISH MUSEUM

opened December 2000

D0322941

The Archaeology of Celtic Britain and Ireland

C. AD 400–1200

LLOYD LAING

WITHDRAWN

CAMBRIDGE
UNIVERSITY PRESS

CAMBRIDGE UNIVERSITY PRESS
Cambridge, New York, Melbourne, Madrid, Cape Town, Singapore, São Paulo

Cambridge University Press
The Edinburgh Building, Cambridge CB2 2RU, UK

Published in the United States of America by Cambridge University Press, New York

www.cambridge.org
Information on this title: www.cambridge.org/9780521547406

© Lloyd Laing 2006

This publication is in copyright. Subject to statutory exception
and to the provisions of relevant collective licensing agreements,
no reproduction of any part may take place without
the written permission of Cambridge University Press.

First published 2006

Printed in the United Kingdom at the University Press, Cambridge

A catalogue record for this publication is available from the British Library

THE BRITISH MUSEUM
THE PAUL HAMLYN LIBRARY
WITHDRAWN

936.1 LAI

ISBN-13   978-0-521-83862-7 hardback
ISBN-10   0-521-83862-2 hardback

ISBN-13   978-0-521-54740-6 paperback
ISBN-10   0-521-54740-7 paperback

Cambridge University Press has no responsibility for
the persistence or accuracy of URLs for external or
third-party internet websites referred to in this publication,
and does not guarantee that any content on such
websites is, or will remain, accurate or appropriate.

Contents

Figures

vi

Preface

When I wrote the first edition of this book, some thirty-five years ago, I had been hired to teach university students early medieval archaeology. In my first academic post I did not realize how difficult it would be both for them and me, to find our way through the hotch-potch of conflicting, inadequate data, dubious source material and incomprehensible papers in obscure journals. I felt I had no option but to try to make some sense of it.

The world has moved on, and many areas which caused problems are now seen as irrelevant, unimportant or solved by modern technology and new approaches. There has also been a revival of interest in the Celts, who currently inspire literature, films, fashion, art and popular events.

The one fact remains: the term Celtic is one of the most emotive in the European past. The concept is strong from Spain to France and Switzerland, and Celtic peoples have included the Galatians of the Bible and Caesar's opponents, the Gauls. It is no less strong in the areas which border the Irish Sea, that are the subject of this book – present day Wales, Scotland, Ireland, the Isle of Man and the south-west peninsula of England (often termed the Insular Celts as opposed to the Continental).

The most enduring image of the Celts includes firelit feasts where druids recited poetry, and the exploits of heroes and kings. It is the world of Caratacus, Queen Boudicca, King Arthur, and (on the Continent), Vercingetorix who fought the Romans and gained historical fame. It takes only a small feat of imagination to deck the halls with sumptuous treasures and a few fey, spirited red-haired maidens for good measure. For less secular moments we can indulge in images of clerics defending church treasures against the Viking looters or painstakingly applying rich colours to sumptuous manuscripts.

Particularly thirty years ago, this picture, gleaned mostly from poetic sources, did not fit the dry, mundane realities of the archaeological material.

The time-span covered in this book roughly coincides with the period between the Roman presence in Britain and the Norman presence in Britain and Ireland. Thirty years ago, the end of the Roman period in Britain (traditionally, AD 409) was still seen as a cut-off point, despite the fact that many traditions were seen to have started well before that time and to have continued past 800. In 1970 not only were technological advances such as pollen analysis, tree-ring dating or geophysical survey relatively undeveloped for this period and area, but study of literary sources was less well advanced.

Even the basic question 'Who were the Celts?' has created academic turmoils. For most of the twentieth century there was major resistance to any suggestion that the Celtic areas were influenced from outside. In search of the 'pure' Celtic culture, some scholars approached the subject by trying to prove or disprove points for which there was simply insufficient data available. Other difficulties were created because forceful personalities could not be questioned.

Sometimes, it seems, individual scholars were simply determined not to agree. Over the centuries the Celtic areas became separated from one another not only linguistically and politically but by religious beliefs. By the nineteenth century they were often in competition with one another on many fronts, so academic study of the past became drawn into their controversies.

The fact that research grants and promotions have been largely unavailable for the writing of syntheses has furthered the compartmentalizing of interests and a certain introversion in which not all evidence available has been taken into account.

Interpretation of both the written and material remains has often kindled bitter controversies which, if traced to their origins, can sometimes be seen to have been based on what (by today's standards of scientific investigation) appear to be the most tenuous of arguments and flimsiest of evidence.

There has been a tendency to assign a site to the period on the grounds that it does not readily conform to what is known about sites of other periods: 'if it isn't obviously Iron Age or later medieval, it must be Dark Age.' An example of this is the site at Dalmahoy (Midlothian, Scotland) which has never been excavated, but was assigned to the early medieval period on the strength of a small piece of gold foil found in fieldwalking, and then became the type site in all discussions of similar-looking sites.

Similarly circular arguments were applied in art history. The Tara brooch was dated from the Ardagh chalice, and the Ardagh chalice dated from the Tara brooch, for example.

Today, it remains difficult to gain a balanced survey of the period, less because of constrictions on voicing ideas, than because of the uneven survival of material and equally uneven research fields. However, there is now more interest in the European milieu in which the Celts operated than in any perceived Celtic isolation. This view appears easier to justify at the present state of knowledge.

The situation at present is therefore unsatisfactory. Some areas of knowledge have stagnated simply because there has been insufficient time to reappraise them in the light of advances in other subjects and areas. It has therefore not been possible in this volume to trace every statement or assumption to its origins for minute scrutiny. The positive side of this is that there is still plenty of scope for students to shine through reappraisal of material.

On a more general front, there is a continuing problem over terminology. I have generally speaking used the terms early medieval or post-Roman to mean roughly AD 350–800, depending on the context and region. The many alternatives – Dark Ages, late Iron Age, early Christian, pagan Saxon, sub-Roman are also in common use for the same period, and their usage in other publications is outlined in Appendix 3.

This edition of the book began as a simple 'update'. It has required a virtual rewrite. It has been a back-breaking, time consuming and soul-destroying task. The width of available research methods have both aided and hindered the production of an overview. The subjects used to research the Celts range from the very highly scientific to art history, linguistics, history, archaeology and ethnology. I therefore assume that readers may be familiar with one or some of the subjects, but not necessarily all, and have endeavoured to remove as much jargon as is feasible. For example, those who are immediately familiar with words such as parallelopiped, ingate and skeuomorphic may well not be instantly aware of the implications of MNI, VCP and ARS. My guess is that those cognizant with terms such as argentiferous galena or plough pebbles, may not even be aware the significance of triskeles, peltas, language death, colophons, totenmemoria or the cumdach of the cathach of Columcille.

I have tried to provide a guide to give students and the general reader an insight into the type of material available and the state of knowledge to (approximately) late 2004.

The more complex or obscure arguments have been omitted, while, hopefully, I have pointed those interested in the right direction. The size of the bibliography itself (which is far from exhaustive), will give some idea of the vastness of the subject and the difficulties of creating an understandable outline. I have listed short descriptions of the groups of people discussed in the book in Appendix 1, and some of the individuals mentioned in Appendix 2.

Finally, with the passage of nearly four decades, even the original title of the book *The Archaeology of Late Celtic Britain and Ireland* (which was in itself a change in approach at the time), has become outmoded.

My thanks are due to colleagues, friends and family who have read sections, or all of this book and in particular Graeme Cavers, William Gillies, David Longley, Ross Trench-Jellicoe and Niamh Whitfield, who have made helpful comments on the text. I am also indebted to those who helped with the illustrations, particularly Sophie Brown, Charlotte Jones and David Taylor. Jennifer Laing very kindly cut some 20,000 words from the penultimate draft on the grounds that the general reader would not relish the more abstruse and unintelligible, jargon-ridden arguments and descriptions.

Introduction: Who were the Celts?

In the first century BC, the Iron Age peoples in western Europe, now known as Celts, were organized into tribes, many of which were gradually enveloped by the Roman world. The conquest of Gaul (now, roughly France) was followed after AD 43 by the creation of the province of Britannia which eventually included all of what is now England, Wales and Scotland south of the Forth–Clyde line.

Ireland, the Isle of Man and northern Scotland including the Hebridean and Northern Isles (the subject of this book) were affected by the Roman world to a far lesser degree.

Direct Roman dominance in Britannia lasted less than four centuries. By the late fourth century, a complex of factors including civil unrest as well as pressure from tribes such as the Huns, Goths and Vandals beyond the Rhine and Danube frontiers, led to control of Britannia being gradually run down. In 410, pleas of aid to the emperor Honorius were met with the famous statement that the Britons should 'look to their own defences' (Zosimus, 6.10.2). Society was forced to function with regional and local organization without direction from an overall power source. Historical sources virtually ended – for many reasons, including the fact that Britannia ceased to be of interest to Roman commentators. What happened in the following two centuries has therefore traditionally been termed the 'Dark Ages'. Until the development of archaeology, what happened during this period was open to conjecture.

Historical and archaeological sources agree on the basics: from the early fifth century, the highly Romanized east, central and southern England received immigrations and subsequent overlordship by the Anglo-Saxons from the continent.[1] The first incomers were almost certainly deliberately recruited to help defend Britannia against other raiders and settlers, but there appears to have been a gradual take-over of power. This began in the east and south-east of England and had spread westwards by the late fifth century. It is significant that relations between those outside Anglo-Saxon territories continued to be as hostile to the new overlords as they had been to the Romans.

Significantly, the 'Celtic' world received no Continental migrants, though there were a few movements within the area: the Scots (from Ireland), established the kingdom of Dál Riata in Scotland in c. 500, for example. Anglo-Saxon supremacy over the former Britannia at its greatest extent took over two centuries to complete, so that there were noticeable gaps between Roman and

1

Anglo-Saxon control in southern Scotland and the extreme south-west of England. Pressure was exerted on Wales, but large-scale conquest was not achieved until the thirteenth century. The organization seems to have reverted to the former tribal areas, with distinctly Roman features. It is clear that the late Roman world was seen as a model for many aspects of life and culture (chs. 12 and 13).

Ireland, Northern Scotland and the Isle of Man continued to develop what was essentially the continuation of the Iron Age society of the first centuries BC/AD. However, the areas were also heavily indebted to the Roman world (chs. oo and oo). Even the more remote Celtic lands were forced to take note of what was happening outside. Christianity was already spreading from Roman Britain to the Celtic areas by the later fourth century (possibly earlier), and was reinforced from the fifth with contacts from the Christian continent. St Palladius was allegedly sent to Ireland from Rome in 431. Written records gradually become available to historians once more.

The Angles of Northumbria (which included Bernicia) successfully pressed on the lands of the Britons of southern Scotland from the later sixth century. By the mid-seventh century the Saxon kingdom of Mercia presented a constant threat to the Welsh. The West Saxons (of Wessex) exerted pressure on Dumnonia (the extreme south-west of England) though did not achieve conquest until 838.

Northern Scotland, Ireland, the Isle of Man and to a lesser extent Wales, suffered attacks and settlements from the Vikings (also known as the Norse) from Scandinavia from the end of the eighth century. These events stretched through the ninth and tenth centuries with an impact that lasted until the twelfth. The looting and burning of monasteries was recorded by monks, who were inevitably biassed against the newcomers. More peaceful aspects are also apparent in the settlement patterns and the art of the period.

In 1066 England was invaded by the Normans (themselves originally Vikings who had settled in northern France). The result was, that by the twelfth century, almost all areas of Celtic post-Roman Britain, were subject to Norman overlordship and the world of the late Iron Age/post-Roman Celtic Briton was over.

The quest for the Celts

The mystery of what happened to the British and Irish Celts during the fifth and sixth centuries has attracted much research and speculation over the past three centuries. The areas which did not come under direct Roman dominance were most successful in resisting Anglo-Saxon and Viking inroads and, significantly, retained cultural features that distinguish them from their neighbours. The temptation to trace lines of direct descent from prehistory into modern times has proved irresistible and as a result there have been many heated debates. It has even been doubted (to the intense irritation of those who regard themselves as Celts today) whether it was ever, or indeed is, meaningful to speak of Celts or Celtic society at all.

The main approaches have been through linguistics, history, art history, politics, social history and archaeology and have been applied variously to the period roughly 600 BC to the present day.

The linguistic approach

The concept of the 'Celts' owes its existence to Classical writers (Rankin, 1987). The Celts figure in the writings of Herodotus (*Histories*, 2.33), in the fifth century BC as a group of people who 'lived beyond the Pillars of Hercules' (the Straits of Gilbraltar) at the 'extreme west of Europe'. The Greek ethnographer Poseidonius provided an account of their culture. Caesar was explicit that the Gauls were Celts, but there was a certain vagueness as to which other groups of people the Greeks and Romans encountered were actually Celts, and where the limits of their territories were.

The term 'Celtic' was first used in the context of Britain by the leading humanist and Classical scholar George Buchanan (1506–82), who argued that the clearest evidence for the origins of the population of Britain was to be found in languages (Collis, 2003: 34–40). In the late seventeenth and eighteenth centuries the concept of the Celts as a unified and widespread group was taken up by a Breton monk, Paul-Yves Pezron (1639–1706), who defined Welsh as a Celtic language. An Oxford scientist, Edward Lhuyd (1660–1709), built on the work of Pezron and defined (in his *Glossography*, 1707) two language groups – the P (Brythonic) and Q (Goidelic) Celtic (Collis, 2003: 48–52). This viewpoint remains persuasive – partly because from the fragmentary evidence it is likely that the people Classical writers knew as Celts spoke a language belonging to the same family.

The Celts in the period under review had (as far as is known) no collective noun for themselves. Although Classical writers use the term 'Celts' with reference to some of the inhabitants of Continental Europe, they did not use it in relation to any of the people in Britain during either the pre-Roman Iron Age or the Roman occupation of Britannia. The term was similarly not used by any writer in early medieval Britain, Ireland or Continental Europe.

The eighth-century Northumbrian churchman/historian the Venerable Bede, stated that 'This island . . . contains five nations, the English, Britons, Scots, Picts and Latins, each in its own peculiar dialect' (Bede, *Historia Ecclesiastica* I. 1). However, there is still no firm evidence that the people to whom Bede referred regarded themselves as having a collective identity: he notably did not use the term 'Celt'. The Irish in the early medieval period sometimes called themselves *Féni*, or more often *Goídil* ('Gaels'), a word borrowed from the Welsh *Gwyddyl*, which implies that they distinguished between themselves and other people with whom they came into contact (Byrne, 1973: 8). They regarded their language as unique, but recognized some similarities with British, which they thought were due to British borrowings from the Irish (Russell, 2005: 406).

Until the late tenth–eleventh-century poem, the *Armes Prydein Vawr,* there is no evidence that the inhabitants of Wales described themselves as *Cymry* ('Welsh') (Snyder, 2003: 262), though they most certainly recognized cultural identity with the *Gwyr y Gogledd* ('men of the north'), who spoke Welsh and with whom they shared genealogies. The Dalriadic Scots saw themselves as Irish and the Picts referred to themselves as *Prydyn* (earlier Priteni, i.e. Britons). They were named by their Gaelic neighbours as *Cruithin* or *Cruithni* ('the native people').

Some commentators have argued, by extension from prehistory, that there were no 'Celts' in the period covered by this book, simply because the term 'Celt' was not used by any of the people living at the time. However, even if this were accepted, speaking related languages does give a head start in trade and other communications, and the possibility that the 'Celts' had a sense of group identity cannot be dismissed outright. Large areas of the modern world acknowledge elements of common ancestry through strong interaction and cultural assumptions, whilst having no overall group name beyond being, for example, English- or Hispanic-speaking. Certainly the people of the 'Celtic fringe' areas were seen as having distinctive characteristics that set them apart from the English from the fourteenth century onwards (Pittock, 1999: 45). It is notable that the late eighteenth/early nineteenth-century antiquary John Pinkerton was using the term 'Celtic' when asserting that 'Scotland was held back by its degenerate Celtic population' (Pittock, 1999: 56).

The historical approach

The main difficulty in studying the Celts before the development of modern archaeology has been the sparsity of reliable historical sources. The areas were rarely of interest to the chroniclers of literate societies such as the Roman world, and the Celtic language itself was oral (except for a few Iron Age inscriptions, mainly on coins, in somewhat different languages) and largely without texts until the influence of Christianity in the fifth and sixth centuries. In addition, historical material relating to before the late sixth century in both Ireland and Britain is extremely difficult to evaluate since most was set down long after the events concerned. Conversely, once writing was widely introduced, it was so enthusiastically and copiously embraced in Ireland, that it is overwhelmingly difficult to collate with other evidence, particularly for the period from 650 to 850 (Ó Cróinín, 1995: 8). The surviving written evidence for Britain (both Celtic and Germanic) remains extremely fragmentary.

Contemporary documentation required a knowledge of the Latin alphabet and language, and many documents were written for specific purposes not always helpful to modern historians. For example, many sources simply glorify individual saints, list battles, or were designed to entertain the contemporaneous audiences. As with modern biographies or political tracts, the agenda may well have been covert and at this distance in time, unidentifiable. Several historians of the period have concluded that there is almost nothing prior to the end of the sixth century that can be accepted as fact, and that a great deal afterwards is very suspect (Hughes, 1972: 146; Dumville, 1977: 173–4; Laing and Laing, 1990a: 42–4). Nonetheless, readers should be aware of the sources as well as their deficiencies, for each generation and each individual views material anew and rejects or accepts with new insight.

The archaeological approach

Many heated debates have taken place over the archaeological evidence for Celts in Europe and by extension, over the origins of the Celts in Britain and Ireland. The arguments have revolved around whether there were 'Celts' in later prehistoric Britain and Ireland.[2] Through much of the twentieth century, the Celts were identified with the Continental Iron Age cultures known as Hallstatt and La Tène.[3] Dating from the seventh century BC onwards, these were primarily focused successively on Austria and Germany, and Switzerland and France. It was argued that both Britain and Ireland adopted a 'Celtic' culture (and language) after invasion or settlement by people belonging to these cultures. The 'Celtic' culture was then seen to have been retained from the Iron Age to the medieval period in the non-Roman regions of Britain, and (particularly) Ireland.

However, from the 1960s onwards, the idea of Hallstatt and La Tène invasions of Britain and Ireland was increasingly rejected (Cunliffe, 1991: 18–20; S. James, 1999). Although it is reasonable to say that some Celts (known to Caesar as Gauls) possessed La Tène material culture, it does not follow that all Celts necessarily possessed La Tène culture, nor that all people using La Tène objects were Celts.

But if there were no invasions, it was argued, could it be said there were Iron Age Celts in Britain and Ireland at all? It is not invariably true however, that material culture, ideas and language are spread only by invasion or large-scale settlement. Celtic culture, as well as language, could have evolved over a longer time and in a wider area than is suggested if it is rigidly identified with the archaeological cultures of Hallstatt and La Tène. In addition, during the past twenty years there has been growing awareness that Ireland in particular was influenced by the Roman world. The study of early Celtic culture is therefore under considerable process of change in techniques of data retrieval as well as methodology.

The political and social historical approach

In Ireland, especially, through much of the nineteenth century and first half of the twentieth, research was coloured by political factors, tied up with modern nationalism. Interest in the early medieval Celts spread from a scholarly base, to the mass of the Irish population who saw that they were not the barbarians the English made out, but the inheritors of a great culture (Sheehy, 1980: 7). A number of personalities were important: William Wilde, George Petrie, William Wakeman, William Wood-Martin and others, including Margaret Stokes, worked in Ireland in the second half of the nineteenth century (Sheehy, 1980: ch. 2; Edwards, 2005: 236–7). The Celtic Society was founded in 1845, the year that Petrie's magisterial survey of Irish round towers was published (Fig. 1), and a few years before O'Neill's *The Most Interesting of the Sculptured High Crosses of Ancient Ireland* (1857). Among other pioneering studies were W. G. Wood-Martin's *The Lake Dwellings of Ireland* (1886) and *Pagan Ireland* (1895). Their research was often sound for its time, but was driven by growing national feeling and the more widespread interest in medieval antiquities.

Nineteenth- and early twentieth-century social historians were more concerned with establishing the antiquity of Irish institutions using Irish law codes as the basis for their discussions. These centred on the assumption or hope that Celtic society of the early medieval period (and by extension, later) represented a direct survival from prehistory (N. T. Patterson, 1991: ch. 1). Such commentators were concerned with what they perceived as the reality of the Irish past, but by the 1880s the Celtic Revival was under way, coloured by such literary figures at W. B. Yeats and J. M. Synge, and by the Irish version of the Arts and Crafts movement (Sheehy, 1980: ch. 6). There was also a growing concern for the role of language, and of its roots in an Indo-European past.

The Harvard Archaeological Expedition (1932–36) was the real impetus behind modern archaeological research. Hugh O'Neill Hencken and Hallam Movius' objective was to explore the origins of the Irish, so the idea of 'Celtic origins' coloured their work. Hencken's excavations at Cahercommaun, the two Ballinderry crannogs and most importantly Lagore crannog were landmarks in the study (Cooney, 1995). S. P. Ó. Ríordáin and Joseph Raftery (who had worked with Hencken at Ballinderry) continued fieldwork in this tradition by providing a further series of major excavation reports on such sites as Garranes and a group round Lough Gur in the 1940s. However, work was still coloured by a desire to demonstrate the individuality of Ireland, while at the

Fig. 1 Round tower at Swords, Co. Dublin after Petrie, 1832.

same time trying to see how Ireland fitted into the wider European past. Françoise Henry became established as the leading figure in the study of Irish art of the period. Her work was characterized by a fervent pro-Irish nationalism (clearly exemplified in her work on hanging-bowls: F. Henry, 1936).

There was a similar if less intense nationalist movement in Scotland (Bell, 1981). Celtic historical studies were pioneered by William Skene, whose three-volume *Celtic Scotland: A History of Ancient Alban* (1876–80), despite its flaws, remains a classic, and was coloured by a strong patriotic fervour (Sellar, 2001). Joseph Anderson, a dedicated Scottish patriot, felt that a nation's achievements had to be viewed in as wide a perspective as possible (Graham, 1978; Clarke, 2002). His two volumes of *Scotland in Early Christian Times* (1881) were impressive, and his work with the Welsh art historian Romilly Allen resulted in the magisterial *Early Christian Monuments of Scotland* (1903), frequently cited in this book.

Other writers such as Daniel Wilson and Robert Munro were similarly pioneering an understanding of Scottish early medieval antiquities. Despite their work, however (and the long tradition of antiquarianism in Scotland, stretching back to the eighteenth century), Scottish archaeology tended to lapse into provincialism in the first half of the twentieth century, and interest was not widespread among the population in general. In the 1970s (when the first edition of this book was published), there was comparatively little interest in the Picts, either in the popular imagination or in academic circles, but a huge upsurge of national feeling and interest in what has been perceived as 'Celtic mystery' has led to the Picts becoming a focus of attention, as the 'original' inhabitants of the north of Scotland. While some 'Pictophilia' has probably been detrimental, it has also fostered major advances in learning.

In Wales some pioneering work was done on the inscribed stones by J. O. Westwood, an Oxford zoologist, culminating in *Lapidarium Walliae* (1876–9), but widespread interest in the antiquities of early medieval Wales was not effectively kindled until after the Second World War, and then only in scholarly circles (Laing and Laing, 1990a: 21–4).

The art historical approach

The study of Celtic Christian art commenced in earnest in the nineteenth century, when scholars began collecting data bases of sculpture and decorated manuscripts, and publishing the major pieces of ornamental metalwork. Study of art has been hampered by the lack of context – manuscripts and major pieces of ecclesiastical metalwork, for example, were very mobile, and travelled between monasteries (Laing and Laing, 1990: 44–6). Very few pieces of fine metalwork have been found in association with other material in archaeological contexts, and most of these have been of limited value in studying artistic developments.

Although sculpture rarely travelled far from where it was carved, it is almost always without an archaeological context. The finds of metalwork from Viking graves are provided with a *terminus ante quem* (earliest period before which the objects could not have been made), but the objects were often very old before they reached their final resting places. Studies of the palaeography and comparative study of texts have been of limited value in the study of illuminated manuscripts, but most study has been concerned with the traditional method of comparing individual motifs and trying to arrange a sequence based on guesswork. The result has been a tendency to date to the eighth century anything that was seen as good quality that did not show obvious Scandinavian influence (J. Raftery, 1981: 89).

When art historians joined forces with prehistorians in attempts to find 'pure' Celtic art by tracing certain motifs back to the Iron Age on the Continent, even further problems arose as assumptions and implications were all too frequently piled upon dubious deductions and inferences.

Modern, scientific advances

Since the first edition of this book the greatest advances have been made with the development of scientific methods of investigation – especially in the laboratory and non-invasively in the field. A major series of radiocarbon dates and dates derived from dendrochronology (tree-ring dating) are beginning to remove the chronological problems. The application of dendrochronology has been particularly useful, since Irish sites often contain well-preserved wood from water-logged contexts (Baillie, 1981; 1993). There have also been some advances in field survey, though detailed regional surveys still remain relatively few (but see now Lacy, 1983; Cuppage, 1986; Buckley and Sweetman, 1991; Toal, 1995; O'Sullivan and Sheehan, 1996 for Ireland, and the RCAHM county surveys for Scotland and Wales).

In Ireland, excavations have included work at the two major sites, Deer Park Farms and Moynagh Lough (both in the process of publication), as well as a wide range of more minor ones. Work at Clonmacnoise is currently producing valuable information on monastic archaeology, as did the work on Reask and High Island.

In Britain, the major landmarks have been the excavation reports on Dunadd and Whithorn, and the reports on the series of 'high status' sites investigated by Leslie Alcock, most notably Dundurn, Dunollie and Dumbarton Rock. The final reports on Cadbury Castle and on Cadbury Congresbury have extended understanding of the archaeology of the south-west of England and a series of more minor sites have added considerable knowledge.

1 The Celtic world

An insight into everyday life in the Celtic world of the early Christian period can be gained through studying many sources – from Law Codes, biographies of early saints and churchmen, poetry, to archaeological objects, sites and art treasures. The snippets of available information do not necessarily reflect the overall situation, yet encouragingly they do exist. Information is available on the structure of society (including the role of women and children), health, religion and many pastimes and pursuits. The limitations and constrictions of the written sources and material remains must be considered for each new piece of evidence.

Written sources

Much insight is gained into Celtic culture through study of written material – which simply did not exist until the Latin alphabet was adopted.

Celtic languages

Linguists use scientific rules to study how languages have developed, and can project back to presumed origins. Celtic languages developed from a parent Indo-European root. Indo-European was probably introduced to Europe at the end of the Neolithic/beginning of the Bronze Age (some have suggested even earlier), and it is generally held that Common Celtic developed after 1000 BC and that Celtic was being spoken in Britain and Ireland (as well as on the Continent) in the Iron Age, if not the late Bronze Age.[1]

Two main Celtic language families were spoken in the period and region covered by this book, Brittonic/Brythonic (notably Welsh) and Goidelic/Gaelic (notably Irish) (Ball and Fife, 1993). Many scholars in the past saw them developing rapidly around the sixth century AD, but it is now thought that Brittonic Celtic evolved gradually in the early centuries AD and Goidelic Celtic may have developed around the same time-span from a common Insular Celtic source (Ellis Evans, 1990: esp. 174–5). Some conservative speech varieties probably lingered longer, but the fifth–sixth centuries were a crucial period for the development of the language.

This period probably also saw the development in north-west Britain of Cumbric – a language related to Welsh. The introduction of Scots Gaelic to Scotland was the result of Irish settlement in Argyll and the adjacent islands (the kingdom of Dál Riata) and the subsequent expansion of Irish-speaking people in Scotland in the early medieval period (Gillies, 1993: 145). By a similar process the Isle of Man, Brittonic speaking in the fifth century AD, changed its language to Goidelic as a result of Irish settlement.

Literacy

Latin literacy was well established during the Roman period when even the most trivial records were made (A. C. Thomas, 1998: 35). It did not die out in Britain in the fifth and sixth centuries, but was preserved through Christian writings and inscriptions.

There is a growing opinion, for example, that one of the major surviving illustrated manuscripts of the fifth century, the *Vatican Virgil*, was made in Britain (Dark, 1994a: 184–91). The sixth-century British monk, Gildas, whose florid prose has been seen as highly controversial for historical purposes, was highly versed in Latin and had clearly been trained in the late Roman tradition, since he was familiar with Roman law and had a good knowledge of both pagan and Christian Latin texts. Memorial stones of the fifth and sixth centuries in Wales and southern Scotland show that not just writing, but sophisticated Latin word games, were being played (Howlett, 1998; Thomas, 1998 and p. 233). The Roman alphabet must have reached Ireland within the Roman period, since the Irish based their ogham alphabet on it. The earliest ogham inscriptions probably date from the fourth, possibly the third century AD (Harvey, 1990; Harvey, 2001; McManus, 1991).

Loan words from Latin into Old/Middle Welsh and Cornish include not only words derived from the Roman cultural milieu, but also terms likely to have been used by rank-and-file Roman soldiers. The Latin colloquial *privatus* or private was taken into Welsh as *priod* 'betrothed' (Thomas, 1998: 34).

The earliest surviving text is that of the Springmount Tablets (Armstrong and Macalister, 1920). These Roman-style yew tablets were found in 1914 in a bog at Springmount, Ireland. Six leaves were pierced and joined with a leather thong, and the whole was carried with a leather strap. The wax bore the impression of the texts of Psalms 30, 31 and 32, the palaeography suggesting that they were written in the early seventh century or even the late sixth. The use of wax tablets was so well established that the Irish used the Latin word *caraxare* (literally, 'to carve') for writing (Herren, 1982).

Irish schools were greatly admired in the time of Bede (late seventh century), and had probably been established much earlier. There is some indication that education was extended on occasion to women: the Life of St Ciarán of Clonmacnoise records how the daughter of the king of Tara was sent to Finnian at Clonard, to study the psalms and other texts, though not without causing some unease among the other monks (Ó Cróinín, 1995: 181).

Historical sources

Written sources are rarely reliable or unbiased and must be used with caution, since their original aims may well not coincide with the modern researcher's aims or wishes.

Narrative histories

There are very few narrative histories as such. A few Classical sources provide limited information about Roman contacts beyond the frontiers of Britannia within the Roman period, and events after the Romans had withdrawn from the province. These include Ammianus Marcellinus (a fourth-century Greek officer in the Roman army) and Sidonius Apollinaris (A Gaulish letter-writer). Of native sources, only the Venerable Bede and Gildas provide early accounts.

The historicity of the *De Excidio* of Gildas is vigorously debated since he was, like the monastic scribes during the Viking period, unashamedly partisan and partial to a colourful turn of phrase (Lapidge and Dumville, 1984). The *Historia Brittonum*, a ninth-century compilation of texts of different dates, used to be attributed to Nennius (a ninth-century monk) but is now regarded as a compilation which lacks any attempt at critical appraisal (J. R. Morris, 1980; critical discussion of dating, authorship and reliablity in Dumville, 1975–6; 1986).

Written sources for Ireland

The documentary soures for Ireland are varied (Hughes, 1972: chs. 2–4).

Annals

These are the main sources for the history of Ireland: catalogues of events listed chronologically, some of which represent compilations from earlier sources, others of which are based on contemporaneous historical knowledge. The key annals are the *Annals of Ulster*, the earliest surviving text of which dates from the fourteenth century; *The Annals of Tigernach*, which down to the middle of the tenth century used the same source; the *Annals of Clonmacnoise* and the *Annals of Inisfallen*. *The Annals of the Four Masters*, an important source since it contains material otherwise now lost, was compiled in the seventeenth century.

Law tracts

These were first set down in the seventh and eighth centuries, as textbooks for the guidance of legal scholars. There are many, including the *Senchas Már* ('the great old knowledge') compiled in the early eighth century, and the *Crith Gablach* ('the branched purchase'), which dealt with the organization of the *túath* (tribe) (Richter, 1988: 87–90). In addition to secular laws, there was a body of Canon Law, the *Collectio Canonum Hibernensis*, compiled in the early eighth century.

Genealogies and saints' lives

There is copious information derived from royal genealogies, and the lives of saints. Adomnán's *Life of Columba*, Cogitosus' *Life of Brigit*, Muirchú's *Life of Patrick* and Tirechán's *Collectanea*, which relates to St Patrick and a supposed journey he made in northern Ireland (Charles-Edwards, 2000: 9–15), are of particular value.

Written sources for Wales

All the sources are of varying degrees of unreliability, since it is difficult (sometimes even for specialists) to determine fact from fiction, exaggeration and convention (W. Davies, 1982: 198–218).

Annals

The *Annales Cambriae* are notable. The earliest version is bound in with the collection known as the *Historia Brittonum*, attributed to Nennius.

Genealogies

These are king-lists compiled to provide an ancestry (not necessarily strictly accurate) for a ruling dynasty. Notable among existing genealogies are those incorporated in the British Library Harley MS 3859 (which are added with the *Annales Cambriae* to a text of 'Nennius').

Inscriptions

Historical information can sometimes be provided by inscriptions: most of these are simple memorials on tombstones, though a few monuments, such as the Pillar of Eliseg, near Llangollen, provide more information (Bu'lock, 1960a).

Law codes

Of these, the most notable are the *Laws of Hywel Dda*, dating from the tenth century (Charles-Edwards, 1989a).

Other documentary sources

The remaining documentary sources were never intended as historical writings, and consist of Lives of Saints, homilies and other religious tracts, and poetry, notably historical narrative poems such as the *Gododdin* of Aneurin (B. F. Roberts, 1988).

Written sources for Scotland

Southern Scotland is poorly documented. Some information is provided in king-lists and annals, mainly preserved in Welsh sources. Of these, the Harley 3859 is the most useful, though there are others, including two which survive in copies no earlier than the fourteenth century (Chadwick, 1949: 137). For the period of the Anglian advance there is Bede.

The Picts

The Picts are badly documented from internal, native sources. It has been argued that a series of historical factors led to the disappearance of documentation relating to the Picts and Scots. A year-by-year chronicle was irrelevant to them, and legend and factual history were intermixed (K. Hughes, 1980: 20). The only surviving 'native' text is a king-list (formerly termed the *Pictish Chronicle*) which survives in two versions, one set down in a fourteenth-century copy alongside a *Scottish Chronicle* (the whole now forming the *Chronicle of the Kings of Alba*: Paris, Bib. Nat., Latin MS 4126). Both may date back to the tenth century (M. O. Anderson, 1949; Dumville, 2000).

Between about 760 and 840 there are more references in the Irish Annals to the Picts, and it has been suggested this data was derived from records compiled in a Pictish monastery, perhaps Applecross (I. Henderson, 1967: 167–8; K. Hughes, 1980: 1).

Apart from these Celtic sources, references to Picts and Scots appear in Roman authors, in Bede and other English writers, and in such sources as Adomnán's *Life of St Columba* (Anderson and Anderson, 1991). As in other areas of early medieval Insular history, accounts of events before the late sixth or seventh centuries are highly suspect.

The Scots

The history of the Scots of Dál Riata is again very inadequately documented. The principal sources are the *Senchus fer nAlban* (a genealogy of the kings of Dál Riata, its divisions and expeditionary strength), an account of the Convention of Druim Cett (which discusses Irish Dál Riata) (Bannerman, 1974: 157–70), and the *Duan Albanach*, an eleventh-century poem about the kings of Scotland (K. Hughes, 1980: 1).

Archaeological sources

As reflected in the chapter titles of this book the archaeological remains include settlements, art, and a wide variety of objects which relate to every-day life in many occupations. A preponderance of the work has been carried out in Ireland, which means that inevitably comparisons have been drawn and generalizations made, which were then projected to Britain, not necessarily always meaningfully. Although a huge number of sites believed to belong to this period have been identified in Ireland (45,000 ringforts, 1,500 crannogs, 3,000 souterrains have been suggested figures), only a very tiny proportion have been sampled by archaeological excavation.

In contrast, almost no known sites can be attributed with any confidence to the period in Wales. One review (Edwards and Lane, 1988) listed only ten settlements known to be certainly of the period, one of which was Anglo-Saxon; only a few more can now be added.

There are only two certain Manx settlements of the period and seven in the south-west peninsula of England. Southern Scotland has ten, though the number of suspected sites in northern Scotland is somewhat greater, though still sparse.

Although potential ecclesiastical sites are more abundant in Wales and Scotland, without excavation it is impossible to tell if any remains survive from this period, and until very recently excavations on such sites have been comparatively rare. Throughout the region covered by this book, there has been a tendency for researchers to concentrate in particular on rich or 'high status' sites, which are likely to yield the most archaeological material. The selectivity of the excavated sample is further distorted by the circumstances through which sites come to be investigated, the main factor in all areas being the random chance of threat from development. Because they have long attracted the attention of archaeologists concerned with a variety of periods, some areas, such as the Northern Isles of Scotland, have received more attention than others.

Furthermore, sampled sites may not be typical of the period or region as a whole, and may have been wrongly interpreted by the original excavators. The limited number of universities in which research in the period is carried out has hindered development of the studies. Some types of material changed so little during the period (and indeed some settlement types appear to have remained similar in terms of superficial appearance from the Iron Age to the seventeenth century!) that it is often impossible to date features or objects to closer than the nearest century or two.

The structure of Celtic society[2]

On the available evidence, the general shape of society in all the areas concerned showed kings and high kings leading nobility within tribal structures. A class not represented as such in modern society included such diverse professions as judges, smiths and poets. Farmers must have made up the bulk of the population.

The Irish law codes of the seventh and more particularly eighth centuries provide a valuable insight, albeit formalized to a considerable degree, into the functioning of Irish society. The sources outside Ireland, which include a body of (later) Welsh laws, suggest that a similar social organization operated there. The written and other evidence for the various areas do reflect broadly similar societies – for example, generally similar kinship systems are described in both Ireland and Wales (Charles-Edwards, 1993: 477).

Attempts to correlate historical or quasi-historical information with the archaeological evidence have experienced difficulties.

The structure of Irish society

From the Irish law codes it appears that the major building blocks of early Irish society were the clan (*cenél*) and the lineage or kin-group (*fine*). This comprised a group composed of all the males who had a great-grandfather in common, up to and including second cousins. Within the *fine* each member might be responsible in part for another member's actions – if a man killed someone and could not pay the honour price (see p. 17), then the *fine* was liable for it. The *cenél* had a corporate unity in law equal to that of the individual in modern society. The clan collectively was concerned with producing enough surplus to maintain its own warrior aristocracy, that took part in battles and cattle-raids.

Society functioned smoothly through clientship. The lord handed over a 'gift' in return for defined dues. This was in two parts, the first usually amounting to a number of cattle equal in value to the 'honour price' of the client. The second part was a larger number of cattle – twelve in the case of farmers of higher rank – in return for which the client gave such items as meat, cheese, bread, honey, leeks, malt and candles, as well as physical help in erecting a bank round his lord's rath, bringing in crops, and so on (N. T. Patterson, 1991: 1995). A large number of querns found at the hillfort of Dunadd, Scotland (over fifty came from the early excavations) might have been for the processing of grain for such food rents from a wide area (Nieke and Duncan, 1988: 12–13).

Kingship

The highest ranks were the over kings (notably the kings of *provinces*), who demanded tribute from those of lesser status (Gibson, 1995). By the Viking Age high kings (*ard-rí*) appear in Irish history, who seem to have outranked them. Their legal position is unclear. In Ireland kings ruled over the *túath* (tribal territory), which could include members of more than one clan (extended family) (Binchy, 1970; Byrne, 1973: ch. 2; Charles-Edwards, 2000:

ch. 13). Geographically, the *túath* typically extended to an area about 16 km across, and was very comparable with baronies in the later middle ages (N. T. Patterson, 1991: 88–93).

In the sixth to eighth centuries evidence suggests that there were 100–150 kings in Ireland (Byrne, 1973: 7). The king was the personification of the *túath* – he led his nobles and freemen into battle, and if he died, the battle was lost. Kingship involved ritual and formal obligations, and carried taboos and privileges. The king however did not have any powers of legislation, or the maintenance of law. He protected his *túath*, and presided over the *óenach* (the assembly of those with political power). Under him, the nobility was obliged to provide the king with hostages, tribute and hospitality as he travelled about his lands.

The kingship of the tribe was open to every male member of the royal lineage whose great-grandfather had been king. In this respect, though usually patrilineal, the inheritance did not depend on primogeniture. To avoid disputes, a king's successor was often nominated in his lifetime, a process known as *tanistry*. In the absence of organized administration, government depended on complex economic and hereditary law codes, which were based on an archaic native structure which was periodically adapted to changing conditions.

In the sixth/seventh century and probably earlier, the king along with the poet (*fili*) had an *honour price* (the equivalent of the Anglo-Saxon *wergild*) which set him above the law, but from the eighth century he seems to have had to atone for his misdemeanours in the same way as lesser ranks. Below the king there were two main classes: the nobility and the free peoples, below which were the unfree, including slaves. A further rank comprised the professionals (*áes dána*) who included the poets, legal scholars and experts in genealogy and history, as well as the druids and skilled smiths. The status of the highest-ranking was often comparable to that of the nobility. Freemen had an *honour price*, owned land and owed military service in wartime. The nobility had a retinue (*céle*) of freemen. Within the main classes were many ranks of lordship (dependent on the number of clients each lord had (Binchy, 1941)), and the farmers were equally classified according to their degree of self-sufficiency. Superior lords made political alliances with their inferiors, by giving gifts such as weapons, horses, dogs and slaves (Dillon, 1962). The Irish shared with the Anglo-Saxons and other societies the idea that any crime or wrong-doing had a price attached (the equivalent of modern court sentencing laws). Instead of imprisonment a material price was set (cows or slaves – coinage was not used until the eleventh century). With the advent of Christianity, the bishop had the same honour price as the king.

Matriliny

It has been actively debated whether the Picts had a matrilineal society. There are two pointers to this: Bede relates that the first Picts were allowed to take wives from the Irish on condition that, where royal succession was in doubt, they should choose their kings from the female rather than the male line, and an Irish source which says much the same thing. One argument contends however that Bede never said that the royal succession in Pictland was always matrilinear, but that it was employed only in certain circumstances (Smyth, 1984: 58). It has been suggested that as the fathers of Pictish kings are named in king-lists, this argues against matriliny (Smyth, 1984). This view has however been vigorously disputed (Anderson, 1987: 9–10; but see also Woolf, 1998).

The warrior band

Decisions over wars and raids fell to the kings, whose obligations included initiating the muster of war bands (hostings) and the seizing of booty. The excuses for war included the desire for plunder, the taking of prisoners: as slaves, or most notably in the case of noble hostages, to facilitate the control of relations with neighbours. Vengeance, blood-feuds and territorial expansion were inherent values and aims, and this has been seen as persisting into the post-Roman period (L. Alcock, 2003: ch. 9). In Ireland and Scottic Dál Riata, regal inauguration involved a demonstration of the king's fitness to rule by organizing a cattle-raid on a neighbouring kingdom (L. Alcock, 2003: 119). This in itself is illuminative of attitudes and values at the time.

The warrior was not a professional soldier, enjoying a social rank by virtue of his employment, but he provided military service to his king or lord. The concept of the 'hero' (a strong man who fought on behalf of his king) was fostered in literature not only of Celtic derivation, but in other cultures such as Dark Age (Homeric) Greece (for example, Hercules or Achilles) and the Anglo-Saxon world (such as Beowulf). Many of the accounts are clearly written to entertain, and since the heroes often fought the heroes of other tribes there is more than a suggestion that these were the equivalent of modern super-sportsmen. How far warfare itself was 'heroic' in the early medieval period is a matter for debate.[3]

The professionals – artists, jurors and smiths

Society differed from modern developed cultures in that it recognized a group of highly regarded professions (second only to kings and some nobility) which embraced a wide variety of occupations. Under the category of *áes dána* (literally, 'men of art') came smiths, jurors, poets and bards.

Some evidence of the status of smiths is contained in documentary sources. For example, in early Irish literature, smiths are recorded as being free, owning and inheriting property, entering into contracts and attending assemblies as members of the *nemed* class. They were involved in the business and mysteries of the tribe (F. Kelly, 1988: 10; Gillies, 1981: 76–7). Coppersmiths (*umaige*) and workers in precious metals (*cerd*) were of a status equal to judges and physicians.

In the *Táin bó Cuailnge* Caulann, the master smith, was able to invite king Conchobor and his followers to a feast in the smith's fort (O'Rahilly, 1976: 17). Blacksmiths (*gobae*) had comparable status and almost magical powers (B. G. Scott, 1990: 184–212). The druids (pagan priests, p. 28) were in this category until Christianity became dominant and they were superseded by churchmen.

Women, marriage and breakups

Women enjoyed a considerable amount of independence not found elsewhere in Europe pre-1200.[4] In marriage both man and woman contributed jointly to the marriage goods, and on dissolution of the marriage each spouse took back what they had put into it, together with any profit accrued since the marriage had taken place. The division was regulated by the formula that one third went to the partner who provided the stock, one-third to the partner who provided the land and one-third to the partner who provided the labour. In this, the wife's work on the farm was given full recognition. In 'no-blame' divorce the division was equal, but the apportionment was reduced for a partner who was seen to have misbehaved (Ó Cróinín, 1995: 128–34). Fourteen grounds for divorce were listed, including the failure of a man to provide sexual satisfaction because of his impotence or sterility; because he was bisexual or homosexual; because he discussed his love-life with all and sundry; or because he abandoned his wife for a life on the road.

A Welsh legal text shows a range of types of recognized marriage, including one in which a woman moved into her husband's house with goods from her family, one in which a woman stayed in her home and is visited there openly by her man, and secret marriages, where sex took place out of doors. The code seems to echo early Hindu texts, suggesting it is based on a system both old and widespread (Charles-Edwards, 1980).

Women in Ireland seem to have acquired increasing rights in the early medieval period. They could acquire and dispose of personal property and they could own land. They were not normally allowed to give legal witness (they were considered 'biased and dishonest'), but their testimony was accepted in matters concerning sex and marriage (F. Kelly, 1988: 207).

If a woman considered her husband impotent, she could call on a panel of 'women dignitaries' to carry out a physical examination (Ó Cróinín, 1995: 131). She could refuse sex if she believed herself to be pregnant, and the cravings common in pregnancy – *pica* – were catered for in a law known as 'Bee-Judgements'. This ruled that the owner of a swarm of bees had to give free honey to any of his neighbours' pregnant wives if they had a craving for it (Kelly and Charles-Edwards, 1983: 64). Although there is no evidence of such high status among women in the real world, Irish myth told of a woman jurist, Brig (Ó Cróinín, 1995: 131). Similarly, myth had the legendary hero Cú Chulainn trained in warfare by Scáthach, a female who ran a training camp for young men and was also a prophetess (Kinsella, 1969: 31). This work contains material that is obviously intended to be humorous (gross exaggeration) so care must be exercised in making assumptions.

Welsh women were less liberated, being regarded as part of some male. Honour price for a woman was half that of her brother before she was married, and a third that of her husband when she was (Owen, 1980: 43).

Children

Irish law accorded special status to children up to the age of seven. Not so the Welsh, though this age was also seen by them as marking an important rite of passage, when girls could 'go on oath' and boys could additionally swear on their own account and take on the 'yoke of God' (McAll, 1980).

Both girls and boys (of the nobility at least) in Ireland went into fosterage (i.e. did not remain with their birth parents), though the fee paid to the foster parent was higher for a girl than a boy. For boys this ended at seventeen, for girls when they became marriageable, normally fourteen. In Wales fosterage was not an option for girls – they stayed at home until marriage arrangements were in place (McAll, 1980: 8–9). It was unthinkable in Wales, as it would have given them a greater opportunity to lose their virginity – this made them unmarketable to potential husbands. In Ireland virginity was not so highly prized (McAll, 1980: 9–10).

The law set out liabilities for injuries incurred by children when at play, which has poignant modern overtones. Certain games were regarded as exempt from incurring penalties: hurley, ball, 'boundary pillar', 'excavating small dwellings', jumping, swimming, hide-and-seek, juggling and board games, were seen as low risk activities. Competitive games were seen as more dangerous, and therefore liable to incur penalties. A third category incurred serious penalties for misdemeanours: one-against-all, cross-pelting and throwing a wooden javelin into an assembly (Ó Cróinín, 1995: 133).

Slavery

There is little evidence for slavery before the Viking period, though it is clear from the sources that it existed, including the autobiographical *Life of St Patrick*, who was taken from Britain as a slave along with a great many others. In his *Letter to the Soldiers of Coroticus* he mentions the fact that the Picts had been buying Christian slaves from Britons in southern Scotland. The finds from Lagore include what has been identified as a slave-collar, which is more probably a shackle for hostages or even a dog collar (Scott, 1990: 106–7). An Irish source, the *Fragmentary Annals*, records how a couple of Viking raiders brought black slaves from Africa – 'and those black men remained in Ireland for a long time' (Ó Cróinín, 1995: 241).

Population figures

Population figures are notoriously difficult to calculate for past societies and can never be much more than guesswork.

The Irish population may have been c. 500,000–800,000.[5] A figure of 10,000 inhabitants in Dál Riata, and 80,000–100,000 for Pictland[6] has been suggested. Figures for Wales are almost impossible to compute, but may have been appreciably lower than in either Scotland or Ireland. Population decline in the late Roman period has been suggested (Arnold and Davies, 2002: 40), and this may have continued into the post-Roman centuries. Figures for the south-west peninsula of England (computed for the Roman period (Pearce, 2004: 29)) suggest there were between 300,000 and 500,000 people.

Life expectancy

There are ethical and other objections to investigating burial sites, so information is limited and random. At Dunmisk, Carrickmore, a cemetery of 535 excavated graves of the latter part of the period suggested that the average life expectancy was around twenty-four years, and that life was 'punctuated by periodic bouts of extreme stress caused by malnutrition and endemic disease' (Ivens, 1989: 59).

The teeth indicated that the population had a tough, abrasive diet with small amounts of sugars and soft foods. As a result, dental caries was less pronounced than in post AD 1200 populations, a recurrent feature noted in early medieval period burials. A similar life expectancy seems to be indicated from the population at Millockstown (O Donnabháin, 1986).

In Scotland, a series of burials in long-cist cemeteries echo the Irish findings. At the Catstane cemetery, Kirkliston, burials were almost entirely of teenagers and young adults. None was under 11–12, and there were no elderly

(Cowie, 1977–8: 196). The story is repeated at Longniddry, where one female burial was over 45, and where there was one child of 10–11 (Dalland, 1992: 204). These two cemeteries belonged to the fifth to seventh centuries.

At Hallowhill, St Andrews, the cemetery continued in use to the ninth century. 145 burials were excavated, displaying a peak of deaths in the age bracket of 20–5, and with an average life expectancy of around 26–9. In keeping with the general pattern, dental caries was low, but increased with age. Arthritis was found in several bodies, and there was a possible case of leprosy. One man had been trepanned in his twenties, but had survived the operation (Lunt, in Proudfoot, 1996: 145).

The burials in the sixth–seventh century cemetery at Whithorn seem to have been generally of older people, 75% of the burials being of adults, with none of the children younger than 7. No fewer that 21% were late middle aged or old. The average height of men was 1.75 m, and that of women 1.67 m. Again there was evidence of much trauma and disease, with three probable cases of tuberculosis and with evidence of spinal anomaly. It was suggested that the Whithorn burials may have been predominantly of diseased high-status males, perhaps seeking a miracle cure at the monastery (Cardy, in P. Hill et al., 1997: 519–92). Caries was not apparent again until the 25–35 age group.[7]

There are few excavated burial grounds in south-west England to provide meaningful statistics, but the figures from the late Roman cemeteries at Henley Wood and Poundbury show that most people died in their late teens to early forties, though a few survived into their seventies. At Henley few women survived past thirty-five (Pearce, 2004: 75).

Significant information comes from the large cemetery at Cannington (Rahtz and Hirst, 2000). Here females slightly outnumbered males (1.6: 1) and two thirds of the burials comprised adolescents and young adults. Only 7% were over fifty years old. Stature was slightly less than at Whithorn – males averaged 1.67 m, women 1.62 m. Congenital defects suggested some inbreeding, but dental caries was low (lower than in many Romano-British cemeteries), though joint disease, especially of the lumbar region, was fairly common. One person seems to have died of cancer, and there were two lepers, the disease possibly introduced from the Mediterranean (Rahtz and Hirst, 2000: 464).

A strangely health-endangering phenomenon was encountered in Ireland at Church Island, where a rectangular cell had a tank which had been fed by water filtered through a midden and a human burial, leaving speculation as to the use of the water (O'Kelly, 1958: 125).

Plagues

Considerable attention has been focused on the possible effect of a global climatic event in the 530s or 540s (possibly prompted by a volcanic eruption) which may have resulted in colder temperatures, crop failure and the spread of plague (Gunn, 2000). An outbreak of plague in 565 killed the Byzantine emperor Justinian, and there is evidence for an outbreak at this time in the Irish Annals. In Ireland it was succeeded by the 'Yellow Pestilence', an outbreak possibly of relapsing fever (MacArthur, 1949). 'Yellow Plague' allegedly killed Maelgwn, king of Gwynedd in Wales (p. 253) around 550, though the annalistic reference has been questioned (Dumville, 1984).

Plagues are documented in Wales in the fifth and seventh centuries as well as the sixth (W. Davies, 1982: 31). Adomnán seems to have been a survivor of an outbreak of (probably) Bubonic plague in 664, which is also documented by Bede, who asserted that it first ravaged southern Britain and then spread to the north. Adomnán seems to have believed there were two outbreaks, with a second in 685 (Alcock, 2003: 25). The impact of plague on the population has perhaps been over-estimated however, as in the Celtic areas settlement was scattered and plague was unlikely to spread very rapidly, except perhaps in the closed environment of the monasteries in which the chroniclers were based.

Medicine

A tombstone of a doctor in Wales (*medicus*) called Melus, datable to the sixth century, stands at Llangian (Nash-Williams, 1950: no. 92; Fig. 2). There is some evidence from Howe, Orkney, for the use of herbal cures through the use of lesser celandine and juniper, the former known to have been used as a gargle for sore throats, the latter as a digestant and antiseptic (J. Hunter, 1997: 19).

From a sixth-century cess pit at Whithorn has come evidence for the use of plants which had medicinal uses: mustard (a diuretic and emetic), chickweed (an emollient, used for wounds and itching, and taken internally for rheumatism) and dog rose (a mild laxative). In addition, there was coriander and dill (neither native to Britain and here probably cultivated in a herb garden), black mustard, blackberry, redshank and fat hen. These could have been used in a culinary context, but since they occur with the others noted above it is likely they were medicinal, used in the treatment of stomach troubles – coriander and dill were used to cure flatulence (Hill et al., 1997: 124). Another slightly later pit at Whithorn contained a wide variety of plant remains, some of which may simply have been growing locally, but could have also been medicinal. Elder (used for a variety of problems, including colds, influenza and breathing problems), woundwart (used for wounds and taken internally for cramps and joint pains as well as diarrhoea), hemlock (a sedative) and nettle (diuretic and astringent) (Hill et al., 1997: 128).

Fig. 2 Stone commemorating Melus, a doctor, Llangian, Gwynedd

Pastimes

There are a number of stone boards for games, the most popular being an Irish war game called *brandub*. Stone boards for playing this have been found at Dun Chonallaich (Argyll, Scotland; Fig. 3) and Buckquoy, Orkney, and wooden boards of the Viking period are known from Ballinderry 1

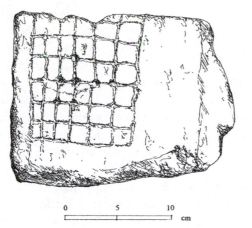

Fig. 3 Gaming board, Dun Chonallaich

crannog in Ireland (Ritchie, 1987: 60–2). There are a few examples of bone or jet knobs with metal shanks, usually taken to be pins, but which could have been used as playing pieces pegged into boards. Examples are known from Clatchard Craig, Ballinderry 1 crannog, and Mote of Mark (Close-Brooks, 1986: 166). Knuckle-bones may have been used in games, which would explain the bone with incised Pictish symbols from Burrian, Orkney (Macgregor, 1972–4: 88).

Drink and feasting

Drinking was a popular pastime, which also carried important social connotations. Law tracts make it clear that it was the obligation of the upper social orders to provide drink and appropriate drinking vessels (De Vegvar, 1995: 81). Ale seems to have been an acceptable substitute for sick maintenance, and a text which refers to a 'king of the mead-round' notes that the weekly order of kings' duties starts with 'Sunday for drinking ale, for he is no rightful ruler who does not provide ale' (De Vegvar, 1995: 81). Individual drinking horns were related to their owner's status, and were on occasion given names (De Vegvar, 1995: 83).

A drinking Pict appears on a slab from Bullion, Invergowrie, where the bird's head terminal on his drinking horn has been bent round to look at him, perhaps as a joke (Stevenson, 1958–9: 44; Fig. 4a). The bird's head terminals of drinking horns and the knob-shaped mounts for affixing to their pointed end have been found in Ireland, for example at Ballinderry 1 (bird's head) and at Clonmore (knob) (De Vegvar, 1995: 82–3). Mounts for drinking horns come from Burghead (here an Anglo-Saxon import) and the Tummel Bridge hoard.

Feasting is a prominent feature of the *Gododdin* poem, traditionally composed in the sixth century by the Welsh poet Aneurin. The date and historicity of the *Gododdin* poem have been questioned (Dumville, 1988; Koch, 1997; G. Isaac, 1990), but presumably reflect the character of early medieval feasting. The mead-hall used by Mynyddawg, a British king in the poem, was hierarchically organized, with the place of honour at the end of the couch. Food is not mentioned in the poem, but there is an account of ritual drinking; 'the pale mead was their feast, and it was their poison' (K. H. Jackson, 1969: 118). Horns, glass vessels and metal vessels of gold and silver were all employed in the quaffing of strong liquor.

Glass cone beakers, presumably for holding drink, were among the imports from France in the later sixth and seventh centuries, and are represented at a number of sites including Dinas Powys in Wales and the Mote of Mark in Scotland (p. 138).

Hunting

Hunting was a popular aristocratic pursuit, and stag hunts are common subjects on Pictish stones. Other animals appear to have been hunted, including boars (to be seen on the Dupplin cross and St Vigeans 1). Falconry seems to have come late to the Celtic world, probably ultimately from the French court of the Carolingian kings where it was regarded as a noble pastime. Falconry is depicted on Pictish stones from St Andrews, Elgin and Fowlis Wester (Carrington, 1996).

Riding

Horsemen abound in Celtic sculpture, riding to the hunt or to war (Laing and Laing, 1984a: 284). Horsewomen are known in Pictish sculpture, riding sidesaddle (for example on the Hilton of Cadboll stone). Bridles are apparent (and parts of some survive), but horses were ridden both bareback and with saddles, the mounts for which also survive. Some depictions in Pictish sculptures have long saddlecloths, such as on Meigle no 4 (Fig. 4b). There is no evidence however for the use of stirrups. Riders are less frequent in the art of other areas, but figure on stones from south-west Scotland (for example at Govan), Ireland (for example on the base of the Kells Market Cross) and Wales (at Llandough).

Music

Musical instruments are known from depictions in sculptures. Two types of harp are illustrated – small harps balanced on the knee and large ones

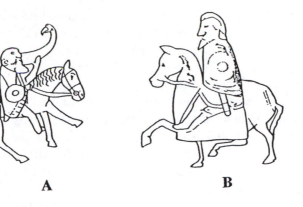

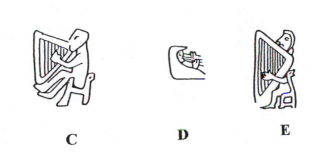

Fig. 4 Pictish pastimes from sculpture:
a. Bullion, Invergowrie;
b. Meigle 4;
c. Monfeith 4;
d. Ardchattan;
e. Dupplin.

that stand on the ground (Fig. 4C–E). The latter are represented on the ninth-century Dupplin Cross; on other Pictish stones at Nigg and Monfeith (Trench-Jellicoe, 1997), and in Dál Riata on the slab at Ardchattan (Laing, 1995a). These are the earliest true harps represented in Europe.

Blast horns appear on a number of stones, such as at Barochan in Renfrewshire, and a triple pipe at Ardchattan and on a Pictish stone at Lethendy, as well as at Clonmacnoise and Monasterboice in Ireland (Laing and Laing, 1984a: 285). The Ardchattan stone also shows what may have been a barrel drum. A figure from the stone at Nigg seems to have cymbals, but these may have been copied from an imported manuscript. A horn of the period is known from Lough Erne (Purser, 2002), and studies of representations of triple horns in sculpture suggest that they were in use in Ireland in the period (Ramsey, 2002).

Documentary and archaeological evidence provide abundant information about music in Ireland (Buckley, 2005: 741–64).

Poetry

Heroic tales and mythic history narrated by bards were part of the cultural life of the Celts.[8] The most famous is the *Táin bó Cúailnge*, set in a mythical

Iron Age past, which concerned a war fought between Ulster and Connaught over a much admired bull, 'The Brown Bull of Cuailnge (Cooley)'. In this the young hero Cu Chulainn played a major part. There are a great many related stories pertaining to what is termed the Ulster Cycle, including *The Exile of the Sons of Uisliu* (beloved by the nineteenth-century Celtic Revivalists as Deirdre of the Sorrows) and the stories of the Burning of Da Derga's hostel and Bricriu's Feast. In addition, there are myths about the prehistory of Ireland, carefully re-worked to fit a Christian milieu by monks from the late sixth/seventh centuries onwards. The major collection is that known as *The Book of Invasions (Leabhar Gabhala Eireann)*, of which the earliest surviving text dates from the twelfth century, but which was being worked at continuously from perhaps as early as the seventh up to the eleventh century (Mac Canna, 1996: 54). Such literary traditions were not peculiar to Ireland, for the Welsh have the *Four Branches of the Mabinogi*, which though very much altered to suit Christian, medieval taste, contain elements of much greater antiquity (MacCana, 1996: 72–81). Pagan gods and cult practices, albeit in disguise, flit through the narratives, and provide an occasional insight into pagan Celtic religion.

Religion

It is not known to what extent Christianity survived in the former Roman areas after the early fifth century though new information increasingly suggests that it did (p. 225). In the non-Roman areas in particular however, paganism survived through the sixth century – well after formal Christian missions were carried out by Sts Columba, Patrick and Ninian. There are many references to druids in Irish sources of the sixth and seventh centuries (Charles-Edwards, 2000: 190). It is difficult to find archaeological evidence for continuing paganism after the fourth century in the Celtic areas but by the sixth century the conversion of the Irish and the Britons had largely been accomplished, and of the Picts, by the seventh century.

There is little archaeological evidence for surviving paganism after the conversion period, though this is vouched for by the documentary sources from Ireland. When St Columba visited the court of the Pictish king Bridei in the sixth century, he had to enter into a competition of wonder-working skills against the king's wizards (Adomnán, *Life of Columba*, 2.34). Irish sources refer to druids and Christian writers frequently condemned them, which would hardly have been necessary had pagan cults been totally suppressed. The most credible evidence is to be found in in the Laws, Monastic Rules, and casual references in the *Life of St Brigit*.

In the middle of the eighth century Aed mac Diarmata meic Muredaich, an Irish king, was hailed in a panygyric which wished him 'every good of gods or ungods', while incantations were still made naming the pagan deities Goibniu and Dian Cécht as cures for common problems (Ó Cróinín, 1995: 33). Although paganism is still alluded to in Wales as late as the ninth century, it is usually in the context of foreigners in the region. Thus Rhigyfarch wrote of the Irish pagan priest Baia and his wife, who were frightened that their magic was less powerful than that of St David (W. Davies, 1982: 169).

Among the archaeological material relating to paganism is the evidence for a surviving bull cult at Burghead, Moray. No fewer than thirty-two incised bull carvings are documented among old finds from the fort, and a further six have been found in more recent times. The well at Burghead, with its twenty rock-cut steps ending in a rock-cut chamber, is now dedicated to St Triduana, but it may well have originated in a pagan water cult still surviving into historical times (Ritchie, 1989: 14).

The Picts apparently practised the drowning of prisoners, and human legs protruding from a cauldron depicted on the stone at Glamis Manse may depict some ritual drowning drawn from a pagan past (Ritchie, 1989: 14). Other allusions to pagan tradition have been seen in Pictish art – for example in the depiction of a tree decorated with human heads at Eassie, and a few representations in Ireland have also been seen as pagan in origin, such as the supposed depiction of the god Cernunnos at Clonmacnoise.

Burghead is also notable for a fire-festival, the Clavie, which is still enacted each January, when a barrel of tar on a pole is carried round the village and finally deposited on the rampart of the fort (Ritchie, 1989: 14–15). At Covesea in the same county excavations discovered a large number of human bones with evidence for nine beheadings as well as what appeared to be offerings of Roman tweezers, nail cleaners and coins of the fourth century, which were perhaps connected with cult practice (Benton, 1931: 205). Similar conversion of pagan water cults is reflected in Ireland and Wales where 'holy wells' were dedicated to saints, most typically in Ireland to St Brigit, who had a pagan Celtic goddess as her counterpart (MacCana, 1996: 34).

The bullaun stones (stones with a hollow) found associated with Irish monasteries and often connected in tradition with miracles, may in fact be Christianized pagan artefacts (Ó Cróinín, 1995: 31). Elsewhere, it is noted how the choice of Christian burial sites seem to show reverence for pagan tradition (p. 224). Later folk customs in the Celtic lands seem to represent survivals of pagan cult practice, among them the shrine containing three stones still re-roofed each year at Tigh na Cailliche (the Hag's House) in Glen Lyon, where stones are taken out in the spring, or the Beltain fire-leaping ceremonies still practised at nearby Fortingall until 1924.[9] There is a wealth of written material on such pagan customs as head hunting, for which virtually no hard evidence exists at the present time. One may wonder, however, what the significance of isolated skulls from archaeological contexts might be, such as that found deliberately buried associated with an iron hook (for its suspension?) in a ninth-century souterrain at Cahercommaun, which also produced an outstanding example of a silver penannular brooch (Hencken, 1938: 23).

2 Settlements

Settlement studies are rapidly changing as new technology is applied to archaeological material. During the past thirty years new thoughts and theories on the way society was organized have been applied to the main settlement types. As a result, a considerable amount is known about everyday life in some settlements, whilst others cannot even be dated.

In Ireland the overall characteristic of the period is expansion of settlement from the fifth and more particularly the sixth century onwards, which does not seem to have been held back more than briefly by the plagues and years of bad harvests that are attested in the documentary records (pp. 22 and 65). Not all researchers accept that the expansion was as great as has been inferred. It has been pointed out that the documentary evidence is weak and it has been suggested that Ireland experienced the same population trends as the rest of Europe, with a population decline of c. 545–70, spurts of growth 700–850 and stagnation thereafter.[1]

The strongest argument in favour of population expansion is archaeological, marked by the distribution and density of ringforts in Ireland, which as a general rule are not found in areas unsuited to farming communities, but located predominantly in areas of good quality soils, effectively in the areas today most favoured for farming.[2] Some ringforts however are also found on poorly drained soils, especially in the Irish areas of north Munster and Connaught, which are unsuited to tillage but are capable of supporting livestock, a reflection of the importance of animal husbandry in early Irish society.[3]

A similar story is apparent in Britain, though to a much less marked degree. Here there was climatic deterioration at the end of the Roman period which does not seem to have much affected the economy. In the region near Hadrian's Wall there is evidence for continued levels of forest clearance from the Roman occupation until the early seventh century (R. Collins, 2004: 125–6). In Wales all but three of the seven pollen sequences for the period show signs of stability or increased use of farmland; the same can be said for the Scottish sequences.[4] In south-west England, pollen diagrams suggest continuity of farming round greater Exmoor until the later eighth century AD, with some intensification of cultivation closer to peat bogs, possibly connected with population expansion, though there was abandonment of high upland in the fourth to sixth centuries (Fyfe and Rippon, 2004: 38–9).

Settlement types

Settlement types range from major fortifications to small open settlements. The largest and most impressive clearly required considerable and deliberate organizational effort, and at least some must have reflected the warring nature of society depicted in the literature. The smaller are more likely to have evolved through subsistence farming needs. Some types are numerous (an estimated 45,000 ringforts, though the date of occupation has never been established for the vast majority). Others are rare (there is only one example of a crannog in Wales).

Generalization is therefore of dubious benefit, and interpretation is more than usually open to contention. Study of Irish sites is hampered by the sheer numbers of sites that have survived over several millennia with relatively little damage, since meaningful patterns cannot be identified from what must be proportionately small samples excavated. The relative lack of threat from urban development in most of the areas in question has often led to a lack of systematic study, with many surveys having been driven more than usually by whim or chance.

Furthermore, certain simple enclosures (whether on hilltops or the flat) can belong to any period from the prehistoric to medieval and later. Even excavation or core sampling may produce no datable material due to the use of perishable materials for building and everyday goods, combined with climatic factors. Much attention has been given, especially in the 1970s and 1980s, to dating certain Irish sites, when it was thought they might belong to the Iron Age rather than the early medieval period (p. 279). The development of scientific techniques of dating (dendrochronology, pollen analysis and radiocarbon for example) is likely to continue transforming the study where suitable material exists for testing in appropriate contexts.

Despite this background, settlements have been categorized sufficiently for a basic overview of knowledge at the present time to be attempted. Some sites barely or not mentioned in this chapter which are important in their regions are found in the relevant regional chapters.

Categories of settlement

The great majority of the known and diverse settlement sites are known simply as 'enclosed places', that is, are defined by an enclosure, usually one or more banks and ditches, or natural water. The most easily recognizable, due to their prominent nature in the countryside, are **hillforts** (which are found in all areas concerned, with fewer in Ireland than outside, and which comprise a number of sub-groups); **stone walled forts** (in Scotland and Ireland, with duns in Scotland); **ringforts** (which include raths and cashels in

Ireland and rounds in south-west England). The fortifications of such sites display some variety. In addition, there are some enclosed hut groups, found in Wales and North Britain.

Enclosed sites, defined by the presence of water (such as promontory forts which are found in all areas, and crannogs which are found almost exclusively in Ireland and Scotland) include artificial or natural islands usually termed crannogs.

There are, in addition, open settlements. Some sites fall into more than one of these categories.

Identifiable within many of these settlements are structures including halls, houses (of various types), and underground or semi-underground structures (**souterrains**). Buildings are sometimes found in isolation.

There is evidence from the eighth century AD onwards that defended settlements waned. Open settlements (which were already in existence) became the norm and include halls and isolated or clustered round, rectilinear and cellular (where the interior is divided into compartments or rooms) homesteads. Attempts have been made to understand society through speculating about the functions of the settlement types. It is tempting, for example, to see the change from enclosed to non-enclosed sites as a reflection of less warfare or skirmishes between neighbouring regions, probably accompanying the rise in both Christian ideals and larger, more effective ruling units or kingdoms. It is, however, not proven that all enclosures were for defensive purposes against other people – some (as in monastic establishments) could have been symbolic, have denoted an area of rights over land, ownership, status or simply for the protectection of young children or stock.

Defended settlements

Hillforts

First built in Britain and Ireland during the Neolithic, hillforts (enclosures built on hilltops) proliferated in the later Bronze Age and Iron Age.[5] Since banks and ditches are more resilient than (say) purely wooden structures, they remain features of the landscape that outlive political or social change. Significantly, in some areas (most notably south-west England), a few Iron Age forts abandoned under Roman policy were re-occupied in the late and post-Roman period (Burrow, 1981 for those in south-west England). Others were newly built from the third century AD onwards.

The works were first called 'hillforts' because they were seen as primarily military in function and a natural adjunct to a warrior society; the banks and ditches which typically enclose them were seen as defence against enemies. This simplistic explanation has been questioned, though in some cases the term can be justified since comparable sites during (for example) the Roman advance in southern Britain are known to have been vigorously defended.

No category of hillfort can confidently be ascribed to the early medieval period on the basis of appearance alone, although attempts have been made (Dark, 1994b). The distribution of such sites is clearly related to the natural topography, and a general characteristic of those with post-Roman/early medieval occupation is a coastal situation. In Scotland, Wales and south-west England only Cadbury Castle and New Pieces respectively are over 20 miles from the sea (L. Alcock, 1987a: 159).

There is a growing awareness that some sites which have been categorized as forts had other functions beyond defence. The smaller examples were probably ordinary farmsteads (as in the case of, for example, raths). The larger examples required a considerable degree of man-management to construct and maintain, suggesting that a measure of 'high-status' organization must lie behind their construction.

Hillfort sub-groups

Hierarchically organized forts[6]

This term embraces forts with multiple, randomly shaped enclosures, (formerly termed 'nuclear' forts: R. B. K. Stevenson, 1948–9; Fig. 5) . Such forts are typically sited on craggy outcrops, often dominated by adjacent hills, and are notable for having a central focus (often termed the 'citadel'). Sections of walling usually link up with rock outcrops to produce outer enclosures, of random shape and size and uncertain function. These characteristics differ from those on forts of Iron Age origin (below, p. 36).

The majority are found in Scotland where several major examples such as Dunadd (Lane and Campbell, 2000) and Dundurn (Alcock et al. 1989) (Fig. 5) have been shown to have been built and occupied in the post-Roman period. A few of similar character are found in Wales (for example, Bryn Euryn) and the Isle of Man (Cronk Sumark), and there is a possible example in Ireland at Doonmore. Originally thought to be of one build, the type seems to have evolved over time, since the link between the central focus and the outworks may not have been part of the original scheme. The final plans at both Dunadd and Dundurn, for example, were not part of single-period designs.

At Dumyat and Moncrieffe, and King's Seat, Dunkeld, a stone-walled dun (see below for type) created a focal point that was imposed on pre-existing ramparts (Feachem, 1966: 73). A clearly defined citadel is however not necessarily a key component of the type, and Dinas Emrys (Edwards and Lane, 1988: 55), and Cadbury Congresbury (Rahtz et al., 1992) have at least two enclosures of apparently equal 'value'.

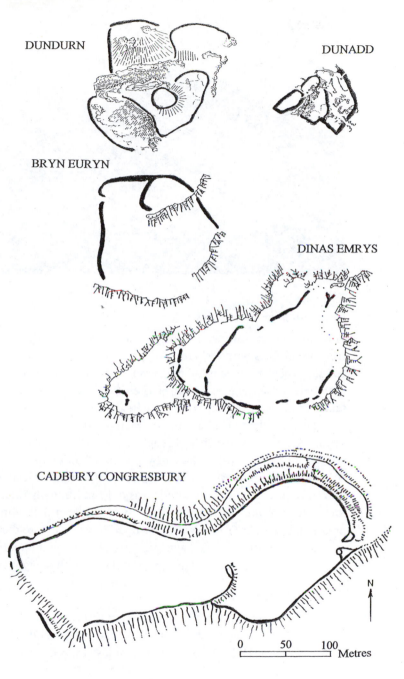

DUNDURN

DUNADD

BRYN EURYN

DINAS EMRYS

CADBURY CONGRESBURY

N

0   50   100
Metres

Fig. 5
Hierarchically organized forts: Dundurn; Dunadd; Bryn Euryn; Dinas Emrys; Cadbury Congresbury.

Fig. 6 Dundurn

Forts with single enclosures

This amorphous category is found in the whole area under review, and ranges from small forts with a single rampart (such as the Mote of Mark: Laing and Longley, 2006), to substantial multi-ramparted forts (such as Cadbury Castle, or Clatchard Craig; Fig. 7). Some of these are refurbished Iron Age forts (e.g. Cadbury Castle: L. Alcock, 1995); others (such as the Mote of Mark) appear to have been newly built in the post-Roman period. In Ireland at Clogher, a late Bronze Age stone-walled fort was replaced in the Iron Age with a dump rampart and accompanying ditch, dated by associated finds to the first century AD (Warner, 1971; 1972; 1973; 1974; 1979; 1988). Within this a second wide flat-bottomed ditch and inner palisade was dug; additionally this had an external low, timber-framed bank with one or more lines of palisading, enclosing an area about 50 m in diameter. This occupation was dated to the fifth to seventh centuries, and after a period apparently of abandonment a large ringfort c. 70 m in diameter was built and occupied in the seventh to eighth centuries.

Inland promontory forts

Some hillforts include inland promontory forts (which have a defensive line of one or more ramparts cutting off a headland or cliff). Examples of these include Crickley Hill (Dixon, 1988) and Dinas Powys (L. Alcock, 1963; Fig. 8).

Fortifications in hillforts

Fortifications show considerable variation, though little investigation has been attempted.

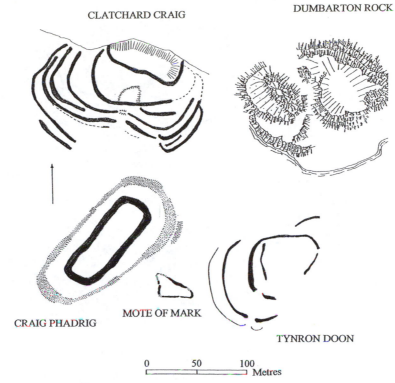

CLATCHARD CRAIG

DUMBARTON ROCK

CRAIG PHADRIG

MOTE OF MARK

TYNRON DOON

0   50   100
                                    Metres

Fig. 7 Hillforts of Iron Age appearance: Clatchard Craig; Dumbarton Rock; Craig Phadrig.

Gateways have been investigated only at Cadbury Castle, where there seems to have been a timber tower 3.4 m × 3.1 m with four corner posts linked by timber sill beams. It may have had double-leaved gates (L. Alcock, 1995: 131). Roman fort gateways have been seen as the inspiration.

Palisades on their own are extremely rare, though represented at Portknockie (Ralston, 1987) and possibly at Cruggleton (Ewart, 1985).

Timber framing or reinforcing is found in both earth and stone ramparts. The classic example in England is Cadbury Castle, where there was an outer timber facing for the stone bank, 4.5–5 m wide with tie-beams running back into the core of the rampart. This appears also to have been the type of defence employed at Dumbarton Rock, where the uprights had been set in a trench and tied back to horizontal tie-beams in the rubble rampart (Alcock and Alcock, 1990: 108–10).

Elsewhere in Scotland a combination of vertical, transverse and horizontal timbers are found, sometimes fastened with nails or spikes (for example at Burghead or Dundurn). Timbers may also be sometimes laid in two directions,

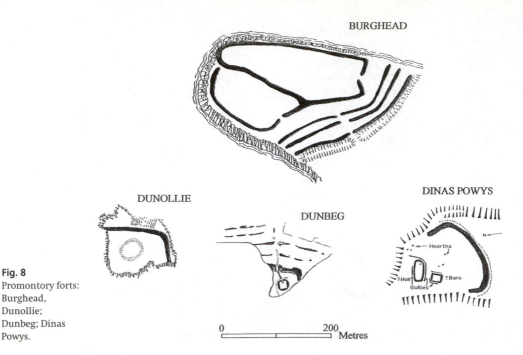

Fig. 8
Promontory forts:
Burghead,
Dunollie;
Dunbeg; Dinas
Powys.

but not touching. At Green Castle, Portnockie, it was found that squared timbers and planks were employed, the verticals sometimes morticed into the centre of the transverse beams (Ralston, 1987). Clatchard Craig had transverse and longitudinal timbers between front and rear revetments, but no evidence of joined timbers (Close-Brooks, 1986: esp. 131–3).

At the Mote of Mark there was evidence for horizontal beams but only very limited evidence for verticals. Here the rampart was partially vitrified. Vitrification is a feature of a number of forts.

Stone ramparts were frequently constructed with a facing of carefully laid stones at the front and rear, and with a rubble core. This was the case at the Mote of Mark, Burghead and Bryn Euryn. At Burghead one of the ramparts was constructed on top of a layer of carefully fitted boulders. Here the front revetment to the rampart still stood to a height of 2.9 m, the rear revetment 0.9 m. The width was about 7.3 m. This may be considered as exceptional (L. Alcock, 2003: 193–5).

Stone-walled forts

This category of site is found in Scotland (where small examples are known as duns), and in western Ireland.

DÙN FHINN

ARDIFUIR

KILDALLOIG

KILDONAN

DUN CUIER

Fig. 9 Argyll duns: Dun Fhinn, Kildalloig, Ardifuir, Kildonan, Dun Cuier.

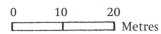

0   10   20
Metres

Stone-walled forts and duns in Scotland

A few larger stone-walled forts exist in Scotland similar to those in western Ireland, such as Clickhimin, which appear to be of Iron Age construction. The majority are small, known as duns, and seem to have begun in the pre-Roman Iron Age (Gilmour, 2000; Jon Henderson, 2000a: 122–3; Fig. 9). Only one in Argyll has produced evidence of being of Iron Age date (Rahoy: Childe and Thorneycroft, 1938). They are found in Argyll and the Inner Hebrides, with similar monuments in Perthshire, and they generally enclose an area not

Fig. 10 Staigue Fort, Co. Kerry.

greater than 375 sq m. Presumably they would normally have accommodated a single family. Characteristics include entrances with door checks and intramural chambers, sometimes at the entrance (effectively, guard chambers). Some small duns with a diameter of 15 m or less may have been roofed. These have been termed 'dun houses', and as many as 66 per cent of those in Argyll could have been roofed.

It is probable that duns displaying rectilinear planning are post-Roman, since it is likely that this feature was adopted from Roman models. Exclusively post-Roman finds came from Dùn Fhinn, Ardifuir, Ugadale Point, Kildalloig and Kildonan (all in Argyll).

A small group of duns which have outer enclosures may belong to the post-Roman period. These are well represented on Mull, where 48 per cent of all duns have outworks (L. Alcock, 2003: 186–9).

Stone-walled forts in western Ireland

A characteristic settlement in south-west Ireland has massive walls; terracing; narrow, lintelled entrance passages that are checked for doors; and staircases up to wall walks. Some also have *chevaux de frise* (stones or stakes) set to deter direct external assault (Jon Henderson, 2000a: 130–1). A few, such as the Staigue Fort, are traditionally believed to be of the post-Roman period but have never been excavated (Fig. 10). Most, if not all, are probably pre-Christian constructions with later occupation.

The Grianan Aileach is traditionally assumed (on no firm evidence) to have enjoyed some importance in the fifth century. Its destruction is recorded in the *Annals of the Four Masters* for the year 1101, but limited excavation provided no conclusive dating (Jon Henderson, 2000a: 137–8). At Dun Aonghasa finds included a late burial and a radiocarbon date of c. 658–851 cal. AD (Cotter, 1995: 10), though the fort may have pre-dated this.

At Dunbeg prehistoric occupation was followed by the construction of four banks (with a possible palisade on the innermost), five ditches and a stone inner wall furnished with a complex entrance with guard-chambers, checked internally for a door (Barry, 1981). The stone wall is probably of early Iron Age date. A stone house built within the site has been dated to the tenth century AD.

Ringforts

Ringforts are the dominant settlement types in Ireland (Stout, 1997; V. B. Proudfoot, 1970; N. Edwards, 1990: ch. 2; Mytum, 1992: 152–9; Limbert, 1996), with about 45,000 estimated to survive. They comprise raths, platform raths and cashels. Of those which have been excavated, the majority were occupied in the post-Roman period. Fewer than fifty sites have provided scientific dating evidence for the occupation (Stout, 1997: 24). However, some show signs of being built and occupied earlier and some were certainly occupied as recently as the seventeenth century. Such a long period of popularity causes problems in interpretation especially since the overwhelming majority have not been excavated at all.

Raths (*ràth*)

These are small ringforts with earth ramparts, and (usually) quarry ditches (Figs. 11–12). They are typically circular (though oval and pear-shaped enclosures are known) and over 80 per cent in most areas have a single rampart and ditch, sometimes with a slight counterscarp bank outside the ditch (Stout, 1997: 17). On rare occasions they have multiple ramparts (under 2 per cent in Co. Down). Garranes, Co. Cork, with three concentric banks and ditches, is a classic site (Ó Riordáin, 1942).

The banks of raths generally enclosed areas which range from diameters of 15.5–75 m, but diameters between 20 m and 44 m are in the majority. The banks have usually spread to over 3 m wide, and survive to a height of less than a metre. Excavation has shown that the ditches tended to be up to 3 m in width and 2 m in depth, either V- or U-shaped (Stout, 1997: 15).

Some ringfort banks (for example at Lissachiggel and Killyliss) had a palisade. On the latter site there was a light wattle hurdle with a framework of split oak uprights, poles and saplings (Ivens, 1984). There are documentary

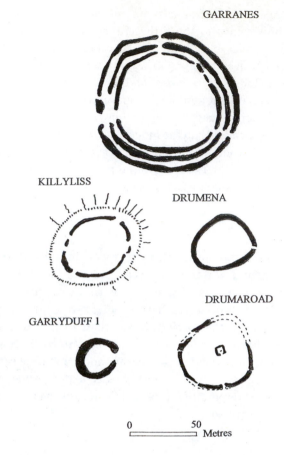

Fig. 11 Raths and cashels: Garranes; Killyliss; Drumena; Garryduff 1; White Fort, Drumaroad.

sources for the use of defences topped with blackthorn hedges (Ó Corráin, 1983: 249).

Timber revetments were sometimes provided for both ramparts and ditches (N. Edwards, 1990: 20). Some raths do not appear to have accompanying quarry ditches, but this is probably due to the ditches having been infilled. Entrances were usually undug causeways and were normally in the east or south-east sector of the forts, regardless of the lie of the land (Stout, 1997: 18).

An unusual rath at Lissue may have had a ritual function (Bersu, 1947). Here concentric rings of posts inside the bank may have been to support a roof which covered the entire ringfort.

Platform raths[7]

These are artificially built up in the interior to a height of on average 1.43 m above the surrounding ground level to raise the site above the water

Fig. 12
Reconstructed
rath interior,
Craggannowen.

table – some can be raised 2 m or more, as at Deer Park Farms (for the site generally: Lynn, 1989). In some cases the interior was raised in stages (there were four stages at Rathmullan: Lynn, 1982), in others it seems to have been built in one. In the case of Big Glebe it was built to a height of 6 m with an access ramp, surrounded by a ditch (N. Edwards, 1990: 14).

Cashels (*caiseal*)

These are 'raths' with stone walls. They occur only in areas where stone is abundant. Cashels tend to be smaller than earthen raths, many having diameters between 15 and 24 m, but the walls can be substantial, as in the case of Drumena, where the wall varied between 2.7 and 3.6 m across and was carefully built, with inner and outer facing and rubble core (N. Edwards, 1990: 21).

Rounds

These are small enclosures found in Devon, Dorset and Somerset (as well as in Brittany). In Cornwall, where there may be as many as 1,000, they are known as rounds, but further west they are not so called. Excavation has shown that they span the period from later prehistory to the sixth century AD or later, the majority being of the Roman era (Pearce, 2004: 29–43).

There is at present no known round that is purely of post-Roman period date. They are generally fairly small, from 0.25 to 2 ha with a single entrance and

TRETHURGY

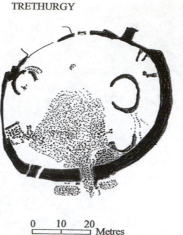

Fig. 13 Round, Trethurgy.

0   10   20 Metres

insubstantial defences. Inside are round houses. They have varied shapes, few being round. The classic site, totally excavated, is Trethurgy (Fig. 13; see p. 243).

The function of ringforts

Some were undoubtedly defensive, although a display of status may have been a factor behind the construction of ramparts. They were probably designed as protection against raiding rather than warfare. There is evidence that they were inter-visible, perhaps providing mutual support in times of trouble. One ringfort in Co. Antrim has been shown to have been visible to seventeen of its neighbours (Stout, 1997: 20). A few ringforts, such as Garryduff 2 appear to have been unoccupied by humans, and may have been intended as enclosures for keeping livestock safe (O'Kelly, 1962a: 124).

The dating of ringforts

Chronology has been vigorously debated (Edwards, 1990: 15–19; Stout, 1997: ch. 2; Lynn, 1975; 1983; Barrett and Graham, 1975; Caulfield, 1981; Laing and Laing, 1990: 149–50; Limbert, 1996). Scientific dating evidence for forty-seven sites (dendro and C-14) provides a date range between AD 236 (probably from occupation underlying the fort and thus pre-dating its construction) and AD 1387. Of these sites, 54 per cent provide dates between AD 540 and 884, and 66 per cent of the total provide dates between AD 600 and 900 (Stout, 1997: 24).

Despite disputed claims that some ringforts continued to be built into post-medieval times,[8] there is little firm indication that they were much in use after AD 1000. In Ulster, sites such as Glenkeen and Drumee have produced occupation material datable to the twelfth to sixteenth centuries. The rath at

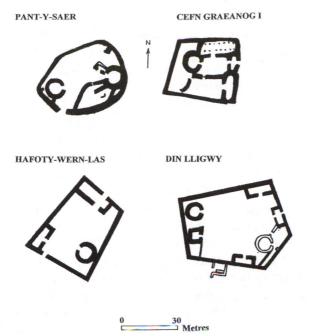

PANT-Y-SAER   CEFN GRAEANOG I

HAFOTY-WERN-LAS   DIN LLIGWY

0   30
               Metres

Fig. 14 Hut groups in Wales: Pant-y-Saer; Din Lligwy; Graeanog; Hafoty-wern-Las.

Beal Boru may have been occupied until destruction in 1116 (O'Kelly, 1962a). A few sites such as Thady's Fort and Garrynamona, produced finds of seventeenth-century date, though the context for them is not clear.

The Ordnance maps of the nineteenth century show occupied ringforts, though these may well simply be cottages built within existing rather than newly built examples. There is a growing body of evidence that some of the ringforts at least were preceded by earlier settlements on the same sites, for example at Lisnagade 2, Langford Lodge, and Sallagh, the two at Castle Skreen, Dressogagh, Glenloughan, Croft Road, Holywood and Lismahon.

Whether any of the ringforts is pre-AD 400 is more controversial:[9] the Rath of the Synods at Tara appears to have been, as does the site at Lugg. It has been suggested that an enclosed site at Lislackagh, which had a single-phase single rampart enclosure radiocarbon dated to around the first century BC, provides a possible prototype, but the dating evidence is ambiguous (G. Walsh, 1995; Limbert, 1996: 283).

Enclosed hut groups

A category of settlement with origins in the Roman Iron Age is the enclosed hut group (Fig. 14). These sites comprise one or more huts, usually round, but sometimes displaying some rectilinearity, which are enclosed within a stone wall, usually furnished with a single entrance. Most of the Welsh evidence comes from the north-west, where there is a long tradition of stone-built hut groups. The enclosures fall into three main categories: (1) oval with thick walls; (2) oval with thin walls; (3) polygonal. In the last, an enclosing wall was set out in straight lines and angles, enclosing both round and rectangular huts. The entrance usually led through one of the rectangular buildings, which may have been a porter's lodge.

The best examples are those from Hafoty-wern-Las, Din Lligwy and Graeanog (Hogg, 1966). The hut groups represent the homes of single families, though they may also have accommodated labourers who perhaps lived in the isolated huts sometimes found nearby. The main homestead stood in a block of farm-land, usually about 6 ha, divided into terraced fields of various sizes. Most of them are on high ground, and some have produced evidence of metal working. Generally, on excavation they indicate a low level of prosperity. Some show signs of continuing occupation or re-use in the early medieval period. Din Lligwy on Anglesey produced a penannular brooch of sixth- or seventh-century date, and radiocarbon dating indicates that Graeanog was similarly occupied as late as the tenth or eleventh century, with an associated corn-drying kiln.

In northern England and southern Scotland there is a similar tradition of stone-built enclosed hut groups in the Roman period, some of which may have continued in use later. The best example is at Huckhoe, Northumberland (Jobey, 1959).

Enclosed places defined by water

Some sites, comprising coastal promontory forts and crannogs, are partly or wholly defined by surrounding water.

Coastal promontory forts

Some of these widespread forts may have Iron Age origins; others appear to be exclusively early medieval. Burghead is a classic example of the type (Small, 1969; Edwards and Ralston, 1978; L. Alcock, 2003: 192–7). Essentially, they are formed by cutting off a peninsula with one or more ramparts. Although not uncommon in Ireland, only a few have been excavated. To judge by the finds, some of the promontory forts were of high status, for example Dunbeg (Barry, 1981), Burghead, or the exceptionally large Tintagel. At Larrybane a single clay rampart with a stone core 5.18 m wide and 2.6 m high was accompanied by an external ditch. Inside, hearths and pavements were found in excavation, with rectilinear structures in the final phase (Proudfoot and Wilson, 1962). At Dalkey Island a dump rampart with external ditch was constructed at a secondary stage in the period (N. Edwards, 1990: 42–3).

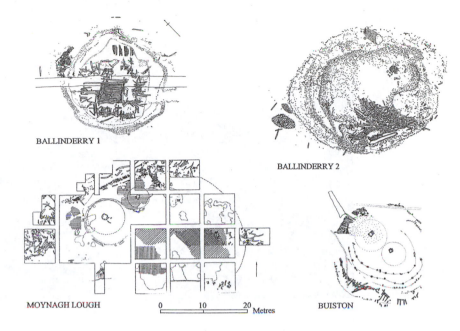

BALLINDERRY 1

BALLINDERRY 2

MOYNAGH LOUGH

BUISTON

0   10   20
Metres

Fig. 15
Crannogs:
Ballinderry 1;
Ballinderry 2;
Moynagh Lough;
Buiston.

Crannogs

Crannogs are circular or oval islands in lakes, which are either totally or partially man-made (main surveys for Ireland: A. O'Sullivan, 1998; 2000; Fredengren, 2002; For Scotland: I. Morrison, 1985; Crone, 1993; Figs. 15–16). They are found in Ireland and Scotland, and a solitary example is known in Wales, at Llan-gors (Redknap et al., 1989). Because they are partially or totally waterlogged, they produce a wealth of organic finds.

In Scotland the great majority of crannogs belong to the pre-Roman and Roman Iron Age, and it could be argued that the few post-Roman examples in the west are due to Irish influence.

In Ireland they seem to date almost exclusively from the late sixth to thirteenth centuries AD (i.e. contemporary with ringforts), one of the earliest being that at Coolure Demesne, Lough Derravarragh, apparently constructed at the beginning of the fifth century (dendro dating for the palisade suggesting the timbers were felled AD 402–9).[10] However, there are Bronze Age crannog-style settlements – although there has been debate over whether these have direct connection with the later settlements (A. O'Sullivan, 1998: 69–95). A recent series of radiocarbon dates from two sites on Lough Gara, KILA 16 and KILA 46, indicate Iron Age construction (around the end of the first millennium BC) (Fredengren, 2000). The claimed Iron Age occupation at Rathtinaun, and the existence of other 'Iron Age' crannogs such as Lisnacrogher, is now in serious doubt (A. O'Sullivan, 1998: 97–9).

Fig. 16
Reconstructed
crannog,
Cragganowen.

There are at least 1,200 crannogs in Ireland (A. O'Sullivan, 2000: 11), mostly in the midlands, west and north-west, especially in Counties Monaghan, Cavan, Leitrim and Fermanagh, where there are many lakes and fens. They vary considerably in size, from 10–15 m in diameter (such as Ballinderry 1) to 30–40 m in diameter (such as Moynagh Lough and Lagore) (A. O'Sullivan, 2000: 15).

The normal construction method was to lay a foundation of planks and timbers on the bed of the lough, which was anchored with vertical piles. On this base was constructed layers of peat, heather, brushwood, timber and stone, until the mound cleared the surface of the water. The island was then furnished with a wooden retaining palisade or revetment. This type of construction is sometimes termed *packwerk*. Some, post-AD 1200 crannogs, were revetted with stone walls (A. O'Sullivan, 2000: 16).

The man-power required to construct crannogs (which has suggested high-status occupants) is debated.[11] Some, such as Lagore, were royal residences (Warner, 1986; 1994a); others, such as Moynagh Lough, seem to have been the residence of a smith (Bradley, 1991; 1993). The sparsity of finds from Sroove has prompted the suggestion that this was of low status (Fredengren, 2001; 2002: ch. 10; Boyle, 2004).

Open settlements

There is a diversity of small, apparently unenclosed settlements in both Britain and Ireland during the period (Figs. 17–18). The most common are coastal, usually sand-dune habitations and seem to comprise a house or

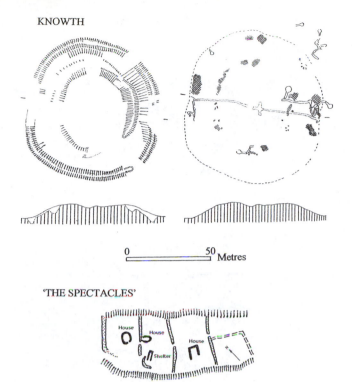

Fig. 17 Open settlements: Knowth; 'The Spectacles', Lough Gur.

houses frequently with an associated midden. They have tended to go unrecognized, as they leave few surface indications until exposed by natural erosion. Due to the nature of sand deposition and erosion, stratification is far from clear, and structural remains are very fragmentary. They include settlements with stone-walled houses, such as the wheelhouses and cellular buildings of the northern and Western Isles of Scotland.

Open settlements in Ireland

Open, sand-dune sites are distributed round Counties Kerry, Donegal, Derry, Antrim and Down. Classic sites include Dooey, which had a habitation area with fire pits and a shallow ditch, as well as a substantial midden (Ó Ríordáin and Rynne, 1961). On Beginish, Co. Kerry, (O'Kelly, 1956), eight stone houses were associated with field systems and cairns. The best-preserved house had two rooms, one circular and partly subterranean, the other rectangular. Occupation was indicated in the eleventh–twelfth centuries. It has been suggested however that Beginish is a Viking settlement – the finds are for the most part not diagnostic. At Lough Gur, The Spectacles comprised two stone

GWITHIAN

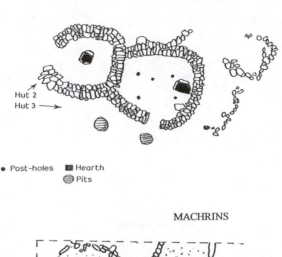

- Post-holes   ▪ Hearth
              ◉ Pits

MACHRINS

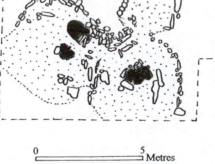

Fig. 18 Open settlements. Gwithian; Machrins, Colonsay.

0   5
▭▭▭▭▭▭▭▭▭ Metres

round houses, with two other structures in an adjacent field (Ó Ríordáin, 1949) and an isolated house was investigated at Inishkea North (F. Henry, 1952).

Rather more extensive, and probably of high status, the settlement at Knowth appears to have had early medieval period occupation on the site of the Neolithic chambered tomb. The first phase involved digging a double ditch broken by a causeway round the burial mound, dated by imported pottery to between the sixth and eighth centuries. It was succeeded by an open settlement which covered the infilled ditches, with at least nine rectangular houses and two souterrains, the latter dated by two tenth-century Anglo-Saxon coins from one (Eogan, 1973; 1974; 1977).

Open settlements in Scotland

Scattered open occupation on sand dunes has been identified at Luce Sands, Stevenston Sands and Culbin. There are also unenclosed settlements at the Udal in the Hebrides and at a number of other locations in the northern and

Western Isles and north Scottish mainland. These are discussed below under houses (see p. 56). Open settlement is also found in north-east Scotland to the north of the Tay (Perthshire and Angus), and is discussed under Pitcarmick houses (see p. 60)

Open settlements in Cornwall

At an open sand-dune site at Gwithian angular stone-built houses were butted against one another after the manner of some houses in Ireland and the 'figure-of-eight' cellular houses of Atlantic Scotland (p. 57), without any apparent defence (p. 242) (Thomas, 1958). In Scilly and Cornwall are located some courtyard houses: in a few cases they are grouped into villages, but most are single houses or small clusters. They seem to have been Romano-British in origin, but some had post-Roman occupation, such as Porthmeor and Halangy (Pearce, 2004: 33). Also in this category is the settlement of rectilinear houses at Mawgan Porth (see p. 242).

Open settlements in the Isle of Man

There is some ambiguity about the settlement at Ronaldsway which seems to have been a secular open settlement of six huts, four of which belong to a secondary phase, but all lying apparently in the sixth to eighth centuries. These were subsequently converted into an enclosed monastery (Laing and Laing, 1990b).

Halls and houses

These may be isolated or in groups and include halls, round and rectangular houses, wheelhouses and souterrains (the below-ground elements of above-ground houses).

Halls

It is notable that the excavated structures bear little similarity to the impressive buildings that are suggested by literary evidence to have existed in the period in Ireland or Britain (Murray, 1979; British halls: S. Evans, 1997: ch. 7; Fig. 19). Documentary sources describe large timber halls with thatched roofs, as well as smaller round buildings of wattle with domed wicker roofs and subsidiary complexes of pigsties, calf and sheep houses.

The law tract known as *Crith Gabhlach* gives a formalized specification for the buildings and equipment appropriate to the various ranks of farmer. Since only one measurement is given for each building (presumably the

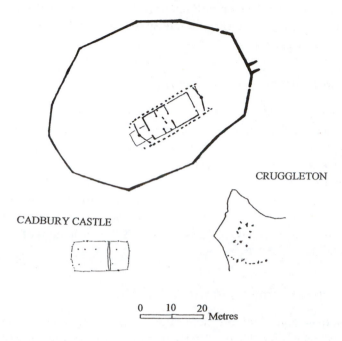

Fig. 19 Halls:
Doon Hill;
Cadbury Castle;
Cruggleton.

length of the ridge-pole or the diameter if the house was round), the information is of limited use (Murray, 1979: 81). Archaeological evidence indicates one main dwelling with a few subsidiary barns, which were sometimes butted on to the inner revetment of the bank. There is some evidence from the literary sources indicating that kings' houses were generally larger than most, but did not differ in construction.

The clearest evidence comes from Cadbury Castle where the post-hole alignments imply a double-square plan with gables of open-book formation, 20 × 9.15 m approximately overall, divided by a partition, and with arcades for roof-supports dividing up the interior in the proportion of 1:2:1 (L. Alcock, 1995: 134). This building possibly dates from the sixth century. At Cadbury Congresbury one building of generally similar date was about 8 × 3 m, its rectilinear plan indicated by a pattern of post-holes (Rahtz et al. 1992).

The evidence from Dinas Powys in Wales is dubious, as the presence of a rectangular building was inferred from a supposed eaves-drip (L. Alcock, 1963: 32–3).

In Scotland at Court Hill, Dalry, a rectangular timber building, just under 15 × 7 m, appears to have been buried under a Norman motte, though it need not have much pre-dated the motte itself (J. Scott, 1989). This seems to have been constructed in a manner similar to Viking-period buildings in Dublin or Anglian-period buildings at Yeavering in northern England, with grooved split-oak timbers, with opposed entrances in the long sides and a putative stone bench along one narrow wall. This dating fits in with that of a rectangular building underlying the bailey bank of a Norman motte-and-bailey castle at Hen Domen (building XXXI: Barker and Higham, 1982: 26–8).

Timber halls occur in the areas taken over by the Anglo-Saxons, for example at Sprouston, Doon Hill and Cruggleton. Because of its similarity to Anglian sites further south in Northumbria, Sprouston has been assumed to be Anglian, but need not have been (I. Smith, 1991). At Doon Hill, Dunbar, there were two phases of hall building. The second phase was Anglian, but the first, Hall A, which was burnt down, was seen to be British, and set within a single palisade. It measured 21 × c. 9 m. This has been suggested as being of sixth-century date (L. Alcock, 1995: 136). Like Cadbury Castle, Doon Hill A and Sprouston appear to have parallel long walls, gables of 'open-book' formation, and an internal division one third of the way along.

Romano-British models for the building tradition have been suggested, and timber halls have been encountered at Birdoswald on Hadrian's Wall which were built over a Roman granary at the end of the Roman period but continued in use during the fifth century. One of these measured 23 × 12 m (Willmott, 1997; 2000). The hall at Cruggleton consisted of a post-built structure, 6 × 3.7 m, defined by four large posts, with gable ridge-support poles. Radiocarbon dates indicated construction in the period AD 650–980, which means it could be either British or Anglian (Ewart, 1985). The same may be said for the enigmatic building at Kirkconnel, Waterbeck, which was probably Anglian rather than British (Clough and Laing, 1969). Although not very substantial, the building at the Mote of Mark which survived only as post-pads was rectilinear, and perhaps in the same tradition of buildings derived from Roman Britain.

The use of post-pads is encountered fairly widely, for example at Birdoswald, Portknockie, Pool, or the Dod (I. Smith, 1991; Ralston, 1997: 24).

A series of sites detected from the air in southern Pictland are exemplified by Lathrisk, and appear to be halls with curved annexes usually set within palisaded enclosures, and averaging about 25 × 9 m (Maxwell, 1987). A building at Monboddo is nearer a double square in plan, but otherwise similar (Ralston, 1983).

Houses

Houses in Ireland

Most archaeological information about house types comes from Ireland, where around 250 ground-plans survive from c. AD 400–1200. It has been suggested that round houses were succeeded by rectangular (Figs. 20–1). In Ireland the former were normal up until c. AD 800, but they were gradually

DRESSOGAGH

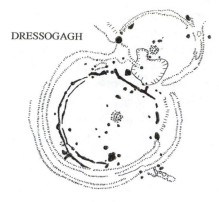

WHITE FORT, DRUMAROAD

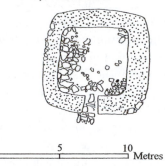

Fig. 20 Irish houses, round and rectangular: Dressogagh; White Fort, Drumaroad.

0   5   10
                                Metres

replaced by the latter, so that by AD 1000 a rectangular plan was the norm (Lynn, 1978b; Lynn, 1994: 85). This does not however appear to be the case with ecclesiastical buildings (other than the churches themselves), where circular cells were still being erected to the end of the period and possibly beyond. The reason for this change in secular planning is not clear: Viking influence has been discussed as a possibility, as has the influence of Church planning (Lynn, 1994: 85–6).

There is evidence that there was usually more than one house in a rath or on a crannog, and they tended to face east or south. The circular buildings before c. AD 800 were wicker or post-and-wattle structures without regular roof supports. The rectangular houses usually had drystone and/or turf lower walling. Remains of the timbers are rare, but were found at Lagore, Killealy, and Deer Park Farms. There were the remains of over forty houses on this site, essentially round buildings built with concentric rings of hazel uprights (over 100 in each house), with horizontals woven between the uprights in a spiral. Between inner and outer ring there was 'cavity wall insulation' of moss, straw, grass and heather. Timbering was also found in the construction of the souterrain at Coolcran (B. Williams, 1985).

A

LEACANABUAILE

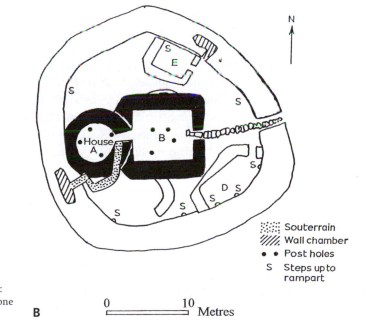

N

House A
B
S
E
D

Souterrain
Wall chamber
Post holes
S Steps up to rampart

Fig. 21
Leacanabuaile:
cashel with stone
house.

B

0 ——— 10 Metres

A' CHEARDACH MHOR

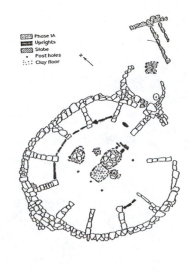

Fig. 22
Wheelhouse,
a' Cheardach
Mhor.

0   3   Metres

The average size of both round and rectangular houses was about 45 sq m, with two diameter sizes in round houses of 4–5 m and 6–10 m. The largest house was at Moynagh Lough, which was over 10 m in diameter, and was a high-status building. The walls of drystone houses tended to more than 1 m thick; their interior diameters were correspondingly smaller. There was a tendency in Ireland to build timber houses in the seventh and eighth centuries to a figure-of-eight plan, as for example at Dressogagh rath. Rectangular houses were usually built of drystone construction, or sometimes had kerbstones possibly facing low clay walls. The interior was frequently paved, and these houses were often connected with stone-built souterrains.

Scottish wheelhouses

These are round, stone-built dwellings in which stone piers radiate like the spokes of a wheel dividing the interior into cells, with an open space in the centre or hub (Armit, 1997: 41–3; Harding, 2004: 251–62; Fig. 22). They were sometimes dug into the sand, and thus partly subterranean. Found in Shetland, notably at Jarlshof and Clickhimin, they are widespread in the Hebrides. They are essentially an earlier Iron Age type of monument, perhaps flourishing between the first century BC and second century AD, though in the Hebrides some seem to have been occupied or re-occupied in the early medieval period, such as a' Cheardach Mhor, Foshigarry and Garry Iochdrach.

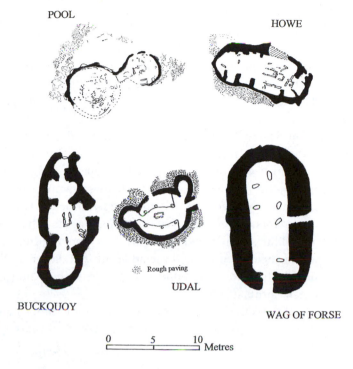

POOL

HOWE

BUCKQUOY

Rough paving

UDAL

WAG OF FORSE

0   5   10 Metres

Fig. 23 Cellular houses: Pool, Howe; Buckquoy; Udal; Wag of Forse.

Scottish cellular houses

The cellular house, of which a special development is the figure-of-eight or 'jelly baby' house (a rounded central room and smaller, rounded annexe) is the dominant type of building in the early medieval period in the Atlantic province of Scotland (Fig. 23). Cellular houses are sometimes found on earlier sites where there were complex round houses and are sometimes even built within them. The earliest date from the third century AD onwards.

They are present at Gurness, Aikerness (MacKie, 1994), and the Howe (Ballin Smith, 1994), at the Udal (Crawford and Selkirk, 1996), Dun Vulan (Parker Pearson and Sharples, 1999), and at Loch na Berie (Harding and Gilmour, 2000). Cellular houses also replaced wheelhouses at Cnip (Harding, 2004: 270) and a' Cheardach Mhor (Young and Richardson, 1959–60). These cellular houses often have cupboards, a central hearth with three sides, and the use of vertical slabbing. Single and double vertical slabs are found at the entrances to the same cells, which often have low entrances (Gilmour, 2000: 163). In Shetland at Upper Scalloway (Sharples, 1998) and Old Scatness in the Pictish-period cellular houses are set semi-subterraneously (V. Turner, 1998: 98). At Kebister in Shetland, where the construction was not sunk into the ground, a radiocarbon dating indicates construction before AD 400 (V. Turner, 1998: 98).

The figure-of-eight house seems to represent the latest stage in the development of cellular buildings. This is the case at Loch na Berie, Dun Vulan and Scalloway, as well as on the classic site at Buckquoy which was built where there had been no earlier roundhouse. At Buckquoy the buildings were constructed with upright slabs and drystone walling (Ritchie, 1977). The earliest had a series of sub-rectangular cells. This was replaced by a trefoil-shaped house.

In the third phase before the Viking period, dated to the eighth century, the house was much larger, with three rooms and an entrance vestibule, approached by two entrances, one paved and opening on to the main hall, the other leading through a vestibule into an ante-chamber. In the centre was a hearth, with a stone kerb, possibly for wooden benches. Part of the building had a hipped roof, but another part used for storage may have been corbelled. Similar buildings are known from Yarows and Nybster. There is some evidence for them in Argyll and the adjacent islands, where they have been identified at ten sites, including An Caisteal on Mull (Gilmour, 2000; An Caisteal: Fairhurst, 1962).

In Ireland the cellular structure of some houses within ringforts (see p. 53) has been seen as a parallel development, though the form they take is rather different (Gilmour, 2000: 163).

Rectilinear houses outside Ireland

Some of the cellular buildings seem to have been built with angles, such as a house at Howe, Stromness, which was dated to the late Iron Age, probably before AD 650. At Pool, Orkney, there were also indications of a transition from round to rectilinear planning during the Pictish–Norse interface period (J. Hunter, 1990).

These show a remarkable similarity to other rectangular buildings with curved ends encountered in northern Scotland, in Orkney and Caithness. These *wags* as they are termed (from the Gaelic for a cave) are usually about 14 × 5 m, with interiors divided up into compartments with slabs. They are best represented at the Wag of Forse, Caithness (Harding, 2004: 278–80).

The key site for rectilinear buildings in Pictland is Easter Kinnear, where roughly square buildings of oak post-and-wattle walling sometimes had shallow cellars. These are fairly late in the early medieval period, and may have been influenced by Anglian building traditions. They were grouped in small hamlets of three or four houses (Driscoll, 2002: 55–7).

In Wales a series of rectilinear houses, some joined to one another, has been identified at Gateholm, now an island but originally a promontory defended by a landward ditch (Edwards and Lane, 1988: 73–5). Two of the excavated structures consisted of houses 8 × 6 m and 15 × 7 m, with turf

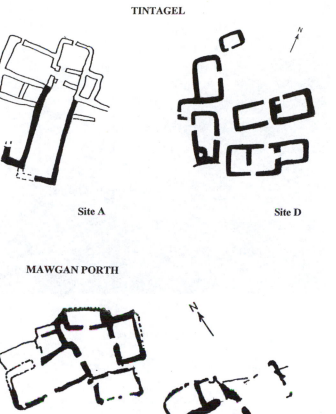

TINTAGEL

Site A

Site D

MAWGAN PORTH

Fig. 24
Rectilinear
houses: Tintagel
and Mawgan
Porth.

0   15 **Metres**

walls, in one case with internal rough stone facing. The larger building had
opposed entrances. A long period of use for the site is indicated by the finds,
but the buildings may be of late Roman and early medieval date.

In Cornwall stone-built rectilinear houses are known from Tintagel and
Mawgan Porth (Figs. 24–5). At Tintagel insubstantial sub-rectangular buildings were investigated dated to the fifth–sixth centuries, as well as more
substantial structures dated to the same period originally investigated in the
1930s, and confirmed in recent excavations to be of generally similar date
(Radford, 1935; Morris et al., 1999). At Mawgan Porth the buildings are later,
of the ninth to eleventh centuries. Two main clusters have been investigated,
comprising courtyard houses built of a stone facing with core of earth and
slate. The key element in the buildings was a long room, partitioned off at the
end for livestock and which opened on to a courtyard (Bruce-Mitford, 1997).

Fig. 25
Reconstructed
buildings:
Tintagel.

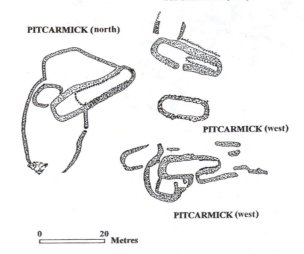

PITCARMICK (west)

PITCARMICK (north)

PITCARMICK (west)

PITCARMICK (west)

Fig. 26
Pitcarmick type
buildings:
1. Pitcarmick
(north);
2. Pitcarmick
(west);
3. Pitcarmick
(west);
4. Pitcarmick
(west).

0   20 Metres

Pitcarmick-type buildings

Named after a site in Perthshire, these have slightly curved, sometimes
bowed sides, rounded ends, a trapezoidal plan and sometimes annexes
(Fig. 26). A single entrance is located in one long side. They appear as low
earth banks, with random stones, and excavation suggests that they were
of clay or turf. The excavated example, at Pitcarmick itself, indicated

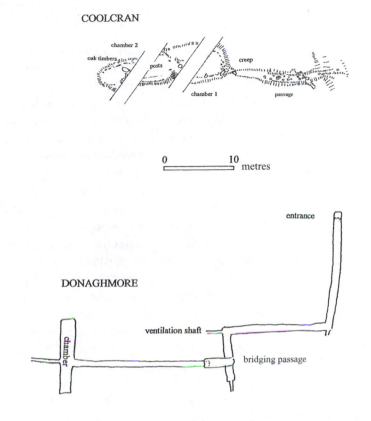

Fig. 27 Irish souterrains: Coolcran; Donaghmore.

occupation in the last few centuries of the first millennium AD (RCAHMS, 1990; J. Stevenson, 1991; Ralston, 1997), and a date in the eighth–ninth centuries AD has been suggested for their origins. They were possibly for summer pastures.

Souterrains

Souterrains or 'earth-houses' are subterranean or partly subterranean passageways, normally connected with above-ground structures (Fig. 27). Their function has been disputed since there is literary evidence to suggest that they were used as places of refuge, but there are also some indications that they were underground stores, particularly used for dairy produce. The souterrain at Oldcourt had been used to hide a moss-wrapped bell (Ó Cuileanáin and Murphy, 1961), and at Shanneen Park, Ballyaghagan, there were depressions in the floor of the chambers which might have been to hold containers for dairy produce (N. Edwards, 1990: 30). There are regional characteristics for those in Scotland and Ireland.

Souterrains in Scotland

On the Scottish mainland, souterrains appear to have been a short-lived type of structure in settlements that were occupied from the mid-first millennium BC (or earlier) until the sixth or even ninth centuries AD. They are particularly common in Fife and Angus, with outliers further south (F. Wainwright, 1963; Maxwell, 1987). Radiocarbon dates from Douglasmuir showed that an underfloor passage of a type probably ancestral to a true souterrain was constructed in the first half of the first millennium BC. A souterrain at Dalladies 2, Kincardine, was dated to the first century BC (Watkins, 1978–80a: 66).

   Although the settlements on which they were constructed continued into the early medieval period, for example at Bankfoot (occupied until the eighth century AD), the souterrains themselves appear to have been dismantled deliberately around the second or third centuries AD (Watkins, 1978–80b). It has been suggested that because it was associated with a 'jelly baby' shaped house similar to that found at Birsay, Orkney, the souterrain at Carlungie, though producing no evidence later than the third century AD, should in fact be reassigned to the early medieval period (Alcock, 2003: 270). Souterrains are also found further north on the Scottish mainland and in the Northern Isles, but here there is slight evidence for their use into the early medieval period, for example in the case of the souterrain-related 'passage house' at Jarlshof, Shetland (Hamilton, 1956: 80–3). The recently excavated souterrain at Langskaill, Westray, Orkney, was on a site occupied from the second or third centuries AD to the eighth, though there were no finds of early medieval date from the souterrain itself (Moore and Wilson, 2005: 335) .

Souterrains in Ireland

Irish souterrains appear to have been more or less exclusively of the early medieval period. They are particularly common in Ulster, but are widespread, with considerable numbers also in Counties Cork and Louth. They are found in a wide variety of contexts: in ringforts, promontory forts, on ecclesiastical sites and on open sites. It has been calculated there are in excess of 1,000, one estimate putting the numbers at around 3,000 (Thomas, 1972; Lucas, 1975; Warner, 1979; 1980; N. Edwards, 1990: 29–32; Clinton, 2001).

   The only firmly dated example was that at Coolcran where dendro dating indicated the timbers used to line the passageway were felled in around AD 822 (B. Williams, 1985). Since they are most often associated with rectilinear houses it is probable that they are particularly a feature from the ninth century onwards. As in Scotland, the souterrains were originally associated with above-ground buildings, but traces of these often have been ploughed out.

The construction of souterrains

Two main types of souterrain are found, with occasional hybrids, employing two different techniques of construction.

In the simpler structures the chamber was made by simple tunnelling. In the more sophisticated, a passageway was lined with drystone walls. The gap between wall and trench-side was infilled, then slabs laid across the walling to form lintels before the ground surface was levelled off. This type was also found partly (or sometimes wholly) projecting above ground. In the case of Coolcran an entirely wooden construction was employed. Here an earth-dug passage, 6.5 m long, led to a sub-rectangular pit, 9 × 3.5 m, lined with forty-eight inwardly sloping oak timbers with indications of wattles between them. Two posts may have divided the interior up into two chambers (Williams, 1985).

Souterrain plans

Souterrains vary considerably in size and plan. Some have several passages joined by 'creeps' (sections where the passage has been narrowed so that it is necessary to crawl from one section to the next). A few have vertical creeps through the roof. Wooden doors were sometimes used to close creeps. Side recesses could be used as guard chambers, and ventilation shafts, drains, cupboards and benches are all encountered (Warner, 1979; 1980).

3 Farming

The economy throughout the entire Celtic area was primarily based on farming with a number of crafts and industries carried out on or near the sites where they were required (ch. 4). Very few farming settlements have been investigated to modern standards, so the data base is limited and much remains conjecture. The seventh- and eighth-century jurists in Ireland provide a unique insight into farming practices through the law codes (F. Kelly, 1997).

Change in climate affected the entire area and has been studied recently with significant results for population trends and changes. The study is not without complexity however; although plagues and bad harvests are recorded in the documentary sources, there is disagreement over how far they may have affected the general population trends.

The climate and soils

In Ireland high rainfall, poor drainage and low evaporation inhibit the growth of crops (J. Evans, 1975: 172). The best areas for cultivation (and therefore habitation) are scattered round the perimeter and along some of the better-drained river valleys, the best soils being found east of the Shannon. Extensive bogs in the interior were partly the result of prehistoric over-cultivation (N. Patterson, 1991: 64). All in all, about one third of Ireland was inhospitable to settlement in the early medieval period. Widespread climatic changes have been identified through scientific analysis of, for example, pollens (p. 31).

In Scotland, most of the best soils for cultivation fringe the east coastal region, extending south of the Forth–Clyde line to most of the coastal regions and to parts of Orkney (Bibby et al., 1982; Davidson and Carter, 1997). In Wales, the poor soils restrict good farming areas to south-west Anglesey, the south of the south-west peninsula, Gower and the Lowlands of Glamorgan and Gwent, some of the eastward-running valleys of the borders, and small pockets elsewhere (Bowen, 1975: 112–13). In the south-west peninsula of England high relief is less pronounced, but areas of good soil are scattered (A. Fox, 1964: 18–19).

Climatic change and population

In the early medieval period (as well as in later prehistory) natural events (particularly volcanic eruptions) in other parts of the world had knock-on effects. There is a complete lack of oak in Irish archaeological contexts between

64

95 BC and AD 540, for example, and there seems to be a correlation between climatic change and the eclipse of the flourishing Iron Age society. Since there is a decline in archaeological evidence for human activity in the early centuries AD, this factor may be related. For example, there was a steady decrease in the number of tree pollens at Red Bog (Mitchell, 1976: 117–21). Pollens from cereals and weeds of cultivation disappeared sharply around 300 BC, when hazel (followed by ash, oak and elm) increased.

From c. AD 300 there was apparently an increase in agriculture, attendant on what has been termed the 'destruction phase' in Irish woodlands (Mitchell, 1976: 166; Weir, 1995). This was an ongoing process: the pollen diagram from Garrandrean Townland indicated forest clearance between the fifth and eighth centuries AD, presumably attendant on a revival in farming (Culleton and Mitchell, 1976).

Pollen analysis spread over much of Ireland shows a similar pattern of woodland clearance and renewed agriculture in the early medieval period, with increased pastoralism on some sites and extensive tillage pre-dating the introduction of the mould-board plough.

There are indications of a downturn in the climate in the sixth and seventh centuries, however, with an increase in temperatures again from the tenth to the thirteenth centuries (Lamb, 1981). A further upsurge in agriculture is attested in some areas of Ireland in the ninth century (Hall, 2000: 368). Minor climatic changes which may have had an effect on the population are reflected in the documentary sources. A rainy summer in AD 759 was followed by a famine the next year, and a snowy winter was followed by a drought in 764. In 892 a windstorm blew down trees and blew houses and churches from their foundations.[1] A dust veil in the 640s may have dimmed the sun and led to snow in summer, crop failure, famine and plague.

Dietary needs

It has been estimated that one farmer would have required between 16 and 32 ha to supply the needs of his farm (Proudfoot, 1961: 119). It has been similarly shown that in Co. Down, if raths are plotted in relation to potential cultivable land, there is adequate land for 25-acre farms for each settlement. Some potentially cultivable land does not, however, appear to have been utilized by rath farmers. These gaps in distribution may be explained by other forms of settlement which have left no trace, and it has been suggested that they might have taken the form of clustered undefended settlements appearing as the placename element *buaile* (bally), and occupied by farmers of inferior status to rath owners (Proudfoot, 1961: 119). There are however other possible explanations for the gaps, such as areas of forest which were subsequently cleared.

As far as can be deduced, specialization in either crop cultivation or animal husbandry to the exclusion of the other was very rare.

Animal husbandry

The economy in Ireland, Scotland and Wales was predominantly pastoral, to judge from the bones from excavations as well as literary sources. There are virtually no figures for south-west England.

Comparing figures from different sites is problematic, since some data bases give proportions in terms of weight of bones, some in terms of numbers of bones, and others in terms of the minimum number of individuals (MNI). None of these methods is wholly satisfactory, as large animals (such as cattle) have heavier bones, and calculating MNIs has inbuilt difficulties.

Cattle

In **Ireland**, the fertility of the land was graded according to the cattle it could support, and farmers' status depended on the number that they owned.

In general terms, in Ireland 46% of all bones on sites after c. AD 400 are of cattle (on the basis of MNIs) (F. Kelly, 1997: 27). At Cahercommaun, the percentage was argued to be as great as 97.

Of the different breeds attested in the documentary sources, the main type was probably similar to the modern Kerry, though a white, red-eared type seems to have been a separate breed (F. Kelly, 1997: 33). Growing evidence suggests that cattle were kept not only for meat, but for dairy produce (Lucas, 1989: 4). Bull calves seem to have been slaughtered and milk cows kept (McCormick, 1983). Literary sources provide abundant evidence for the use of milk and milk products, including cream, butter, buttermilk and cheeses (F. Kelly, 1997: 323–30).

In **Scotland**, cattle constitute the major percentage in bone assemblages. On the Pictish and Dalriadic sites of Dundurn and Dunollie, they amount to over 60% of the total assemblage of bones, but as these figures are for numbers of bone fragments not minimum number of animals represented, they may be over-inflated (L. Alcock, 2003: 112–13).

On the Pictish site at Buckquoy 50% of the bones were of cattle, and at Dunadd the percentage amounted to 76. Despite a suggestion that in Scotland (in contrast to Ireland) cattle were kept for meat rather than dairy produce, the fact that they were kept until they were quite old might support that here too they were kept for dairying. At Dunadd there was a general lack of skulls, implying slaughter away from the site.

A similar absence of skulls was apparent at the Mote of Mark, where cattle comprised the majority of the stock. Here the bones were 86% by weight of cattle (74% of all identified bones), with a sufficiency of young animals to suggest breeding near the site. At both the Mote of Mark and Dunadd the bones were of especially small animals, suggesting that Roman improvements in stock had not reached beyond the frontiers.

In **Wales**, the original analysis of finds from Dinas Powys indicated cattle bones comprised 20.2% of the total assemblage. A more recently studied sample which examined the bones from both phases of the occupation arrived at 27.9% and 36.7% (MNI) respectively. The original analysis suggested that cattle were killed at between two and three years, but the most recent study suggests that two thirds were over three years old at slaughter, and one third of these (% of the total) were over four (Gilchrist, 1988: 36). It was suggested that the cattle were brought to the site for butchery, and that the age pattern is supportive of the view that they were kept primarily for dairying.

Pigs

Pigs were second in importance to cattle and well-suited to partially-cleared woodland. In Ireland 31% of bones (MNI) are of pigs. At Moynagh Lough 67% were shown to have been slaughtered between their second August and the following spring (F. Kelly, 1997: 85). The bones from excavated sites suggest a slender breed.

Pig bones predominated at Dinas Powys, making up 61.3% of the original bone record, or 40–45% in the more recent sample by MNI (L. Alcock, 1963: 192; Gilchrist, 1988: 57). They were slaughtered before maturity, suggesting they were kept primarily for meat (Gilchrist, 1988). Elsewhere the numbers were lower. At Dundurn and Dunollie their bones amounted to 31% and 19% of the total number (L. Alcock, 2003: 113), at Buckquoy 20%, at Dunadd 10% , at Whithorn 24% and at the Mote of Mark 16.5%. Similar percentages are apparent in Ireland. The animals were kept for meat and presumably also leather, and as a result tended to be young – there were almost no adult pigs at the Mote of Mark.

Sheep and goats

It is extremely difficult to differentiate between sheep and goats from surviving bones. At Armagh in Ireland a specific analysis was carried out to determine whether any bones were of goat, and none were found (V. Higgins, 1984: 154). The literary sources from Ireland suggest they were not very important (F. Kelly, 1997: 78–9).

At Deer Park Farms (p. 280), sheep/goat constituted about 20% of the animal remains, and there was evidence for sheep ticks, lice and whipworms near the houses. Ked (parasites living in sheep wool) were absent, suggesting that fleeces were not kept on site.[2]

The breed of sheep was small and stocky, some with two horns and some with four, probably similar to the modern Soay (Jope, 1953). Each might have produced about 1.5 kilos of wool (enough to produce a modern sweater). Their suitability for meat was probably outweighed by their importance for wool.

In the promontory fort at Larrybane there was a much higher proportion of sheep bones, probably to be accounted for by the suitable chalk-land grazing adjacent (Proudfoot and Wilson, 1962). In Ireland, the bones of sheep/goats comprise about 23% of the overall assemblage (F. Kelly, 1997: 27).

The dearth of sheep/goat bones from sites may be partly the result of the animals being kept for wool rather than for meat. What have been assumed to be sheep shears are relatively common finds on sites in Ireland (p. 99).

In Scotland, two goats were identified on each of the Mote of Mark and Dunadd. At Dundurn and Dunollie sheep represent 8% and 17% of the assemblage; at Dunadd 12%, at the Mote of Mark 9.1% but at Buckquoy they constituted about 30%.

Sheep were not kept in large numbers in the wetter Lowlands, being more suited to the hilly regions. Their comparative abundance in Orkney might be explained by the greater suitability of the terrain for sheep rearing. The pattern apparent at Buckquoy is also detectable at Howe (J. Hunter, 1997: 20). At Dunollie, sheep seem to have been slaughtered under the age of eighteen months, implying that here at least their value as meat was appreciated. The evidence from the Mote of Mark also suggested that they were kept for meat as well as wool. At Whithorn, sheep were poorly represented in the earliest monastic occupation (the seventh century), amounting to 8% of the bone assemblage, but this percentage increased in the late eighth to ninth centuries, when the wool trade was becoming more important: there is a corresponding increase in spindle whorls and carding combs at this period (Hill et al., 1997: 607).

In Wales the latest survey at Dinas Powys suggested that sheep comprised 20.7% of the total sample by MNI, declining to 10.2% in a late phase, a previous sample suggesting that the total proportion of sheep bones in the assemblage amounted to 13.4%. The sheep appear to have been slaughtered late – 50% were older than three years, pointing to their being kept for wool rather than meat (Gilchrist, 1988: 57).

Horses and ponies

Ponies may occasionally have been eaten, as the evidence from the Ballinderry crannogs suggests (where bones were found split as if for marrow extraction) (Hencken, 1942: 72; 1936: 234), but were more usually used for riding or draught. There was a relatively high proportion of horse bones at Garranes (9%), but this was possibly because the site is traditionally the seat of the Eóganacht chieftains, who might have required mounts. Only two bones from horses were represented at Dunollie, and occasional horse bones are found on many sites (for example Whithorn and Dunadd), though none from the Mote of Mark.

Poultry

Evidence for poultry-keeping is slight, domestic fowl being represented on only a few rath sites. The chicken was probably introduced from the Roman world, though there is no evidence for it in the law codes before the seventh century. Three fragments of domestic fowl came from the Mote of Mark, two probably from the same bird. One was found at Dinas Powys (L. Alcock, 1963: 193). At Ballinderry 2 they were rather better represented by several dozen bones (Hencken, 1942: 74). Bones from large varieties were represented at Lagore and Lough Faughan, and there are depictions of cocks in the Book of Kells and on a Pictish sculpture from Meigle.

Cats and dogs

Dog bones are common in site assemblages, and bones probably gnawed by dogs are also apparent, for example at the Mote of Mark. Irish wolf hounds were mentioned in Roman sources, and deer hounds are also documented. In addition to working dogs, smaller breeds were kept as pets.

Evidence of both large terriers and lap dogs was present at Lagore. Cats, which were probably introduced from Roman Britain (F. Kelly, 1997: 121), seem to have been kept as rodent catchers – two cats watch two mice biting a Church wafer in the Book of Kells. They were also kept as pets, including in monasteries,[3] though they were particularly associated with women and children. Some slept indoors in a basket, or on a pillow beside their mistresses (F. Kelly, 1997: 122).

There is a nearly complete cat skeleton from Seacash (Lynn, 1978a). Cats and dogs are represented at Dunadd, and evidence of dogs was found at Cadbury Congresbury and Duckpool (Pearce, 2004: 74).

Other animals were kept as pets. Most notable were the *corr* (a bird of uncertain type), crows and jackdaws (F. Kelly, 1997: 127–9).

Wild animals

Hunting of wild animals is known from literature, and is supported by archaeological evidence. Apart from deer and wild boars (see p. 70 below), a wide variety of species has been found in excavation.

At Dundurn and Ballinderry 2 heron remains were found, and remains of a sea eagle were found at the Mote of Mark. Ballinderry 2 produced evidence of a crane, a jay (possibly a pet), various species of duck, teal, goose and gull (Hencken, 1942: 73–4). On Iona, grey seals constituted 7.4% of the total bone assemblage, and there was also an otter, probably caught for its pelt (L. Alcock, 2003: 114).

Wild birds were represented at Leacanabuaile and Carraíg Aille (Leacanabuaile: Ó Riordáin and Foy, 1943; Carraíg Aille: Ó Riordáin, 1949: 102). Remains of foxes are occasionally found in animal bone assemblages, for example at Dunadd and Whithorn. At Church Island, grey seal was well represented, with a few otter, as well as a variety of sea birds, namely gannet, shag, cormorant, and whitefronted goose, ducks, sparrows and finches, though it is unlikely that many of these were eaten (O'Kelly, 1958: 133–4).

A similar variety of sea birds to that at Church Island was present in Orkney: at Howe there were gannets, cormorant/shag and auk, possibly gathered from cliff habitats some 6 km away, while at Pool there was quite a number of cormorants and shags. At Skaill was found the now extinct great auk (Hunter, 1997: 21).

Deer and wild boar

Despite the importance of hunting in the literature, and in Pictish sculpture, bones from deer are poorly represented. A few antlers were found at Dundurn and Dunollie. On Iona about 33% of the total number of bones came from wild species. These included red deer (14.8%), and roe deer (3.7%). At Edinburgh Castle red deer comprised 9% of the total number of animals represented by bones (L. Alcock, 2003: 114).

Deer were probably larger than their modern counterparts and would have been a good source of protein (McCormick, 1981: 317; Noddle, 1982). At Howe on Orkney red deer decreased in importance in the Pictish period, possibly because herds were reduced, or because sheep were increasingly exploited (Ballin Smith, 1994: 143), but at Skaill and Pool the decline in deer was not linked to an increase in sheep. Whole carcasses may have been brought to Pool from nearby Eday (J. Hunter, 1997: 21). In Wales, deer were represented at Dinas Powys, mainly by twelve loose teeth (L. Alcock, 1963: 192).

Wild boar were probably hunted (they are depicted in Pictish sculpture) but it is very difficult to distinguish wild from domesticated species.

Shellfish and fish

Fish bones and shells are on the whole poorly represented, possibly because they are easy to miss in excavation, though it is also possible that fish played a relatively minor role in the diet, even in coastal areas, until at least the Viking Age. A few fish bones were found at Lagore, and at Oughtymore a midden contained a number of eel and cod bones as well as some flatfish, salmon and possibly haddock (Mallory and Woodman, 1984). Winkles and cockles predominated in the midden, but there were also mussels. At Pool and Howe limpets, periwinkles and mussels were found, and at Howe fish included saithe and eels, with some cod and ling (J. Hunter, 1997: 22).

At Rathmullan, mussels, limpets and a whalebone were discovered (Lynn, 1982: 154). Cetacean bone (i.e. from marine mammals) was generally represented in Orkney, presumably also from beached animals. Only three fish bones were present at Dunollie (which overlooks the sea), and there was very limited evidence for fishing from Buckquoy before the Norse period. Line sinkers are not common. Cod and wrasse bones were found at Church Island (O'Kelly, 1958: 134).

Oyster was present at Longbury Bank in Wales and at Dunadd. At Dinas Powys, although the diet was predominantly derived from land species, remains included limpet, oyster, whelk, cockle, periwinkle and mussel, as well as salmon or sea trout (L. Alcock, 1963: 39–40).

Cultivation

The direct evidence for the cultivation of land is meagre, but the picture is filled out by literary references (M. Duignan, 1944; V. Proudfoot, 1958; 1961: 104–9). Some information is becoming available through aerial photography and ground survey, but it is often impossible to assign field systems to any specific period.

Evidence for the crops themselves is increasingly available through analysis of pollen and deductions may be made in the absence of direct evidence from tools and mills (p. 75).

Field layouts

The Irish Laws imply that although most fields were fenced and were family property, there was also a certain amount of common land with elaborate rules for its use.

In Ireland, at The Spectacles, Lough Gur (Ó Riordáin, 1949: 61), and at Cush (Ó Riordáin, 1940), field layouts can be traced (Fig. 28). At Cush, the fields were defined by banks and ditches, the latter about a metre deep. Earth and stone boundaries were employed at The Spectacles, where each house was set in its own small field. It is possible that the fields and huts at Caherguillamore and Two Mile Stone were contemporaneous. Those at Two Mile Stone are large and irregular, bounded by short lines of walling, and would have been used for

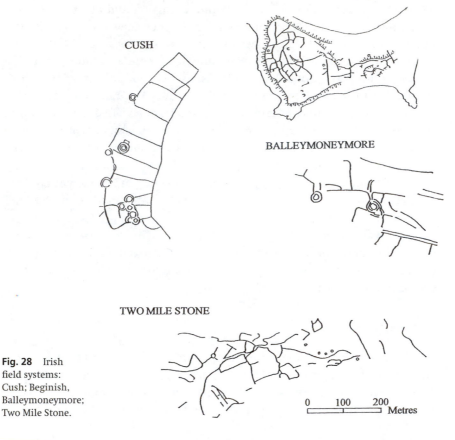

Fig. 28 Irish field systems: Cush; Beginish, Balleymoneymore; Two Mile Stone.

pasture (O. Davies, 1942). Terraces on the slopes below the settlement were possibly used for cultivation. In the main, fields were small and irregular, formed without any overall planning. At Rathangan the fields seem to have radiated out from a central rath (Norman and St Joseph, 1969: pl. 35). In some cases fields have been found under raths – for example at Lisduggan North.

Ridge-and-furrow is fairly widespread in Ireland, and certainly appears to pre-date the arrival of the Normans. Irish texts refer to sowing on wide earthen ridges or raised beds, which may in some cases be taken to indicate ridge-and-furrow.[4] Ridge-and-furrow appears in long rectangular fields at Goodland where pollen diagrams suggested it may date from c. 600 (Mitchell, 1986: 162–4). It was out of use by the fifteenth or sixteenth century. Ridge-and-furrow is also attested at Cush, though the date is less certain (P. J. Fowler, 1966).

In Scotland there is some evidence for ard cultivation in the early medieval period at Portmahomack overlain by later ridge-and-furrow cultivation (Carver, 2004: 19). Terracing, including on the slopes of the summit of

Dundurn (Alcock et al., 1989: pl. 12.1), probably in some instances belongs to the period, while some of the narrow rig plots often dug with hand tools near Lairg may also be of this date (Carter, 1994). The plough pebbles from Whithorn indicate that by the seventh century the mould-board plough was in use there (Hill and Kucharski, 1990). Associated with some of the 'Pitcarmick' houses in Perthshire, notably at Glen Derby, Benachally and the Hill of Cally, were fairly extensive systems of narrow sub-rectangular fields with low terraces and stony banks (RCHAMS, 1990, 12 and passim).

In Wales ridge-and-furrow was found to pre-date the Norman motte at Hen Domen, in the Welsh Marches (Barker and Lawson, 1971).

In south-west England, at Gwithian, a field dated to the late fifth to sixth centuries measured 27×40–100 m (Fowler and Thomas, 1962). The northern long side was demarcated by a wide, shallow boundary ditch, and the southern side was a terrace above the mud flats of the estuary. The field was some distance inland from the houses. At the base of the plough soil in one cutting, stripes of sands separated horizontally and vertically by bands of dark soil were interpreted as the turned furrow-slices produced by a fixed mould-board plough. Field systems have been studied south and west of Tintagel, where about ten enclosed settlements were replaced in the period by about thirty open settlements, which employed a system of small, roughly square fields and trackways. Some fields seem to have been re-structured for strip cultivation, perhaps after 850 (Rose and Preston-Jones, 1995: 54; Pearce, 2004: 44–6).

Crops

Seven grain crops are known from both literary and archaeological sources: 'red' (possibly emmer) and bread wheat, spelt wheat, oats, two- and six-row barley and rye (F. Kelly, 1997: 219). The archaeological evidence is sparse and random and includes other plants about which deductions must be made with caution.

Wheat is generally absent from Scotland, but is better represented in Ireland. Straw was found at Lagore (Hencken, 1950: 242). Literary sources indicate different types.

Oats were cultivated at Dunadd as the main crop from the seventh century, supplemented by barley (which appears to have been grown nearby). Oats were widespread in Orkney in the Pictish period, appearing for the first time in the archaeological record at Pool (J. Hunter, 1997: 18). Oats and barley were the main crops grown at Scalloway from the fifth to the eighth centuries, with oats becoming more popular later (Holden and Boardman in Sharples 1998: 99–106). Oats and barley were represented at Dundurn.

Barley was commonly the six-row type known later as *bere*, and occurs in both hulled and naked varieties. Two-row barley is also possibly mentioned in literary sources (F. Kelly, 1997: 223). Naked barley would have been used for broth; hulled barley could have been used to make bannocks.

Flax seeds were found at Lissue, and the plant is mentioned in literature along with various vegetables including kale, onions, leeks, garlic and dye-plants. Flax is attested at Buiston crannog, and Easter Kinnear. Flax appeared in Orkney in the Pictish levels at Howe and Pool, and later was more intensively cultivated in the Viking levels. It was used for both fibres and oil (Bond and Hunter, 1987; J. Hunter, 1997: 19). Other plants attested in the literary sources are peas, broad beans, cabbage, chives and root crops (F. Kelly, 1997: 248–56). Fruits mentioned include apple and plum (F. Kelly, 1997: ch. 8).

Tools and structures associated with cultivation

Tools and structures can indicate the methods of cultivation and occasionally the type of produce.

Corn-drying kilns are known from a number of sites such as Letterkeen, Ballymacash and Garranes, and possibly also Uisneach and Nendrum (corn-drying kilns generally: Monk, 1981). At Cush grain may have been stored in **granaries** supported by four posts, while grain storage pits of Iron Age 'Little Woodbury' type are known. Rotary querns, often decorated in the early medieval period with lines and rings in relief, are found on Irish sites.

According to literary sources **ploughs** were pulled by a team of two, four or six oxen (F. Kelly, 1997: 468–77). Two types of plough are known; the light two-ox plough without a coulter, wheels or mould-board, usually known as an 'ard', used in cross-ploughing and widely present in prehistoric Europe and the heavy coultered plough, often with wheel and mould-board. The latter was suited to heavier soils, and though known from Europe as early as the fifth century BC does not appear to have been introduced to Britain until the second century BC. Thereafter it was common, but it has been argued that it did not reach Ireland until the tenth century (F. Kelly, 1997: 470).

Two wooden **ards** have been found at Buiston, a variation of a type known as a crooked ard. They are made from branch joints deliberately selected so that the beam curves away to the right of the sole: this had the same effect as a mould-board (Crone, 2000: 118).

Relatively few sites have produced coulters or shares, which are only known from major crannogs, Dundrum, and a few raths. They indicate the use of a fairly heavy plough as well as a type of ard (p. 104).

Sickles and reaping hooks were used for cutting the crops, as well as for fodder and thatch (p. 99). The scythe does not appear to have reached the Celtic world until the fifteenth century – reaping was invariably done with a sickle, the ears being cut at the top of the stalk.

An iron spade (or rather the shoe for one) has survived (p. 99), and cut turves and peat of the period are known.

For **threshing** a stick was used rather than a true flail (F. Kelly, 1997: 481–2). Corn was sown directly on the furrow and harrowing is mentioned in the *Crith Gabhlach* law code, though the date of its introduction is unknown (F. Kelly, 1997: 478).

Mills

There is no evidence for windmills in this period, but there is a growing body of evidence for watermills. This is largely due to the good preservation of woodwork in waterlogged conditions in Ireland, and the advances made in Irish dendrochronology for the period. There are two types of watermill: the horizontal and the vertical.

A **horizontal wheel** under the mill was powered by water coming in through a wooden trough which was splayed internally to give the necessary pressure to the water. There were no gears: the waterwheel's axle was directly connected to the upper millstone (Lucas, 1953). Widespread in the Mediterranean, such wheels were introduced to Ireland by the second half of the sixth century (Rynne, 1989: 23). Several survive sufficiently well-preserved for the study of the mechanism, most notably a ninth-century example at Cloontycarthy (Rynne, 1989: 23) and an eighth-century example at Drumard (Baillie, 1975).

A more developed type of horizontal watermill is represented at Nendrum, on Stranford Lough, which has the earliest documented tidal mills in Europe.

Three mills were found at Nendrum, the earliest being constructed between AD 619 and 621, with an embankment built to contain tidal water. The later mills were more sophisticated. Mill 3, constructed in or around 787, had a stone-built wheelhouse and tidal tailrace. The housing for the wheel was built as an open rectangle, like a tidal dock, and survived to a height of c. 2.1 m. Finds from it included parts of the granite millstones, parts of the wooden wheel paddles and some grain. The flume, which was of sandstone, was wedge shaped, and funnelled the water to force it through an oval hole, 16 × 15 cm, on to the paddles of the millwheel (McErlean, 2001: 14).

Ballinderry 1 produced a sandstone millstone 70 cm in diameter and 29 cm thick. Although fragmentary, it weighed 158 kg and must have been used in a water-driven mill due to its weight.

Watermills with **vertical wheels** were introduced to Ireland by the seventh century, as shown by the dendro-dated examples of undershot mills at Little Island which were built c. 630 (Rynne, 1989: 26).

4 Everyday objects and equipment

Between c. AD 400 and 1200, a variety of everyday artefacts were produced in materials such as wood, bone, pottery, textiles, leather and metals. Rarer ceramics and glass were imported (ch. 6). A considerable range of production techniques, activities and creativity is indicated. The assemblage available for study is entirely dependent upon chance survival of non-durable materials; the skill of investigators; technological methods of retrieval available at the time, and the sites chosen for research. Water-logged sites have yielded a high proportion of wood and leather, which was then subject to the conservation tehniques available at the time of finding.

Wood

There is some evidence that woodworking production centres existed in Ireland and Scotland notably from Deer Park Farms, Lagore, Lissue, and the monastic sites of Clonmacnoise and Iona. Evidence includes unfinished staves, waste cores and roughouts. It is unknown whether some products were traded.

Wooden objects

The most common domestic vessels were of wood. Many wooden items are so similar to recent examples, that they can be dated only from find context (if known). Most wooden objects are relatively simple; typical examples are shown in the illustrations. Most of the wooden objects from the period are vessels (such as buckets, troughs, bowls and tankards), and utensils (such as mallets, paddles, handles, spindles, clubs, pegs, scoops, knobs, lids and spoons).[1]

Amongst the rarer items are dugout canoes. A fine gaming board and part of what is possibly a pack saddle was found at the crannog site known as Ballinderry 1 (p. 281) (Hencken, 1936: 170–90). A shoe last was found at Deer Park Farms (Earwood, 1993: 100). The bases of bentwood boxes are known from Ballinderry 2 and Lagore (Earwood, 1993: 105).

Wooden troughs were found at Deer Park Farms and at Loch Glashan crannog (Earwood, 1990). Artefacts from the latter site included spatulae, pegs, pins and handles, wedges, balls (possibly for a game) a spindle whorl, a paddle and a paddle-shaped tool which may have been used for beating flax.

Buiston crannog produced two wooden ards, a spindle, possible loom pegs, a shoe last, a textile comb and a hobble of twisted birch stems which was probably used to restrain yearling calves (Crone, 2000: 118).

Furniture does not survive, with the exception of an eighth-century bed end from Deer Park Farms, from which site has also come a complete door frame, door lintels and jamb. The bed ends were made of split oak into which were fitted woven panels, and the bed itself was filled with brushwood and other organic materials, probably including cloth. One end was built into the wall.

There is evidence for furniture from art. Chairs with animal headed knobs at the back are depicted in Pictish sculpture, for example on a stone from Kirriemuir (Allen and Anderson, 1903: fig. 239b) and the pommel from such a chair, decorated however in Viking style, was found at Fishamble Street, Dublin (Lang, 1987: 175 and fig. 1). Elaborate chairs with decorative pommels, stretchers and other ornament appear on the Pictish slab from Dunfallandy (Allen and Anderson, 1903: fig. 305b), while another slab, Fowlis Wester 2, depicts clerics seated on chairs with coiled terminals at the back and intricately carved side panels (Sutherland, 1994: 160).

Carpentry techniques

Woodworking techniques include stave-building, lathe-turning and carving. A few items were decorated.

Stave-built vessels

Most vessels seem to have been stave-built (Fig. 29). Some staves had projections at the top with a hole to take a metal handle, often of twisted iron. The handles are common finds. The hoops were made of a branch split lengthwise and fastened with an iron clamp. The bottom was set in a groove in the staves. A small, complete bucket from Ballinderry 1, consisted of nineteen staves and two hoops. Two pegs supported each of the hoops after they were hammered into place (Hencken, 1936: 141). From Lissue came a churn of oak, dating from around AD 800, wider at the base than at the top, with wooden hoops and an iron rim mount, together with two iron hoops. The churn could have been suspended from cords which passed through two iron rings attached to the central iron hoop. Such churns, which were swung to and fro to make butter, were used in Ireland until the nineteenth century (Bersu, 1947: 53). The lid of a stave-built vessel, probably a barrel, was found at Buiston, though it may have been an import, introduced to the site filled with wine (Crone, 2000: 114). The lids of two plunge churns were also preserved there (Crone, 2000: 118–28).

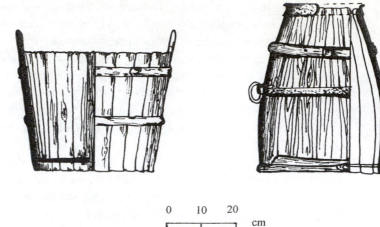

Fig. 29 Wooden stave-built vessels, Ballinderry 1 and Lissue.

0   10   20
cm

Lathe-turned vessels

Lathe-turning seems to have been particularly common in the ninth and tenth centuries AD (Earwood, 1993: 94). A series of lathe-turned wooden bowls from Ballinderry, Lagore, Moynagh Lough, Lissue, Dublin, Buiston, Iona, Loch Glashan crannog and Deer Park Farms show the types that were in use (Fig. 30).

Ballinderry 2 has produced parts of fifteen lathe-turned bowls and one platter (Hencken, 1942: 58–61). A cord or a pole-lathe was employed – waste material from the manufacture of bowls has been found at Iona (Barber, 1981: 335), Moynagh Lough (Earwood, 1993: 284), Buiston (Crone, 2000: 112) and Lagore (Hencken, 1950: 166), among other places. Lathe-turning required specialist equipment and training, though Irish laws mention lathe-turners as craftsmen of fairly low status (MacNeill, 1923: 280).

A recent study has defined three main groups of lathe-turned vessel, which seem to have been inspired by imported pottery (Classes A and E: pp. 139–41) (Earwood, 1991–2).

> *Group 1* Usually has a footring and upright profile. Decorated with incised horizontal lines or cordons. Fairly uncommon. Have been seen as inspired by imported A Ware (p. 139) which suggests a date of the late fifth or early sixth century.

> *Group 2* Appears to be inspired by E Ware imports (Earwood, 1993: 94–100). All main types of E Ware are represented, Ei jars (at for example at Loch Glashan crannog and Lissue), Eii jars (for example at Lissue and Iona) and Eiii bowls (at Lagore and Lissue). Unlike the pottery versions, however, the wooden bowls often have cordons or incised decorative lines. Although the

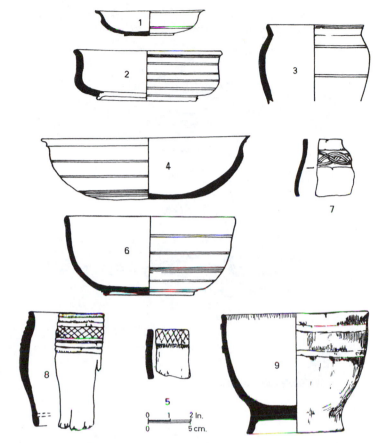

Fig. 30 Wooden turned vessels. 1, 2, 4, 6: Lagore; 3. Lissue; 5. Ballinderry 2; 7, 9: Ballinderry 1.

earliest instances appear to be contemporary with E Ware, the wooden bowls continued to be made or used into the ninth or even the tenth century.

Group 3 Comprises bowls without ceramic parallel but which are decorated – they have been found at Ballinderry 1 and Dublin, and are presumed to belong to the Viking Age.

Carving

Apart from items carved out of the block (Fig. 31), carved wood has rarely survived, except in the Viking levels at Dublin. There is a carved wooden figure of a nude man from Lagore (Hencken, 1950: 168), and a gaming board from Ballinderry 1 (Hencken, 1936: 175–90). This example has a human head and an animal head at opposite sides as handles, and is decorated with ring-chain, key or fret patterns and interlace. The board was probably used for a version of Fox and Geese.

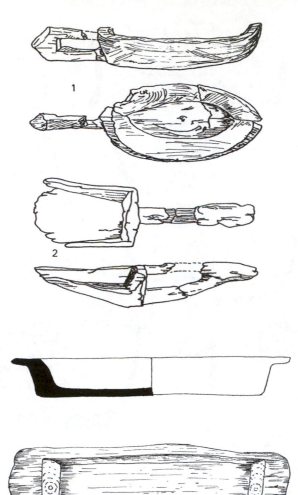

Fig. 31
Wooden scoop,
shovel and
trough: 1. Lagore;
2. Ballinderry 1;
3. Loch Glashan.

A wooden gaming counter was found at Moynagh Lough. A lid with perfor-ated lug came from Buiston and may have held a fastening bar (Crone, 2000: 115–17), such as was found on kegs from Letterkeen, Co. Mayo, and Rosmoylan, Co. Roscommon (Earwood, 1993: 112–13).

The finest example of carved wood however is a Pictish wooden box from Birsay, Orkney, cut from a block of alder with a sliding lid, and probably of the eighth century. It is decorated with chip-carved running scrolls and C-curves. It was probably the toolbox of a leatherworker, and when found contained eight handles from leatherworking tools (Stevenson, 1951–2).

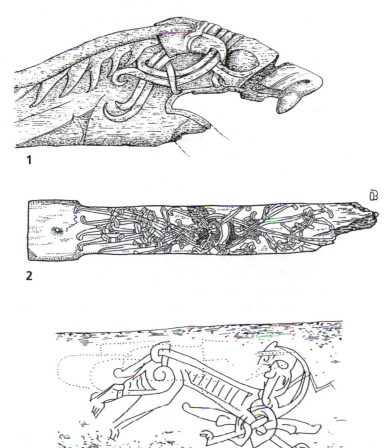

Fig. 32
Decorated
woodwork from
Dublin. 1. chair
pommel,
Fishamble St;
2. box lid,
Fishamble St;
3. spatula, Christ
Church Place.

Decoration

Ornate decoration other than simple ruling or ribbing is relatively rare on domestic vessels (Fig. 32). A wooden tub from Ballinderry 1, decorated with trellis and cordon ornament, was made by hollowing out a piece of trunk, a groove being cut to take a separate bottom plate. This difficult technique of producing wooden vessels is known from post-medieval Ireland.

Interlace decorated a wooden trial piece from Ballinderry 1 and a very elegant bowl from a bog at Cavancarragh (both probably of the ninth or tenth century: Earwood, 1993: 114–15). Platters and troughs were normally rectangular or oval, and were frequently furnished with a pair of lugs to facilitate lifting (Earwood, 1993: 102).

The skill of the Celtic woodcarver is apparent in the range of decorated woodwork from the Viking occupation at Dublin, which included such items as a series of crooks or curved handles; a yoke, and part of a carved boss from a wooden example of a High Cross (Lang, 1987: 174; Lang, 1988). Non-Viking products from Dublin include the roof of a house shrine, a stylus, a decorated box, and a figurine (Lang, 1988: 4–8).

Bone

Bone and antler were worked domestically as well as on a larger scale, notably at the monastery of Clonmacnoise, where an antler workshop has been excavated.

Bone objects

Apart from pins, needles and combs (p. 83) a variety of small objects was made in bone, most notably weaving equipment, handles, bobbins, toggles, shuttles and mounts for such items as wooden boxes.[2] As a substitute, antler was sometimes used for combs or for toggles or handles.

Bone dice are widespread in Europe in both area and time. Around the second century AD they appeared for the first time in Scotland, and may have spread thence to Ireland (D. Clarke, 1970: 217–18). In Scotland they were a feature of the Atlantic region from the Iron Age onwards, and at sites such as Bac Mhic Connain, Foshigarry or Dun Cuier may have been used during the early medieval period.

In Ireland they were found at Lagore and Ballinderry 2 and occasionally turn up as stray finds. One from Ballinderry 2 is wooden, and another has on one face the ogham sign for the Roman numeral V, instead of the normal five dots (Hencken, 1942: 55, no. 45). They were probably used not for scoring throws, but for a game in which four dice are used together and thrown in the air, to fall on a blanket or cloth (D. Clarke, 1970: 226). All these dice are long (parallelopiped) and are marked on four faces, the ends being open. Bone dice-boxes are also known.

Gaming pieces were found at Dun Cuier, Barra (A. Young, 1955–6: 319–20) and simple, round gaming pieces of bone, stone, and occasionally glass, occur in a variety of contexts in the early medieval period.

Comb making

A specialized form of bone working was used to make combs which were current throughout the period and occur on most sites (MacGregor, 1985: 74–98). Bone was a cheap substitute for ivory, the most suitable material for combs, though wood was used on occasion, for example at Buiston.

The composite bone comb (the most common type) originated in the Romano-British period. Some combs have ring-and-dot decoration, a type of ornament used in both the Celtic west and on the pagan Anglo-Saxon combs. Composite bone combs predominate – most are double-sided and are thus difficult to make out of a single piece of bone.

It is possible that combing and hair cutting were part of an inauguration ritual in the pagan world which was adopted by Christians (Alcock, 1963: 155), a factor which may account for the abundance of combs. It is unlikely that all double-edged combs were worn in the hair, though references in the *Mabinogion* (a collection of Welsh tales) imply that some combs were worn in this way, though as the text of these stories dates from the later middle ages, they may not refer to the period covered by this book.

The double-sided comb was retained as a design even when the original reason for having two sides – that one side could have fine teeth and the other coarse – was lost during the period, when the teeth on both sides became of moderate coarseness.

Comb types

A scheme for Irish combs categorizes all combs from early medieval and later periods by letter, of which A to G are from the period covered in this book (Fig. 33).

A   Simple single-edged comb with high curved back.[3] They may span the entire period covered by this book, though one sub-type seems to be eighth century and later.
B   Double-edged composite comb with straight sides. This is the most common type and appears to have been current until the tenth or eleventh centuries, on the evidence afforded by a comb with Viking-period decoration from Ardglass.
C   Single-edged composite comb with ornamental back.[4] The finest example comes from a seventh-century context at Dun Cuier, Barra, where the head has a zoomorphic form. This date would be compatible with apparently early finds at Lough Gara and Killealy (Dunlevy, 1988: 357). A characteristic feature of combs of this type is the median plate which is riveted along each side but does not extend to the ends of the comb. Other examples tend to have backs of tribolate form, and occur at Lagore and Carraíg Aille. The type was popular in the sixth-seventh century, but may have continued later.
D   Double-edged composite comb with teeth of reducing length at the ends (wide end-teeth). Three sub-varieties span the entire period.[5]
E   Double-sided comb with two braces on each side.
F   Single-sided long comb with humped back. This is a common Viking type of comb, current from the ninth to twelfth century and later. It appears at

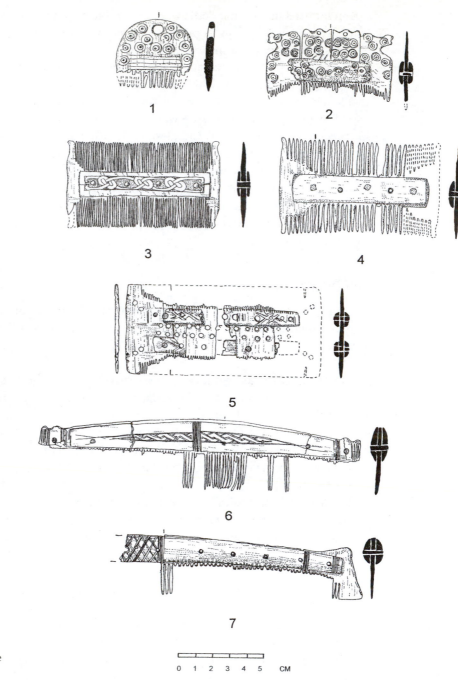

Fig. 33 Bone comb types.

0 1 2 3 4 5   CM

Lagore, Dublin, Carraíg Aille and Lagore in Ireland as well as Jarlshof and Skaill in Scotland.

F2 Handled one-sided comb. This is a Viking-period type, which is simply a variant of type E.

G Single-edged composite highly polished comb with straight back and straight end-teeth. There are simpler and ornate versions (Dunlevy, 1988: 367–9). They appear to date from the ninth to the eleventh or twelfth centuries.

Pottery

Following the withdrawal of the Roman legions, the Romano-British pottery industry soon declined, though it would appear that Romano-British kilns were producing wares for local use into the fifth and sixth centuries in for example, Lincoln and Oxfordshire. A distinctive Romano-British pottery known as black-burnished ware continued in production in Dorset into the fifth century (Dark, 1996b: 58–60; Sparey-Green, 1996: 123–6).

There is some evidence for Romano-British potting surviving on a local basis in the west of Britain, but fine, wheel-made potting seems to have ended at some point in the fifth century. The Anglo-Saxons introduced into southern and western England new types from the Continent, but no such impetus, however, was given to the Celtic-speaking areas which uniformly produced extremely mundane wares undoubtedly due to the lack of source materials as well as skills.

Except in the Atlantic province of Scotland, native pottery of the period is so uniformly poor in quality that it cannot normally be used as a viable indicator of culture or date. The term sometimes used is VCP (Very Coarse Pottery). In addition to these very coarse wares, there are six distinct groups of western native pottery: (1) surviving Romano-British pottery in south-west England; (2) grass-tempered ware; (3) Irish souterrain ware and its relatives in Scotland; (4) Cornish grass-marked ware; (5) Atlantic province pottery; (6) Viking period wares.

Native pottery

Very Coarse Pottery

This was produced throughout prehistory after the Neolithic and in early historic times, making it impossible to date except from its context (unless it displays some distinctive feature). Clearly, in Very Coarse Pottery both fabric and form are related since the lack of suitable clay necessitated large, straight-walled pots with simple rims and elementary decoration. Whether the choice of very heavily gritted clay was a necessity, or a matter of taste, rims were inevitably either upright or slightly everted, slightly rounded or flattened.

(1) *Romano-British potting traditions in south-west England*   In south-west England there is some evidence for a lingering tradition of Romano-British potting. At Ower, on Poole harbour, the production of black-burnished Roman-style pottery continued on a seasonal basis during the fifth and possibly also the sixth century. Pottery from this centre may have been traded to Exeter, Bath and Dorchester, and finds are widely distributed in Hampshire, Dorset and Somerset (Sunter and Woodward, 1987; Gerrard, 2004). In Cornwall pottery in Romano-British forms made from gabbroic clays from the Lizard peninsula turns up on sites such as Trethurgy, Carvossa and Reawla; at Reawla it may have been in use through much of the sixth century, while at Trethurgy it was in use as late as 500. It appears associated with imported pottery of the fifth–sixth centuries at Bantham (May and Weddell, 2002: 421), and it also occurs at Mothecombe, Tintagel, Gwithian, and St Michael's Mount (Turner, 2003: 27). At Heliggy fourth-century-style pottery was associated with a North African Red Slip bowl of the late fifth century (Pearce, 2004: 71). Cumulatively, this suggests that native pottery production in the Roman style continued in Cornwall into the sixth century.

(2) *Grass-tempered pottery*   This has organic tempering: typically chopped grass was mixed with the clay to strengthen it. Grass-tempered pottery was found on the Irish monastic site of Reask. It was of light, porous, light-brown to buff ware, to which burnt food residues adhered. Associated with it was a more compact coarse pottery with large sandy grits. Dating was provided by radio-carbon and by overlying Biii imported pottery (p. 139), implying it has been in use probably in the fifth to sixth centuries (Fanning, 1981: 112–3). Two tiny sherds were identified at Dunadd (Lane and Campbell, 2000: 104), and similar pottery is documented at Iona (Campbell and Lane, 1988; Barber, 1981: fig. 43, 234–2), where one sherd was also grass-marked (Campbell and Lane, 2000: 104).

Grass-tempering was a feature of the late Roman and post-Roman period in south-west England (Rahtz, 1974: 99). In Gloucestershire it is found in the latest levels of the villas at Frocester Court and Barnsley Park. It appears to represent a late Roman tradition which survived into the fifth century (Rahtz, 1974: 98–9).

(3) *Souterrain ware*   This term for a category of Irish pottery is misleading since it is found more often in raths than souterrains (Fig. 34A). It has been found in east Ulster, Wicklow and Tyrone, and where the grits are identifiable appears to have beeen of local manufacture (Ryan, 1973: 623). Souterrain

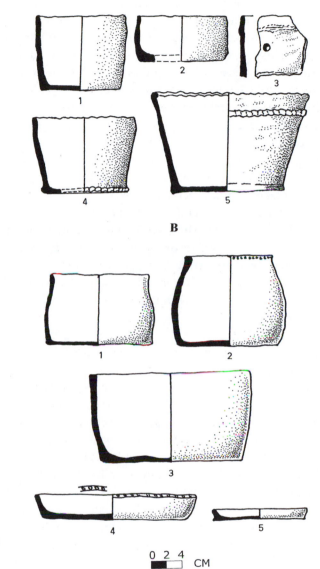

Fig. 34
A. Souterrrain
ware:
1. Dundrum
Sandhills;
2. Lough
Faughan;
3. Nendrum;
4–5. Lissue. B.
Grass-marked
pottery,
Cornwall:
1. Chun Castle;
4. Tean; 2, 3,
5. Gwithian.

ware pots are flat-bottomed and 40% are grass-marked. Unlike grass-tempered pottery, the clay vessels were set on chopped grass to dry out, which left grass impressions on the base.

On present evidence, souterrain ware seems to have come into use during the seventh or eighth centuries, and continued into the twelfth or thirteenth centuries (for example at Doonbought, Co. Antrim: McNeill, 1975). There seems to have been a phase with undecorated pots (represented in the earlier ringfort ditch at Lissue, Co. Antrim: Bersu, 1947), followed by a phase with plain cordons (for example at Lissue: Bersu, 1947: 51 and Langford Lodge: Waterman, 1963), in turn followed by a period of pots with incised ornament and finger-tipping (Proudfoot, 1958). The decoration is confined to finger-tipping the rim or fingerprinting a cordon around the vessel (Waterman and Collins, 1966: 133–5). It seems likely that souterrain ware should be seen as a continuing tradition of prehistoric potting techniques.

In a few cases, souterrain ware was clearly associated with E Ware (for example at Ballyfounder and Langford Lodge). At Rathmullan (Lynn, 1982) and Gransha (Lynn, 1985), E Ware has been found in the earlier layers; souterrain ware in the later. At Drumard a sherd of souterrain ware lay under a timber in a horizontal mill, which was dated by dendrochronology to AD 782. However the sherd could pre-date the mill (Bailey, 1986).

At Larne (Waterman and Collins, 1966: 133) the site produced both souterrain ware and a radiocarbon date of 480 ± 120 AD. Related to souterrain ware is a small group of sherds from Whithorn, where it was suggested they belonged to the eighth to twelfth centuries (Campbell in Hill et al., 1997: 358). There is also a small amount of souterrain ware from Iona (Campbell and Lane, 1988: 208).

(4) *Grass-marked pottery in Cornwall and Scilly (Fig. 34B)*   The pottery sequence in Cornwall was originally set out on the basis of finds from Gwithian. However, the evidence from Gwithian is not as clear as was originally suggested (Preston-Jones and Rose, 1986: 175). At Samson grass-marked ware appears to post-date E Ware in the late sixth to seventh centuries (C. Thomas, 1985: 186) and it has been argued that in both Ireland and Cornwall grass-marked pottery post-dates the importation of E Ware (Campbell, in Hill et al., 1997: 358).

The Cornish grass-marked wares are extremely coarse, and range from browns to grey and black (A. Thomas, 1968a: 322–3). They appear in two basic forms: the platter and the cooking pot. The cooking pots, which are usually carbonized externally (suggesting that they were used in the fire), are normally either flat-rimmed or slightly rounded off with some thickening. There are a few vessels with slightly everted rims. Frequently the pots are slightly narrower at the mouth than at the base, which is flat. It has been suggested that grass-marked pottery was introduced to Cornwall by Irish settlers in the sixth century (Thomas, 1968a: 327). This view is now not widely maintained.

Among the pottery from Gwithian were grass-marked sherds of 'bar lug' pottery, which was hand-made and globular in shape. It has high 'ears' (hence its name) covering bridge spouts, presumably to protect the suspension strings from the fire. It was originally suggested these pots were introduced to Cornwall in the early ninth century from the Low Countries (Thomas,

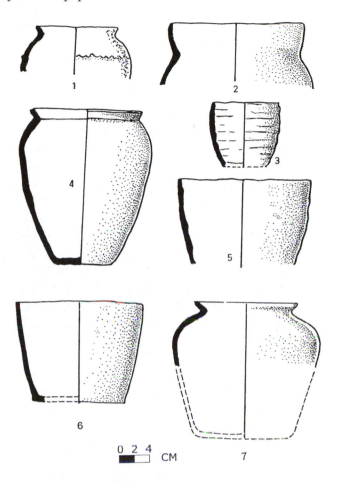

Fig. 35 Atlantic province pottery. 1–4: a' Cheardach Mhor; 5: Dun Cuier; 6–7: Jarlshof.

1968a: 313). More recent appraisal suggests there is no evidence for Frisian settlers in Cornwall and that it was a purely local development.[6] There are indications that grass-marked pottery continued in use until the twelfth century (Preston-Jones and Rose, 1986: 176).

(5) *Atlantic province pottery*   In the Atlantic province of Scotland native Iron Age pottery traditions continued until the time of the Viking settlements (Fig. 35). In the Northern Isles the pottery sequence differs from the Hebridean sequence, but represents a parallel series of developments.

Pottery in Orkney

In Orkney a radiocarbon-dated sequence has been established at Howe where in the fourth to ninth centuries AD pottery comprised upright jars with slightly everted rims. Where decoration occurred at all it was minimal, having a neck cordon, combed or dragged incised lines, or in one case a possibly painted design (Ballin Smith, 1994: 252–6). Wheel-finishing was employed in the earlier part of the Pictish period. A comparable ceramic tradition existed at Pool and Skaill (Pool: J. Hunter, 1997: 30–1; Skaill: Buteux, 1997: 202–3).

Pottery in Shetland

In Shetland there are slight differences between the pottery found at Jarlshof and Clickhimin. At Jarlshof 'buff ware' made its appearance some time after AD 100 (Hamilton, 1956: 81–3). New forms were made in this ware, the most common being a large open bowl with a slightly inverted flat-topped rim. The bases are often slightly splayed. A second class of ware of similar date is grey or grey-black with a smooth, burnished surface. The rims of these pots are sharply everted and the curved shoulders suggest fairly rounded vessels. Finally, just before the arrival of the Vikings, the associated pottery is thin-walled and crude, and represents a degenerate form of 'buff ware'. At Clickhimin all the earlier forms survived, the most common being a large cooking pot with everted rim, plain or fluted (Hamilton, 1968: 144), with simple pottery similar to the degenerate buff ware at Jarlshof in its final phase (Hamilton, 1968: 159). Generally similar pottery is documented from Scalloway (Sharples, 1998: 136).

Pottery in the Outer Hebrides

In the Outer Hebrides, the chronology of pottery from 500 BC to AD 800 has been actively debated in the last fifty years (Young, 1966; Lane, 1990). The key to understanding its evolution lies with the long sequence of occupation at the Udal where between the third/fourth century AD and the eighth or ninth centuries hand-made, undecorated pottery with flat bases and bucket and shouldered-jar shapes are found, termed 'Plain Style'. Similar pottery has been found at a' Cheardach Mhor and at Beirgh (Harding and Gilmour, 2000) as well as at Dun Cuier (Young, 1955–6).

The sequence outlined above is somewhat different from that represented at Dun Vulan where pots with sharply everted rims and decoration involving feather-based incisions, curved parallel lines and channelled arches (a type of pottery termed 'Clettraval Ware' at Dun Mor Vaul: Lane, 1990) were current in the fifth to sixth centuries and were succeeded by largely plain vessels with flaring rims with cordons and applied curved arches ('Dun Cuier' style) current in the sixth to ninth centuries (Parker Pearson and Sharples, 1999: 210).

Viking-period pottery

In the Outer Hebrides during the Viking Age a new style of pottery is found. This is characterized by sagging and flat-based cups and bowls and flat platters, sometimes associated with 'Plain Style' pottery. Some of it is grass-marked, and some simply decorated rims are found. Influence from souterrain ware has been argued (Lane, 1990: 123).

Textiles and textile production

Although few textiles themselves survive, their production is attested by a variety of pieces of weaving equipment.

Looms

Although a circular stone weight from Shaneen Park, Belfast, has been claimed to be from a warp weighted loom, it is more likely that the textiles represented at Lagore were made on a two-beam vertical loom or (for narrower weaves) a backstrap loom (Hodkinson, 1987). What may be a loom is depicted on a Pictish slab from Kirriemuir (Allen and Anderson, 1903: fig. 239b).

Spinning and weaving equipment

A variety of implements for spinning wool and weaving both wool and flax have been found.

Flax

This was used for making linen. After hand-harvesting, the plants were dried and the seeds removed by the heads being pulled through a coarse comb (Earwood, 1993: 125–31). The plants were immersed in water ('retting') to soften the fibres before being dried again and beaten. Four comb-like objects from Deer Park Farms may have been used for this purpose. At the same site slotted beams were found for a wooden wall reaching waist height. It has been suggested from the nearby presence of flax seeds that it was used for flax beating. Wooden beaters probably used for this are known from Lagore and Ballinderry 1 and 2, where flat beaters were employed.

Wool

Wooden spindles for wool spinning are well attested from crannogs, and were typically bulbous, ranging in length from 50 to 268 mm.

At Deer Park Farms the type employed measured from c. 100 to 180 mm in length, was fatter in the middle and had pointed ends. These examples compare with Viking-period examples from Haithabu, Sweden (Earwood, 1993: 35). Wooden spindle whorls and hand distaffs are also known from Ireland (Earwood, 1993: 136–7).

Two forms of bone hand distaffs are known from Ireland, one from a Lough Faughan crannog, the other from Lagore and Ballinderry 2 where they were originally described as 'spindles' (Patterson in A. Collins, 1955: 81–2). Other implements connected with weaving are pin beaters, made from sheep or goat bones (metatarsals or tibia) sliced off at the end to form a point and used

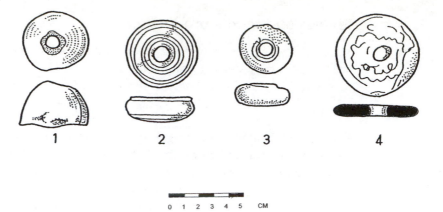

Fig. 36 Spindle whorls: 1–2. Cahercommaun; 3-4. Carraíg Aille.

to pack the thread down on the loom (Crowfoot, 1945). A weaving sword is known from Littleton Bog (Mitchell, 1965).

Spindle whorls

These were made of bone and were sometimes decorated, a feature rare before AD 400. Many were simply made out of a piece cut from the top of a femur and drilled through – such were current at all periods from 500 BC to AD 1500. They belong to four basic types (Fig. 36):

Plano-convex cut from a femur   A very common type, current from 500 BC to AD 1500 (Fig. 36.1).

Plano-convex or bowl-shaped   These were worked to this shape, and were the most common type at Cahercommaun and Lagore (Fig. 36.2).

Bun-shaped   This type occurs in the Roman period, for example at Wroxeter and Richborough, and continues into the early medieval period, for example at Dinas Powys, Ballinderry 2 or Carraíg Aille (Fig. 36.3).

Flat-disc shaped   This is more often found in other material (e.g. stone), but occurs in bone at Ballinderry 2 (Fig. 36.4).

Cloth dye

There were many different sources for dyes. Madder appears to have been used for dyeing one piece of cloth from Lagore, and madder or bedstraw on a piece of tabby (i.e. plain over and under) weave from Deer Park Farms. At Inishkea North the extraction of dye from the *purpura* shell appears to have been a minor industry (Henry, 1952: 173–7). Literary references imply that blackberry juice was used as a dye and documentary sources (saints' *Lives*) provide information on bleaching and dyeing – there is evidence that during these processes there were taboos against the presence of men (Plummer, 1968: 120).

Leatherwork

Leatherworking must have been a common domestic craft. Most of the evidence for it takes the form of shoes, though there is also a surviving fragmentary leather book satchel from Loch Glashan crannog. Among the evidence for leatherworking is a workshop in the monastery at Portmahomack apparently dedicated to making vellum for manuscripts, clearly not a general activity (Carver, 2004: 18).

Blacksmiths' products

Smithing techniques are discussed in Chapter 5. The items produced ranged from edged weapons to domestic implements, horse gear, iron sheets and some items that are not specific to this period.

Weapons

While stratified weapons are lacking from sites in Britain, with the exception of Dunadd and Buiston which have both produced spearheads, they are more common from Irish sites, and the major crannogs have produced a range. The weapons were the sword and the spear, the axe being used only occasionally and probably not before the Viking Age. Many axes claimed as weapons are probably woodmen's tools. The sword was probably confined to the nobility; this would account for the number found at Lagore, which was a royal dwelling. Weapons however are depicted in sculpture, and this provides information on sword pommel types.

Swords (Fig. 37)

Irish swords are both double-edged and single-edged (Hencken, 1950: 88–94). The characteristic features of the double-edged sword are square shoulders, a central ridge and a V-shaped point with parallel sides. It appears to be descended from the Roman *gladius* and *spatha*, which were themselves derived from Iron Age types (E. Rynne, 1982). One of the Lagore swords has sloping shoulders – a feature of Iron Age swords. Examples of the *gladius* type of Irish sword come from Teeshan and Ballinlig (B. Scott, 1990: 103). A longer, more slender sword seems descended from the *spatha*, and is represented at Lagore and Craigywarren crannog (B. Scott, 1990: 103).

A second type of double-edged sword is generally similar but has a broad, flat or rounded tang, with a blade wider near the point than at the hilt. This type is represented both at Lagore and Ballinderry 2, and there are other examples from Ireland. They may belong to the sixth to seventh centuries,

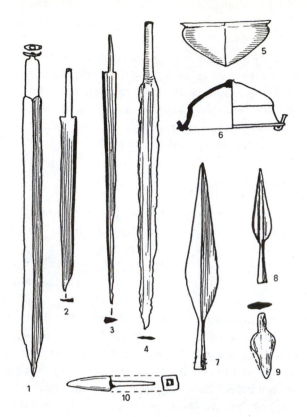

Fig. 37 Iron weapons, all Lagore except 9. Carraig Aille.

though some could be earlier (B. Scott, 1990: 103). A distinction has been made between the 'expanded ended' and 'crannog' varieties, the former of which have flattened tangs, the latter rounded (Rynne, 1982). One example of the 'expanded end' type was found in the River Lung, and has copper alloy hilt plates with interlace, pointing to a seventh- or eighth-century date. A unique sword from Lagore is of bronze and has straight sides and a flat straight blade with a similarly straight guard. The blade type is that of the Anglo-Saxon *spatha*; the guard is of a type used on Viking swords.

The single-edged sword is the Germanic *scramasax* type. The Irish versions of these weapons are distinctive, and appear to derive from at least two ultimately Continental prototypes. All the Irish single-edged swords are smaller and lighter than similar weapons found in the Anglo-Saxon world. There are examples from Lagore and Cahercommaun.

Pommels

There is little direct evidence for pommel types, though a bronze pommel of seventh-century Anglo-Saxon type decorated with interlace is known from

Culbin Sands (Laing, 1993: 238), and there are two examples in Pictish style, both in silver, one from the St Ninian's Isle hoard and one from Beckley (Graham-Campbell, 2003: 38). These are of the late eighth to ninth centuries.

In the ninth century the guards were turned down and the pommel guard turned up (Laing, 2000b: 86–93). This type continued probably into the tenth century and in Scandinavia is known as Petersen Type L. In the tenth century the straight guard again became dominant, and is apparent on Viking swords from Scotland and Ireland. There are Scottish examples of swords of the ninth century with curved guards from Harvieston, Clackmannan and Torbeckhill as well as Gorton (Laing, 2000b: figs. 7–9).

Spears

As in Anglo-Saxon England, spears were far more common than swords in the Celtic world (Fig. 37). What are normally called spearheads in archaeological literature are javelins (throwing spears), lances (hand-held cavalry weapons) or pikes (infantry hand-held weapons). Spears or their equivalents were used for hunting as well as for war.

Two basic types of spearhead occur in Irish contexts. One is leaf-shaped, the other shouldered. Both types were already present in the European Iron Age and were current in Britain, but in later contexts the leaf-shaped spear is more typical of Romano-British weapons and the shouldered spear is more typically Germanic, occurring in Anglo-Saxon graves. The presence of one rivet is an Iron Age phenomenon, the presence of two is indicative of Viking influence. One of the many spears from Lagore, of leaf-shaped type, has false damascening (a technique of ornamental ironworking) on the blade of the type found on Viking examples. Other distinctive features of Irish spears are to be seen on some with lunate depressions with thickened cutting edges on either side of a midrib (Scott, 1990: 105).

The arrival of the Vikings had considerable impact on the types of Irish weapons (Rynne, 1966). Spears from Ballinderry 1 and Lagore are clearly Irish imitations of Viking weapons with several rivets. Spear ferrules sometimes occur on Irish sites. Those from Lagore have plain tapering covers for the shafts, though a spear butt from the same site has a square section and a long tang for insertion into the shaft (Fig. 37, 10). It may be presumed that in Britain the same types of spears were in general use, and ferrules are widespread. The spearhead from Buiston, however, has the addition of incised grooves on the socket.

Bows

The longbow and arrow were used, though rarely. A bow, 183 cm long, and originally slightly longer, was found at Ballinderry 1, and can be presumed to be tenth-century (Hencken, 1936: 139). Flat arrowheads were found at Carraíg Aille, Dunollie and Dunadd, and more substantial bolts at Buiston, Dunadd and Cadbury Castle. These appear to have been for crossbows, the nuts for which have been found at Buiston and Castle Urquhart (A. Macgregor, 1976: 317–20; 1985: 158–61; L. Alcock, 1987a: 246–7; 1995: 77).

Armour

Apparently the only armour possessed in the Celtic west was the shield – round targe-like shields are depicted in the Book of Kells and in Irish and Pictish sculpture, in the latter case sometimes carried with a thong round the neck (Laing and Laing, 1984a: 281). Shield bosses are known from Lagore, Ballinderry 2 and Lough Faughan. The Irish shield bosses are comparatively small, and it is interesting that the Viking examples from the cemetery of Kilmainham-Islandbridge in Dublin were also small, presumably made under the influence of native tradition. The Saxon type of sugar-loaf shield boss is absent, and the Irish examples are more like the Roman.

Edged tools

A variety of iron edge tools are encountered in the period, most of which have Iron Age and Roman antecedents. The following are the main types: knives, axes, shears.

Knives

Knives of the period are not particularly distinctive, and are closely related to both Roman antecedents and medieval forms. The basic types are not peculiar to the west and north, and related forms occur in Anglo-Saxon graves and on Middle Saxon sites. Although there are a few differences, the series from Celtic sites corresponds broadly with the typology based on those from the Anglo-Saxon cemeteries at Norton (Sherlock and Welch, 1992: 51) and Dover (Evison, 1987: 113), or in the series from the Trier region in Germany (Böhner, 1958: 2). It is often difficult to assign knives to particular types as they are usually worn or badly corroded – for this reason the form of the cutting edge should not be accepted as a determinant of form, the profile of the blunt side being used for identification. The following are the basic types (Fig. 38).

Knife with curved, backed blade, tang and straight cutting edge Worn examples have a shoulder jutting from the cutting side with the rest of the blade offset

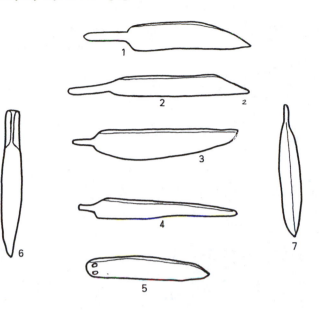

Fig. 38 Iron
knife types.

to the tang. They occur in the early Iron Age, at Traprain Law during the
Roman period, and throughout the early medieval period (Fig. 38.1).

Knife of scramasax form   These have a tang, a straight cutting edge, and a back
which runs parallel to the cutting edge before running at an angle to the
point. The type appears in Iron Age contexts in Scotland and Ireland, later
becoming common throughout post-Roman Celtic and Saxon Britain. It
survives after 1200 (Fig. 38.2).

Knife with tang, straight back parallel to the tang, and curved cutting edge   Some
variants of this type have a straight cutting edge running at an angle
to the back. This is a common early medieval type with Roman antecedents
and occurs in Anglo-Saxon and Viking contexts. It persists after 1200
(Fig. 38.3).

Knife with tang, straight back and cutting edge, tapering or pointed at the end   These
knives have Roman antecedents and occur throughout the early medieval
period, continuing after 1200 (Fig. 38.4).

Knife with flat tang and riveted handle   The blade takes many forms. This type is
current from Roman to 1200+ (Fig. 38.5).

Knife with socketed handle   This type occurs in Roman Britain and on a
few early medieval sites. It does not appear to have continued after 1200
(Fig. 38.6).

Flame-shaped knife   This is a rare form and could be a surgical knife. It has
Bronze Age and Iron Age European parallels as well as Roman. It could also
have been used as a fleshing knife. It is represented at Lagore.

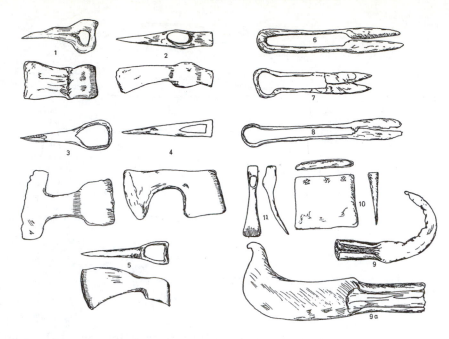

Fig. 39 Iron blade tools. Axeheads: 1. Carraíg Aille; 2, 4, 5. Lagore; 3. Lough Faughan. Other tools: 6. Carraíg Aille; 7. Garranes; 8–10. Lagore; 11. Ballinderry 2.

Axes

There are five main types of axehead (Fig. 39).

(1) This has a small head – the socket is formed by the iron being folded over in a loop and joined to the blade. A good example comes from Buiston, and others, one slightly 'bearded', from Lagore, and a simpler example from Carraíg Aille 2 (Fig. 39.1).

(2) This is, strictly speaking, an axe-hammer, since there is a projecting head used as a hammer on the opposite side of the handle from the blade. It occurs at Lagore, Lough Faughan and Cahercommaun in Ireland, and Cadbury Castle and Buiston in Britain (Fig. 39.2).

(3) This is the T-shaped axe, which is ultimately of Frankish origin. It occurs widely in Viking contexts and is illustrated in the Bayeux Tapestry. It is found in England down to the middle of the fourteenth century. It was used for dressing wood. It occurs at Lough Faughan (Fig. 39.3).

(4) This is the 'bearded' axe which was current in Europe from Viking times to c. 1300+. It is represented at Deer Park Farms (Fig. 39.4).

(5) This is similar to the Frankish and Anglo-Saxon francisca; it occurs at Lagore and is probably derived from Anglo-Saxon models (Fig. 39.5).

Shears

There are several types of shears (Fig. 39).

(1) A simple type with normal bend and straight-shouldered blades. Shears occur as early as the Iron Age period in Europe, and this general type is undatable. There is one from Garryduff 1, and one from Deer Park Farms may have been used for hair or fine textiles (Fig. 39.6).

(2) This type has a loop at the junction of the arms, a feature which is first noted in pagan Scandinavian graves during the tenth century. It is recorded among the 'old' finds at Lagore, and may be a Viking period type (Hencken, 1950: 113). It also occurs at Garranes and Garryduff 1 (Fig. 39.7).

(3) This type has semi-circular recesses at the top of the blades. It occurs very rarely in Scandinavia in pagan Viking burials of the tenth century; in England it does not occur before the thirteenth century. It is recorded among the 'old' finds at Lagore, and may be a Viking period type (Fig. 39.8).

Other edged tools

Pruning knife or sickle   This is related to the billhook, and is little different from its modern equivalent (Fig. 39.9).

Billhook   This is a fairly common object on Irish sites, and continues later than the early medieval period. One from Lagore has a curled tip and ash handle, and there is an example from Deer Park Farms. Another comes from Dinas Powys (Fig. 39.9a).

Spade shoes   These are rare, being represented by an iron shoe for a wooden spade from Ballinderry 2 (Hencken, 1942: 47; Fig. 39.10).

Adze   This common woodworking tool is similar to its modern equivalent. One was found at Whithorn in the debris of the earliest monastery and another from Ballinderry 2 (Hill et al., 1997: 424; Fig. 39.11).

Horsegear

This is relatively rare, and is confined mainly to bits, though a number of harness fittings in bronze are known from Viking graves in the Isle of Man and Scotland (Laing, 1993a: nos. 164–7; Fig. 40).

Snaffle bit   This is represented in the Celtic world only at Lagore and Whithorn. It is a two-piece bit and has plate cheekpieces with expanded terminals. The general type is represented from the grave at Hintschingen, Baden, dated to the seventh century. Part of one was represented at Whithorn in a phase prior to the late seventh century. Moulds for axe-shaped plates from the Mote of Mark may have been for their production (Fig. 40.1).

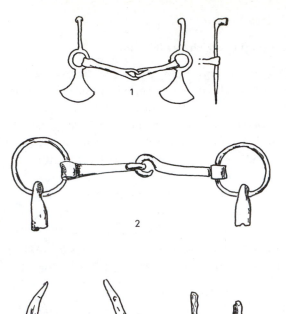

Fig. 40 Iron
horsegear:
1–3. Lagore;
4. Ballinderry 1.

Another type of *snaffle bit* occurs at Carraíg Aille 1 and has simple ring
cheekpieces. What may be a bit is depicted on a Pictish slab from Meigle 8
(Allen and Anderson, 1903: fig. 317; Fig. 40.2).

Horseshoe There is some doubt as to the antiquity of the horseshoe from
Lagore, and horseshoes do not occur stratified on any other site of the early
medieval period in the Celtic area except at Whithorn, where a similar type
of shoe was found in a context dated to the early eighth century or earlier
(Hill et al., 1997: 421; Fig. 40.3).

Prick spur This is represented only by one badly preserved example from
Ballinderry 1 (Hencken, 1936: 146). The spur, current in Europe among the
Carolingians, was probably introduced to Britain by the Vikings, though
there are Iron Age and Roman examples. Given the likelihood that the occupation on this site was by Vikings (see p. 281), this is the likeliest explanation for its appearance here (Fig. 40.4).

Linch pin One is represented at Whithorn, in a context of the mid-sixth
century (Hill et al., 1997: 411).

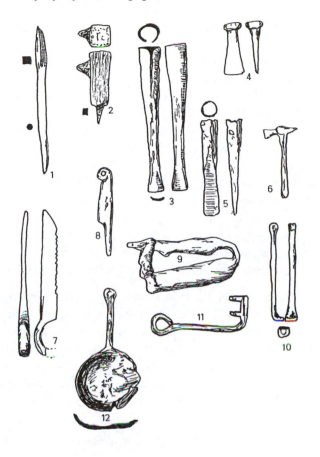

Fig. 41 metal- and wood-working iron tools: 1, 3–7, 11. Lagore; 2, 8–10, 12. Garryduff.

Metal and woodworking tools

These are fairly common types of iron objects. The axes and adzes listed above were also used for woodworking. The main types are as follows (Fig. 41).

Awl This simple object occurs frequently in a wide variety of forms (Fig. 41.1).

Anvil A small anvil with a spike for setting it in a wooden block and a projection on the side was found at Garryduff (O'Kelly, 1962a: 56). It was probably for ornamental metalworking (Fig. 41.2).

Gouge There are two basic types, one large and socketed (intended for use with a hammer), and one smaller (for use by hand). They occur on a number of sites, including Lagore and Cahercommaun (Fig. 41.3).

Punch or wedge These occur at Carraíg Aille and Lagore (Fig. 41.4).

Chisel A socketed chisel was found at Lagore (Fig. 41.5).

Smith's hammer A small hammer of Viking date was found at Kilmainham, Islandbridge, Dublin, and others are known from the Mote of Mark,

Garryduff (O'Kelly, 1962a: 64), Garranes (Ó Ríordáin, 1942: fig. 9, 239), and Dundurn (Fig. 41.6).

Saw   The round-handled type is relatively rare: one example is known from the 'old' finds at Lagore. The smaller, Irish varieties are more common. An unusual long, narrow saw blade was found at Cadbury Castle which may have been used for relatively delicate work. Although found in the post-Roman rampart, it could have been a late Roman survivor (L. Alcock, 1995: 77–8). A saw from Deer Park Farms had fine teeth, possibly for bone working (Fig. 41.7).

Arms of dividers   have been found at Dunadd, Cahercommaun, Oldcourt and Garryduff (Coatsworth and Pinder, 2002: fig. 10). Dividers had probably been used to produce a grid layout on a motif piece from Ballinderry crannog, and pennanular brooch designs at Nendrum (O'Meadhra, 1979: no. 150) and Dunadd (Youngs, 1989: no. 155). A study of the 'Tara' brooch (p. 160) has shown how circles were used in its design (Stevick, 1998; Fig. 41.8).

A range of tools from Dunadd could have been used in smithing, and included awls, punches, chisels, bits, shears, a hammerhead, files and cold chisels. One punch seems to have been for very delicate work (Lane and Campbell, 2000: 211). In addition, a stake used for hammering sheet steel metal vessels has come from Moynagh Lough – it would have been set in a wooden block (Youngs, 1989: 213). There are other possible examples from Mote of Mark and from Cadbury Castle, Somerset (L. Alcock, 1995: 81).

Miscellaneous ironwork, mainly domestic

There are a number of objects which do not readily fall into the above classes, mostly connected with the home (Figs. 41–42).

Barrel padlocks   These were used in the Roman period and continued until at least the sixteenth century. Examples (or parts of them) have been found at Garryduff, Cahercommaun, Lagore, Buiston and Dundurn. Those from Buiston and Dundurn are both large, and were probably for doors. Keys for such padlocks are common. The Garryduff padlock was dissected, and it was found that the barrel and bow were all of one piece (O'Kelly, 1962a: 54–5). The Buiston spring, however, seems to have had the bow attached (Fig. 41.9).

Barrel padlock keys   A number of these have been found, but they seem to have been made more frequently of bronze than iron. Eight iron keys, however, come from Garryduff (O'Kelly, 1962a: fig. 6), and there is another possible example from Cahercommaun. The type is standard, consisting of a flat bar of metal bent over into a right angle with a normally rectangular hole (Fig. 41.10).

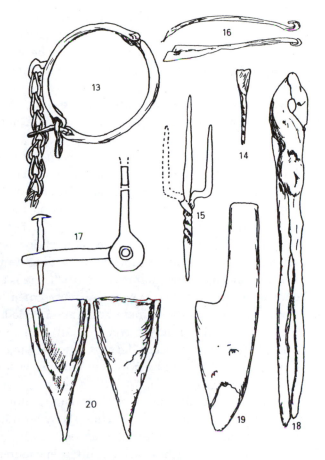

Fig. 42
Miscellaneous
ironwork: 13, 15,
19–20. Lagore;
18. Garranes;
14. Carraíg
Aille; 17.
Cahercommaun.

Tumbler lock key The only example known is from Lagore. This is a Roman type of padlock (Fig. 41.11).

Ladle Shallow ladles somewhat reminiscent of Roman paterae were found at Garryduff and Ballinderry 2, while similar objects have come from Lagore and Strokestown. These are now believed to be used in glass working (see p. 122; Fig. 41.12).

Tethers These are sometimes found with chains attached. They consist of hinged shackles of various forms and sizes. They are probably animal tethers, perhaps for guard dogs, though the larger examples may be for prisoners. The example from Lagore displays considerable technological skill in its manufacture (B. Scott, 1978; 1990: 105). The general type occurs in the early Iron Age (e.g. at Llyn Cerrig Bach), as well as post-1300 (Fig. 42.13).

Stylus This was used for writing on wax tablets and also probably for sketching designs on other materials such as bone. They are fairly common on ecclesiastical sites, but occur also in secular contexts, for example, the Mote of Mark, and usually have an expanded, flat head (Fig. 42.14).

Fork   A large trident occurs at Lagore and may have been used in fishing. Three-pronged and two-pronged forks were represented at Deer Park Farms (Fig. 42.15).

Bucket handles   Characteristically of a twisted rod of iron, these seem to be derived from Roman antecedents. They occur at Lagore and several other sites (Fig. 42.16).

Door hinge   The pivot door hinge seems to have been the type used in the early medieval period. One was found at Cahercommaun (Fig. 42.17).

Tongs   These were used mainly for lifting crucibles from hearths, and accordingly are found on several Irish early medieval period sites (p. 115). They may have also been used for a variety of other purposes (Fig. 42.18).

Plough coulter   The coulter of the early medieval period was heavy and sharply angled, and its ancestry is probably to be sought in the Romano-British coulter, which is related to Iron Age types. There is a general similarity between the Irish coulters, which are represented at Lagore and Ballinderry 1, and those of the Germanic Migration Period, which are in turn descended from the Iron Age type current on mainland Europe. Probably the plough coulter reached the west from the Anglo-Saxon world. The Irish coulters seem to have been used in ploughs with a heavy team, possibly on wet ground (Fig. 42.19).

Ploughshares   These are found either with or without reinforcements at the sides, and occur at Lagore and Leacanabuaile. The type without reinforcements is known from La Tène contexts (Fig. 42.20).

Firesteel or pursemount   One of these objects, often encountered on Anglo-Saxon sites, was found at Dunadd (Lane and Campbell, 2000: 166–7), and consists of a bar with scrolled ends. There is one from Whithorn dated to the seventh or eighth century (Hill et al., 1997: 424).

Candlestick and rushlight holder   These were represented at Deer Park Farms, the one with a central spike for a candle, which was fastened on to a wooden stick and had lateral rush holders.

Structural ironwork

Nails of all sizes are common finds, ranging from very large (used in fastening together the timbers of a rampart at Dundurn: L. Alcock, 2003: 101), to small (perhaps used in furniture). The shanks tend to be square-sectioned. A group of nails with tiny heads in use in the earliest monastery at Whithorn may have been 'hidden' nails used in finely finished work (Hill et al., 1997: 406). Clench nails, iron rivets, bolts, hinges, chains, hooks and joiner's dogs are all encountered.

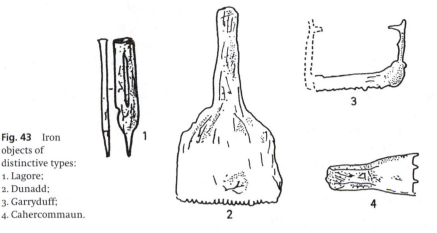

Fig. 43 Iron objects of distinctive types: 1. Lagore; 2. Dunadd; 3. Garryduff; 4. Cahercommaun.

Sheet iron objects

Sheet iron was worked into a variety of objects, the best known of which are bells, which were sometimes plated with copper alloy. Good examples come from Oldcourt, which typically had riveted seams (Murphy, 1961), or one from Birsay (C. Curle, 1982: 50–1). Other sheet iron objects include vessels from Lagore (Hencken, 1950: 113 and fig. 46) and Deer Park Farms (Scott, 1990: 105).

Objects of types not current at other periods

Most of the iron objects from early medieval period sites are of types which remained current in later times. A few objects, however, are more distinctive (Fig. 43).

Slotted object   This has a flat expanded head with an elongated slot and a shank, which was fitted into a handle. Examples are known from Birsay, Lesser Garth Cave, Keiss broch, Gwithian, Scalloway, Dunadd and a series of Irish sites, including Lagore, Cahercommaun, Lough Faughan, Carraíg Aille 2 and Uisneach, in contexts from the seventh to the tenth centuries. Various suggestions have been put forward as to its use: that it was used as a bodkin in weaving some coarse substance such as rush matting (Hencken, 1938: 53); that it was a type of auger (Ó Ríordáin, 1949: 79); that it was a strike-a-light (Hencken, 1938: 53).

　　None of these explanations seems totally satisfactory. A more recent suggestion is that it was used in ornamental metalworking, to hold rivets (Lane and Campbell, 2000: 164; Fig. 43.1).

Small single-handled saw   This object occurs at Dunadd and Garryduff and seems to be peculiar to the early medieval period. The tang was set in wood and the edge was possibly used for cutting wire (Fig. 43.2).

Two-handled saw   Strictly speaking this is a one-handled saw, since the two handles connected a wooden cross-piece, producing an effect rather like a modern fretsaw. The early medieval saw, however, could not be adjusted for tension. Examples of this type occur at Garryduff and Carraig Aille (Fig. 43.3).

Socketed pronged object   This implement has a socketed blade with three or four sharp teeth. These implements tend to be small, and have been found at, for example, Lagore, Garryduff, Dunadd, Whithorn, Cahercommaun and Ballinderry 1. They belong to a general class which occurs in simpler form in the Roman period. The Migration Period examples are usually of bronze and more elaborate than the Irish – they also occur in Frisia in the eighth and ninth centuries AD. Their function is uncertain though the Roman examples might have been used for scoring tiles (S. Piggott, 1958: 194). A more probable explanation is that they were weaving tensioners (Hill et al., 1997: 425; Fig. 43.4).

Industry and technology

Technological development is dependent upon markets, transportation, availability of raw material, the skills to work and develop it and surplus food production in the community to support such work. The evidence implies that technological skills were used by the Celts in the period on an *ad hoc* basis rather than to support organized industries. Many of the products were used within the community with comparatively few being traded or exchanged outside the locality of manufacture (Chapter 6).

The most important technological skills (excluding pottery making: see ch. 4) were in metalworking, though glass and stoneworking played a notable role. In most of these cases the raw materials were probably available within the Celtic world, which would have obviated the need for far-reaching trade as well as aided production within well-defined geographical limits.

Metalworking

Objects were created by smithing and casting, using a variety of metals – iron, bronze and copper, gold, silver and lead. There is written and archaeological evidence for many aspects of the industry, which generally speaking was carried out on a small scale – akin to cottage industry. However, recent excavations at Clonmacnoise have in particular produced evidence for ironworking on an almost industrial scale.

Iron sources

Iron ores have rarely been found in association with ironworking sites. Documentary evidence suggests that mines were worked in the period, though references to mines and miners are vague (B. Scott, 1990: 101). As with all ancient mining activity, later workings are likely to have obliterated any trace.

Bog Iron   It has often been assumed (on scant evidence) that local sources of bog iron ore were used in Ireland (B. Scott, 1990: 153). Bog iron ore has been found at Ballyvourney and Lough Faughan; limonite at Garryduff 1 and Oldcourt, and haematite at Ballyhenry (B. Scott, 1990: 154).

Water-borne iron ores   At the Mote of Mark, the ores used were tabular and massive haematite, which were abraded and may have been collected from a stream or beach (Crew in Laing and Longley, 2006: 38).

107

Copper sources

The mining of copper and tin is not clearly demonstrable in the period, though smelting, and possibly related mining, was carried out at Ross Island, Co. Killarney around the eighth century AD. A cave on the island seems to have been used for smelting in the period, possibly using Ross Island ores (W. O Brien, 2004; Comber, 2004).[1] it is quite possible that the location of the Mote of Mark reflected the proximity of copper ores (Macleod, 1986: 132–3).

Fragments of copper ore at Bryn Euryn (north Wales) may indicate the continuing use of the copper mines on the Great Orme which had been actively exploited in prehistory,[2] and it is likely that copper and tin were mined in Ireland. Apart from the finds at Ross Island, the strongest argument for the mining of copper in Ireland is provided by the analyses of copper-alloy artefacts – bronze seems to have had a high tin content (over 10%) in contrast to Roman copper alloys which had small and irregular amounts of tin, lead and zinc. This suggests that Roman scrap was not recycled in any great measure, a situation in marked contrast to that in Anglo-Saxon England (Oddy, 1983: 955; Craddock in Youngs, 1989: 170).

Tin sources

There is some documentary evidence that tin continued to be mined in Cornwall into the seventh century AD (Penhallurick, 1986). Additionally, there are tin ingots from Praa sands, Breague, radiocarbon dated to the seventh century (Bick, 1994). Of particular interest are the forty ingots of tin found at the mouth of the Erme in Bigbury Bay, attributed (though without firm evidence) to the period (A. Fox, 1995). There is a tinner's oak shovel from Boscarne, radiocarbon dated to the period under review and evidence for tin smelting and working for a series of sites in the south-west of England, notably Penwithick, Trethurgy, Killigrew, Halangy Down and Penhale (Pearce, 2004: 237).

Gold sources

Gold may have been recovered in small quantities in Ireland, Scotland and Wales (map of raw materials: L. Alcock, 2003: fig. 25). Gold can be found as native gold, alluvial gold, and under iron cap. In Scotland there are usable sources of gold at Wanlockhead (Dumfries), and Cononish (Perths.) (L. Alcock, 2003: 91).

In Ireland, there are some literary suggestions that gold was imported, but the evidence is ambiguous. The mineral is found in fifteen of the thirty-two counties of Ireland – and the relative abundance of Irish gold-work in the eighth to ninth centuries in contrast to the Anglo-Saxon areas (where an early abundance of gold in the sixth and seventh centuries was due to imported coin) might point to a native source. Later documentary evidence supports this; Gerald of Wales (a twelfth-century source), called Ireland the 'golden island' and argued that the gold resources made the country too valuable to be lost by the Normans (Whitfield, 1993a: 127).

Silver sources

Silver was used in Ireland for decorative purposes, and a range of techniques were used to work it.[3] Roman silver, derived from hoards such as those from Coleraine and Balline, may have provided a source in the fifth to sixth centuries, but by the seventh this must have been in short supply. Certainly the Old Irish word for silver, *airgid*, is derived from Latin *argenteus*, and suggests that the concept of silver working came from the Roman world (Ryan, 2002: 5). From the ninth century onwards the chief source of the raw material was probably re-used coin introduced by the Vikings, but a hoard of silver ingots weighing over 30 kg of pre-Viking date is known (Ryan, 2002: 10), and the notable lack of Anglo-Saxon and Carolingian coinage in Ireland discounts these as a source in earlier centuries.

Argentiferous galena (i.e. lead, from which silver can be extracted) is fairly widespread in Ireland, and silver-producing deposits were mined there between the seventeenth and nineteenth centuries (Ryan, 2002).

Scotland probably enjoyed a greater supply of Roman silver. An analysis of early Pictish silver has shown it to be composed mainly of re-used Roman metal (Stevenson, 1954–6b), and some Pictish silver is very pure (Close-Brooks, 1986: 167). It is notable however that the quality of silver declines as we move towards the Viking Age – the silver used in the St Ninian's Isle Treasure was very debased (Small et al., 1973: 46). There are deposits of silver-bearing lead in several parts of Scotland, though not in Pictland where silver is best represented.

Lead sources

There is some evidence that lead (which is often associated with silver ore) may have been extracted in the post-Roman period at Draethen, Glamorgan (Dark, 1996: 61) and there may have been silver extraction adjacent to Lesser Garth Cave in Glamorgan, as well as iron mining (Campbell, in Edwards and Lane, 1988: 86–7).

Re-cycled metals

There is more evidence to suggest the re-use of silver, gold, bronze and lead. Some of the scrap bronze at Dinas Powys probably originated in Anglo-Saxon buckets (L. Alcock, 1963: 105). Scrap bronze from Cadbury Congresbury was probably intended for re-use. From Clea Lakes crannog comes a sheet of bronze folded up ready for melting down, and similar bronzes come from the Mote of Mark.

Ironworking

Iron extraction (smelting)

Virtually all the sites of the period in the Celtic areas of Britain have produced evidence for metal (particularly iron) working. At Dunadd, there was no evidence for iron smelting, only smithing (McDonnell, in Lane and Campbell, 2000: 218), but at the Mote of Mark dense flows of tap slag suggested smelting (the extraction of metallic iron from the ores) as well as smithing (the working of the smelted iron into objects) (Laing and Longley, 2006: 38).

Furnaces Similar furnaces and equipment were probably used in both bronze and ironworking. They could be simple pits or more elaborate structures with bellows. The deliberate carburization of iron to produce steel appears to have been a regular procedure, to judge from a series of iron-edged objects in Ireland which suggested that 40% had been deliberately carburized. It appears that low carbon iron was produced initially, followed by secondary carburization (Scott, 1990: 146). Low carbon content probably accounts for the worn state of some utensils.

Bowl furnaces The only smelting furnaces in Ireland are of the simple bowl type, now identified on a number of sites (Scott, 1990: 159). It is difficult to be sure whether these bowl furnaces used in smelting had a superstructure – no evidence for one has so far been found in Ireland or in Britain. Among the sites to have produced evidence of bowl furnaces is Kilpatrick, a monastic site with occupation in the seventh to eighth centuries AD, where there was a bowl furnace 45 cm in diameter and 20 cm deep, with a thick clay lining over a packing of stones. Associated were plano-convex blocks of slag ('furnace bottoms') up to 25 cm in diameter and 10 cm deep (Swan, 1973; Scott, 1990: 161).

On another monastic site at Reask, the excavators found evidence for ironworking inside two monastic cells. In structure D three pits represented the remains of bowl furnaces, filled with slag and charcoal, one 45 cm in

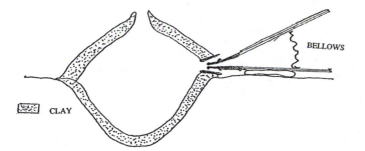

A

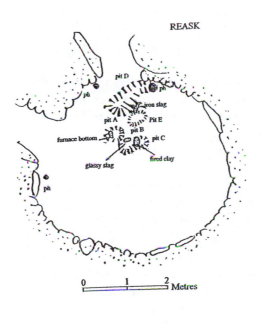

B

Fig. 44
A. Reconstructed furnace; and B. Plan of metalworking area at Reask.

diameter and 10 cm deep, a second 30 cm in diameter by 13 cm deep, both cut by a third 42 cm in diameter by 22 cm deep. Outside the structure were the remains of a peat stack and signs of heavy peat burning, along with a deposit of slag (Fanning, 1981: 106–7; Fig. 44).

At Garryduff 1, six small bowl furnaces ranged from 30 to 45 cm in diameter and from 23 to 30 cm deep (O'Kelly, 1962: 101). Associated were lumps of

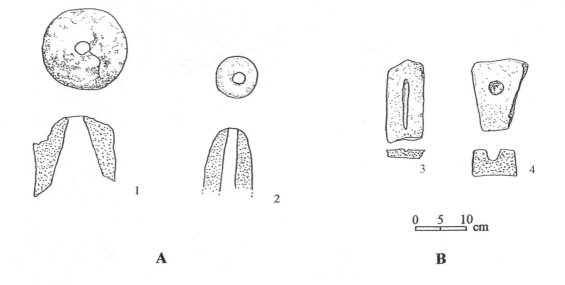

Fig. 45
A. Tuyères:
1. Ballyvollen, Co.
Antrim; 2. Lagore.
B. 3–4. Ingot
moulds.

slag and burnt clay, and by pieces of tuyères (clay casings for the nozzle of bellows). Limonite, the ore used, was found associated, and experiment suggested that some had been roasted before smelting. The site also produced 440 'furnace bottoms' or more accurately, smithing hearth cakes. It was probably used for both smelting and smithing.

Tuyères   These were used to direct the draught from the bellows into the furnace – they have been found at Garryduff, and are fairly common finds elsewhere (O'Kelly, 1962: 101–2. Tuyères mapped in Dark, 1994: fig. 36; Fig. 45a). When complete, a tuyère measured c. 45 cm long and up to 30 cm in diameter, and was cylindrical externally, funnel-shaped internally. Two bellows with wooden nozzles were used, both of which were inserted into the wide end of the tuyère and worked alternately. Heat of 1100° or 1200° C. was required to reduce the ore, which at Garryduff was of poor quality and found locally. Charcoal was mixed with the ore in the furnace. The heat of the smelting caused one end of the tuyère to fuse into pottery, coated with slag, while the other end remained unbaked clay and after the smelt tended to crumble away, so that complete tuyères are very rarely found.

'Furnace bottoms'   Lumps of slag which take the shape of the bottom of the furnace and are due either to slag collecting higher up in the furnace during the smelt and subsequently sinking, or to a failed smelt, when the whole mass sinks to the bottom. The roughly worked iron was lifted from the furnace by tongs, and then hammered into shape with frequent reheating.

Iron smithery

There is more evidence for smithing than for smelting. At the Mote of Mark, for example, there were smithing hearth cakes, an iron billet and bars, which represented stages in the refining and smithing (Laing and Longley, 2006: 38). The billet of iron from the site was a wedge-shaped block, 100 × 50 mm, which may have been brought from elsewhere. A tuyère from the same site seems to have been used in iron smithing. Smiths were able to carburize iron to produce steel; this was sometimes done in the smelting process, but was normally done outside the furnace.

Technological advances in ironworking

Celtic smiths were able to weld steel edges on to blades which were subsequently heat treated (Scott, 1990: 146–7). There is some evidence for relatively sophisticated techniques in the production of wrought iron work, well exemplified by a dog collar and chain from Lagore with a herringbone pattern perhaps inspired by Anglo-Saxon work (Scott, 1978). An axe from Ballynahinch, displayed a sandwich construction – a piece of low-carbon iron was folded over round a bar (which formed the socket) and a piece of high-carbon metal then sandwiched between the ends of the blade before the whole was welded together (Scott, 1990: 133, no. 51).

Copper, bronze and goldworking

Remains of copper, bronze and goldworking are less frequently found than those of iron smelting, but even so are fairly abundant. Copper alloy, which was used for most purposes in the pre-Roman Iron Age, was mostly used for ornamental metalwork in the period under review. Bronze-working furnaces were generally similar to those used in ironworking, and are attested on a number of sites, most notably at Moynagh Lough (Bradley, 1993) and Mote of Mark (Longley, 2000; Laing and Longley, 2006).

At Moynagh Lough a bowl-shaped furnace had a maximum diameter of 35 cm and a depth of 14 cm, and was deliberately stepped so that one part was higher than the other. There is no clear evidence of smelting at the Mote of Mark or Moynagh Lough, but both sites produced abundant evidence for smithing, and are notable for producing evidence for separate workshop areas given over to bronze and ironworking.

Goldworking is attested from a number of sites, most notably Moynagh Lough. A crucible with a gold residue was found at Clogher (Youngs, 1989: no. 220), dating from the sixth to eighth centuries, and the same site produced a gold rubbing stone perhaps for use with gold leaf (Youngs, 1989:

221). Possible touchstones are also known from Portmahomack and the Mote of Mark.

Other evidence for goldworking in the form of residues on crucibles comes from Dunadd (Lane and Campbell, 2000: 201), Buiston (Munro, 1882: 236), Dumbarton Rock (L. Alcock, 1975–6: 107–8), and Dinas Powys (L. Alcock, 1963: 147). There is some evidence from finds from the Mote of Mark and Movilla Abbey that the gold may have been deliberately alloyed (Whitfield, 1993a: 130). Shallow clay dishes known as 'heating trays' were probably used to separate gold from silver and for fire-assaying – they have been found at Knowth and Dunadd (Bayley, 1991; Whitfield, 1993a: 131).

Treatment of raw materials

Raw material seems to have been first cast into small ingots or billets in stone ingot moulds, which were then melted down in crucibles for pouring into two-part clay moulds.

Ingot moulds

Ingot moulds are attested on a number of sites, including the Mote of Mark (where a billet or ingot of copper alloy was also found), Dunadd (Lane and Campbell, 2000: 207), Lagore (Hencken, 1950: 170), Moylarg crannog (where a copper alloy ingot was also found) (Youngs, 1989: 174, no. 150), and Garranes (Ó Ríordáin, 1942: 108; Fig. 45b).

Crucibles

Small crucibles are among the most common finds that attest the smithing of copper alloys in the period. Dunadd produced evidence for a minimum of 60 crucibles, as did Brough of Birsay, Orkney. Lagore had a minimum of 55 crucibles represented, while Dinas Powys had a minimum of 11. The assemblage from Garranes amounted to 2,500 crucible fragments, with at least 50 complete crucibles surviving (Lane and Campbell, 2000: 205). At the Mote of Mark a minimum of 24 crucibles was represented (Laing and Longley, 2006: 26).

Considerable variety is shown in the crucibles, but characteristically their fabric contains much quartz. They are generally small, with a capacity to fill only one mould at a time. They were probably heated from above (Tylecote, 1986: 99–100) – probably by the use of a blowpipe. The clay nozzles of blowpipes have been found at Garryduff, Lagore and Garranes (O'Kelly, 1962: 99).

The different forms seem to have been used for heating different metals. It was shown at Dunadd that one type (A), was used for silver and the lidded type (C) was used for base silver alloys. A third type (E) seems to have been used exclusively for copper alloys. Dunadd seems to have had more crucibles used for silverworking than for copper alloy (Lane and Campbell, 2000: 206). Some crucibles seem to have been re-lined, though this was not invariable.

The crucibles from the Mote of Mark were apparently mostly used for copper alloys, though at least two were used for gold. A series of sixteen Irish crucibles were examined in the 1920s, and in almost all cases the main trace elements were of copper, with iron second, and tin, lead and other metals thereafter (Moss, 1927). Examination also showed slag from copper pyrites adhering to the sides of the crucibles, which suggests that they may have been heated in copper-smelting hearths.

Precious metals only seem to have been melted in crucibles on a few sites: at the Mote of Mark, Dunadd, Buiston and possibly Cadbury Congresbury where scraps of gold were associated with them.

Ceramic *crucible stands* are sometimes found, notably at Garryduff (where they were believed to be crucibles), Clogher and Nendrum (where a stone example was found).

Types of crucible

Until recently it was usually thought that the standard crucible of later prehistoric Britain was hemispherical and heated from above, but it seems that this type, which continued into the period under review, is less common than the triangular, which is easier to grip with tongs. By the post-Roman period, a wide variety of new crucible types were in use. They were normally lifted from the fire with tongs, and examples used presumably for this purpose are known from Garranes and Garryduff. The impression of the tongs is sometimes preserved in the slag on the outside, as for example at Dunadd and the Mote of Mark, where the tongs had a serrated grip. Handles to facilitate lifting were common in a variety of forms.

The lidded crucible seems to have appeared during the Roman period. Lids helped to reduce oxidization in the molten metal, to retain the heat while the metal was being poured, and to prevent ash from contaminating the crucible's contents. Lidded crucibles occur at Dunadd, Dinas Powys, Garryduff, Moynagh Lough and less certainly Buiston and Iona. Lids appear to have been added to whichever shape of crucible was in use, although at Garryduff the triangular crucibles were adapted slightly to take lids.

Crucibles were made of local clay and sometimes had linings the function of which has been seen as to prevent contamination from the material previously melted. This feature occurs on both lidded and unlidded examples. The lining of unlidded crucibles at Dinas Powys and Iona was probably to

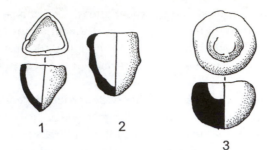

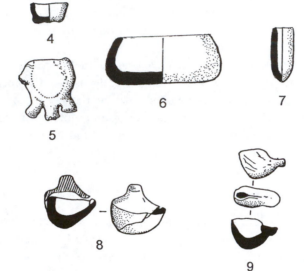

Fig. 46 Crucible types: 1. Ballinderry 2; 2, 4, 5. Lagore; 3. Garranes; 6–7. Dunadd; 8. Dinas Powys; 9. Ballinderry 2.

provide a springing for the lid. Many crucibles show signs of having a partially vitrified 'pumice'-like fabric and heat-crazed exteriors.

The crucibles in use in the period can be divided into ten basic types (of which one is however likely to be a heating tray). All except the triangular-mouthed are rarely found (Fig. 46).

Triangular-mouthed crucible[4] (Fig. 46.1).

Bag- or cup-shaped crucible   These have round mouths and profiles tapering to a pointed or rounded base. The type is Iron Age in origin and extends throughout the early medieval period (Fig. 46.2).

Hemispherical crucible[5] (Fig. 46.3).

Shallow circular crucible with flat base and straight sides   This type often has an inturned rim. It does not appear to occur before the early medieval period but was current probably through much of it. It is represented at Lagore and Dunadd, where it is Type B3–5. This may in fact be not a crucible but a heating tray, as in Fig. 46.4.

Three-legged crucible   This type is only represented at Lagore where it is round-mouthed and somewhat bag-shaped with a lug on one side (Fig. 46.5).

Rectangular crucible with vertical sides and rectangular flat base   This type occurs at the Mote of Mark (A. Curle, 1913–14: 158 and figs. 18–19). It may be a heating tray.

Cylindrical crucible   This occurs in the Iron Age, but in the post-Roman period only at Dunadd, where it has been designated Type A, and where it was suggested it was used for silver smithery, though it is also known in Viking-age Scandinavia (Lane and Campbell, 2000: 134; Fig. 46.7).

Handled crucible, without lid   This type first appears in the early Iron Age, but is rare before the early medieval period. There are a number of different varieties. It is Type D in the Dunadd series (Lane and Campbell, 2000: 141), and was the main type represented at Birsay, Orkney (C. Curle, 1982: 40–1). In Ireland it is found at Carraig Aille 2 (Ó Ríordáin, 1949: 91–2), and it has been suggested that it was a western Scottish type later taken to Ireland and Scandinavia (Lane and Campbell, 2000: 141; Fig. 46.9).

Lidded crucible   These first appear in Roman Britain, but are extremely rare before the early medieval period when they are fairly widespread. They occur at Dunadd, where they were designated Type C (Lane and Campbell, 2000: 134), and are common in Ireland, for example at Lagore (Hencken, 1950: fig. 60, no. 1278) and Garryduff (O'Kelly, 1962: fig. 21, 374; Fig. 46.8).

Saucer- or dish-shaped vessel with round or triangular mouth, sometimes with a spout   This is more probably a heating tray, used in the cupellation of silver or for fine working. Some may have been used as crucible stands. Such objects are represented at Moynagh Lough, Lagore, Garryduff, Garranes, Birsay and the Mote of Mark. At Dunadd they were designated Type B. They seem to have been heated from above (Fig. 46.6).

Moulds for artefact production

Moulds for making small objects are fairly common on Early Christian sites. Nine hundred fragments were found at Dunadd (Lane and Campbell, 2000, 106) and many hundreds at Birsay. These are normally of clay (though stone moulds also occur).

Different techniques seem to have been used in mould-making. It would appear that a wax model was used to create a clay mould, from which a lead die was cast to impress on subsequent moulds from which the copper alloy objects were cast.

A lead-alloy model for the head of a loose-ringed pin was found at Dooey (Youngs, 1989: no. 185) and another of different type was found at Moylarg crannog (Youngs, 1989: no. 187). A lead brooch pin was among the finds at Clogher (Youngs, 1989: no. 188). A lead disc from Birsay, Orkney, with a design

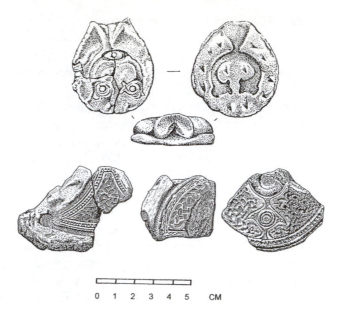

Fig. 47 Clay brooch moulds: *above* Birsay; *below* Mote of Mark.

0 1 2 3 4 5   CM

similar to many hanging-bowl escutcheons may have been for making moulds, as it appears to be negative, though could be a motif piece (C. Curle, 1982: 48–9; Fig. 48.3). For simpler objects bone was used for the dies – this was the case at the Mote of Mark (A. Curle, 1913–14: 147) and Birsay (C. Curle, 1982: 94). In these cases bone pins were found in their moulds. A lead model for the terminal of a penannular brooch was found at Dinas Powys, though whether it was for making moulds or a trial casting has been debated (L. Alcock, 1963: 121). One suggestion is that the casting was a failed attempt to make a die from a wax model (Graham-Campbell, 1991a: 225).

Construction of moulds

Moulds were of two-piece construction, and seem to have been used only once, being broken to remove the casting (Fig. 47). A *former* of wood or bone was used to impress an *ingate* and the two halves of the mould were positioned with keying, different methods being used on individual sites, including pegging and marking with a knife tip. At Birsay, it was suggested that different techniques were the 'trademarks' of different craftsmen (C. Curle, 1982: 39).

At Birsay different clays were used for different types of casting, more quartz being included in clays for coarser casting (C. Curle, 1982: 36–7). The clays seem to have been carefully prepared, and at the Mote of Mark a pile of clay and another of sand for mixing with it was found in the main metal-working area. A similar clay pile was noted at Moynagh Lough (Longley, 2001: 79; Bradley, 1993: 79).

The basal pad of clay usually shows signs of bevelling, the top pad being curved over it. After the die or model had been removed, the two halves of the mould were keyed together, cased in a skin or *luting* of clay, and oven-dried prior to casting. The moulds were set on edge, perhaps in sand, for the casting process. In the case of simple objects several could be cast from one mould, pins being set to radiate out from the ingate, larger objects being joined by a runnel.

Motif pieces ('trial pieces')

These were pieces of stone or bone, bearing craftsmen's designs (Fig. 48). They occur in Ireland and Dál Riata.[6] The few from outside these areas include one from Aberglaslyn (Redknap, 1991: 35), two from Birsay, Orkney (C. Curle, 1982: 24, fig. 11 and fig. 45, no. 606), and some from Tintagel (Laing, 1996: 134) and Jarlshof, Shetland (Hamilton, 1956: pl. xxi). The majority of the 350 plus motif pieces known from northern Europe are from Ireland, where they have been found at over thirty sites (O'Meahdra, 1987b: 159). They were particularly common in the Viking period, but there is an example of the sixth to seventh century from Dooey.

These are usually regarded as artists' sketches – attempts at working out the design before setting it down on the mould or working on the face of the metal. Some may have been simply 'doodles', and a few might be apprentices work, as they are often technically incompetent. Some may have been talismans.

Some of the bone trial pieces (for example, from Lagore), may have had a more immediate use as dies in making the moulds themselves, or as dies for stamping the designs on metal. This would explain the great intricacy and care shown in their execution. A series from the monastery at Nendrum comes from the ruins of the 'school' and presumably constitute exercises, which include letters as well as drawings of animals (Lawlor, 1925: 144).

One stone trial piece from Dunadd is for a penannular brooch, while another, dating from the last days of the occupation, is purely a decorative scheme (Lane and Campbell, 2000: 243–4).

Techniques used ornamental metalworking

Wire-work

Modern gold wire is produced by drawing a thread of gold through a hole in a plate, but in the period under review, the metal was cut into thin strips from a gold sheet which could then be hammered into a circular section or could be twisted into a solid cable. Such wires show seam lines (Ogden, 1992: fig. 30).

More universal however was block-twisting, where rectangular strips were twisted (Whitfield, 1987: 78). Beaded wire was created by running a grooved tool

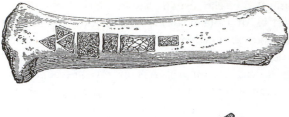

1

2

Fig. 48 Motif pieces and die: 1. Lagore (bone); 2. Kingarth, Bute (stone); 3. Birsay, Orkney lead die with triskele design.

3

over a round wire (Whitfield, 1987: 78). Twined or rope-twist wire (i.e. twisted cables of several wires) was used for edge decoration among other things.

Trichonopoly work involved knitting wire using a perforated block with four pins, after the manner of knitted wool work still made by children (Coatsworth and Pinder, 2002: xv–xvi). This was successfully used on a number of major pieces of metalwork, such as the Derrynaflan paten (see p. 180). A more substantial method of interlocking metal cables was employed in a necklet from the Pictish Gaulcross hoard – a special tool had to be developed in order to make a replica of it (Stevenson and Emery, 1963–4).

Filigree

Filigree involves the use of fine ornamental gold wire soldered on to a metal plate. It is often found in conjunction with granular work, in which tiny beads of gold are applied to a baseplate in the same fashion (Whitfield, 1987). The technique was used in the Classical world and was developed by Byzantine metal smiths, who may have been influential in its spread among at least some of the barbarians, such as the Lombards. It was widely used among both the Celtic and Germanic peoples of the Migration Period. It is a feature of Anglo-Saxon jewellery, notably Kentish, but in Ireland developed along separate lines.

Celtic filigree could be attached to either a plain backplate or one which had been stamped. A distinctive technique was 'hollow platform work' in which there were two baseplates, one a relief backplate which was attached to a plain backplate. This was used on the Hunterston and 'Tara' brooches among other pieces. One of the earliest examples of filigree work from the Celtic arena is a tiny gold bird from Garryduff, but also early is a foil from Lagore (Whitfield, 2001a).

Granulation

Granulation involves setting tiny droplets of gold on a baseplate. The granules are produced by applying heat to tiny pieces of gold on charcoal. These tend to flatten on cooling on the charcoal bed, but can be made round by making pits in the charcoal base (Maryon, 1959: 53).

Die stamping

Foils were sometimes embossed by pressing them down on a die, and this technique, known as *pressblech*, is found on a number of pieces such as the Moylough Belt Shrine and the stand for the Derrynaflan patten (see p. 180). It may be an import from Anglo-Saxon England.

Sheet metalworking

Sheet metal was made into both iron and copper alloy objects. Classic examples are the ecclesiastical bells, which were folded and riveted. Bowls were produced by raising – hammering the sheet on a special anvil or a stake. Both this and the technique known as spinning were employed in the production of bowls. Hanging-bowls (p. 175) were spun using a pole-lathe, which left a hole in the base where it has been attached to a plate. Most hanging-bowls were produced by spinning from a single bronze sheet (Brenan, 1991: 6).

Plating

Gilding was the most common form of plating, but tinning (to give a shiny appearance similar to silver) was also employed (La Niece, 1990). Some items in the Donore hoard (p. 180) were tinned. Silver plating was comparatively rare.

Chip carving

Chip carving is derived from woodworking. Chips of metal were cut away to leave depressions similar to inverted pyramids, to reflect the light. True chip carving is very rare; normally the effect is simulated by casting. The technique had a long life, and was widely used by the barbarians in Europe down to the eighth century AD. It is mainly a Germanic technique, and probably came to the Celtic west through Anglo-Saxon England (Henry, 1965: 96–7).

Glass and enamel working

Glass making

Until recently it was assumed that glass working was unknown amongst the Celts of the period under review, who were thought to have relied on imported material that was re-worked into enamels and inlays. Investigation of a glass-producing site at Dunmisk has reversed this view since it revealed all stages of glass production on a considerable scale (Henderson and Ivens, 1992; Henderson, Julian, 2000). Occupation on the site extended from the sixth to the tenth centuries, with glass making during the latter part of the period.

Glass working was also carried out at Dunmisk, where products included glass studs and millefiori rods.

Evidence for glass working includes an iron plate, possibly for rolling rods from Armagh, and a series of iron pans that may have been used for melting glass. Glass working was also carried out at Clonmacnoise and Portmahomack.

Enamelling

In enamelling, powdered glass is heated until it fuses into an opaque mass (Butcher, 1977; Bateson, 1981; Haseloff, 1991. Irish enamels: Henry, 1933 and 1956). Red was the chief colour used in Iron Age Europe, though in the first century AD yellow, blue and later other colours were introduced. Enamelwork in Roman Britain seems to have been employed particularly on brooches (notably the dragonesque and plate types) and harness fittings, and is associated with native rather than Classical taste. The technique employed was champlevé, in which the areas to be set with enamel were cut away leaving sockets or cavities. In Ireland there is some evidence for it on items such as some of the Iron Age horse-bits and the Petrie Crown (Raftery, 1994: 157–8), but it is not common before the period under review.

Evidence for enamel workshops is rare, though at Garranes a fragment of red enamel and a bronze button decorated with a red champlevé pattern were among the refuse of the industrial activity (Ó Ríordáin, 1942). champlevé enamel was fairly common in late Celtic Britain until at least the eighth century. It is probably a survival from the Roman Iron Age.

Enamel in the post-Roman period, however, is somewhat different in its composition from that employed in Roman Britain. It has been shown that the reds are not based on the coloration of soda-lime-silica glass, but involved the re-use of metallurgical slag. A further suggestion has been made that red enamel was produced as a by-product of metallurgical slag (Stapleton et al., 1999).

The enamelwork of the sixth and seventh centuries consists mainly of red inlays with spiral or whorl patterns, and it is probably to the sixth century, rather than the fifth, that many of the enamelled hanging-bowl escutcheons should be assigned. In the eighth century the spiral tended to disappear from champlevé work and was replaced by angular patterns, which were possibly influenced by the shape of millefiori settings or equally probably by the wide-spread fashion for step pattern cloisonné work in the Anglo-Saxon jewellery of the seventh century. Red and yellow were the predominant colours of the eighth century, occasionally coupled with blue bosses. Area enamel super-seded restricted inlay – on eighth-century enamelwork very little of the surface of the bronze is visible (Henry, 1965: 96).

Millefiori

The technique of millefiori involves fusing together rods of different coloured glass to form a single rod with a coloured pattern running through it. It is still made, and enjoyed a particular vogue in the nineteenth century for paper-weights (Fig. 49).

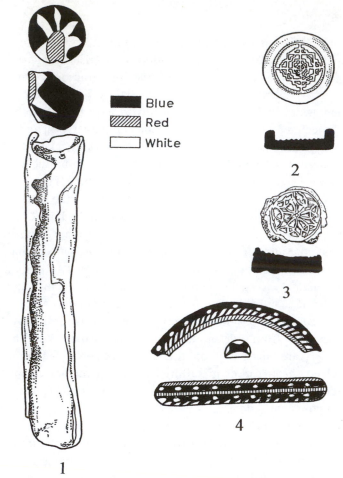

Fig. 49 Glass working: 1. millefiori rod and holder, Garranes; 2. glass stud mould, Lagore; 3. glass stud, Iona; 4. glass armlet, Lagore.

In the period under review, millefiori was only used in the form of slices taken from the fused rods, for panels of decoration. The technique originated in the east and was developed in the Roman Empire. There is evidence for the presence of millefiori in Roman Britain from the second to fourth centuries. Different classes of millefiori have been recognized, Class 1 being represented by round or square panels of different-coloured millefiori floated in red enamel. Class 2 has squares of two colours of millefiori in a chequer pattern again floated in a red 'sea' and Class 3, panels of blue and white fused together (Carroll, 1995).

It has been suggested that the Class 1 millefiori was imported from the east Mediterranean in the fifth or sixth century, and that it was replaced by Class 2 in the seventh, the latter being of Romano-British derivation (Carroll, 1995:

55–6). It is however more probable that all types originated in Britain (Laing, 1999).

A workshop has been excavated at Garranes, where a glass-melting crucible was found as well as millefiori rods, one in its metal holder (Ó Ríordáin, 1942: 118–20), and there is further evidence for millefiori working at Lagore, Dunmisk and Armagh.

Sticks of millefiori have been found in Scotland and Wales, the one a stray find from Luce Sands (Cramp, 1970: 333), the other from the excavations at Dinas Powys, where it may have been part of the stock of an Irish glassworker.

Millefiori, which was initially used to decorate hanging-bowls, penannular brooches and a few buckles (Youngs, 1993), was sometimes used to decorate Anglo-Saxon pendants of the early seventh century and it also appears in the Sutton Hoo jewellery. A rod of millefiori was found at the monastery at Jarrow, in what appeared to be a workshop, and more millefiori was found in the sister monastery of Monkwearmouth (Cramp, 1970: 331–2).

Glass studs

There are two types of glass studs for ornamental inlays: those that are simple castings with relief ornament, and those that have inset metal grilles (Fig. 49.2–3). A particularly fine stud of the former type, only 1 cm in diameter, decorated with a raised pattern of interlace, was found at Garryduff (O'Kelly, 1962: 72–4). At Lagore one was found in the open clay mould in which it had been cast (Hencken, 1950: 129–30).

Other clay stud moulds were also found at Lagore, along with glass rods which presumably had supplied the raw material (Hencken, 1950: 132). The Lagore stud had a stepped geometric pattern. Moulds for making glass studs are also represented at Iona (Graham-Campbell, 1981: 24). All seem to be of the eighth–ninth centuries AD. The second type of stud, inset with a metal grille in a geometric design to imitate cloisonné, is represented in eighth-century metalwork such as the Ardagh chalice. They seem to have been made at Clonmacnoise. An isolated stud with gold wire grill was found in an eighth-century context at Deer Park Farms (Lynn, 1989), and there are fine studs from Portmahomack.

Niello

This black silver sulphide or copper sulphide material is fused into engraved areas on metal, though in the period under review was not truly fused but inlaid. Although it is found at an early date in the Mediterranean, it is in the Roman Empire that it became popular (La Niece, 1983). In Roman Britain copper sulphide niello was particularly favoured, but there are also found combinations of copper and silver sulphide niello which had a low melting point (680° C) and could be fused without melting the underlying metal. It was used commonly in the Viking Age, and may have been influenced by Anglo-Saxon work, as niello was particularly popular in Trewhiddle-style metalwork in ninth-century England.

Stone

Stone was used for a diversity of purposes including querns (see below), hones and whetstones, rubbers, pot lids, polishers, spindle whorls, weights, ingot moulds (p. 114), hammerstones, anvils, pestles, palettes, querns and millstones, as well as motif pieces (p. 119) bracelets (p. 147) and beads (p. 148).

Worked flints

These were sometimes re-used from prehistoric times, and are fairly common on sites of the period. A prehistoric assemblage was re-used at the Mote of Mark (Laing and Longley, 2006: 100) and at Dinas Powys (L. Alcock, 1963: 168–75), and stray prehistoric flints have been found at Lagore (Hencken, 1950: 178–9), Ballinderry 2 (Hencken, 1942: 64), Carraíg Aille (Ó Ríordáin, 1949: 101), Dunadd (Lane and Campbell, 2000: 199), Whithorn (Hill et al., 1997: 68), Dundurn and Dunollie (Alcock et al., 1989: 220–1). Studies of Irish material have suggested that over 50% of ringforts have small assemblages of flints (Harper, 1974: 32–41; N. Edwards, 1990: 96), leading to the belief that flint implements were not only re-used but worked for the first time.

Querns, whetstones and hones

These may have been produced by specialist quarrymen, though the historical evidence, afforded by a text in Cogitosus' *Life of St Brigit*, suggests that even these were quarried as required by members of the community (*Vita Secunda*, quoted in Thomas, 1971: 210–11).

No detailed petrological survey is available of millstones and quernstones of the period, but where reported the source for quernstones is usually a local outcrop. The querns at Dunadd seem to have been worked on the site, and for the most part were of the standard disc form found in the earlier Iron Age (MacKie, 1987: 5–110). Some however had oblique or side handle holes, and in one case a projecting handle. They also had rind slots cut into the underside of the top stones, and it was suggested by the excavators that they were cut down upper stones from horizontal mills, or influenced by them (Lane and Campbell, 2000: 185).

A feature of some of the Dunadd querns was decoration on the upper surface (Campbell, 1987), and they were generally flatter than their Iron Age counterparts. The querns at Lagore were similarly made on the site, and were also flat (Hencken, 1950: 173–5). The whetstones and hones are mostly rectangular in section and elongated, some with suspension holes. The latter feature was absent from the whetstones found at Dinas Powys, Dundurn or the Mote of Mark, but is found among the old finds at Dunadd, and on Irish sites.

6 Trade and communications

The evidence for trade in the Celtic world in the early medieval period mostly relates to overseas transactions, though internal trade was more important in society than the mere buying and selling in markets. It was also part of complex social ties, including gift exchange (Doherty, 1980). Trade over more than a few miles is dependent upon good communications and transport as well as reasonably amicable relations between the traders. Goods were taken directly from A to B, but must also have been passed through long trading chains with no direct contact between the place of origin and the final place of use.

Transport

Extensive trade of raw goods or manufactured items relies on good communications, as do itinerant workers, such as craftsmen, and the Celtic world under review had developed roads, bridges and a variety of vehicles. The most important method of trading transport was likely to have been the sea: the ease of water travel for the ancient world is often overlooked.

Roads and bridges

Roads and bridges are known mostly from references in literature. Different classes of roads are indicated, some of which may have been modelled on the Roman (De Paor and De Paor, 1958: 98–9). Very substantial roads, albeit possibly for ritual purposes, existed in Ireland in the Iron Age. The Corlea Road, for example, was dated to 148 BC by dendrochronology, and seems to have run for at least 2 km. This large undertaking involved laying split oak planks across the surface of a bog (Raftery, 1994: ch. 5).

While such ancient roads may have been utilized as late as the early medieval period, there is firmer evidence of a few early medieval period tracks, mostly associated with raths and ecclesiastical sites. The cobbled path at Hallow Hill, St Andrews, ran between the long-cist burials – it was sunken, and between 2 m and 4 m wide (Proudfoot, 1996: 441). Other roads include the more substantial paved roadway on Iona – the 'Bothar na Marbh' (Road of the Dead) – which ran through the later monastic cemetery and appeared to be heading for the primary monastic settlement (Barber, 1981: fig. 5).

Surviving bridges are rare (ferries may have been used, which would have left little or no evidence). A substantial monastic example was recently investigated, spanning the Shannon at Clonmacnoise which was dated by dendrochronology to c. AD 804 (Moore, 1996; O'Sullivan and Boland, 2000). The bridge spanned 160 m and was constructed with 36 vertical posts in pairs 4–5 m apart. Transverse beams and planks served as baseplates. The vertical beams had been hewn by axes to a near-square section, and the planking had probably been quarter sawn with rip saws. Bridle joints were employed, and some nails used in the superstructure.

Wheeled vehicles

Archaeological evidence for wheeled vehicles in the early medieval period is rare. A wheel from Lough Faughan crannog survives only as a fragmentary hub. However, from this it seems that the wheel probably had twelve spokes, the end sections of which were rectangular. It seems too crude to have belonged to a chariot, but could have come from an agricultural wagon.[1]

The Lough Faughan hub raises the question of the origin of the chariot in Ireland (Harbison, 1969; 1971; D. Green, 1972). References in Irish saga literature indicate that the chariot was known in early medieval Ireland, though some references seem almost certainly to be partly derived from Classical literary traditions. There are, however, a number of depictions of chariots on high crosses, notably the North Cross at Ahenny, Flann's Cross at Clonmacnoise, the tall cross at Monasterboice, the cross of St Patrick and Columba at Kells and the Kilree Cross. The Ahenny, Kells and Clonmacnoise chariots seem to have had eight-spoked wheels, reaching as high as the horse's back. References in Irish literature imply that the Irish chariot of early medieval times was closely related to modern farm carts, and there are allusions to certain features, such as the use of rereshafts which do not appear in the sculptures.

An unusual wheeled vehicle with an awning, depicted on a (now lost) Pictish stone from Meigle, had two wheels and raised sides, and was drawn by two horses with braided tails. It had two occupants as well as the driver. It may have been a surviving example of the Roman *carpentum* (Fig. 50b) (Laing and Laing, 1984: 277–8).

Boats

Boats of various constructions were clearly in use in the period and could have been used for both internal and long-distance trade. Documentary sources show that the Scots of Dál Riata had a fleet: *The Annals of Tigernach* in an entry for 733 noted that 'Flaithbertach took the Dál Riatan fleet to Ireland, and a great slaughter was made'. In 729 the same source relates 'a hundred and fifty Pictish ships were wrecked at Ross Cuissine' (L. Alcock, 2003: 129). According to a muster in the *Senchus fer nAlban*, the Dalriadic fleet comprised 140 ships (L. Alcock, 2003: 129). Adomnán's *Life of St Columba* is more detailed

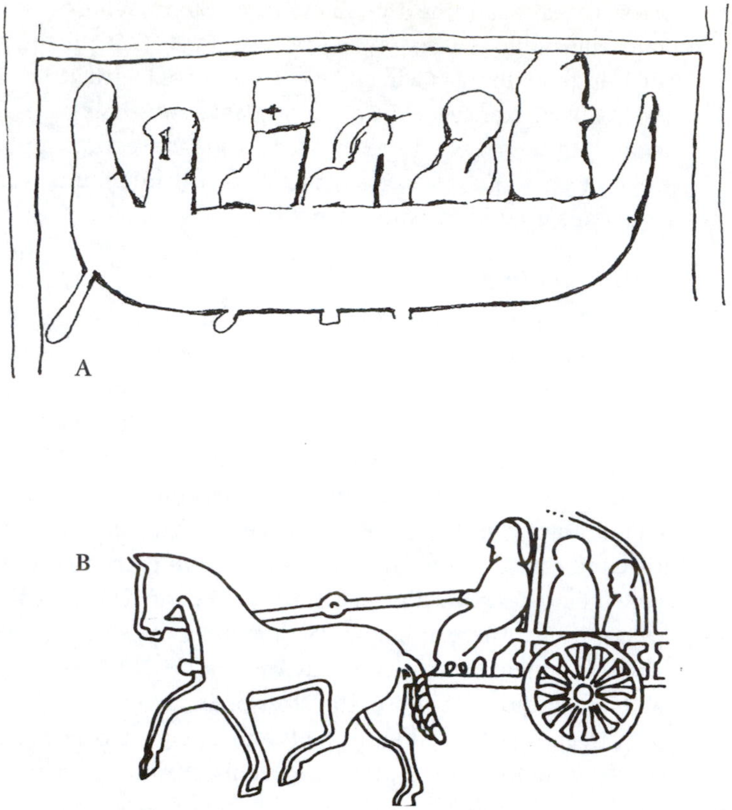

Fig. 50 A. Depiction of a Pictish boat on St Orland's Stone, Cossans, Angus; B. lost depiction of a Pictish wheeled vehicle, Meigle, Angus.

in the information it provides – it suggests ships with both oars and sails were used.

The only boats to have survived from the early medieval period are dugout canoes, such as that from Buiston crannog (Munro, 1882: 237) or that from Ballinderry 2 crannog, which was 7.5 m long (Hencken, 1942: 60). Dugouts could only have been used for travel from the water's edge to a crannog or for a limited amount of river travel and fishing.

A group of nine dugouts was found associated with the bridge at Clonmacnoise (above) (O'Sullivan and Boland, 2000). These survived ranging from 5.5 m to 3 m, with a typical width of 60 cm. They were carved with axe and adze from roundwood trunks. Some were long narrow vessels with round bottoms for fast travel, others were squarish and flat-bottomed. One canoe had separate frames put into its lower hull. Some of these were perhaps for ferrying. Three of the boats contained tools – a whetstone in one, and woodworking axes in two others.

It is probable, however, that larger boats existed. A carving of a boat on a pillar at Bantry shows what appears to be a rowing boat with four pairs of oars and a steering oar (Johnstone, 1964). Although weathered, the overall appearance of the Bantry boat is of a skin-covered vessel similar to the *currachs* used for inshore fishing in Ireland as late as the twentieth century.

Skin boats seem to have been successfully used even in long-distance sailing (cf. the *Voyage of St Brendan*). A boat of uncertain date, depicted on the wall of Jonathan's Cave, Wemyss, is a low vessel with high prow and was probably made of skin. It has five oars, a rudder, and a single occupant and is likely to be Pictish (Johnstone, 1980: 152–3; Ritchie and Stevenson, 1993: 204 and fig. 25.6).

A boat depicted on St Orland's stone (a Pictish slab from Cossans), is a plank-built vessel with high prow and stern. It has a rudder, and what appear to be oars (Fig. 50A; Foster, 1996: 102). Depictions of sailing boats on stones have been found at Jarlshof, Shetland, and though usually assumed to be Viking, could be Pictish (Ritchie, 1989: 50). There are depictions of boats on Irish crosses, but since they represent Noah's Ark, they may not reflect Irish vessels. One, on a cross at Camus-Macosquin, has a dragon prow and curved stem post, reminiscent of Viking vessels (F. Henry, 1967: fig. 25). A dragon prow appears on a motif piece from Jarlshof, Shetland, as well as depictions of masted ships, though these are probably of the Viking Age.[2]

One of the finds from the earliest watermill at Nendrum was an oar (McErlean, 2001: 12). Some timbers from Portnockie, re-used in the ramparts, may have been from boats (Ralston, 1987: 22), and there are re-used boat timbers from Ballinderry 1 crannog (Hencken, 1936: 137).

Internal trade

Most evidence indicates that Celtic artisans obtained raw materials locally 'as and when'. Some rare materials seem to have been traded over quite long distances: lignite worked in Bute and the Isle of Man may have originated in north-west England, and the jet found at the Mote of Mark probably originated in the area round Whitby, for example. Production of ornamental metalwork, for example, at Birsay (p. 117) and Dunadd (p. 117) suggests a scale of manufacture too great solely to serve the local community. The products of the brooch 'factory' at Clogher have been found in a fairly restricted area in Ulster but with an outlier from Killucan (Kilbride-Jones, 1980a: 63–7). A type of brooch pin which has been suggested as originating in the Clogher 'factory' has been found as far afield as Inishkea North (Kilbride-Jones, 1980a: fig. 50, no. 144).

There are some indications that querns and millstones were traded distances of some kilometres. Two querns at Dunadd were made from stone quarried between 15 and 35 km away and one may have been carved with a cross by a cleric from Iona (Campbell, 1987).

Markets certainly existed, but in the Celtic world there was no growth of urban *emporia* on the Anglo-Saxon or Continental model. Royal or princely citadels maintained (among their many functions) a role as markets, from which goods seem to have been distributed to sites of lesser standing. This pattern is reflected in the distribution of imported pottery and glass (p. 135). A few beach sites, such as that at Bantham (p. 242), Mothecombe (A. Fox, 1961; Turner, 2003: 27), St Enodoc, Carnsew or Gwithian, in south-west England (Pearce, 2004: 240), or Dooey in Ireland (Ó Riordáin and Rynne, 1961) seem to have been primarily concerned with trading.

By the eighth century, monasteries were centres of production not only for their own domestic use, but for further afield. The monastic fair (*óenach*) was operated, which is first documented in 799 at Lusk (Doherty, 1980: 81). Ornamental metalwork may have been produced for trade in secular work-shops, such as those at the Mote of Mark or Moynagh Lough (see pp. 301 and 282). The types of objects involved in such small scale trade are discussed in Chapters 7 and 8.

External trade

Documentary evidence for external trade

There is strong written evidence, especially for Ireland. In the fifth century the Atlantic ports of Aquitaine which had already been operating in the Roman period continued to trade with Spain, the British Isles and northern Gaul. By the sixth and seventh centuries this trade was well established (James, 1977: 221).

An element behind the trade may have been the cult of the fourth-century St Martin, which reached Ireland at an early date (Mayr-Harting, 1972: 84–6). The references are sparse, though illuminative. Columbanus, an Irish monk who founded monasteries in Italy (see below, p. 134) was expelled from Burgundy and taken to Nantes in order to board a ship which, significantly for our purposes here, was engaged in trade with Ireland (Ó Cróinín, 1995: 21). A *Life of St Cybard* by Nicasius of Angoulême (albeit in a late text) recorded that when a Church was founded at Bordeaux 'ships from Britain equipped with sail and oar arrive at the port of the city to do trade there' (E. James, 1977: 23).

The importance of the wine trade with Gaul has been given much promin-ence in the past, although some of the key references are from later sources and may reflect the situation after the period to which they refer (Wooding, 1996: 70). There is no doubt, however, that wine was consumed in Ireland, as is made clear from Adamnán's *Life of St Columba*.

A lost Irish legal text, *Muirbretha*, lists the cargoes of wrecked ships: 'hides and iron and salt . . . foreign nuts and goblets and an escup of wine or honey, if there is good wine or honey in her'. Other versions add gold, silver, furs and British horses (Wooding, 1996: 73).

Archaeological evidence for external trade

There is strong evidence for contact and influence from outside Celtic lands, of which the most prominent is the spread of Christianity. Evidence for long-distance trade, however, is primarily documentary or confined to finds of pottery and glass which originated on the Continent, with an increasing number of different categories of non-Celtic finds. Evidence for trade with the Anglo-Saxon world is notably not plentiful.

Trade with the Mediterranean world

Many sherds of pottery and glass made outside the Celtic areas have been found and their significance has been vigorously debated. The types of pottery and glass are outlined below; the most important categories of pottery for this period being Classes A, B, D and E Ware.

Other material is rare, but varied. What appears to have been part of a Frankish chatelaine was found on a settlement that also produced E Ware, at Tean in the Scillies (C. Thomas, 1990: 18), for instance. A native imitation of a Frankish S-brooch was found at Ronaldsway, Isle of Man (Laing and Laing, 1990: 404). A list of possible Frankish finds from Lagore includes a probable horse-bit and possible shield bosses. A pin from Garranes has been seen as Frankish (Laing and Laing, 1990: 404).

Of particular interest in terms of Frankish connections are the recently discovered mounts for a saddle from Hillquarter, which may have been made by an Irish person with good knowledge of Continental saddles (E. Kelly, 2001). A Frankish gold coin (a *tremissis*) was found at Trim, and two dubious Byzantine coins from a garden in Ballymena (Hillgarth, 1963: 177). Other exotic imports include a flask from the shrine of St Menas in Alexandria, from the now-submerged coastal trading base at Meols (Bu'lock, 1972: 35 and pl. 2).

In addition, there are a number of other exotic items which imply overseas trade: a Frankish bead from Dunadd (Lane and Campbell, 2000: 243); a German arm ring from Blackness (R. Stevenson, 1983: 474–6); a disputed eighth-century Frankish helmet from Dumfriesshire;[3] a hoard of *Vestlandkesseln* (bowls) from Halkyn Mountain; and a few finds of later Frankish material from Ireland and the Isle of Man.

Apart from a few items of Irish origin in Merovingian France (E. James, 1982: 381), and some from Scandinavia, there is no evidence to date for reciprocal trade.

Monastic trade

Pigments needed by monasteries for manuscript art came from far afield: orpiment (a yellow mineral) was found at Dunadd, where it was possibly in transit to Iona (Campbell, 1987). Ultramarine, which was derived from lapis lazuli, was used in the Book of Kells, and in the later middle ages came, ultimately, from Afghanistan.

Books were not strictly trade items, since many were probably gifts or exchanges, but they were among the commodities that passed between Celtic Britain and the Continent. Columbanus, an Irish monk, founded monasteries at Luxeuil, St Gall and Bobbio in Italy. In the latter foundation a school of Irish monks working in the scriptorium took up Italian scripts but used their own distinctive systems of abbreviation and decorative devices.

Some manuscripts were taken from Ireland to Bobbio, such as the *Antiphonary of Bangor*, while some manuscripts produced in Bobbio went to Ireland, such as the *Codex Usserianus Primus* (Hughes, 1966: 93; Henry, 1965: 62). At Bobbio Columbanus reputedly carried a North African manuscript of the fourth or fifth century in his book satchel (Lowe, 1934–63: iv, 465).

A characteristic of the Irish monks is that they were frequently driven into exile as a penance, which took them far afield in Europe and undoubtedly led to much dissemination of both ecclesiastical items and ideas.

Trade with the Anglo-Saxon world

Evidence for trade with the neighbouring Anglo-Saxon world is generally lacking, which may reflect the hostile relations between the two areas. A scatter of Anglo-Saxon finds in Scotland extends as far north as Orkney, but the majority come from the south, from areas which were for part of the period under Anglo-Saxon control (Proudfoot and Aliaga-Kelly, 1996). Outside this zone Anglo-Saxon finds are so few that they cannot be seen to represent trade. Very recent excavations however may have changed this situation since there was evidence of Northumbrian contacts from the artefact assemblage from Dunadd (Lane and Campbell, 2000: 241). Until recently there has been a similar dearth of Anglo-Saxon finds from Wales, where apart from the metalwork from Dinas Powys, a buckle from Dinorben, and a few other items from Glamorgan and Gwent, there was nothing to point to any form of organized trade. Recent metal detecting activity has, however, produced material particularly in the border areas (Redknap, 1995: 60).

In Ireland, Anglo-Saxon finds are sparse, with most finds coming from Lagore. In south-west England there are putatively Anglo-Saxon tweezers from Gwithian, but most of the Anglo-Saxon finds in Dumnonia belong to the period when there was Anglo-Saxon pressure in the ninth to eleventh centuries. This is best exemplified by the Trewhiddle hoard, which comprises ninth-century Saxon silverwork and coins (Wilson and Blunt, 1961).

There seems to be more direct evidence of trade to than from the Anglo-Saxons. It is clear, for example, that the Anglo-Saxons not only acquired penannular brooches from their British neighbours, but also produced their own iron versions of a type of brooch current in the fourth to fifth centuries (Class C penannulars: Laing, forthcoming, 2006).

The Anglo-Saxons similarly acquired hanging-bowls made by the British Celts, which they also, on occasion, copied (p. 176). Other Celtic imports into Anglo-Saxon England include a Pictish brooch found in York (Hall, 1984: 102), a hinged pin found in Northampton, an Irish glass stud inset into a linked pin set found at Roundway Down, and another from Camerton (Meaney and Hawkes, 1970: 48–9). The well-known Sutton Hoo whetstone was made from stone that probably originated in Dumfriesshire (Evison, 1975).

There is some doubt about a boss from Steeple Bumpstead, but if it is taken to be an ancient import rather than a modern loss (Youngs, 1993b), it would fall into the same category as the reliquary hinge from Breedon-on-the-Hill; the Ribchester boss; the Brougham horn mount and the Markyate mount, as examples of Celtic decorated metalwork which passed into Anglo-Saxon hands (Laing, 1993b: nos. 242, 244, 252, 258).

The overseas pottery trade

Late Roman trade in pottery from overseas was concentrated south of the Thames, but the focus began to shift to the Severn and west of England (Lane, 1994: 105). In the later fifth and sixth centuries, Mediterranean pottery (Classes A–D) of this date shows that trade was focused on the Severn estuary, the south-west peninsula and the extreme south of Ireland.

It has been argued that this trade was conducted from or via the Mediterranean (especially the Byzantine world) in return for tin from Cornwall and lead and silver from south-west England and south Wales (Fulford, 1989; C. Thomas, 1988; Lane, 1994; Campbell, 1996a; 1996b). There is certainly growing evidence for the exploitation of tin in the period in the south-west (p. 108) and the *Life of St John the Almsgiver* mentions that a ship from Britain returned to Alexandria half laden with *nomisma* (small bronze coins) and half with tin (Penhallurick, 1986: 245). It has been suggested that the Byzantine Empire may have had diplomatic links with kings in south-west England, and that there may even have been a Byzantine trading community at Tintagel (Harris, 2003: 141–52).

The argument is further supported by a scatter of Byzantine coins (from, for example, Exeter and Ilchester); a Byzantine censer from Glastonbury; and a Byzantine coin weight from Entwhistle (Pearce, 2004: 237). The Byzantine trade route may have continued further north – a Byzantine ring bezel was found at Cefn Cwmwnd, Anglesey (p. 260) (Denison, 2000).

Although it is usually assumed that the Byzantine trade was direct, it is equally possible that it was a secondary trade from France (Bowman, 1996: 102). There are a few 'stray' finds of imported pottery (A and B Ware) further north, from Whithorn, the Mote of Mark, Dumbarton and Iona. The relatively scarce D Ware mortaria from western France seem to belong to the sixth century, and to provide a bridge between the earlier trade and that of E Ware in the later sixth and seventh.

By the seventh century the existing trade was in E Ware from France, and had extended in a broad belt through Ireland and along the west coast of Scotland. Imported glass, now known from forty or so sites, also mostly from France, turns up in the same contexts as E Ware.

Although it has been suggested that all the surviving A and B Wares are so rare that they could represent the cargo of a single ship (Thomas, 1988), the surviving material is sufficiently varied to suggest more regular exchange – as the 1,500 identified vessels from Tintagel in Cornwall would seem to indicate (Thomas, 1993: 93; L. Alcock, 2003: 89). Cargoes would not have comprised entirely pottery, and other perishable commodities would have figured, such as wine, dyes,[4] or other luxury items (Lane, 1994: 107).

There are indications that some pottery reached coastal trading bases from which it was distributed – possible distribution centres being Dalkey Island near Dublin, Tintagel (Thomas, 1993), Bantham (L. Alcock, 1995: 144–5) and possibly Caldey (Campbell, 1996: 95), in south Wales. Most of the finds seem to be concentrated in high-status centres such as Dunadd, Dumbarton, Clogher or Garranes, which are located close to the sea or major waterways. Thus the eastern find-spots of pottery at Dundurn and Clatchard Craig, may have been supplied from Dumbarton via Loch Lomond and the Tay, while Craig Phadrig near Inverness could have obtained its supply from Dunollie via the Great Glen (L. Alcock, 2003: 87).

The traders were probably not Celts, but from the Continent. Adomnán, who in his *Life of St Columba* spoke of a ship from Gaul arriving in Iona around 680, also states in another source that bishop Arculf, a Gaul, arrived at Iona after a shipwreck on the western coast of Britain. The evidence for trade with Gaul represented by imported pottery and Frankish glass, discussed below (Thomas, 1990), is corroborated by documentary references which certainly suggest that Frankish traders were reaching the Atlantic coasts from the seventh century onwards.

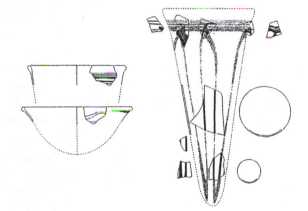

Fig. 51
Imported vessel
glass and map of
its distribution.

Overseas glass trade

In the Celtic west, vessel glass is known from at least forty-four sites
(Campbell, 1989; 1995; 1996a, b; 2000. For Ireland, E. Bourke, 1994; Fig. 51).
Originally, this was believed to have been imported from Anglo-Saxon
England as cullet (scrap glass for melting down). It is now apparent that apart
from material on a few sites such as Cadbury Congresbury, Dinas Powys and
Whithorn, virtually the entire corpus is vessel glass that was imported intact

from the Continent. When such vessels were eventually broken, it seems that they were re-cycled into beads and inlays. At Dinas Powys deep blue, brown and green glass was selected for this purpose in one area of the site, while the clear glass was randomly discarded (Campbell, 2000: 37).

Particularly favoured were fine clear cone beakers often with white trailed decoration, usually marvered into the vessel, and occasional bowls (Campbell, 2000: 39–43; his Group C/D vessels). The cone beakers were suitable for drinking from at feasts, and they may have been imported as an adjunct to the wine trade. Other vessels in deep blue, green, brown and red glass appear to be later, of the eighth century (Lane and Campbell, 2000: 171).

It would appear that this glass was being manufactured in the neighbourhood of Bordeaux in the fifth to seventh centuries AD and in Britain and Ireland is associated with the imported pottery D and E Ware (which came from the same area, below). It was imported in the late sixth to early seventh centuries AD (Campbell, 1996: 90). It is noteworthy that with the exception of one sherd from Reask, no glass in Ireland has been associated with an ecclesiastical site (E. Bourke, 1994: 180).

At Whithorn a distinct type of vessel occurs – with thicker walls, different decorative schemes and a characteristic rim. Such vessels occur in late sixth-century contexts (Campbell, 2000: 43). It is likely that this glass was a local attempt to imitate the imports for a short period in the sixth century.

In Ireland a few vessels of the seventh to ninth centuries ultimately came from the Carolingian world. These include a late palm cup from Dalkey Island (associated with E Ware and datable to the period around AD 700), and some later vessels from the same site and Lagore. They probably represent a continuation of the later wine trade with Aquitaine (E. Bourke, 1994: 179). A fragment of Spanish glass is documented from Tintagel (Pearce, 2004: 241).

The most unusual glass of eastern origin comprises gold leaf tesserae, believed to be similar to those used in Byzantine mosaics. Such tesserae seem to have been imported to Scandinavia as a source of scrap glass in the eighth century and have been found at Dunadd, Birsay and Whithorn. The example from Dunadd was found in a seventh-century context, and may indicate trade with Scandinavia in the pre-Viking Age (Lane and Campbell, 2000: 173). A piece of what may have been a glass tessera was also found at the Mote of Mark.

There is very little eastern Mediterranean vessel glass, though a few vessels (with wheel-cut and abraded decoration) datable to the fifth century, could have come from many locations as far apart as Egypt and Spain. Four vessels dated to the fifth century have been identified from Tintagel (Harden, 1956: 155), and there is another from Trethurgy, while four others come from Whithorn (Campbell, 2000: 39 – his group A). A phial base from St Andrews with an opaque white marvered trail on the body is probably eighth to tenth century and from the east (Harden, 1956: 155).

Imported pottery

Imported pottery is particularly important for establishing a chronology for sites which produce it. A wide variety of sites in western Britain and Ireland have produced sherds of imported wares. These were first generally recognized following the publication of a group from the monastic site of Tintagel in 1956 (Radford, 1956), and since then intensive research has built up an impressive list of sites with imported pottery, the study and dating of which has been refined.[5]

Class A Ware

This consists of a series of bowls and dishes in a brick-red fabric with slightly glossy or red-brown slip (Fig. 52a).

Two separate groups of wares have been identified:

Phocaean Red Slip Ware (PRS)　also sometimes known as *Late Roman C,* which was produced and traded in the east Mediterranean, except for a brief period when it was traded to Britain and Spain, from the mid-fifth to mid-sixth centuries AD (Hayes, 1972; 1980). Virtually all the imports in Britain seem to date from the period AD 475–525 (Campbell, in Edwards and Lane, 1988: 124).

North African Red Slip Ware (ARS or NARS)　was produced in the vicinity of Carthage (Fulford and Peacock, 1984: 14–15), and imported to Britain at a slightly later date, perhaps mainly around the mid-sixth century.

Class B Ware

This consists of a series of amphorae or storage jars with handles (Fig. 52b). They are in red, pink, buff and creamy coloured fabrics and very frequently have grooves on the body in a continuous spiral to aid handling. They have been divided into four main sub-classes.[6]

Class C Ware

This pottery comprises small bowls and dishes with a dull red or buff fabric with considerable inclusion of grits. It is widespread in Britain, and is of uncertain origin.

Class D Ware

This consists of mortaria – bowls for mashing fruit and vegetables that were descended from the Roman form (Thomas, 1959; Rigoir, 1968; Ferdière and

A

B

Fig. 52A.
A Ware, Tintagel
and map of its
distribution;
B. B Ware, Dinas
Powys and map
of its
distribution.

Rigoir, 1972; Rigoir and Meffre, 1973). Class D vessels are in soft, grey ware
with a blue-black wash (Fig. 53A). They frequently have a small spout for pouring, and like their Roman predecessors have grits to aid grinding. Related to
the mortaria are smaller bowls and other vessels with external rouletting,
and a few larger bowls with stamped decoration.

As a whole, this class belongs to a family of wares found in France which
were once thought to be Visigothic but are now known to be descended
from local Roman wares. Examples of this ware are widespread in southern
and western France in the fifth and sixth centuries, and the closest parallels
for the British imports are from the region round Bordeaux, though they
may have been produced at other centres, notably in the Loire valley. The

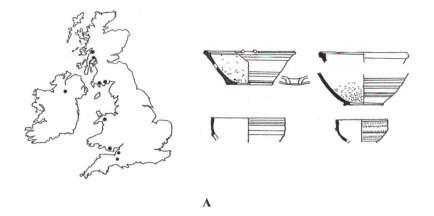

A

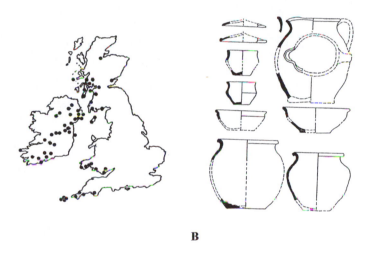

B

Fig. 53A. D Ware, Dinas Powys and map of its distribution; **B.** E Ware and map of its distribution.

date span of its use is not certain, but it appears to be spread through the sixth century.

Class E Ware

This type is the most frequently found and comprises cooking pots, bowls, jars, jugs and beakers (Thomas, 1959; Thomas and Peacock, 1967; Campbell, 1988). It is characteristically hard-fired (almost to stoneware) and pimply to the touch (Fig. 53B). The colour is usually dirty white on the interior with a grey or yellow exterior shading through to ochre and red or dark grey. The fabric includes quartz and other grits of a white or red colour. On the base there is frequently a raised whorl. The type has turned up on thirty or more sites, and more than 100 vessels are represented. Long regarded as Rhenish, more recently the grits in E Ware sherds were examined petrologically and were found to compare most closely with those from the Paris basin and more particularly Aquitaine. While no E Ware has yet been identified with certainty in this area, present opinion places its production around the Charente.

It is dated only by association with other imports of datable material in Britain, but does not appear to have been imported prior to 525–50. It continued until about 700 or slightly later.

Class F Ware

This pottery comprises some thin-walled but large vessels with a laminated fabric and a pearl-grey to pink colour. Its provenance is unknown, and it occurs at only a few sites notably Dunadd and Dalkey Island.

7

Clothes and jewellery

Much is known about Celtic hairstyles and clothing from art, particularly from sculpture, though a small amount of cloth also exists. Leather items such as shoes have occasionally been found. By far the largest body of material comprises ornamental dress accessories, most of which were attractive as well as functional – brooches, different classes of pins, buckles and studs. Due to their durability, dress-fasteners have attained a prominence in academic studies that is disproportionate to their importance either to the Celts themselves or to understanding their society. Purely decorative items such as beads and glass or shale bracelets were also worn.

A further body of evidence consists of surviving examples of durable items from which it is possible to make inferences about lost material – spindle whorls and weaving equipment, for example.

Hair and clothing

Clothes are represented on high crosses (p. 202) and in literary sources but evidence is very sparse for everyday wear. By inference, people of high status wore a probably linen tunic (*leine*) secured by a belt of wool or leather, under a probably woollen cloak (*brat*) that was fastened with a pin or brooch at the breast. While the *brat* was usually wrapped round the body several times, on occasions it was allowed to drag behind. The *brat* sometimes appears to have been of several colours. The *leine* was normally white, with an ornamented border. In Viking period Ireland, a tunic and breeches seem to have been worn by the lower social orders, and in this period, too, silk seems to have been in use (De Paor and De Paor, 1958: 101–5).

Irish law codes relating to the fosterage of children (p. 20) dictate which colours were to be worn by which social ranks. The sons of the ordinary freemen could only wear dun-coloured, yellow, black or white garments, but the sons of lords could wear red, grey or brown. Only the sons of kings could wear purple or blue (F. Kelly, 1997: 263).

Some depictions of clothing appear on ninth- and tenth-century Irish crosses. The West Cross (Cross of the Scriptures) at Clonmacnoise shows two figures, each dressed in an ankle-length linen *leine*, and with a woollen *brat* fastened at the shoulder with a brooch. Each person wears a beard, one pointed, the other bifurcated. Two figures (believed to be king Flann and abbot Colman) beneath the first pair wear respectively, a short tunic and an

143

Fig. 54 Arrest of Christ from Cross of Muiredach, Monasterboice, showing brooch and trousers.

upper garment and long robe. The garments of both appear to have embroidered borders.

Figures on the Tower Cross at Kells appear to be wearing trousers, and Christ, in the depiction of His arrest on the cross of Muiredach at Monasterboice, wears an embroidered robe and a penannular brooch. The two soldiers wear breeches, cut off above the knee (Fig. 54).

Both sexes usually wore their hair long in the early medieval period: art also indicates the wearing of pigtails, for example on a shaft from Banagher, or on a Pictish slab from Golspie. Clerics are depicted in sculpture and manuscripts as cleanshaven, while laymen often have drooping moustaches and fork-pointed beards. Hairstyles were often elaborate, particularly by the end of the period, as shown by the styles represented on the eleventh-century *Breac Maodhóg*.

To judge from Pictish sculpture, clothing in Scotland was similar to that in Ireland, except that trousers do not figure. Women wore their hair shoulder-length (one depicted at Monfieth having hers in bunches) and men wore moustaches and beards. The figures on a Pictish slab at Birsay had their hair tied back. The clerics on Fowlis Wester 2 wear vestments that appear to have been embroidered all over, with noticeable borders.

Virtually nothing is available about fashion from the Welsh monuments, as figural artwork is very rare.

Cloth

Very little cloth has survived, and evidence must be pieced together through inference from more durable objects, associated with the wearing or production of material. The sparse evidence suggests that cloth production was carried out at local centres rather than 'at home' (Hodkinson, 1987: 49).

An exceptional survival is the woollen hood from St Andrews Parish, Orkney, which has been dated to between AD 250 and 615 (Wood, 2003). It was apparently woven on an upright loom, with a tablet-woven border, and with long tassels. Such hoods are shown worn by Picts in sculptures.

Some cloth from Ballinderry 2 crannog shows that tabby (i.e. simple over-and-under weaving) existed in sixth-century Ireland (Hencken, 1942: 58). Tabby weaving was represented at Deer Park Farms.[1] From Lagore the evidence is more abundant and shows that although tabby weaving was predominant other techniques were known. Some diagonal weaving was carried out.

Tablet weaving was widespread among the Germanic peoples of the migration period (Crowfoot and Hawkes, 1967), and, since evidence for it occurs in Anglo-Saxon graves, it is possible that it came to Ireland by way of Anglo-Saxon England. It is represented by a leather tablet at Deer Park Farms, which could have been used for weaving either borders or bands.

Wool was the material mostly used for weaving – some was carded before being spun. Goat's hair was also used. Flax is represented in the form of seeds from a few sites (Monk, 1986), but the only linen found was from the crannog at Llan-gors (Granger-Taylor and Pritchard, 2001). This charred textile, which probably came from a shirt, was embroidered with silk, and dated from the end of the ninth or early tenth century. The stylized ornament included pairs of small, confronted lions with vinescrolls and birds, inspired by Asian models.

Leatherwork

The small amount of surviving leatherwork is mostly very fragmentary and unidentifiable. Part of a book satchel (originally identified as a jerkin), as well as fragments of knife sheaths were found at Loch Glashan crannog,[2] and there was part of a purse from Iona (Barber, 1981: 320), but most other leatherwork is footwear.

Shoes

Many shoes have been recovered from waterlogged deposits (Lucas, 1956; Fig. 55). A large collection of shoes, made from the skins of calf, horse, deer, seal and goat or sheep, was recovered from Iona, dating to AD 585–618. Sole and upper were joined using a closed seam, while careful and skilled sewing and thonging was used for what appear to have been frequent repairs (Barber, 1981: 319). The 'thread' used was of animal origin, possibly from the muscular tissue of the intestine wall. Decoration was of impressed small circles in

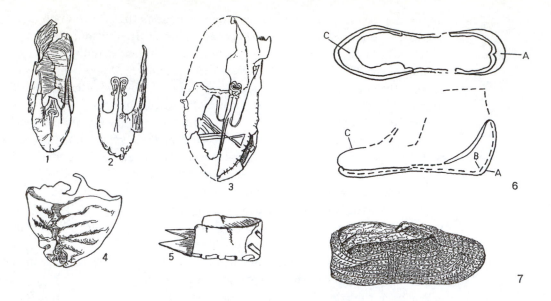

Fig. 55 Leather shoes, Ireland: 1–2. Craigywarren crannog; 3. Ballinderry 2 crannog; 4–5. Lagore; 6. Lissue, shoe construction: A. outer sole; B. inner sole; C. Upper; 7. decorated shoe, Dundurn.

different patterns (Barber, 1981: 319). One shoe, which could be reconstructed, would have fitted a modern UK size 7 foot.

Such turnshoes (made inside-out, with a separate sole) had tongue-shaped stiffeners sewn flesh to flesh inside the heel (a feature otherwise unknown between Roman and late medieval times), and a tongue-shaped riser at the back (Groenman-van Waateringe in Barber, 1981: 318–20).

Two types of shoes were recognized at Ballinderry 2 (Hencken, 1942: 56). Most had a longitudinal join from the toe to the tongue along which were lace holes. This type is also represented at Lagore. In the Book of Kells, the St Matthew evangelist figure is wearing similar footgear. A second find had a tongue with holes for laces round the front decorated with interlace and a scroll.

It was not possible to relate uppers to soles at Ballinderry 2, though at Lissue (Bersu, 1947: 54–6) shoes could be shown to have been made in three pieces; an upper (missing at Lissue), an insole and an outsole. The edges of the insole and the outer sole of the Lissue shoe were folded together and a welt seems to have been used to join upper and sole. A boot of similar type is known from Craigywarren crannog.

A very decorative shoe was found at Dundurn – of a one-piece construction, with an all-over stamped design (L. Alcock et al., 1989: 217 and illus. 16).

The finds from Lagore and Buiston include wooden shoe lasts (Hencken, 1950: fig. 86, no. W146).

Toilet articles

What may be a mirror handle is known from Inishkea North (Henry, 1952, 169–71), and mirrors occur as symbols on Pictish stones (p. 312). Bone was

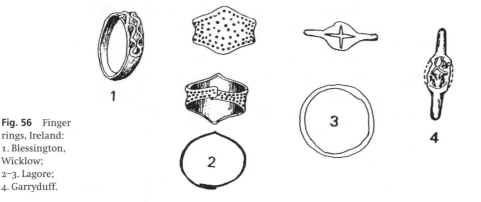

Fig. 56 Finger rings, Ireland: 1. Blessington, Wicklow; 2–3. Lagore; 4. Garryduff.

used for a type of pin with an expanded, curved point similar to nail cleaners or Roman ear scoops. Examples from Lagore are very ornate, with animal or human heads in two cases (Hencken, 1950: 190). They seem to be derived from Roman antecedents.

Jewellery

Finger rings and bracelets

Finger rings from the early medieval period are rare (Fig. 56). The design on one example, in the collection of the Royal Irish Academy, is closely related to that on some penannular brooch terminals, and is therefore probably contemporaneous (Coffey, 1909: 23). A bronze finger ring from Garryduff 1, with an oval flattened bezel, was decorated with incised lines and chip-carved triangles. The bezel from a similar ring from Lagore was incised with a cross. A spiral bronze finger ring was among the finds from Garranes. Fragments of what might be two glass finger rings of the late first millennium AD were found at Whithorn (Price in Hill et al., 1997: 358).

Bracelets are not common finds before the Viking period, with the exception of one series of glass armlets and a series made of shale, jet, cannel coal or lignite. The jet or shale armlets are very similar to those found in the Bronze Age and in Roman Britain (Lawson, 1976), except that in contrast to the Roman they are usually D-shaped in section. They seem to have been manufactured at Ronaldsway on the Isle of Man (Laing and Laing, 1990: 409), at Little Dunagoil, Bute (Laing, Laing and Longley, 1998: 557), and also seem to have been made at Whithorn (Hill et al., 1997: 441) and Armagh, where the discs left after their production have been found. Their chronological spread is wide, certainly from the sixth century to the ninth or tenth century at Jarlshof, Shetland (Hamilton, 1956: 121 – but these have circular sections), and possibly even into the twelfth century at Kingarth and Little Dunagoil.

There are a few bracelets of bronze with limited decoration.

Glass armlets were produced in north Britain in the second century AD from re-used Roman glass (Kilbride-Jones, 1937–8; R. Stevenson, 1954–6; 1976). In Ireland examples have been dated to between the seventh and tenth centuries (Carroll, 2001; Fig. 48.4). They are plano-convex in section and decorated with cable-patterned bands, akin to some of the beads (p. 149). Threads of white glass were twisted round a blue rod, which was drawn thin, the cable thus formed being applied to the body of the bracelet. The cables were pressed into the wall of the bracelet, and do not project above the surface. White spots were also used for ornamentation.

Two groups have been distinguished in Ireland, the first comprising lighter-coloured bracelets close in style to the Romano-British, and which are concentrated in Co. Meath. The second group is without a visible core and is dark blue, sometimes without a raised cable or dots. Glass bracelets have been found in the Northumbrian monasteries of Monkwearmouth and Jarrow where glass was worked, and it has been suggested that they were developed from Roman examples in Northumbria, and taken to Ireland where they were copied (Carroll, 2001: 109).

Beads

Beads for necklaces are among the most common finds from settlement sites (Fig. 57). Although they were sometimes made of amber, bone or stone, glass was the most popular material. Some glass beads, notably plain dark blue (and possibly spotted types), were probably produced in the Celtic west. Many were almost certainly imported from the Germanic world. Trade connections are also implied from the material used: amber (which was also used to decorate penannular brooches) probably originated in the Baltic, and rock crystal possibly came from Anglo-Saxon England, where they may have been imports from the Continent (Huggett, 1988: 70). The different colours chosen may reflect fashions or regional ethnicity, though they must also have been dictated by availability. Non-glass beads are normally round and undecorated, though some bone beads may be cordoned or ribbed, being lathe-turned.

Most beads are undatable (Fig. 57 for types), except for the following.

Opaque red bead   Plain round beads of this type, sometimes with a marvered spot, are common Germanic types and occur in Anglo-Saxon graves. They are rare in the west – a single example was found at Dinas Powys. A type of brownish-red bead was also represented at Dunadd and in a Viking burial at Ballinaby, Islay, where they were dated to the ninth century (Guido in Lane and Campbell, 2000: 176).

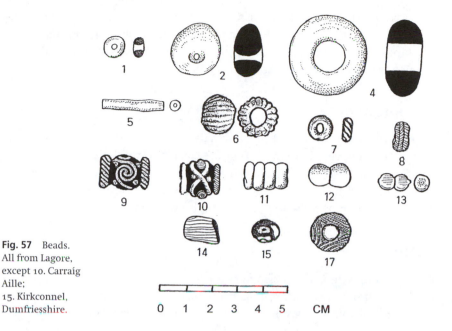

Fig. 57 Beads. All from Lagore, except 10. Carraíg Aille; 15. Kirkconnel, Dumfriesshire.

Cable bead This was made by twisting together one or more cables of different coloured glass threads. Termed reticella beads on the Continent, they are commonly of blue with white herringbone designs. Some in Scandinavia have been regarded as Irish imports. Three types were recognized at Lagore (Hencken, 1950: 137): (1) annular beads made with one cable; (2) zig-zag beads, which have herringbone cables and occur at Dunadd, Lagore, Ballinderry 2 and Cush. They have been dated mostly from the ninth century and later, though it has been suggested that they may start as early as the seventh century (Guido in Lane and Campbell, 2000: 176); (3) beads with cables at each end (also termed a 'string' bead).

Horned eye bead This category includes all beads with applied bosses or knobs, decorated with spirals of differently coloured glass. It is predominantly an Iron Age type which is rare in western Europe in the early medieval period, but also occurs in the Viking period.

Eye bead This is distinguished by trailed white opaque glass with central dark-coloured glass spots (usually dark blue) against a dark blue or other dark-coloured background. Examples appear to be mainly sixth- to seventh-century in date, and occur at Trier as well as in Anglo-Saxon cemeteries. British finds include one from Kirkconnel, and many from Ireland. A variant form is dark blue with trailed white interlace, and appears to belong to the period c. AD 800–850. Finds include examples from Dunadd, Moylarg crannog, Lagore and Westness, Orkney (Guido in Lane and Campbell, 2000: 176).

Amber bead These appear to be a feature of Viking-period sites, being represented in Viking burials on Islay and Colonsay (Ritchie, 1993: 85, 87), and in Viking-period contexts at Whithorn (Hills et al., 1997: 359). Amber also was being worked in the pre-Viking period, for example at Armagh.[3]

Dress-fasteners

These very varied items are difficult to date precisely, with some pin types in particular being very long lived. They are clearly very closely related to style and function of dress as well as availability of materials. Basic forms probably had a long currency, but decorative schemes were shorter lived. Some of the brooches are important works of art in their own right.

Buttons

Buttons were used as dress-fasteners as early as the late Neolithic in Europe, but thereafter various classes of pins and brooches seem to have been favoured. Buttons are rare in the Celtic post-Roman/early medieval period. Possible examples have been found at Garryduff 1 and Lagore (O'Kelly, 1962a: 38).

Latchets

The characteristic features of the latchet are the S-bend in the shank, the central expansion and the plate-head. Spirals of wire were wound round the stem of latchets and the bends in the shank – the coil of wire could be turned in the cloth like a corkscrew to grip it securely. In a few cases the spirals still survive. Experiments have shown them to be highly effective. A lost find appears to have comprised two latchets linked by a chain (Greene, 2003). About 25 latchets are known, 24 of which were found in the eighteenth or nineteenth century, and all are without authoritative context (Fig. 58). The type may have evolved out of a type of Iron Age pin that has a bent neck (Smith, 1917–18; Greene, 2001). Their extreme rarity suggests that they may have been badges of rank – the fact that most have been found in or near rivers may be significant.

Due to the absence of finds from excavations a chronological scheme for latchets cannot be established, but it is probable that examples at various stages of the typological sequence existed contemporaneously. The series probably belongs to the period from the fifth to the seventh or early eighth centuries AD, and on stylistic grounds most of those with decorated heads belong to the period after 600.

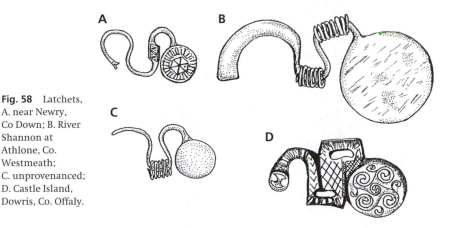

Fig. 58 Latchets, A. near Newry, Co Down; B. River Shannon at Athlone, Co. Westmeath; C. unprovenanced; D. Castle Island, Dowris, Co. Offaly.

Buckles

Buckles (for belts) were comparatively rare in the period, and are mostly known from moulds (Fig. 59). The earliest series comes from the Mote of Mark, where they were characteristically small, and the buckle loop was cast in one piece with the plate (Laing and Longley, 2006: 144) – a feature of some late Roman buckles. The pin seems to have been attached by being looped round a bar formed by leaving a hole in the plate. Occasionally the device is found in the Frankish world, and on a few early buckles from England (for example Leeds, 1936: 103, fig. 21).

At Dunadd the buckle moulds seem to follow the design of some Anglo-Saxon three-piece buckles with a hinged loop, current in the seventh century (Campbell and Lane, 1993: 55; Lane and Campbell, 2000: 127–9). One mould had silver in it from a casting. A buckle of similar design from Lough Gara had a sub-triangular body and inlays of glass and enamel (Youngs, 1989: 58, no. 46). A similar buckle was found near Melton Mowbray though it seems to be of a simpler form, with buckle and plate cast in one (Youngs, 1993a: fig. 2).

Buckles probably came to Ireland in the sixth century as a result of contact with later Roman Britain, or the Anglo-Saxon world. The Irish examples are closely comparable to the Anglo-Saxon. One of the Lagore buckles has a square plate, rather more elongated than the majority of Anglo-Saxon examples. A second buckle from Lagore has a triangular plate, an early seventh-century form known from Anglo-Saxon graves. The third Lagore buckle, of the eighth century, while inspired by triangular Germanic types, is without doubt a native development, having a slightly triangular plate from which extends a stem for the strap attachment. The plate is richly decorated.

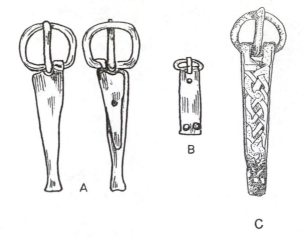

Fig. 59 Buckles and studs. Buckles: A, B. Lagore; C. Peel, Isle of Man; studs, Lagore.

An unsual buckle decorated with millefiori was among the finds from Derry. This lacks a plate, and presumably the belt was looped round it in the manner of later buckles (rather than being riveted or sewn to it). It is probably of the seventh or eighth century.

In the Viking period buckles probably became more common in the Celtic west, due to Viking taste, and examples are known from Viking graves in Scotland. A recent study has shown that they were of native manufacture, and suggested that they were produced in Scotland and also in centres such as Dublin (Patterson, 2001). They have hinged loops with elongated plates, and incised ornament, sometimes combined with enamel on their loops (as in the case of one from Bhaltos, Lewis, or one from Ballinaby, Lewis). The Viking-period buckles include those with plain, rectangular plates; those with domed studs and an elongated, waisted profile; and those with an elongated, narrow waist (Laing, 1993a: 38).

Tanged studs

Domed studs with tangs are fairly common finds, a less common form having a flat head like a button (Fig. 59). It is possible that they were for sword belts or harness. They appear at Garranes, Cahercommaun, Creevykeel, Cush and Lagore in Ireland, and at Dinas Powys in Wales. The type first appears in the

Roman Empire, and they are fairly common in Migration Period graves in Switzerland.

In Ireland and Wales the prototypes are probably Anglo-Saxon and the finds from Sutton Hoo include one such stud. In Ireland, they seem to span a period from the sixth century to the ninth. The heads are frequently decorated.

Brooches

The main types are pennanular, ring and kite brooches. Some designs of ornate brooches seem to incorporate Christian symbolism. The motifs were positioned so they could be 'read' by the wearer. Both the celebrated Hunterston and 'Tara' brooches (p. 179) display such symbolism (Stevenson, 1974; 1983). Some brooches seem to have been produced in monastic workshops, such as Nendrum and Armagh (Nieke, 1993: 130).

Penannular brooches

The most common type of dress ornament in the early medieval period was the penannular brooch – basically a hoop of metal with two confronted terminals and a pin which runs along the hoop. The brooches originated in Roman Britain, and came to Ireland in the fourth or early fifth century. It is probable that the continuing popularity of penannular brooches was partly the result of renewed contact with Roman and Byzantine fashion second-hand, through Germanic fashion which was inspired by it (Whitfield, 2004: 70).

Representations in Irish sculpture suggest that the brooches were worn with the pin pointing obliquely upwards (for example on the Cross of Muiredach at Monasterboice: Henry, 1967: pl. 79). The decorative schemes on some of the more ornate brooches support this. Pictish brooches in sculpture similarly appear to have had the terminals pointing down and with the pin horizontally across (Fig. 60).[4] Men seem to have worn brooches at the shoulder, women at the breast. Some of the later ornate examples were almost certainly ecclesiastical and may have been used for fastening chasubles (priests' tent-like robes), but both the simpler brooches and probably many of the ornate examples were worn by laity. A number of Irish documentary sources refer to brooches including the *Senchus Mór* (a collection of law tracts), which related the wearing of brooches to rank, according to the metal from which they were made.[5]

The dates of penannular brooches can be established only in relative terms. Almost all the more ornate examples are stray finds or come from Viking-period contexts when they are often arguably much earlier than the date of burial. Most of the earlier, simpler types are either without association, or not associated with closely datable material. Typology is a useful way of organizing

Fig. 60
Penannular
brooches worn in
Pictish sculpture:
1. Monifeith 2;
2. Hilton of
Cadboll.

the material, but can be taken only as a rough guide to date (see below, p. 155). Both simple and ornate forms remained current until the Viking period, when new types enjoyed a currency – Viking women may have regarded 'foreign' (frequently penannular) brooches as status symbols. The more ornate forms of penannular and pseudo-penannular brooches do not seem to have outlived the Viking period, the annular brooch being preferred thereafter. The different types of dress-fastener which are related to the penannular tradition are:

A *pseudo-penannular brooch*: the terminals of the hoop joined together, the former penannular shape being preserved through the decorative scheme.
A *ring brooch (sometimes termed brooch pin)*: a penannular or pseudo-penannular brooch in which the hoop's diameter is less than a third of the length of the pin – normally the hoop has a diameter not greater than 4 cm.
A *loose-ringed pin*: the hoop is a simple ring without terminals and in which the length of the pin is at least three times the diameter of the ring.
A *ring-headed pin*: has a fixed ring, made in one with the shank.

Terminals

At the time when there was very little material to work on from the period and research techniques were in their infancy, investigators exercised considerable ingenuity and industry in trying to extract any intelligible data. Brooches and pins were therefore subjected to classification, usually based on typology. For this purpose, the most important element was the terminals, though the form of the pin attachment was also significant.

The simplest forms of penannular brooches developed in Britain about the third century BC and continued to be used during the Roman occupation along with more ornate forms of brooch. In the late Roman and early medieval periods there was a marked revival in the popularity of the type, perhaps due to their value as indicators of status in society, but also perhaps due to changes in dress fashion. Penannular brooches also occur in some numbers in pagan Saxon contexts, hinting at British influence in the population (Laing, 2006: forthcoming).

Fifth- and sixth-century brooches were derived from Roman forms and generally were of 'zoomorphic' type (i.e., with animal-headed terminals, often stylized beyond recognition). Ornament on the terminals was limited, but during the sixth century some more elaborately decorated types began to appear and continued into the seventh. The period from the end of the sixth century is also characterized by the increasing tendency to flatten the terminals into expanded flanges: the majority of the ornate eighth-century brooches are derived from this type. While the true penannular remained current in Britain, the pseudo-penannular evolved in Ireland.

The typology of penannular brooches

The scheme normally followed in classifying penannular brooches down to the end of the sixth century uses an alphabetical system of classification (E. Fowler, 1960; 1963; J. Raftery, 1941; Savory, 1956). In the scheme that follows this is cited in brackets for each type. Other schemes have been proposed for some of the material.[6]

The main types are:

- Brooches with thistle-like knob terminals, possibly current in the Viking period (A5) (Fig. 61.1).
- Brooches with terminals bent outwards: probably datable to the seventh century (B3) (Fig. 61.2).
- Brooches with terminals consisting of three ribs separated by deep, squared grooves (D7) (Fig. 61.3). The type probably had a long life, current at least until the seventh century. A variant form which has been termed the South Shields type (Snape, 1992; Cool, 2000: 51), is found in fourth–fifth-century contexts, and has the terminals flattened vertically into rectangular plates.
- Small brooches with zoomorphic terminals on which the features of the animal's head are all discernible (E) (Fig. 61.4). The type became popular in the mid-fourth century, and occurs on Roman military sites.
- Larger versions of the above; (F) (Fig. 61.5–8, 62.5). Of these, it is possible to distinguish many sub-groups, a few of which are distinctively Irish.
- A more elaborate, specialist form of Fig. 61.4, in which the terminals have rounded, projecting 'eyes' and are inlaid with enamel or millefiori (F3) (Fig. 61.9). There is a tendency on these brooches for the pin to become

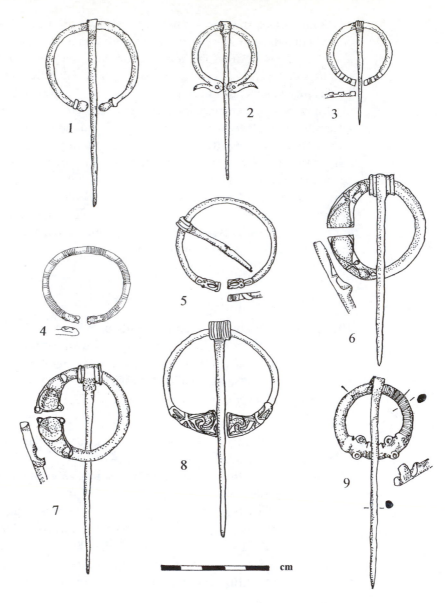

Fig. 61
Penannular
brooches:
1. Lagore;
2. Ballyfallon;
3. Ballycatteen;
4. Lydney, Glos.;
5. Barnton,
Edinburgh;
6. Mullingar, Co.
Westmeath;
7. English, Co.
Armagh;
8. Belcoo,
Enniskillen, Co.
Fermanagh;
9. Ireland,
unprovenanced.

longer, and the type is almost exclusively Irish. It is probably a sixth- to seventh-century form (Newman, 1989; 1990).

• These have squared or faceted terminals, with a central dot or diamond containing four dots (G) (Fig. 62.1–4). The type is probably of Roman origin. A feature of many of the brooches is the silvering or tinning that they show. The group has been seen to comprise several different series, and have been sub-divided into four groups (Graham-Campbell, 1976), and further sub-divided into a complex scheme (Dickinson, 1982).

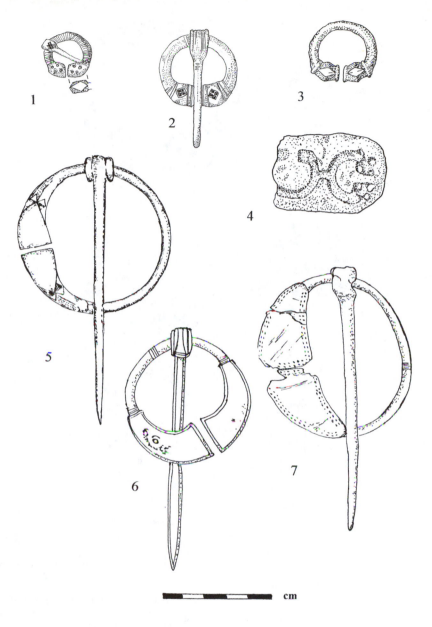

Fig. 62
Penannular
brooches:
1. Sleaford, Lincs.;
2. Trewhiddle,
Cornwall;
3. Dunadd (from
a mould); 4. Mote
of Mark (mould);
5. Toomullin, Co.
Clare; 6. Pant-y-
Saer, Anglesey;
7. Tummel
Bridge, Perths.

- This type (H) has expanded, flattened sub-triangular terminals, and is a fore-runner of the pseudo-penannular brooch tradition (above) (Fig. 62.6–7). These too are capable of sub-division.[7]
- These brooches have flattened round terminals (Fig. 63.1–2). They fall into different groupings and probably start at the end of the Roman period.
- This is a small group of brooches characterized by terminals in the form of confronted animal heads, of more sophisticated form than appears on the

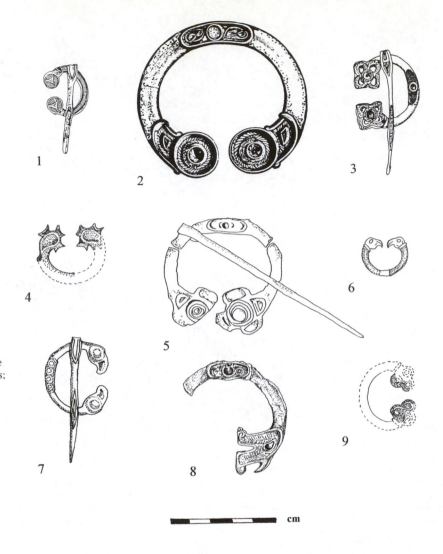

Fig. 63
Penannular
brooches: 1. Luce
Sands, Wigtowns;
2. Croy; 3. Loch
Glashan, Argyll;
4. Dunadd;
5. Machrins,
Colonsay;
6. Dunadd;
7. Clogh, Co.
Antrim;
8. Freswick,
Caithness;
9. Dunadd.

F3 brooches (Fig. 63.6–8). They can be sub-divided. There are a number of sub-types.

• This group comprises all the pseudo-penannular brooches that appear to have evolved in Dál Riata or Ireland in the later seventh century and which span the eighth and ninth centuries (development in Stevenson, 1974, but see also Smith, 1913–14). In contrast to the other brooches, they have joined terminals and a pin which is fastened to the hoop with a hook. They may be sub-divided on the basis of the design of the terminal into a number of sub-groups (Developed H; Fig. 64, 1–2).

• This small group comprises brooches with terminals contoured round bosses (Fig. 63.9). The starting point is a brooch mould from Dunadd

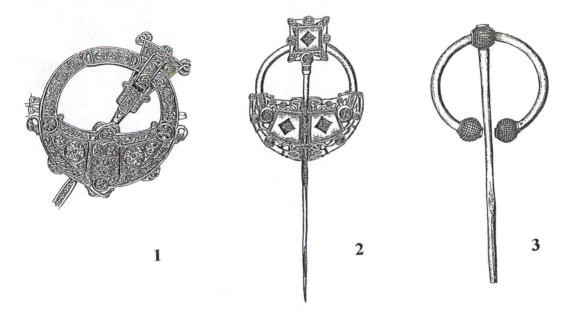

1   2   3

Fig. 64 1. The
Tara brooch;
2. pseudo-
penannular
brooch; 3. thistle
brooch; 2–3
found with the
Ardagh chalice.

of the seventh century (Lane and Campbell, 2000: 116, no. 454). Actual brooches are known from Rogart, Sutherland, of the eighth to ninth centuries (Fig. 63.9).

- Brooches of this type are usually termed 'thistle brooches' and have this-tle-shaped terminals and head to the pin (Graham-Campbell, 1983). They can be either brambled or plain, with engraved decoration. They are a product of Viking culture, were developed in Ireland in the late ninth and tenth centuries (Fig. 63.4).

The decoration of penannular brooches

True penannulars were still made after the seventh century, but the pseudo-penannular is the more common type found in Ireland. In Scotland true penan-nulars were the normal type, and in several cases imported Irish brooches had the junction between the terminals removed to convert them to the penan-nular form, the most notable example being the Breadalbane Brooch.

Of the highly decorated brooches, the earliest display filigree-outlined animals, pseudo-filigree and the device of making an openwork hollow plat-form on the top of gold panels to emphasize the relief of the filigree and gran-ular decoration. The earliest brooches of the series include the finest. The Tara (p. 179), Westness (p. 179) and Hunterston (p. 179) brooches, along with the Dunbeath brooch, belong stylistically to the period of the Lindisfarne gospels and a little later, perhaps the late seventh and early eighth centuries (Fig. 64).

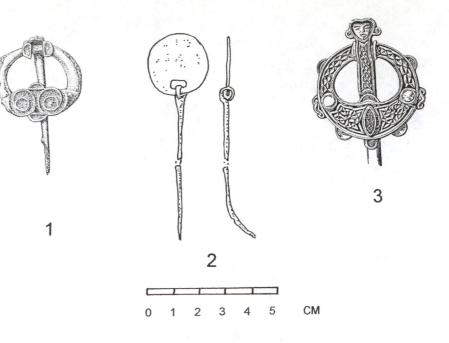

Fig. 65 Hinged pins:
1. Ronaldsway, Isle of Man;
2. Garryduff, Co. Cork; 3. Ireland, unprovenanced.

Study of the design of the Tara brooch and Hunterston brooch has shown that both were devised using mathematical principles, the same governing ratios being employed on each to create a harmony of design (p. 171) (Stevick, 1998; 2003; Whitfield, 1999). A detailed study of the measurements of the Hunterston brooch suggested that it employed a unit of measurement of 9 mm, which may represent a third of an inch based on the Roman foot of 32.4 cm (Whitfield, 1999).

It would appear that the Celts associated different types of brooch with the regions from which they came. An eighth-century Irish law tract includes English and Pictish words for penannular brooches, and implies a widespread awareness of the distinct form of the Pictish version (Etchingham and Swift, 2004). In Ireland brooches of the Tara type with triangular terminals and interlaced animals as a main motif are a feature of the east midlands, lozenge pattern terminals being found in the south midlands, while lobed terminals occur in the north east (and in Scotland) (Ó Floinn, 2002: 177).

Ring brooches (brooch pins)

Closely related to penannular brooches is a series of pins with heads that resemble brooches (Fig. 65). In this 'ring brooch' series, the pin tends to be

Fig. 66 Kite
brooch, near
Limerick.

very long and the head (i.e., the penannular ring) small. There are three
groups:

1. Small, simple penannular brooches with elongated pins (the types are
   identical to the larger penannulars).
2. Hinged pins that have a fixed pin which swivels in a notch or bar on the
   hoop. Apparently they are almost exclusively Irish (there are four examples
   from Scotland) and relatively rare (Stevenson, 1987; 1989). The Westness
   brooch (Stevenson, 1965; 1989) is the most sophisticated example.
3. Disc pins: a flat round plate-head is hinged to the pin. They are closely
   related to penannular ring brooches and are characterized by the absence
   of decoration. It has been suggested that they were derived from the ring
   brooches (Armstrong, 1921–2: 77), but since they appear at Garryduff 1,
   this does not seem likely.

Kite brooches

This rare category of Irish dress-fastener of the ninth–tenth to the twelfth
centuries is characterized by a hinged head attached to a large pin (Fig. 66) (F.
Henry, 1967: 128–31). They became current alongside pseudo-penannular
brooches, but outlasted them (Whitfield, 1997; 2005). They can be large or
small, and made of diverse metals, probably intended for the appropriate
rank of wearer. The hinged head or pendant hangs down from the pin due to
the thickness of the hinge, which suggests that they were used for very thick
material such as fur or leather. A metal chain is usually suspended from the
pendant, to be wound round the pin to secure it. The pendants are richly
decorated and vary slightly in shape, the classic example being one from
Clonmacnoise, now lost. One from Temple Bar West in Dublin came from a

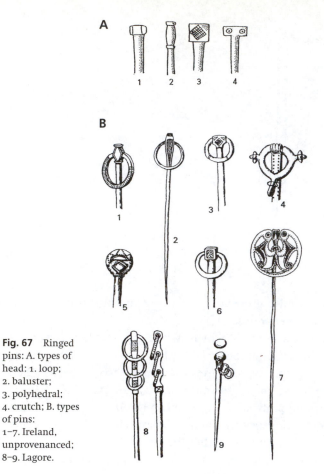

Fig. 67 Ringed pins: A. types of head: 1. loop; 2. baluster; 3. polyhedral; 4. crutch; B. types of pins: 1–7. Ireland, unprovenanced; 8–9. Lagore.

context dated to c. 940–50 (Whitfield, 2005). They sometimes appear depicted in sculpture (Whitfield, 2005: 65).

Loose-ringed pins

The most common dress-fastener in the period, this type survived for almost a millennium (Fig. 67). About 800 examples are known, of which at least 700 have come from Ireland (Fanning, 1994). The spread of the ringed pin was probably due in great part to Viking adoption of the type (they seem to have been used as shroud pins), though evidence from various finds in Scotland shows that some at least were in use on the mainland prior to the arrival of the Vikings (Fanning, 1969; 1983).

A loose-ringed pin has a swivel ring held in a looped or perforated head. The pin was probably kept in place by a cord or wire – the cord from an example from a Viking burial in the Faroes was still attached.

Classification of loose-ringed pins is based on the two basic elements, the ring and the pin-head. From the plain-ringed variety evolved types with increasingly smaller rings, fitting closer to the pin-head. The pin-head also became larger, probably to facilitate a variety of decorative schemes. Pins with larger heads and pins with close-fitting rings were in vogue at the time of the Vikings. From these the kidney-ringed pin evolved.

Loose-ringed pins were normally made of bronze, though iron examples are not uncommon and are of identical types. Silver-ringed pins also occur, the most notable example being the Adare pin. Decoration is usually confined to the pin-head and in the period prior to the Vikings was relatively simple. In the Viking period more elaborate designs appeared.

Spiral-ringed pin   The ring consists of a spiral strip of bronze threaded through the baluster or looped pin-head. Occurs on sites of the fifth and sixth centuries, but probably continued until the Viking period. Rare in Scotland, where their introduction may have been connected with the Columban settlement (Fanning, 1983: 325).

Loop-headed plain-ringed pin   Very long-lived, essentially a shroud pin, it occurs in early contexts along with spiral-ringed pins, and in Viking graves.

Polyhedral-headed ringed pin   The heads are faceted and some bear simple decoration. Pins of this type occur in contexts from the ninth to the eleventh centuries. The pin from Ballinderry 2 has been seen as the only pre-Viking example (Fanning, 1983: 327).

Knobbed-ring pin   Closely related to the loop-headed ringed pin, but has up to three projections on the ring. A relatively rare type, current during the Viking period.

Kidney-ringed pin   Large polyhedral-headed pin often ornamented with brambling (see thistle brooches, p. 159). In the first stages of evolution of the kidney rings the ring was cast separately and fitted on to the pin-head; later it was soldered on to the pin and finally it was cast as one with it. This late form was current in Ireland post-1200 AD, probably lasting until the thirteenth century.

Stirrup-ringed pin   Pins of this type have crutch heads into which the stirrup ring is socketed by means of small tenons. It is a related form to the kidney-ringed pin, also current until at least the twelfth century.

Rib-ringed pin   A rare type in which the ring is segmented with 'spokes' radiating from a central boss, usually placed off centre. The circumference of the ring may also carry knobs, or more frequently sockets for inlay. Most are probably of the tenth century.

Double-ringed pin A relatively rare type, with two rings, one of more regular style, the other passing through the shank lower down. In the case of a pin from Lagore there are three tiers of rings.

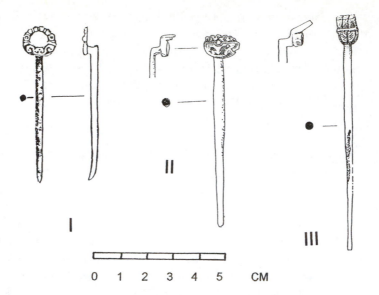

Fig. 68 Hand-pins: I. Oldcroft, Glos.; II. Kirbister, Orkney; III. Dunadd, Argyll.

Ringed pin with secondary ring   These have a second ring, or a bead looped on to the first, as on the Lagore example. Apparently an elaboration of the basic ringed-pin type, examples usually being similar to sprial-ringed pins.

Hand-pins and their predecessors

Although very rare, hand-pins have been much studied. They have a head which projects from the shank, and a plate with beads or 'fingers', which give them the appearance of a clenched hand. Formerly believed to be an Irish development (Smith, 1913), they are now seen as evolving from British proto-types (L. Duignan, 1973; Laing, 1990; Ó Floinn, 2001b: 4–5).

There are three main classes of hand-pin, with sub-divisions (Fig. 68):

Proto-hand-pins   The proto-hand-pin has from three to six beads round the upper part of the ring only. It probably evolved in the third or fourth century AD. They are found in southern Britain in the Roman period. Earlier examples seem to have more beads. Six beads separated by fillets are apparent on the silver example from Oldcroft coin-dated to the mid-fourth century. Where there are only three beads the classification is more difficult, since only one bead need be set higher than the others to produce an arced effect. There are two sub-types.[8]

Early hand-pins   These evolved out of proto-hand-pins. The lower part of the ring developed into a crescentic plate and the upper part, which consisted of beading, straightened out into a row of projections or 'fingers'. The hand-pin appeared in Ireland when fully developed, and evidence suggests that the early stages of its development took place in Britain where the essential elements of hand-pins were already present.

Developed hand-pins The open space between the plate and the fingers diminished to a pinpoint and then disappeared, while the plate itself became a true semicircle of larger size and was more intricately decorated, though the decorative schemes were always fairly simple. Developed hand-pins continued into the eighth century at least.

Stick pins

With the exception of a few rarer types, the remainder of the pin types current in the period are of the 'stick' variety with solid heads (E. Fowler, 1963; R. Stevenson, 1955b; Armstrong, 1921–2; MacGregor, 1972–4: 70–6; Foster, 1990). As with the other types of dress-fastener, they seem to have been for clothing, though their use as hair pins (as in the Roman period) cannot be ruled out.[9] Stick pins were made in metal (normally bronze, more rarely iron), bone or antler – usually the bone pins are of similar type to some of the bronze. The majority of bone pins seem to have been made from pig fibulae, and are simple objects.[10]

Very few bone pin-making sites are known, compared with bronzeworking and it may be that the carving of pins out of cattle bones may have carried social connotations due to the importance of cattle. Antler seems to have been used almost exclusively in the Viking period (Foster, 1990: 150). Bone and wooden pins, of which a few examples survive, probably served as models for moulds for the metal types. Bone pins have been found associated with the moulds made from them at Birsay and the Mote of Mark. Ball-, bead- and nail-headed pins are almost certainly of Romano-British or native Iron Age ancestry, the early medieval examples being, however, shorter for the most part than the Romano-British and frequently having a hip or swelling on the shank to prevent the pin slipping out, a feature which has been noted as pre-Norse (Foster, 1990: 150).

Stick pins are common in Ireland at all periods, but in Britain are relatively rare except in the western and northern isles of Scotland. Very few types from Scotland have exact counterparts in Ireland, and it must be assumed that they are the product of a continuing native tradition. A large percentage of the Scottish pins were of types current at the time of the Viking raids. It is possible that the Scandinavian movements were instrumental in the spread of different types of personal adornment, including stick pins, leading to a period of increased popularity. Stick pins continued to be used into the twelfth and thirteenth centuries, when on occasion types encountered in the early medieval period are also found. Examples come from fourteenth- and fifteenth-century century contexts in Scotland and Ireland.

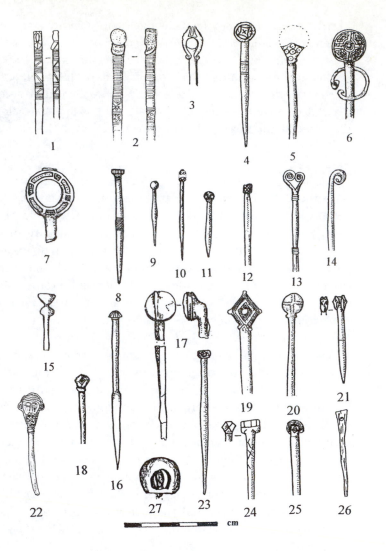

Fig. 69 Stick pins: 1. Traprain Law, E. Lothian; 2. Ireland, unprovenanced; 3. Mote of Mark, from a mould; 4. Orkney; 5. Blackhall House, Strathtay, Perths.; 6. Ireland, unprovenanced; 7. Birsay, Orkney; 8. Berneray Sands, Harris; 9. Broch of Burrian, Orkney; 10. Borerary Sands; 11. Rosemarkie; 12. Vallay, Uist; 13. Ireland, unprovenanced; 14. Lagore; 15. Mote of Mark, from a mould; 16. 'Ross'; 17. Garranes; 18. Culbin Sands, Moray; 19. Birsay, Orkney; 20. Harris; 21. Broch of Burrian, Orkney; 22. Golspie, Sutherland; 23. Kildonan, south Uist; 24. Birsay; 25. Valtos, Lewis; 26. Jarlshof, Shetland; 27. Birsay, Orkney.

It is difficult to construct a 'type series' for stick pins, for although certain types occur with frequency, many are known only from single examples. Those that seem to be datable include (Fig. 69):

Pin with zoomorphic or proto-zoomorphic head   These have long shanks and are closely related to types (E) and (F) Romano-British penannular brooches (p. 155). They continued from the Roman period into the fifth and sixth centuries (Fig. 69.1).

Pin with round head, sometimes enamelled   This has been seen as related to the zoomorphic-headed pins, and several are of silver, including some examples from Ireland (e.g. Youngs, 1989: 10–12). The red enamel dot was sometimes replaced later by geometric designs. The type was current in the fourth to fifth centuries, some surviving perhaps into the sixth. (Fig. 69.2).[11]

Pin with confronted animals on the head   This is represented only from a mould from the Mote of Mark. Sixth–seventh century (Fig. 69.3).

Pin with flattened, round head   Pins of this type may be Pictish. A related type appears to be represented in the Mote of Mark moulds, with a collar between the head and the shank (Fig. 69.4).

Racquet-headed pin   The type is fairly common in later Anglo-Saxon contexts. Although described as a pin, an ornate example of the eighth century with a pair of 'Lindisfarne style' confronted birds engraved on it from Armagh is more probably a stylus (Gaskell-Brown and Harper, 1984: fig. 10.34). A related type of pin seems to have had a fan-shaped rather than round head. This is represented among the moulds from Dunadd (Lane and Campbell, 2000: 125, no. 1804), and there is a similar pin from Machrihanish, for which an eighth-century date was suggested (Batey, 1990; Fig. 69.5).

Ringed racquet pin (Armstrong, 1921–2: pl. xiv, figs. 1.1–2). This is an Irish type with a round head, usually more elaborately decorated than on pins such as Fig. 69.4, and with a wire ring through the shank not far below the head. On the evidence of the decoration on the head, they are unlikely to be earlier than the eighth century (Fig. 69.6).

Wheel-headed pin with fixed ring   These have flat, open wheel heads, frequently inlaid with enamel panels. There is one example from Birsay (C. Curle, 1982: 62 and figs. 39, 421), the others are all Irish. Probably eighth century (Fig. 69.7).

Nail-headed pin   This type is one of the commonest of the pre-Viking Age. It has been suggested the rare bone versions may be late and inspired by Anglo-Saxon versions (Macgregor, 1985: 119). Some were made at the Mote of Mark, Whithorn and Dunadd. Some have glass insets. It is represented in the earliest assemblage at Whithorn (Hill et al., 1997: 364), in the later sixth to seventh centuries. It does not appear to have outlived the Viking period although it occurs in an early Norse context at Jarlshof (Fig. 69.8).

Other types include Fig. 69: (9) *ball-headed pin*; (10) *triskele pin*;[12] (11) *ball-headed pin with settings*; (12) *bramble-headed pin*; (13) *double spiral-headed pin*; (14) *single spiral-headed pin* (normally of iron); (15) *vase- or thistle-headed pin*; (16) *mushroom-headed pin with radial grooves* (in origin the type may Romano-British);[13] (17) *projecting disc-headed pin*; (18) *faceted diamond-headed pin* (probably Viking period); (19) *cushion-headed pin* (again Viking period); (20) *pin surmounted by a round or oval head above a fillet*;[14] (21) *animal-headed pin* (predominantly Viking type); (22) *human-headed pin*;[15] (23) *faceted-headed pin* (also Viking period); (24) *crutch-headed pin* (closely related to the crutch-headed pins of the stirrup- and kidney-ringed pins and of the Viking period); (25) *kidney-ring skeuomorph pin* (Viking and later); (26) *bone pin with triangular head*; (27) *iron pin with bone head*.

8   Art and ornament

The art of Celtic Britain and Ireland during this period has received more attention in the past than any other aspect of its material culture, partly because it includes some major art treasures that have never been lost.[1] Almost all consists of decorated functional or devotional objects which range from manuscripts through portable reliquaries (p. 177) to monumental slabs of carved stone set up in the countryside, though there are also less costly everyday objects such as brooches (see Chapter 7). The art makes use of many motifs and symbols which are either similar to or identical with those in other societies from prehistory onwards. In consequence, it has been argued that it is not art in the modern sense, but should be classed as decoration and craft.

There is no evidence for abstract or conceptual art in the modern sense, although passion and idealism undoubtedly inspired the greatest pieces and society lavished support on those with talent. Unlike today, artists were supported and chosen to reinforce the ideals of society, not to question fundamental beliefs. Inherent in this was a respect for a past.

The resultant deep conservatism makes dating very problematic. Decorative elements seen in, for example, the Book of Kells at the end of the eighth century, recur in many different media thereafter to the eleventh and twelfth centuries. Individual motifs (such as the lion of the Book of Durrow evangelist symbol page) could be copied in different media, for example in sculptures produced in the Northern Isles in the Viking Age (Fig. 70).[2] Moreover, artworks were rarely signed by the artists and were not dated by any method that has so far been identified. When names have survived, these are mostly from the eleventh century onwards, and occur in documents when deaths were recorded or on metalwork (and more rarely in stone). Before the ninth century the chronology of metalwork and sculpture is a relative matter, and experts differ on dates by as much as a century.

Manuscripts were executed in monastic scriptoria; metalwork and stone carving were the products mainly of lay workshops, though these were frequently attached to monasteries. Work for secular patrons seems to have been produced mainly in workshops in the settlements of the rich, perhaps sometimes by travelling smiths.

Artists and patrons

Artists and smiths ranked highly in Celtic society (p. 19), and both monasteries and the rich would have retained their own artisans. The status of the

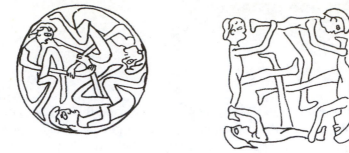

Fig. 70 Book of Kells, linked men and sculptural counterpart, Market Cross, Kells.

craftspeople both explains why they were able to create major works of art, and conversely indicates the importance given to such works.

Itinerant bronze smiths would have produced objects (such as penannular brooches) which were used by most sectors of the community. This fact alone explains both the remarkable uniformity of material culture within the areas under review and the rapid transmission of new styles and ideas. In Ireland from the Viking period onwards (prior to which little evidence survives) most of the ecclesiastical metalwork was produced by lay craftsmen attached to monasteries. The traditions were maintained, with skills being passed on from father to son, so that jobs became hereditary (F. Henry, 1970: 77).

The master craftsman in wood, the *sáer* (whose work could include buildings, boats and mills as well as objects and later came to include work in stone) had counterparts of equal social standing in the *gobae*, blacksmith, the *umaide*, who worked in copper and bronze, and the *cerd*, the jeweller who worked in gold and silver (MacLean, 1995b: 131).

Information is available from eighth-century law tracts about the hierarchies of craftsmen in Ireland, and the high legal and social status that master craftsmen held. The most useful source is the *Uraicecht becc*. The text makes it clear that they were 'dependent professionals', free men who through their arts enjoyed the free privilege of 'noble dignitaries'. Although dependent on their patrons, they had the honour price and maintenance due to the nobility. On occasion their status could exceed that of the jurist.

The code shows that the craftsmen operated in workshops within which there was an ordered hierarchy under a master, the apprentices being clients of the master in the same way that he was the client of his patron. The master provided the apprentice with training, food and clothing, and in return received all the apprentice's earnings, his first earnings on leaving his apprenticeship, and support in his old age (MacLean, 1995b: 130).

With regard to sculpture, an earlier, seventh-century text, the *Life of St Brigit* by Cogitosus, suggests that the same craftsmen worked in wood and stone (MacLean, 1995b:140). The master craftsman who created the overall design of

Fig. 71 Kinitty cross inscription.

free-standing crosses seems to have been accorded more status than the carver who fashioned the details of the ornament. The former was seen as an architect, the latter merely an artist (MacLean, 1995b: 136).

The inscriptions on two crosses, at Kinitty and Clonmacnoise, seem to include the name of the craftsman, Colman, as well as the patron – in the case of Kinitty, Mael Sechnaill, king of Tara (846–62), in the case of the cross of the Scriptures at Clonmacnoise his son, Flann (879–916) (Fig. 71; De Paor, 1987). The same template may have been used to cut the letter forms in both inscriptions.

These crosses, and the literary evidence, make it clear that master crafts-men could be commissioned outside their own monastery or even *túath*, though those that worked under them enjoyed less mobility.

Mathematics and design

Celtic art was essentially the province of the draughtsman. Designs were care-fully laid out using compasses and grid-lines, and in accordance with constructive geometry and specific units of measurement. Pin-pricks and grid-lines survive on the backs of the pages of some manuscripts, such at the Book of Kells, and motif pieces survive showing the laying out of the designs using grids and compass, for example at Nendrum or Ballinderry 1 crannog (O'Meadhra, 1979).

Studies of the Tara and Hunterston brooches have shown that they were designed using compasses and a straight edge, but that their design showed a fundamental grasp of constructive geometry (Tara: Stevick, 1998; Hunterston: Stevick, 2003). A further study of the units of measurement employed suggests that multiples of 9 mm were employed in the design (Whitfield, 1999: 311).

These governing principles seen in metalwork apply equally to the design of sculpture. A survey of high cross design has suggested that it was conceived using a 'continuous chain of constructive geometry proceeding from one given measure' (Stevick, 2001: 227). It has been seen as independent of number symbolism, and not related to the imitation of other crosses. It has been calculated that some Columban crosses in Ireland and Scotland were designed according to Vitruvian (i.e. Classical) principles (D. Kelly, 1996). Each cross was designed anew, using the same creative principles. In contrast, the iconography used to decorate them was borrowed from earlier traditonal compositions.

In the design of manuscript pages the same mathematical principles apply (Stevick, 1994).

Within the overall designs, the design of the ornamental detail is equally mathematically constructed. This was first appreciated by Romilly Allen who studied the repertoire of abstract designs and considered the methods of construction (Allen and Anderson, 1903: ch. 8). In the case of interlace, a limited range of knots (six have been isolated for Ireland and Northumbria) were combined in different ways (Adcock, 1978: 33; Edwards, 1987: 111). Allen reckoned that there were only two basic elements in spiral ornaments, the S-scroll and the C-scroll, and the variety of the basic elements in fret patterns was also limited (Allen and Anderson, 1903: 377; N. Edwards, 1987: 113).

Small-scale art

The scribes and artists who created manuscripts and metalwork took pride in being able to work on a very small scale. The scribe Máel Brigte Ua Máel Uánaig, responsible for the MS Harley 1802 (composed in 1138), wrote in a minute script. On a slip of vellum inserted between two folios he wrote 'had I wished, I could have written the whole commentary like this' (Kenny, 1929: 648, no. 483). Máel Brigte was 28 at the time he composed his work (F. Henry, 1970: 65; Ó Cróinín, 1995: 181). The letters hidden under the rim of the Derrynaflan patten are 1 mm high, but are complete with wedges (M. Brown, 1993: 165). It has been said that the scribe must have been working blind, but a possibility is either that some form of magnifier was used, or that the scribe was afflicted with extreme myopia, a condition particularly common among the young, who appear to have frequently been scribes. The Ardagh chalice (below) has been calculated as composed of 350 parts (Ó Floinn, 2002: 177).

Symbol and meaning

For the Celtic monastic artist, art was a method of reinforcing the Christian message by using symbolism and coded messages that could convey meanings within meanings. While these were probably clear to the designers of the work, it is less clear how far they were understood outside a learned clerical context. One of the simplest forms of symbolism was that concerned with number, which drew upon the text of John Scotus Eriugena, a ninth-century Irish monk living in the Carolingian empire: three (which symbolized the

Trinity), five (the Wounds of Christ), twelve (the Disciples) all figure in many different combinations. Number symbolism was probably employed in the design of the Ardagh chalice (Berger, 1979; Richardson, 1984) and in the assembly of the Derrynaflan patten, where it also dictated the number of studs (12) used on it structurally (Brown, 1993: 163). The triskele no doubt was popular because of its three legs, and a similar explanation may account for the currency of the concave-sided triangle. Swastikas were symbols of the Resurrection.

Animal symbolism was also very significant. The source symbolism is to be found in the *Physiologus*, originally a Greek text which was formulated in the early centuries AD and defined proper Christian behaviour. The 'natures' of animals were interpreted allegorically to show the 'nature' of Christ, Christian doctrine, and so on. The Derrynaflan patten employs complex animal symbolism in its filigree panels: the stag confronting a serpent that appears on one of these symbolizes Christ consuming a demon-dragon and then drinking water to flush out the venom, before shedding the horns and being thus renewed (Ryan, 1983; 1987a: 72). The symbol could thus be read as Christ's triumph over evil and His subsequent renewal, a subject relevant to the patten's use in the Eucharistic feast. The stag can also be read as a symbol of the repentant man.

The *Physiologus* had a profound influence on Celtic (and, for that matter, Anglo-Saxon) artists, and clearly influenced the Picts (I. Henderson, 1996). The occurrence however of animal-headed men in Irish and Pictish art has been seen as representing the survival of pagan myths used to serve a Christian purpose (Roe, 1945). A ninth-century Carolingian copy survives with illustrations, though it is difficult to match the iconography in it with specific occurrences on Pictish or Irish sculptures.

Knots were used in antiquity as charms, and continued to have amuletic qualities in the medieval period, when knots were seen as a method of trapping Satan and warding off demons. Adding animal features to interlacing lines gave them extra force (Kitzinger, 1993: 3). Serpents were particularly common symbols, and the 'snake boss' occurs in Iona sculpture and in Pictish art, as well as in the Book of Kells and in Irish metalwork: it may have been seen as a reference to the Fall, and also an allusion to Eternity, as the snake sheds its skin and comes out of it alive (F. Henry, 1974: 208; I. Henderson, 1987: 64). The use of dogs' heads may represent faithfulness.

The siting and iconography of free-standing crosses was important from a liturgical standpoint. The stepped base symbolized Golgotha, the capstone the shrine set up by Constantine on the site of the Resurrection. The wheel, often found round the head, though probably also a structural element, may have embodied pre-Christian sun symbolism and a reference to the Classical wreath (Richardson and Scarry, 1990: 23–5).

Chronology

Due to the lack of finds from excavations and the dearth of dates provided by the objects themselves, dating works of Celtic art is impossible by the more usual archaeological or historical methods. Lack of provenance is also a deterrent to assured dating. Except in the case of monumental sculpture, provenance is complicated to establish, since any portable objects including manuscripts were taken from monastery to monastery, the most ornate and valuable being the most likely to move from the place of production. As a result, dating is based on very generalized and subjective art historical considerations. The majority of the great works of Celtic art are therefore without firm provenance, creating much room for controversy.

The chronology of metalwork and sculpture before the ninth century is such a relative matter that experts disagree on dates by as much as a century. Because two objects or motifs are the same does not necessarily imply that they are the products of the same centre or of the same date, but only that both were drawing upon the same tradition.

Celtic metalwork before c. AD 650

There is relatively little ornamental metalwork of consequence earlier than the late seventh century. Most of this comprises penannular brooches, and other small articles used as dress attachments (discussed in Chapter 7) and hanging-bowls.

The Origins of Celtic Ornament

It was long held that Celtic art of the Christian period represented a survival or revival of that of the pre-Roman Iron Age, kept alive in particular in Ireland (e.g. F. Henry, 1965: 1–3). That view is no longer tenable. Although there are some decorative devices found in the art of later Iron Age Britain which seem to have persisted into the early centuries AD in Britannia and played a role in the later development of the repertoire of 'Celtic' ornamental devices, the sources of inspiration for the decoration of the early medieval Celts came from later Roman Britain (Fig. 72). Here were to be found the triskeles, peltas, confronted trumpet patterns, scrolls and other motifs that appear in such later works as the Book of Kells. This art seems to have been kept alive in late Roman workshops, particularly in the west of England and Severn basin areas, where it was employed in the decoration of penannular brooches, stick pins and hanging-bowls among other products. From Britain it seems to have been taken to Ireland, to be further developed.

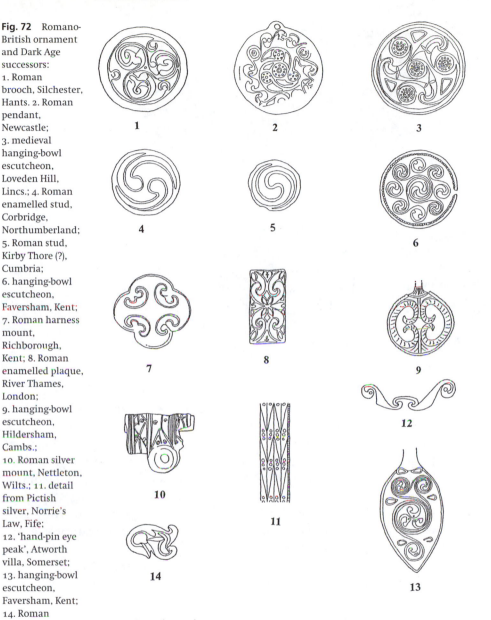

Fig. 72 Romano-British ornament and Dark Age successors: 1. Roman brooch, Silchester, Hants. 2. Roman pendant, Newcastle; 3. medieval hanging-bowl escutcheon, Loveden Hill, Lincs.; 4. Roman enamelled stud, Corbridge, Northumberland; 5. Roman stud, Kirby Thore (?), Cumbria; 6. hanging-bowl escutcheon, Faversham, Kent; 7. Roman harness mount, Richborough, Kent; 8. Roman enamelled plaque, River Thames, London; 9. hanging-bowl escutcheon, Hildersham, Cambs.; 10. Roman silver mount, Nettleton, Wilts.; 11. detail from Pictish silver, Norrie's Law, Fife; 12. 'hand-pin eye peak', Atworth villa, Somerset; 13. hanging-bowl escutcheon, Faversham, Kent; 14. Roman 'trompetenmuster' ornament, Castlelaw, Midlothian.

Hanging-bowls

These represent the greatest known achievements of Celtic art of the fifth to seventh centuries, and are the only large pieces of ornamental metalwork to have survived (Fig. 73). They are generally small bronze vessels (15–30 cm in diameter on average), with three or sometimes four hooks (escutcheons) attached to the outside to take suspension chains, and often with an additional mount or pair of mounts (termed 'prints') on the base of the vessel.

Fig. 73
A. Hanging-bowl,
Wilton; B. basal
print,
Crossthwaite
Museum,
Cumbria;

They were lathe-turned. Over 100 escutcheons and nearly 50 bowls and fragments survive. The majority have been found in Anglo-Saxon graves.

Mystery for long surrounded the place of manufacture and the purpose of hanging-bowls because they were believed by many to be Irish (Irish view: Henry, 1936: 210; recent account and catalogue: Brenan, 1991). At the time it was not proven that, for example, millefiori and enamel working was carried out on both sides of the Irish Sea (Bruce-Mitford, 1987: 31). A more modern viewpoint sees them as produced by late Romano-British craftspeople and their successors which found an Anglo-Saxon market at a time when they were deemed appropriate status symbols to bury with the Saxon dead.[3] A few were imitated by the Anglo-Saxons themselves (Laing, 1993a: 32–3; Laing, 2006).

It seems likely that hanging-bowls were not produced in Ireland until the late seventh to eighth centuries. The discovery of a hanging-bowl escutcheon mould from Craig Phadrig, Inverness, in Pictland (R. Stevenson, 1976: 250), shows that some were being made there, and an unfinished escutcheon from Seagry, Wilts, points to at least some manufacture in south-west England (Youngs, 1998b).

It is probable that hanging-bowls served different functions according to particular requirements.[4]

The most ornate hanging-bowl escutcheons are those with enamel work. Enamelled escutcheons in some instances are also decorated with millefiori (Laing, 1993a). This would appear to be a surviving Romano-British device.

Most of the motifs employed in escutcheon ornament are variants of the standard repertoire of abstract fifth- to seventh-century art, the most frequent being the developed pelta and confronted trumpet patterns, frequently in a triskele arrangement. Christian motifs appear on what seem to be late escutcheons and might imply that some were produced in monastic workshops.

Metalwork c. 650–800

There is ample evidence that the Celts were producing fine works during this period, expertly created using a number of techniques, including enamelling, engraving and high relief casting (Chapter 5). Along with the traditional repertoire of ornament, animals made their appearance, and in addition interlace patterns, ultimately probably of Germanic origin, came increasingly into use. These are in evidence at the Mote of Mark in the late sixth or early seventh centuries. By this date regional styles are noticeable and by the later seventh century a distinctive Irish art had been developed by the church. With the exception of brooches and pins, most of the surviving ornamental metalwork from this period is ecclesiastical. Much of this would have been produced in monastic workshops, and most takes the form of reliquaries or fragments of reliquaries.

Most of the surviving metalwork is Irish, but the achievements of Pictish smiths included items such as the Monymusk reliquary, the Bologna shrine, richly ornamented penannular brooches and the components of the St Ninian's Isle Treasure. The evidence for continuing metalworking in Wales is less strong, but accumulating (Redknap, 1995).

Reliquaries

The cult of relics came to Ireland with St Palladius in 431, who was reported as bringing relics of Sts Peter, Paul and others which were later kept in a casket in a Church now identified with Killeen Cormac (Ó Floinn, 1994: 5). By the seventh century the cult of relics was well established, and relics of local Irish saints became objects of veneration. The possession of relics gave status to churches and attracted wealth.

Relics had a real value, and were collected or sometimes stolen. They had many functions: they were believed to effect cures, they were used for the swearing of oaths, they were battle talismans and they were used in calling down curses. They were taken 'on tour' to promulgate the 'laws' of particular

Fig. 73 C. The
plates from the
Clonmore shrine.   C

saints, and as a result of their travels often were damaged occasioning repair
or alteration.

The making of shrines was very frequently a political statement, connected
with the events in the history of a particular monastery (Ó Floinn, 1994: 13).
Reliquaries could be corporeal (i.e., intended to contain all or some of the
mortal remains of a saint) or incorporeal (i.e., made for an object closely associated with the saint).

Corporeal relics were usually contained in a house-shaped shrine (actually
a copy of a type of tomb found widely on the Continent). Most of them were
small, but a few larger examples intended to stand on or beside the high altar
are known. The earliest surviving is that from Clonmore, on the Blackwater,
and probably dates from the seventh century (C. Bourke, 1991; Fig. 73c).
Specific corporeal reliquaries are rarer and later, but include an arm-shaped
shrine and another for a foot.

The incorporeal reliquaries are most commonly crozier shrines, made to
encapsulate the staffs of early saints. These were shaped like walking sticks,
with a straight drop and usually a crest with knobs on the stem. A simple
wooden crozier found at Lemanaghan was associated with a trackway dated to
AD 596 (O'Carroll, 2000: 24), but the metal croziers are unlikely to pre-date the
eighth century. Shrines were also made for such things as the bells, books or
belts of early saints. Reliquaries of these general types continued to be made

even down to the seventeenth and eighteenth centuries in Ireland (Ó Floinn, 1994: 9). The surviving reliquaries are often fragmentary due to their composite construction, panels of ornament being made separately and riveted.

Major examples of metalwork, 650–800

From the seventh century onwards, interaction with Anglo-Saxon England seems to have stimulated the development of metalworking. Gold filigree and granular work were among the new techniques (Whitfield, 1987), as well as cloisonné work (i.e., in cells) employing inlays (usually amber) or glass. Interlace was adopted as a decorative device, and animal ornament makes its appearance (interlace: Laing and Laing, 1990a: 215–24; animal ornament: Haseloff, 1987; Hicks, 1993). The Hunterston brooch (p. 159: R. Stevenson, 1974; 1983; Whitfield, 1993b) appears to be the earliest that reflects Anglo-Saxon skills and was perhaps made in Dál Riata by someone trained in an Anglo-Saxon workshop in the second half of the seventh century. Richly decorated with filigree and granular work, it has amber inlays.

Closely related but more developed, the Tara brooch[5] (p. 160) was probably made c. AD 700. This was covered with ornament, but the traditional, abstract 'Celtic' elements seem to have been confined to the back.

Similar metalworking techniques and ornament can be seen on the Ardagh chalice (Gogan, 1932; Organ, 1973; Ryan, 1983b, no. 51), found in 1868 concealed under a stone slab with four brooches and another small bronze chalice (Fig. 74). It too was probably made c. 700, although the brooches show that it was not buried until at least Viking times. It is liturgical, and is usually regarded as one of the finest achievements of Christian Celtic art.

It (and the similar Derrynaflan chalice, below) are unlike surviving early medieval European chalices and appear to be inspired by Byzantine prototypes. It has been suggested that these came not directly from Byzantium, but indirectly through versions made perhaps in Rome, the ultimate models being Roman Church plate (Ryan, 2002: ch. 8; Ó Floinn, 1994: 9).

Among the reliquaries, the Monymusk reliquary appears never to have been lost and is a house-shaped shrine dating from c. 750. It is probably of Pictish workmanship (Youngs, 1989: no. 129; Eeles, 1933–4; Wilson, in Small et al., 1973: 128–30; Caldwell, 2001 doubts the traditional identification with the Brecbennoch of St Columba).

One exceptional recent discovery is the Tully Lough cross. Found under water near a crannog in 1986, it is an oak cross encased with metal plates, standing 128 cm high. Its arms are cusped (similar to those on the cross of Cong, below), demonstrating that such crosses were the inspiration for

Fig. 74 The Ardagh chalice.

the design of some of the Irish high crosses. Ornament includes interlace, traditional abstract designs, human figures, and amber studs. It dates from the eighth or early ninth century (E. Kelly, 2000).

Hoards

Apart from the individual works, there are several important hoards.

The Derrynaflan Hoard was found in 1980, on the site of a monastery and comprised a chalice, silver patten, its stand, and a liturgical ladle. When found, these were covered by a plain bronze bowl (Ryan, 1983a; Youngs, 1989: nos. 124–7). The items in the hoard were of different dates, and it was probably deposited in the late ninth or even tenth century. The earliest item is the patten, which dates from the eighth century, probably in the latter part. The stand may have been made later, and has die-stamped panels. The strainer-ladle is probably also of the eighth century. The chalice, which is cruder than that from Ardagh, but in the same tradition, probably dates from the ninth century.

The Donore Hoard was found in 1985, and comprises a collection of items which appear to have been door furniture from a major Church – perhaps

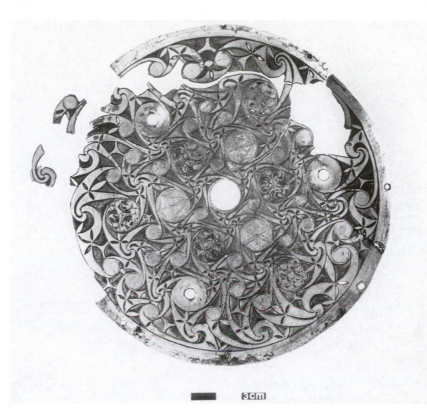

Fig. 75 Handle escutcheon, Donore Hoard.

Dulane or Kells (Ryan, 1987b; Fig. 75). The main item in the assemblage is a door handle comprising a lion head with a ring in its teeth. The hoard dates from the eighth century, and shows the influence of Anglo-Saxon 'Lindisfarne' style work in eastern Ireland at this date.

The St Ninian's Isle Treasure was found in the 1958 excavations at St Ninian's Isle, off the Shetland mainland (Wilson in Small et al., 1973; Youngs, 1989: 108–12; Graham-Campbell, 2003). It consisted of seven silver bowls, a hanging-bowl, two sword chapes, three pepperpot-shaped objects, a sword pommel, a spoon, a single-pronged claw-shaped implement and twelve penannular brooches along with the jawbone of a porpoise (Fig. 76). The objects were probably not of the same date – some, such as the inscribed sword chape, show signs of considerable wear. The date of burial was probably the late eighth or early ninth century.

A case has been made in support of the Treasure being of ecclesiastical function and not secular, though this has not won wide acceptance (McRoberts, 1960–1). Current thinking prefers the view that it was a collection of church treasures (Graham-Campbell, 2003: 23). The chapes have been the subject of

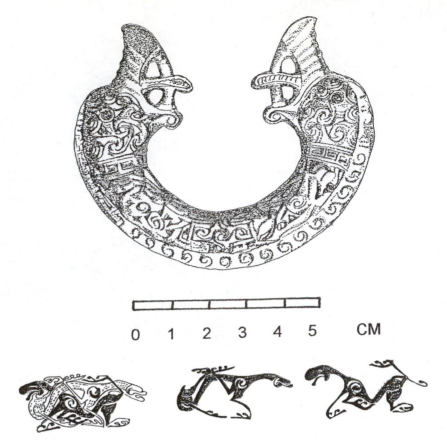

Fig. 76 St Ninian's Isle strap end.

some debate since one bears inscriptions on both sides. The current reading would support the view that the inscriptions on both sides are continuous, and read 'In the name of God, of the Son and of the Holy Spirit, Resad' (Graham-Campbell, 2003: 31–2). Arguments have been advanced that the chapes are of Anglo-Saxon workmanship, but this has not been universally accepted (Graham-Campbell, 2003: 31–2).

Other major works include the Moylough belt shrine (M. Duignan, 1951; O'Kelly, 1965; Harbison, 1981; Youngs, 1989: no. 47); the Rinnigan (Athlone) crucifixion plaque (Youngs, 1989: no. 133; Harbison, 1984 on possible later date; Fig. 77); the Lough Kinale book shrine (E. Kelly, 1993); the Ekerö crozier (Holmqvist, 1955; Youngs, 1989: no. 147); the Bobbio shrine (Ryan, 1990); the Copenhagen shrine (Graham-Campbell, 1980: no. 314; Youngs, 19: no. 131); the Saint-Germain reliquary terminals (Hunt, 1956; Youngs, 1989: no. 138); the Romfohjellen mount (Youngs, 1989: no. 139); and the Bologna shrine (Blindheim, 1984).

Fig. 77
Rinnigan plaque.

Ornamental metalwork in the ninth and tenth centuries

This period was disrupted by the Viking raids and is distinguished by the relatively small amount of surviving metalwork, most of which is fragmentary. The lack may be due to a number of ninth-century pieces being ascribed to the late eighth century, and/or to fairly extensive looting, but is more likely to reflect a general decline in production.

Certain features are typical of the period. Enamelwork became very rare and filigree coarser (F. Henry, 1967: 131). Niello was revived in the ninth century and its appearance in Ireland was probably due to contacts with Anglo-Saxon England (through the Trewhiddle style: Wilson, 1964: 24–35). Interlace in this period was geometric and monotonous. Spirals and peltas that had been current in the preceding centuries fell out of popularity in favour of an increase in the use of foliage, which reflected the widespread revival of acanthus and other leaf decoration that was one of the characteristics of Carolingian art. Such foliage was the result of a conscious Classical revival, and the ultimate ancestry is to be found in late antique manuscripts and sculpture.

Much silver seems to have arrived in Ireland in the ninth and tenth centuries (from 841, when Dublin was founded), presumably with the Vikings. Silver was

Fig. 78 Crozier of Cú Dúilig, ornamental details.

used by native craftspeople to make bossed penannular brooches and thistle brooches (p. 159), kite brooches (p. 161), arm rings and neck and finger ornaments. There are upwards of 150 hoards of silver from Ireland, some of which may have been booty and ransom payments extracted from the Dublin Vikings by the southern Uí Néill in the Irish midlands (Wallace, 2002b: 214).

A 5 kilo gold hoard (now lost) was found at Hare Island, and gold finds have come from Viking Dublin (Wallace, 2002b: 215).

There are a few surviving examples of ecclesiastical metalwork, most notably a series of croziers, the date of which has been fairly vigorously debated (C. Bourke, 1987). They include the Prosperous crozier;[6] the Corp Naomh; and three croziers of similar type (Cú Dúilig, St Dympna and St Mel),[7] the final form of which is probably late tenth-century work.

The **crozier of Cú Dúilig** (named after the personal name inscribed on it, and sometimes known as either the British Museum crozier, or the 'Kells crozier' – despite the fact it has no known association with Kells), lacks enamelling and is decorated with small lozenge-shaped or triangular panels, each panel with a separate motif – interlace, animal interlace or foliage (Fig. 78).

The **Soiscél Molaise** (*soiscél* means book satchel) is a shrine for the Gospel of St Molaise, and in its present form it is generally assumed to date from the early eleventh century (Henry, 1967: 120; Ryan, 1983b: no. 75).

Ornamental metalwork in the eleventh and twelfth centuries

A considerable revival of the art of the metalworker took place in the early eleventh century in response to Viking art (Ó Floinn, 1987; F. Henry, 1970: 74–122). A number of complete, or nearly complete, reliquaries have survived. By its very nature Viking and Irish art was close in spirit. The Ringerike and subsequently the Urnes styles of Scandinavian art had considerable impact on metalwork, resulting in a rich style (F. Henry, 1970: 74–122). The Urnes style was more popular in Ireland than the Ringerike, and indeed was developed there to a degree of excellence surpassing any example in its homeland. Intricacy and detail in design were subordinated to a flamboyant overall effect; nevertheless, some very fine designs were displayed on individual works.

The first centre for the Viking-inspired art was probably Kells, which may have derived its inspiration from work in Dublin (Ó Floinn, 1987: 181). The style may have evolved there around the mid-eleventh century, and can be seen in the repaired knop of the crozier of Cú Dúilig where a pure Ringerike Viking design was used employing acanthus in silver and niello. The foliage of the pure Ringerike, however, was not long popular, and an Irish version replaced it in which the foliage became zoomorphic. This can be seen in the shrine for St Columba's gospels (see below, p. 186).

Other centres probably included Clonmacnoise (where the Clonmacnoise crozier was probably made (Ó Floinn 1987: 181)); and possibly Roscommon, where the cross of Cong may have been fashioned (Ó Floinn, 1987: 186).

The number of fine objects probably represent only a few survivors out of what must have been an impressive catalogue. While it is likely that some metalwork was being produced in Scotland, and less probably in Wales during this period, it is unlikely that this was ever as abundant and impressive as that from Ireland.

Ornamental techniques in the eleventh and twelfth centuries

Earlier techniques such as chip carving continued (F. Henry, 1970: 77–81), though filigree work tended to be coarse. Gilding was not fused on to the metal surface but was plated – a piece of gold foil was used to cover the surface of the worked metal. Enamel continued, but instead of yellow on red, red on yellow was favoured. Niello became increasingly popular, possibly because of the Anglo-Saxon, Viking and Byzantine use of it for inlay.

Two new techniques appeared in the eleventh and twelfth centuries: borders with plaits of red copper and silver wire were hammered into grooves, which were then polished to give a two-coloured rope pattern. The technique was used in Merovingian Gaul and Scandinavia, but by this date was becoming obsolete on the Continent.

Silver ribbons were inset into shallow grooves cut on a bronze ground, usually accompanied by bands of niello on either side. This decoration appears on the Clonmacnoise crozier and the shrine of St Lachtin's arm. Originally it would have appeared as a silver tracery with black borders against a gold ground, since the bronze would probably have been gilded. The technique may be Byzantine in origin.

Major examples of metalwork of the eleventh and twelfth centuries

Inscriptions on metalwork can provide information about metalworkers, who, it appears, were frequently laymen attached to major monasteries such as Armagh or Kells. The items below marked with an asterisk are inscribed and therefore datable.

Fig. 79
St Patrick's bell.

The cumdach of the cathach of St Columba/Columcille (last years of the eleventh century), was the shrine made for Columba's gospels (F. Henry, 1970: 91; Ó Floinn, 1987: 180). The upper plate is fourteenth-century; the others, except for some additions, are eleventh-century.

The shrine of St Patrick's bell (1094–1105) housed the iron bell traditionally used by the saint (Mahr and Raftery, 1941: 159; Ryan, 1983b: no. 79b; Fig. 79).

The Clonmacnoise crozier is closely related in style to the cumdach of the cathach of St Columba (Mahr and Raftery, 1941: 159–60; Ryan, 1983b: no. 77).

The Lismore crozier (1090–1113) has an openwork crest ornamented with three-dimensional terminal animal heads with lappets and moustaches in degenerate Ringerike style (Mahr and Raftery, 1941: 159; Ryan, 1983b: no. 81).

The shrine of St Lachtin's arm (1118–21) dates from the early twelfth century and comes from Freshford (F. Henry, 1970: 103–6; Ryan, 1983b: no. 80). It consists of a wooden cylinder covered with metal plaques, terminating in a clenched fist.

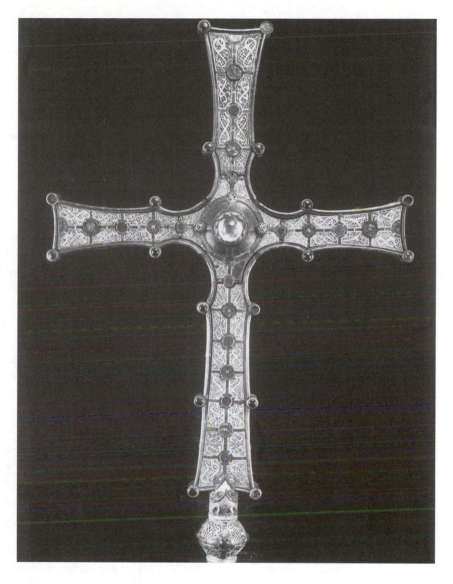

Fig. 80 Cross of Cong.

The cross of Cong (1123–27) is a large processional cross which served as a reliquary for a fragment of the True Cross (F. Henry, 1970: 106–7) made at Clonmacnoise (Fig. 80).

The shrine of St Manchan (60 cm long and 50 cm high), now in Boher Church (Kendrick and Senior, 1937), is made of yew with bronze and enamel fittings. It contains bones, including part of a femur which is traditionally that of St Manchan who died in 664.

Fig. 81 Codex Usserianus Primus and Cathach of St Columba, ornamental details.

There are many other, slightly lesser, pieces, of the twelfth century. These include the Innisfallen crozier (F. Henry, 1970: 85); the Misach of St Columba (Armstrong and Crawford, 1922); the Glankeen bell shrine (made for the bell of St Cuileain, and known as the Bearnan Cuileain) (Mahr and Raftery, 1941: 157 and pl. 83); and the cumdach of the Book of Dimma (Ó Floinn, 1982; Ryan, 1983b: no. 83).

Manuscripts[8]

Manuscript art came to Britain from the Mediterranean, initially probably in the form of imported late antique books. Although there is evidence for book production in southern Britain in the fifth century, if the British provenance of the *Vatican Virgil* is accepted (Dark, 1994a: 185–91), the earliest extant books produced by Celtic clerics were probably written on the Continent.

The Codex Usserianus Primus, now in Dublin, dates from the beginning of the seventh or end of the sixth century AD. The ornament is confined to a framed Chi-Rho between alpha and omega which is purely antique in inspiration (F. Henry, 1965: 62; Fig. 81a).

The Cathach of St Columba is the earliest Insular (i.e., made in Britain or Ireland) manuscript (Nordenfalk, 1947; Fig. 81b). It has large ornamental letters and traditionally was thought to be the work of the saint (though this is improbable). It was probably produced at Iona in the early seventh century. Only fifty-eight pages survive, decorated with sixty-four initials done in red and brown ink and displaying peltas, spirals, trumpet patterns, scrolls and curvilinear patterns, as well as fishes and crosses.

The Book of Durrow has generated considerable debate over its provenance and date. Claims have been advanced in favour of its creation at Durrow itself; in Northumbria; or on Iona (Luce et al., 1960; G. Henderson, 1987; Mevaert, 1989; De Vegvar, 1987; Werner, 1981; 1990; Laing, 1995b; Fig. 82).

Fig. 82 Book of Durrow, fol. 3v.

Most scholars now support the view that it was made in Iona in the second half of the seventh century, though opinions differ as to whether it was early or late in that half century. It is a small volume – 245 × 745 mm – consisting of 248 folios. It is ornamented with framed evangelist symbols, carpet pages and ornamental letters for the opening words of the gospels. The ornament includes both the usual 'Celtic' devices, along with animal ornament of Anglo-Saxon type and interlace.

Pocket gospels and the Book of Kells

A feature of Irish manuscripts in this period is their small size. They are often termed 'pocket gospels', as they were designed to be carried by monks for their own devotions (F. Henry, 1965: 199–202).

The Book of Dimma is named after a monk who was traditionally given one day to complete a copy of the gospels at Roscrea (Alexander, 1978: 69). Fortunately, the sun did not set for forty days, which gave him time to complete the work for the dying St Cronan. However, the Book of Dimma is clearly the work of several hands done with more enthusiasm than genius in rich colours, with attractive evangelist symbols at least two centuries later than St Cronan's lifetime.

The Book of Mulling is more uniform in style than the Book of Dimma, and has three evangelist portraits which have been removed and bound in at the back (F. Henry, 1965: 200; Alexander, 1978: 45).

The Book of Kells is the finest manuscript to survive, and dates from the late eighth or early ninth century (G. Henderson, 1987; F. Henry, 1974; Farr, 1997; Meehan, 1994; O'Mahony, 1994). Claims have been made that it was produced at Kells in Ireland, but it may have been made at Iona, possibly to mark the enshrinement of St Columba, sometime between AD 752 and 767 (G. Henderson, 1987: ch. 5). It may have been produced under the patronage of Oengus mac Fergus, king of the Picts. It is the work of several hands (four major artists have been distinguished), probably with additional input from apprentices (F. Henry, 1974).

There are six main types of ornament in the Book of Kells: (1) canon tables; (2) evangelist symbols; (3) portraits of Christ and the evangelists, on separate pages; (4) miniatures of the Temptation of Christ (the 'Temple Page'), the Virgin and Child and the Betrayal; (5) cruciform pages preceding each gospel (i.e., carpet pages); and (6) decorative text pages, of which the XRI monogram is perhaps the most ornate. In addition, there are decorative details throughout. It was a highly influential work, its ornament influencing both Irish and Pictish sculpture (I. Henderson, 1982).

Ninth- to twelfth-century manuscript art

Nearly all the Celtic manuscript art that survives from the ninth century and later is Irish.[9]

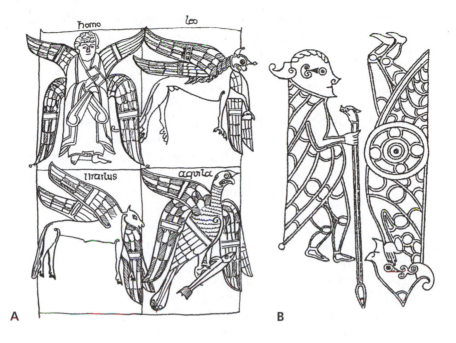

Fig. 83 A. Book of Armagh; B. page from Cambridge, St John's College C.9.

A   B

The Book of Armagh (Trinity College, Dublin) (Meehan, 1998) is noteworthy for its drawing and for an inscription which shows that it was made in Armagh, and from which it can be dated to c. AD 807 (Fig. 83). It is a compilation of several works, including a *Life of St Patrick* and a New Testament.

The Book of Mac Regol (Bodleian Library, Oxford), is perhaps the most significant of the illuminated books, named after MacRegol of Birr, the scribe responsible for it, who died in 822 (Hemphill, 1911–12). The colours are rich and thick, if slightly heavy-handed, and it has evangelist portraits and initial pages.

The tradition of the Irish 'pocket gospels' continued during the ninth and tenth centuries.

The Book of MacDurnan (Lambeth Palace Library), is named after an abbot of Armagh (AD 888–927) (F. Henry, 1967: 102–5; Alexander, 1978: 70). The manuscript was acquired by the Anglo-Saxon king Aethelstan, and remained at Christ Church, Canterbury. It has four evangelist pages, St Mark with his symbol, and decorative initials in each gospel. The interlace, fret and animal patterns are crude, and the colours used sparingly.

There are two notable psalters (books of psalms).

The Cotton Psalter (British Library, Cotton Vitellius F XI), was one of the books seriously damaged in the notorious eighteenth-century fire in the Cotton library (F. Henry, 1970: 47). Two surviving pages show David and Goliath and David as harpist. Two pages from the beginnings of sections, and decorated initials from each psalm also survive. The psalter dates from the early tenth century.

The Southampton Psalter (St John's College, Cambridge C9; Fig. 83B) dates from the late tenth or eleventh century. Three miniatures with simple drawing and limited colours depict David and the lion; David and Goliath; and the Crucifixion (F. Henry, 1960). The animal ornament is reminiscent of metalwork.

A number of manuscripts survive from the twelfth century, showing both Viking and English influence (Henry and Marsh-Michelli, 1962). They represent the last flourish of early medieval Irish manuscript illumination.

Two, the **Corpus Missal** (British Library), and **Cormac's Psalter** (British Library) are of exceptional merit. The latter is a small volume in which a rich red background with intricate interlace was sometimes used.

In Wales, the **Psalter of Rhygyfarch** (Ricemarch) is a manuscript now in Trinity College, Dublin (MS 50), written at Llanbadarn Fawr c. 1079 by a scribe called Ithael, and illuminated by Ieuan. A second Welsh manuscript from the same scriptorium is an illuminated text of St Augustine's *De Trinitate*, now in Cambridge (Corpus Christi MS 199), also produced by Ieuan. Although it has frequently been suggested that the style of these is purely Irish (F. Henry, 1970: 121) it has recently been suggested that it may draw upon a native Welsh tradition as well as other Insular sources, Irish and possibly Scottish (N. Edwards, 1995).

In Scotland, the principal manuscript to survive from this period is the Pictish **Book of Deer**, an undistinguished tenth-century gospel book with two surviving evangelist portraits, inspired by Irish pocket gospels but probably produced locally (Geddes, 1998). The **Edinburgh Psalter**, produced in the early eleventh century, may have been made in what is now Scotland.

Sculpture

There are three main types of relief sculptured monument in Celtic Britain and Ireland – recumbent cross slabs, free-standing cross slabs and free-standing crosses. Some bear Pictish symbols (p. 312), and all display at least a cross, which is usually taken to be Christian in intent. Most are definitely Christian with lavish and complex Christian iconography. Some display both Pictish and Christian symbolism. Sculpture differs regionally with marked groupings in Ireland, Scotland, Wales, south-west England, and the important monastic site of Iona in Dál Riata (p. 328).

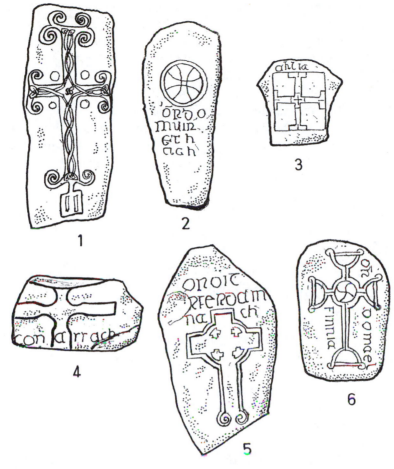

Fig. 84
Recumbant cross
slabs:
1. Inishmurray,
Co. Sligo;
2–6. Clonmacnoise,
Co. Offaly.

Recumbent cross slabs

Found in both Ireland and Scotland, these stone slabs date mainly to the eighth century and later. They bear a cross (incised or later in low relief), and were probably designed to lie on a grave (Fig. 84). They may be Irish in origin, and may be derived from grave markers, though Northumbrian or Gaulish influence has been suggested (possible models, Bailey, 1996a: ch. 2).

Ireland

About 800–900 recumbent cross slabs have been recorded, scattered over the entire country with a concentration in Co. Offaly where a rich collection is located at Clonmacnoise where about 400–500 have been recorded, not all of which survive (Lionard, 1961). Few, if any, are earlier than the eighth century.

A recent study of the chronology of the Clonmacnoise slabs suggests that they belong to three periods: late eighth century; mid-ninth to the early eleventh century; and twelfth century (Ó Floinn, 1995: 257). The earliest datable slab bears the name of a king who died in 764 (Ó Floinn, 1995: 252).

Scotland

The most significant cross-incised slabs in Scotland are at Iona, and are related to the Irish examples. The earliest may be one with an incised Chi-Rho cross of arcs and an inscription on its edge declaring it was 'the stone of Echoid'. This was assigned on epigraphical grounds to the seventh century, though this may be too early (Fisher, 2001: 128, no. 22). There are four others which have been assigned to the eighth century again on epigraphical grounds, but there is no reason why any of these is not late in the century (Fisher, 2001: 128–9, nos. 31, 37a, 46, 47; also RCHAMS 1982: 187).

Free-standing cross slabs

These are found in Ireland, Scotland and the Isle of Man.

Ireland

There are one or two slabs in Ireland executed with incised or false-relief work which have been claimed as early; that from Reask, which has a pseudo-relief cross of arcs with a stem with running scrolls and peltas and which may represent a *flabellum* or processional cross, has a brief inscription which reads DNE (*Dominei* – Lord), the last two letters in ligature. This could date from the end of the sixth or early seventh century (Fanning, 1981: 139–41; F. Henry, 1965: 57). A similar monument stands at Kilfountain, with a similar short inscription naming the local saint, Finten (F. Henry, 1965: 57).

A series of relief decorated slabs in Co. Donegal, most notably those from Fahan Mura and Carndonagh, have attracted extensive published argument over dating. Arguments were advanced for a seventh-century date on account of the presumed dating of an inscription on that at Fahan Mura (F. Henry, 1965: 126–8), but a more convincing case has been advanced for a ninth-century date (Harbison, 1986).

Figural work appears incised on a number of Irish slabs, notably in the form of crucifixions at Inishkea North, and Duvillaun, both in Co. Mayo, but these too have recently been argued as being no earlier than the ninth century (Fig. 85; Harbison, 1987a), and, given their similarities with Scottish and Manx sculpture, could be even later.

Scotland

In the eighth or ninth century relief sculpture on standing cross slabs flourished in Pictland.

Fig. 85 A. slab from Reask, Co. Kerry.

A

The stones were classified into groups by Allen and Anderson in 1903. Class I were the incised symbol stones that carry no Christian imagery (p. 313), Class II were dressed relief slabs with a cross and Pictish symbols, Class III were relief decorated slabs without Pictish symbols.

Class II cross slabs are among the finest works of sculpture produced in Europe in the period between AD 400 and 1100. They fall into a number of stylistic groups, some of which can be related to particular centres of production.[10] Dating is debated, some arguing that many were produced in the

Fig. 85
B. Duvillaun slab,
Co. Mayo.

eighth century, others favouring the ninth for the majority (Laing, 2000a), others seeing them as mostly of the tenth to eleventh centuries. The proliferation of sculpture at this date may have been due to an increase of royal patronage of the Church.

The churchyard stone at Aberlemno (Aberlemno 2; Fig. 86a) is the finest of a group of monuments in comparatively low relief concentrated in that county but with some outliers, which includes stones at Eassie, Rossie, Glamis (Fig. 86b), Menmuir and Kirriemuir (Laing, 2001a; 2001b). It has been suggested that some at least were the work of a community from Iona that settled in Angus in the ninth century, following the sack of the monastery by the Vikings (Trench-Jellicoe, 1999).

Major collections of stones are collected in St Vigeans and Meigle, which may represent two centres where royal patronage was significant (Ritchie, 1995).

A group of monuments at Portmahomack, with a series of outliers including the exceptional slabs at Hilton of Cadboll and Nigg, may represent a monastic school based on Portmahomack itself (Carver, 2004: 14–16).

Class III cross slabs were believed to have comprised work erected in Pictland after the unification with Dál Riata by Kenneth in the ninth century (p. 310), when Pictish symbols were seen not to have been acceptable (Allen and Anderson, 1903: cix). In fact, there is good reason to suppose Pictish symbols

Fig. 86 Class II
Pictish cross
slabs,
A. Aberlemno
churchyard;

A

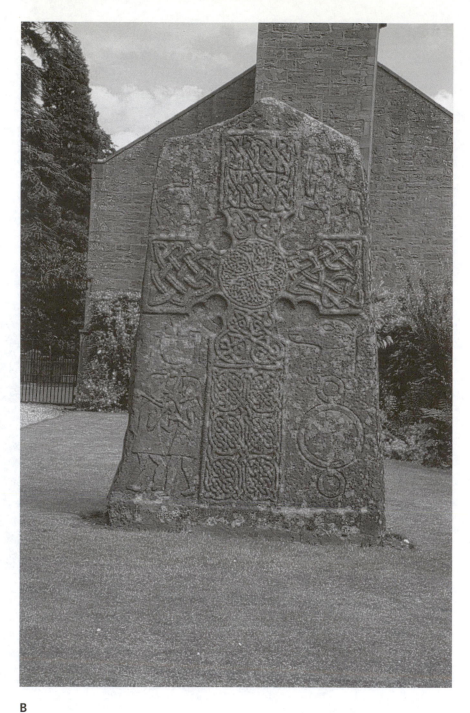

Fig. 86
B. Glamis manse,
Angus.

B

were still in use through the ninth and even into the tenth century (Laing, 2000a). Monuments in this class include Sueno's Stone near Forres, a shaft 6.5 m high, with a battle scene on the back.

The Isle of Man

The sculptural legacy of the Isle of Man is rich and varied, but virtually all of it belongs to the Viking period, and though it displays connections with Pictland, Ireland and Wales, is not part of the tradition of Celtic sculpture. There are however a few important monuments that have been argued as pre-dating Viking influence, probably erroneously, most notably in the assemblage in the monastic site at Maughold, and the others at Lonan and Onchan (Kermode, 1907; Cubbon, 1971. The numbering followed here is the current system, replacing that used by Kermode). These belong to the standing cross slab series. A cross slab from Maughold (no. 96) recalls Scottish monuments, with its seated clerics on either side of the cross shaft. Other notable monuments are a wheel-headed cross of the ninth or tenth century from Braddan (no. 72), and a wheel-headed cross, with poor interlace, probably of the tenth century, at Lonan (no. 73).

Free-standing crosses (high crosses)

Free-standing crosses date from the late eighth to the eleventh centuries and occur in Ireland with a few in Scotland (Dál Riata especially Iona), Wales and south-west England. In Ireland they are usually termed high crosses even though some are little more than 1 m high, some over 7 m. The earliest are found in Scotland (R. Stevenson, 1956; Fisher, 2001: 15–16).

It is uncertain whether free-standing crosses were originally funerary, dedicatory or simply commemorative. Wooden crosses are mentioned in the *Lives of Eastern Saints*, and Adomnán refers to three in Iona existing in the seventh or possibly even the sixth century (Ritchie, 1997: 68). Such crosses, with either small, straight struts in the four angles of the arms or four arc-struts forming a ring head were probably translated from wood to stone in the seventh century – some cross slabs seem to depict wooden crosses complete with skeuomorphic wooden features such as the carpenter's nail heads.[11]

Scotland Free-standing crosses are very rare in Scotland outside Dál Riata, where they represent an extension of the Irish province. In Pictland the notable exception is the cross at Dupplin, which has an inscription in Latin letters, and has been dated to the ninth century (Forsyth, 1995b), though could be later.

Although forerunners may date from the seventh century, no free-standing cross dates from earlier than the mid- to late eighth. It is becoming increasingly

A

Fig. 87
A. Kildalton cross,
Islay.

apparent that the earliest are a group in Dál Riata, which may have been inspired by Northumbrian predecessors of the earlier eighth century.

Of these the first is arguably the cross at Kilnave, Islay (Fisher, 2001: 115), which is flat and reminiscent of some early Northumbrian undecorated crosses at Whitby, Yorkshire (Peers and Radford, 1943: figs. 1–2). The ornament on the Kilnave cross is purely abstract, and consists of spiral, key and pelta patterns. It is linked to the crosses on Iona by its ornament, some of which it shares with the fragmentary St Oran's cross, which has in addition to abstract ornament the use of Virgin and Child iconography and snake bosses, both characteristics of Iona work (Fisher, 2001: 16). The Kilnave and St Oran's crosses both lack a ringed head.

The first cross to display a ringed head is St John's, on Iona. St John's cross was put together with tenon-and-mortice joints from four pieces, four further pieces being added to form a ring at a secondary stage, perhaps to reinforce it

Fig. 87
B. Ahenny, Co.
Offaly.

B

after a fall. Later St Martin's cross on Iona and the Kildalton cross on Islay (Fig. 87A) were both designed to have an integral ring from the outset.[12]

In southern Scotland apart from some Northumbrian sculpture in Dumfries and Galloway and in the Lothians, which includes the finest Anglian free-standing cross at Ruthwell, the surviving sculpture was nearly all produced during the Scando-Insular phase. The most notable series of works are the crosses created by the Whithorn school in the tenth and eleventh centuries, which are distinguished by their use of wheel heads and monotonous inter-lace (Craig, 1991). Apart from the stones at Whithorn itself, fine examples of the school are represented by the Kirkinner crosses and those from Craiglemine, Glenluce and Kirkholm (Allen and Anderson, 1903: 480–4).

A

Fig. 88
A. Clonmacnoise, Cross of the Scriptures, east face.

Ireland

There are between sixty and seventy surviving examples of high crosses, which are characterized by a number of features displayed on nearly all.[13] The distribution of high crosses lies to the centre and north of Ireland, with only one in the south and a few, late examples in the west.

The earliest cannot be dated much before AD 800, and principally comprise the crosses of southern Ossory, notably those at Ahenny (Roe, 1969; N. Edwards, 1983; Hicks, 1980; Fig. 87b). These seem to have been products of a Clonmacnoise workshop and have decoration which indicates the influence of metalwork on their designs, exemplified by the Tully Lough cross. A date may be provided by an inscription on the stylistically early cross at Bealin,

Fig. 88 B. Kells,
South Cross.

                                                                                    B

which appears to name Tuathgal, an abbot of Clonmacnoise, who died in 811
(F. Henry, 1930). The south cross at Clonmacnoise was dated by the discovery
of a recumbant cross slab of Type A under it during recent excavation (King,
1992: 23), and by an inscription on it which names king Maelsechnaill mac
Maelruanaid, who died in 862.[14]

   The dating of the south cross at Kells (the cross of Patrick and Columba)
has been argued to be as late as c. 900 (Stalley, 1997: 135), but many have
seen it as dating from earlier in the century (Fig. 88B). Some scholars have
seen all the main group of high crosses as the work of a relatively short
period in the ninth century, produced under Carolingian influence
(Harbison, 1987b); others have preferred to spread the dating out into the
tenth. Particularly problematic in this context is the date of the south cross

Fig. 89 Cross of
Hwyel ap Rhys,
Llantwit Major.

at Monasterboice (Muiredach's) – the Muiredach named in the inscription is usually taken to be an abbot who died in 924 (but see Harbison, 1992). Roughly contemporary with this stylistically is the west cross (Cross of the Scriptures) at Clonmacnoise, which has an inscription naming abbot Colman and king Flann, and which would thus have been erected in the period c. 904–16 (Fig. 88A).

Discussion of the iconography of the Irish crosses lies outside the scope of this book, but has been the subject of detailed study. Subjects were chosen for their symbolic or spiritual meaning rather than for the stories they told, and therefore should not be seen as a 'Bible in pictures'. There are about ninety subjects selected, but they are not found in the same arrangements. Particular themes are Christ's life and miracles, Old Testament themes that could be seen to foreshadow events in the life of Christ, Sts Paul and Anthony (popular as the founders of monasticism and for their resistence to temptation), the Crucifixion and the Last Judgement (Stalley, 1990; Harbison, 1992; 1994; 1999).

Wales

Welsh sculpture of the period is generally less distinguished than that of either Ireland or Pictland. It was studied by Romilly Allen, and subsequently was the subject of a Corpus compiled by Nash-Williams: a new Corpus is in preparation (Allen, 1899; Nash-Williams, 1950; Redknap, 1991). The majority of the Welsh sculpture of this period is grouped round major monasteries and churches. Dates are provided by inscriptions – the pillar of Eliseg has been dated to the second quarter of the ninth century, a cross at Llantwit Major names Hywel ap Rhys, a king who lived in the later ninth century (Fig. 89), and a cross slab of the late eleventh or early twelfth century at St Davids appears to commemorate the sons of Bishop Abraham (Edwards, 2001: 33–4). It has been suggested that they were symbols of Church power and royal and ecclesiastical patronage, and some were set up to mark Church land (N. Edwards, 2001). Figural work is very limited, and the style of the Welsh monuments very eclectic – vinescroll seems to have been inspired by Northumbrian models, while 'twin beast' designs perhaps originated in Mercia. Key-and-fret patterns may have derived from Ireland, and Anglo-Scandinavian traditions provided ring-chain and various key patterns (Nash-Williams, 1950: 29–32; Redknap, 1991: 69). Of the various categories of monuments, particular groups can be discerned at Margam and Llantwit Major, Glamorgan and St Davids in Pembroke. Among noteworthy monuments additionally are the cross shafts at Nevern and Penally, Dyfed, Llandough, Glamorgan, and Carew, Dyfed. The sculptural traditions seem to have continued after the Norman Conquest.

South-west England

The free-standing crosses of Cornwall span the period from the ninth to the fifteenth centuries, and were erected for a variety of purposes (Langdon, 1896; Hencken, 1932: 203–86; Dexter, 1938). The most important class which dates from the early medieval period (but which overlaps into the middle ages) is that of churchyard crosses. A few of these can be assigned to the ninth and tenth centuries, and some show strong Anglo-Saxon influence.

The general style seems to have been a product of Anglo-Scandinavian traditions in northern England, which spread to affect Welsh sculpture and presumably thence to Cornwall. The decorative schemes used on the Cornish crosses are basically those of the vinescroll and interlace, with ring-chain of Viking origin being particularly favoured, though key-and-fret patterns, step patterns, and triquetras are also common, as are alternately inverted T's. The so-called 'Jellinge beast' and 'Ringerike scroll' were obviously borrowed directly from Viking sculpture. A number of the Cornish crosses have inscriptions in devolved Hiberno-Saxon lettering.

The finest of the Cornish crosses is that at Cardinham near Bodmin. This cross has on one face a very degenerate vinescroll, more reminiscent of a running spiral than true vinescroll, with an interlaced head, while the sides carry step patterns, ring-chain and ring-twist interlace. The ring-chain is of the type first encountered on a cross on Man known as Gaut's, and dates from the tenth century.

Fig. 90
Kirkinner cross,
Whithorn School.

Sarcophagi and miscellaneous monuments

A number of additional artworks survive such as the late eighth-century St Andrew sarcophagus (Foster, 1998).

An incomplete panel from the Isle of Man (the Calf of Man crucifixion slab (no. 61)), displays Christ in a long robe (*collobium*) flanked by the sponge bearer. It probably came from a shrine (Cubbon, 1971: 16). Although it is often claimed to be an eighth-century work, it is more probably of the later ninth, made at a time when Viking influence was beginning to make itself felt, as the bordered beading on Christ's robe suggests.

Later work is represented by the sarcophagus of St Constantine at Govan, which has a hunt scene and interlace and probably dates from the tenth or eleventh century – it is quite close in style to a surviving cross at Barochan, and seems to have been inspired by a Continental shrine (Spearman, 1994).

The monuments erected in Strathclyde at the time of the Vikings are varied in character, with both cross slabs and cross shafts (Craig, 1994; Fig. 90). Most of the stones at Govan belong to the tenth and eleventh centuries, possibly continuing into the early twelfth (Ritchie, 1994). They include hogback stones which are characteristic of Viking influence – hogbacks are also found distributed elsewhere in the region, and along the south-east coast of Scotland (Lang, 1972–4). Apart from the Govan stones, there is a group of monuments (including a hogback) at Kingarth in Bute (Laing, 1998; Fisher, 2001: 17), a related cross coming from Rothesay.

9 The church

Christianity was a major factor in the life of the Celts especially from the sixth century onwards. Historical evidence is plentiful, since those who were responsible for the keeping of records in the early medieval period were mostly clerics, even if the information they recorded is sometimes misleading. The archaeological evidence is similarly plentiful – notably buildings and areas given over exclusively to Christian worship or activity – monasteries, hermitages, churches, chapels, shrines, living cells (*clocháns*), dedicated burial grounds (which had marked features not seen in pagan cemeteries and which can belong to both monastic and non-monastic sites), memorial stones and works of art such as sculptures.[1]

Traditionally, building was in wood – development of stone building appears to have been mainly a phenomenon of the eighth or ninth century onwards.

Historical evidence

Although written material is plentiful from after AD 600 compared with the preceding periods, it is highly biased, often allegorical and very much focused on the Christian message rather than 'historical' information. This is particularly the case with the *Lives* of saints, though some, such as Adomnán's *Life of St Columba* or Cogitosus' *Life of St Brigit*, contain a valuable core of factual information (for these saints and their lives, see Appendix 2, p. 336).

In Roman Britannia, the Christian faith was introduced around AD 200. The first English martyr, St Alban, probably died between 251 and 259, though earlier dates have been suggested (Thomas, 1981b: 50). In 313 Christianity was declared tolerated by Rome, and became the state religion in 395. By the fourth century the evidence for its spread in the province is convincing, as at least five British clerics were documented as attending the Council of Arles in 314. British priests were also present at the Council of Nicaea in 325 and the Council of Rimini in 359 (Birley, 1980: 153). Apart from a considerable number of portable antiquities with Christian associations,[2] there is a growing body of evidence for probable Romano-British churches, some possibly developed from mausolea.[3]

It seems that Christianity spread to the region north of Hadrian's Wall and westward into parts of Wales before the end of the Roman period. It is notable that when the Romano-Briton Patrick (later St Patrick), was abducted into slavery to Ireland, he was there converted by practising Christians. This event is generally assumed to lie in the mid-fifth century, strongly implying that Christianity was already established in Ireland at that time. Furthermore, Patrick may have been preceded by Palladius who Prosper of Aquitaine noted had been sent to Ireland in AD 431 by Pope Celestine.[4]

In Scotland the spread of Christianity was, according to the Anglo-Saxon historian Bede, initiated by St Ninian (St Nynia),[5] who was also active among the Picts. His date and historicity have been debated, though it is likely he existed around the mid-fifth century. No debate surrounds the arrival of St Columba from Ireland and the foundation of the monastery at Iona (in Dál Riata) in 563, whence missionary activity was conducted among the northern Picts (I. Smith, 1996: 21). In Wales, the spread of the belief is associated with Sts Dubricius and Illtud, who were active in the south-east c. 475, and with St David in the later sixth century.[6] South-west England (Dumnonia) had St Samson, also in the sixth century.

Church dedications to sixth- or seventh-century saints are often due to a medieval revival of interest in the particular cult, or to deliberate antiquarianism, though some may be 'authentic' (Bowen, 1954: 7–10). It has been suggested, for example, that dedications to Irish saints in Scotland were derived from commemorative lists in the relevant monasteries. However, there were many saints with the same name, so that without adequate documentation it is not always possible to distinguish them. Conversely, some saints were known by many different popular names.

Placenames can provide information about the existence and/or status of ancient sites of which no trace now survives. However, they are subject to corruption through long usage. Charters, though seldom earlier than the twelfth century, are usually the most informative sources.

A substantial number of ecclesiastical placename elements seem to be exclusively of the period. *Dysert* or *dìsert*, for example (derived from Latin *desertum*, a deserted place), refer to hermits' cells which were sometimes located at a distance from the monastery concerned. The term *abthaine* in Scotland, meaning literally 'abbacy' or 'abbey lands', occurs in medieval charters, sometimes in its Latin form *abthania*, but apparently always refers to early medieval monastic sites. Other Scottish placenames – *annat*, found by itself or in compounds (Macdonald, 1973a); and *teampull* (from Latin *templum*) – are known to refer to specific kinds of church, though their precise meanings remain in some doubt. In wider usage *kil*, *cille*, *llan*, *keeill*, *merthyr*, land, can all provide clues to the presence of small chapel sites (Thomas, 1971: 224).

Memorial stones potentially provide evidence from their find-spots, their inscriptions or their carvings. They may, however, have been moved. During the eighteenth and more particularly in the nineteenth century there was a tendency to move stones into churchyards or churches. In nineteenth-century Scotland, Scottish presbyterianism was sometimes deliberately given an 'ancestry' associated with Ninian and Columba, by the setting up of a Christian stone of early date.

Church organization

In the period immediately following Roman control in Britain, it is likely that ecclesiastical administration was based on urban bishoprics – Caerwent might have survived as one such in south Wales, and Carlisle may have been another from which Christianity was spread in south-west Scotland. Bishops and priests are mentioned on memorial stones of the fifth and sixth centuries in Britain,[7] and bishops are mentioned in documentary sources. Gildas implies that in his day the Church was diocesan, and both Ninian and Patrick are described by their biographers as bishops (Thomas, 1971: 13). With the decline of towns in former Britannia from the middle of the fifth century, it is likely that bishops became attached to courts and royal households, rather than to large, permanently positioned churches in towns (Thomas, 1998: 82–3). Outside Britannia sees may have been focused on major churches closely connected with royal strongholds.

The concept of the Celtic church

There has been a widespread conviction since the nineteenth century that the 'Celtic church' had a distinct identity and character. This partly stemmed from the writings of Bede who created the categorization. He was concerned to represent the Celts as following an inferior form of Christianity from that of the Anglo-Saxons who had been subject to a deliberate mission from Rome by St Augustine in 597. This version of Christianity was essentially urban in its organization, and thus was difficult to adapt to a non-urban situation.

The persistence in viewing the Celtic Church as an entity was furthered by a nineteenth- and early twentieth-century idea that it represented a distinct and unified form of religion which had resisted Rome and displayed (in common with Protestantism, a key issue of the day) a strong desire to look after its own affairs.[8]

The twentieth century also saw a belief that the 'Celtic Church' was somehow more pious; more attuned with the natural world than the 'Anglo-Saxon Church'; and consisted of gentle hermit saints who communed with nature.[9] New Ageists have seen it as retaining something of the 'old wisdom' of the druids.

As far as hard evidence goes, there is nothing to suggest that there was a single entity which could be termed the 'Celtic Church', nor that the elements within it identified themselves as separate. There were regional synods, but they had no 'national' character. The concept has therefore some basis, but like the term Celt itself, is elusive.

Monasteries

The Church in all parts of the Celtic world may have been initially diocesan, but in the absence of towns, this administrative structure was gradually replaced. From the sixth century on, the monastic movement coloured political and economic life as well as spiritual. Almost all the great Christian art treasures were monastic in origin, and some of the larger monasteries have highly visible remains today.

Major monasteries were run by an abbot (though sometimes a bishop) ministering to daughter houses. In Wales, towards the end of the first millennium AD, there emerged a mother Church similar to an Anglo-Saxon minster (the *clas*). This was ruled by an abbot who presided over parishes which coincided with secular territories.

Although some monasteries may have been founded in the fifth century, Ireland became the main stronghold of monasticism in western Europe from the sixth century onwards. St Columba founded Derry, Iona and Durrow (mid-sixth century), St Comgall founded Bangor (555–9) and traditionally St Ciarán established Clonmacnoise (540–550) (K. Hughes, 1966: 57).

The development of learning and art proliferated with the monasteries, which can range from major foundations to hermitages, their status mostly discernible from documentary sources (Macdonald, 1984). They served a variety of functions,[10] being more than merely enclosed religious communities engaged in prayer and scriptural study. By the eighth century they were important as landowners, patrons of the arts, and providers of social services. They were places for fosterage, centres of education, places for hospitality, places of refuge, and treasuries. They were also open prisons for penitent sinners. In monasteries, objects were manufactured, and from them trade was conducted. They were the nearest things to towns in the pre-Viking Celtic lands.

Monastic life is well documented in Irish sources.[11] In early Irish monasteries, for example, there was no adherence to a rule compatible with that of the later monasteries – each monastery followed the rule of its founder. They were not claustral (i.e., they were without cloisters). A characteristic of the Irish monks is that they frequently chose exile as a penance, which took them far afield in Europe.

Kings became important as the patrons of the monasteries, which reciprocally supported their authority. Increasingly, secular law came to be applied to the Church, providing secular support and protection for the Church and its property, and affording socially recognizable ranks for the clergy. Through patronage, monasteries became progressively richer, and the possession of important relics enabled them to exact taxes from the areas to which relics were loaned (Hughes, 1966: 168).

Monasteries gradually became less motivated by religious zeal and more oriented towards the amassing of property and land. By the eighth century in Ireland there were squabbles between rival monasteries, which brought a reform movement led by the *Céli Dé* (Culdees), the 'Servants of God', who stressed meditation and the ideal of the monastic state (Hughes, 1966: ch. 16). Many Culdees were hermits, in southern and eastern Ireland, for example. The movement did not have time to develop as the Viking raids brought about the decrease of the monasteries in Celtic lands. Many survived, however, and there was something of a spiritual revival in the post-Viking centuries.

Monastic location

Major monasteries were often sited in the more prosperous areas, near to royal sites and on good land (the result of patronage) and were frequently located near the coast or on navigable rivers (for ease of communication).

River bends were seen as particularly suitable, as at Old Melrose on the Tweed or Old Deer. The larger monasteries were selected for their convenience. Island monasteries – both major and minor – are not uncommon. The classic example of the withdrawal from monastic metropolitanism is the remote site of Skellig Michael (De Paor 1955; Horn et al., 1990), but there are others, such as Inishmurray or Iniscealtra in Ireland; Iona, Lismore, Birsay and Papil in Scotland; and Priestholm off Anglesey in Wales. Promontories were sometimes utilized, as at St Abb's Head, or the Brough of Deerness, Orkney, both of which probably made use of earlier promontory forts (p. 46).

Monastic layout

The most important feature in a monastery was the enclosure that separated it symbolically and in reality from the outside world (Fig. 91–3). In the larger foundations, the feature is often highly visible – a bank and ditch; a stone wall (usually termed a cashel but not to be confused with the same term used to mean a secular fort); or even a wattle fence or hedge. The enclosed areas varied greatly in size, from c. 2.5 ha at Nendrum to less than 0.2 ha at Church Island. A curvilinear plan was preferred, and the ideal was drawn diagramatically in the Book of Mulling, which shows a double circle (Bitel, 1990: 59). Sometimes natural features were used as rough demarcations before the man-made enclosures were built. Cross-marked stones could serve as boundaries, which were defined by complex ceremonies of dedication (Bitel, 1990: 61–6).

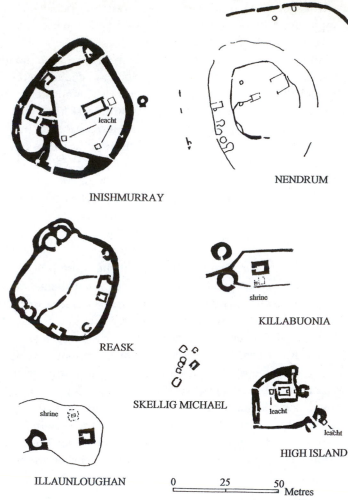

Fig. 91 Irish monastic plans: Inishmurray, Nendrum, Reask, Killabuonia, Skellig Michael, Illaunloughan and High Island.

The *vallum*

The earth bank (*vallum*) was the most common enclosure and could sometimes incorporate earlier secular earthworks, for example at Iona, where part of the western bank seems to pre-date the arrival of the monks by half a millennium (McCormick, 1993; 1997). It seems probable that a number of Irish monasteries were surrounded by stone cashel walls and the area they enclosed, which were originally Iron Age, and were given to the monks by kings and ruling families. This is probably the case with, for example, High Island and Illauntannig.

Some of the larger monasteries had multiple *valla*, arranged in concentric circles to define the zones of the monastery. Adomnán seems to imply a triple boundary at Iona – the outer boundary embracing the farmland; the middle

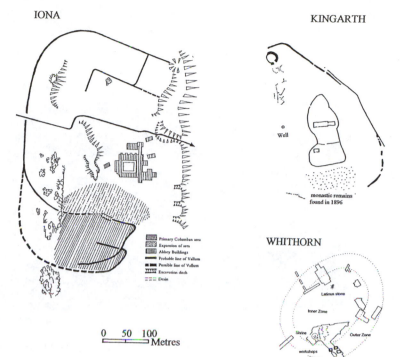

Fig. 92 Scottish monastic plans: Iona; Kingarth; Whithorn.

the monastery itself; and the inner being the enclosure round the church and its cemetery (Macdonald, 2001). Similar patterns occur at Clonmacnoise (Macdonald, 2001: 29); Nendrum (Lawlor, 1925: 95–101); Whithorn (Hill et al., 1997) and Kingarth (Laing, Laing and Longley, 1998).

Sometimes (as at Killabuonia and Kingarth), zones are defined by terraces, and occasionally there are divisions within the zones, as at Inchcleraun and Kiltieran (Hughes and Hamlin, 1997: 56).

The substantial *vallum* at Iona seems to have been the first enterprise of the Columban community. Where it is best preserved it consists of an inner bank about 1.8 m high, a ditch and an outer bank 1.2 m high, with a drop from the top of the bank to the bottom of the ditch of 4 m. At one point (known as Cnoc nan Carnan) the ditch was dug into solid rock, and was over 4 m wide. The entire width of the earthwork was 12 m, and the inner rampart which had been heightened or renewed, was probably topped with a palisade (Barber, 1981: 356; Ritchie, 1997: 36).

Structures within the vallum

Internal structures were positioned according to their importance (Fig. 93). Over a period of time, monasteries often erected multiple churches (tradition-ally, seven), examples of which are at Clonmacnoise, Ardfert, Glendalough,

Fig. 93
Inishmurray
monastery.

Iniscealtra and Inchcleraun (Hughes and Hamlin, 1997: 68). Outside Ireland, the phenomenon can be observed at Iona and Kingarth in Scotland or Maughold in the Isle of Man.

Often associated with a Church was a tomb or shrine of a founder saint, and outdoor altars (*lechta*). The consecrated inner precinct in Ireland (the *termon*) was divided into zones of increasing sanctity. The innermost sanctuary contained the relics of saints (Hughes, 1966: 148). Between the church and the rest of the enclosure was an open space (the *platea*, pl. *plateolae*), sometimes with carefully placed crosses. Only the clergy could enter the sanctuary, but lay people could enter the *platea*.

In hermitages the *plateolae* were confined to clergy. In larger monasteries public spaces were used for the exhibition of gifts and for the display of public monuments, such as crosses (Herity, 1984). Grouped around the *plateolae* were domestic buildings such as the refectory (*tech mór*), where the monks gathered for meals. Adomnán's *Life of St Columba* refers to activities such as reading and the performance of domestic tasks. *The Tripartite Life of St Patrick* suggests the ideal measurement: 8.1 m, with separate kitchens measuring 5.1 m (Macdonald, 1984; Bitel, 1990: 78). A building tentatively identified as a *tech mór* was excavated at Iona (Barber, 1981: 358). Small cells provided accommodation for individual monks; the abbot (or abbess) lived in a separate house which sometimes stood in its own enclosure, as, for example, at Ard Macha (Macdonald, 1981: 310). Other buildings found in monastic enclosures included guest houses, stores, workshops, watermills and animal shelters.

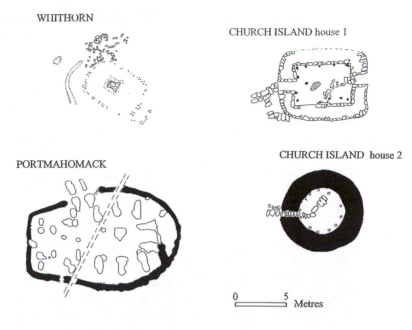

Fig. 94 Monastic buildings: Church Island, houses 1 and 2; Whithorn; Portmahomack.

Mills, corn-drying kilns and souterrains were frequent features (the last confined to Ireland) (Hughes and Hamlin, 1997: 76–7).

At Iona, a complex of about sixty post-holes possibly represented a timber building which dated to the eighth century (Reece, 1974: 42). At Whithorn, in the early sixth century sub-rectangular buildings with external latrine pits and domestic debris were constructed in an area prone to flooding. Two of the buildings were bicameral (with two chambers), one room having a central hearth, the other possibly used for sleeping (Hill et al., 1997: 34). In the developed phase of the monastery, a group of small stake-walled buildings in the outer zone were separated by wattle fences. This segregated the various elements in the monastic population, and included an area used by craftsmen (Hill et al., 1997: 35). A mill and corn-drying kiln were situated in the outer area of the monastery.

At Clonmacnoise, extensive areas on either side of a metalled road were given over to iron, bone, lignite, glass, bronze and goldworking. In one part of the site 60% of the area was covered to a considerable depth with debris which indicated that there was ironworking on a commercial scale.

At Portmahomack, diverse industrial production included workshop areas on each side of a road. Industrial activity included metalworking (gold, bronze, iron), glass working and the production of vellum for manuscripts. In all probability, the products included chalices, pattens, reliquaries and book covers (Chapter 8). One building that was interpreted as a kiln-barn was also used as a smithy. It was curvilinear at one end and sub-rectangular at the other, with a foundation trench filled with beach pebbles. There was also some evidence for the existence of a mill (Carver, 2004: 19–20). The adjacent countryside was farmed by married lay members of the community (the *manaíg*).

Smaller monasteries

Smaller monasteries are difficult to identify since many (in both Britain and Ireland) seem to have been family foundations, with abbot, donors and patrons coming from within the group (Hughes, 1966: 76–7).

Secular origins might explain why some early monasteries, for example, Reask (Fanning, 1981); Millockstown (Manning, 1986); Ronaldsway, Isle of Man (Laing and Laing, 1990b); and Portmahomack (Carver, 2004), resemble forts. It has been suggested that this situation arose through some landowners in the later fifth century converting their rural estates into monasteries to avoid taxation – an example might have been at Llantwit Major (Thomas, 1998: 60–1).

It is probable that a number of the 'chapel' sites in remote situations were hermitages – examples are that on North Rona, to the north of the Butt of Lewis (Nisbet and Gailey, 1962); the scattered remains on Eilean Mor, off Argyll; or the chapel site on Pygmies' Isle off the coast of Lewis. A related category are cave sites which are associated with hermits, such as Ellory, and Weem, near Aberfeldy. St Ninian's cave, Physgyll, is a classic example of the type (Thomas, 1971: 85).

Churches

Many of the smaller churches seem to have been sited on the borders of kingdoms, perhaps following the tradition of siting pagan sanctuaries and royal centres there. The large monastic establishment at Armagh, for example, was close to the pagan centre of Emain Macha (Navan) (N. Edwards, 1990: 105).

Wooden churches

Until comparatively recently the evidence for wooden ecclesiastical structures was entirely literary, but there is now archaeological evidence for timber oratories or chapels. In Ireland a wooden chapel is distinguished from a stone one by the term *duirtheach* ('house of oak': Leask, 1955: 6).

A fifteenth-century manuscript, drawing on an older original, implies that the average dimensions for a wooden church were 4.5 × 3 m (Trinity College, Dublin MS H.3.17), the rectilinear plan being a break from traditional

ARDWALL

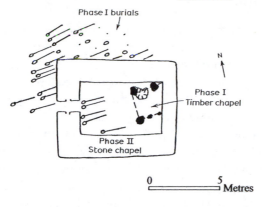

CHURCH ISLAND

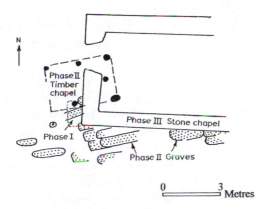

Fig. 95 Timber churches: Ardwall Isle and Church Island.

architecture. The congregation remained outside Celtic oratories which contained an altar and church plate. Early timber buildings were roughly oriented east–west.

There is documentary evidence for substantial timber churches, of which the most fully documented was that of St Brigit at Kildare, described in Cogitosus' *Life of St Brigit*, written in the seventh century (Bieler, 1966: 28; Harbison, 1999: 192).

There is archaeological evidence for timber chapels at a number of sites such as Iniscealtra (Harbison, 1982: 628); White Island (Lowry-Corry et al., 1959); Derry (Waterman, 1967), St Vogue, Carnsore;[12] Barhobble (Cormack et al., 1995); Llanelen (Schlesinger and Walls, 1996: 110); and Burryholms (Hague, 1974: 29–32; Fig. 95).

The classic multi-phase sites are Church Island (O'Kelly, 1958) and Ardwall Island (Thomas, 1967).

Stone churches

The earliest references to stone churches in Ireland are in the *Annals of Ulster* in an entry for 724 and in Tírechán's *Life of St Patrick* (written in the later seventh century) which refers to Duleek. In the Irish Annals for 788/9, a stone chapel (*oratorium lapideum*) is noted at Armagh. References become slightly more common in the ninth century, and are frequent by the eleventh and twelfth centuries (Macdonald, 1981: 306–70).

Dating early church buildings is difficult and controversial particularly over some simple structures such as the Gallarus Oratory (Harbison, 1970); buildings on Skellig Michael (De Paor, 1955; Horn et al., 1990), and those in the Dingle peninsula (Henry, 1957). Traditional dating (Leask, 1955: ch. 6) has now been supplemented by radiocarbon (Berger, 1995; Fig. 96–7).

Unlike Anglo-Saxon churches, Celtic examples were not modelled on Roman architecture (Romanesque influence was not felt until the twelfth century in Celtic areas, after which point church and other records usually exist). There has therefore been a tendency to assume that any simple structure without documentary evidence or Romanesque features, must be of the earliest Christian period.

Clearly, such an approach has given rise to many controversies.

Decorative details which copy techniques irrelevant in stone but essential in carpentry have often been seen as indicative of early date. However, there can be problems. For example, a large amount of attention has been given to butterfly finials (Leask, 1955: 46–7) – winged ornaments that were placed on the apex of the gable. They were believed to imitate similar finials used to hide the crossing of the cruck beams in a cruck-built timber Church.

Scientific dating methods are rarely applicable to simple stone structures and have even more rarely been used. A corbelled oratory on a stone platform at Illaunloughan was dated by radiocarbon to between 640 and 790. It seems to have had a stone predecessor, and before that, two turf oratories (White Marshall and Walsh, 1994). At Croagh Patrick, a larger oratory (8.80 × 5 m), which was probably corbelled, provided a radiocarbon date centred on the seventh century (Walsh, 1994).

The structure of stone churches

Most of the surviving stone chapels which are claimed to be early, are small and unicameral. There was evidence for the use of plaster at High Island for both the interior of the church and the altar, possibly in the eleventh century (White Marshall and Rourke, 2000a: 85). Plaster is attested at Whithorn in its earliest phase (p. 305) (Hill et al., 1997: 81), and at Clonmacnoise on the original south wall of the cathedral, built 909 (Manning, 1995: 30–3). Many early

Fig. 96
Columba's House,
Kells.

chapel walls are bonded with clay, cob or mud. In west and north Scotland it is fairly common to find stones laid in yellow clay.

The presence of a chancel can generally be taken to indicate a date after the eighth century. Adomnán describes an *exedra* (porch) to the timber church at Iona, but this was probably exceptional. Roofs have not generally survived in Ireland unless made of stone. Representations on later hog-backed tombstones imply that churches were roofed for the most part with lapped semicircular shingles, slates or stones.

Features of Irish stone churches

A number of features are commonly encountered in the pre-Romanesque Irish stone churches. Cyclopean masonry (i.e., very large blocks of stone) for example, may have been symbolic. Door jambs are frequently inclined inwards, and surmounted by a substantial lintel, sometimes with another relieving lintel above. Irish churches (and one in Scotland, at Chapel Finian) sometimes have *antae* (a projection of the side walls creating the appearance of buttresses).

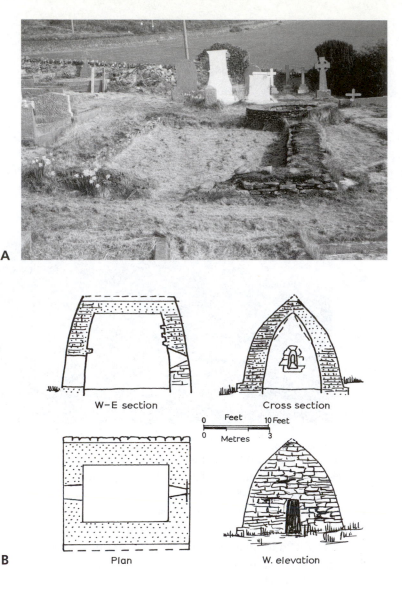

Fig. 97 A. Keeill, Maughold, Isle of Man; B. Gallarus Oratory.

Antae have been seen as skeuomorphs of angle posts in plank walls (Leask, 1955: 56), though it is now generally held that they supported barge boards. There is a good example at Temple MacDuagh (Hughes and Hamlin, 1997: 61).

The earliest churches (where datable) are unicameral, and tend to a ratio of 3:2. Later the double square became more favoured. Many have battered walls (i.e., where the outer long walls of the churches lean inwards slightly). This feature was originally used in drystone buildings to add strength (Leask, 1955: 54–5). A number of doorways (known as architrave lintel doorways: Leask, 1955: 56–8) have a raised border or architrave. In some cases the lintel bears a carved or engraved cross. Good examples of architrave lintel doorways can be seen at St Fechin's Church, Fore, and Clonamery.

The only window was often in the east wall above the altar. Most windows are narrow (sometimes only 15 cm wide). They usually have a single, rounded stone at the head. The interior may be splayed, sometimes with steps down. Flat and triangular-headed as well as triangular windows are sometimes encountered.

Stone roofs were extremely heavy, but were not vulnerable to fire and may have been a response to the Viking raids. Few stone roofs appear to have been built before the twelfth century. There are examples at St Lua's Church at Killaloe and Temple Mac Dara. In the case of Temple Mac Dara there may have been permanent struts of timber propping the roof. Signs of props at St Lua's may have been temporary supports while the cement was setting. The date of these two buildings is in dispute. Although claimed as earlier, Temple Mac Dara may date from as late as the twelfth century.[13] Stone roofs tend to sag inwards halfway up, so a propping arch was devised which also roofed the vault and provided a space known as the croft, which could be used as a room.

A good example is St Columba's House at Kells, where the unicameral building internally measures c. 5.7 × 4.65 m (Leask, 1955: 34–5 N; Fig. 96). It is usually dated to the early ninth century, since there is a reference to a stone church at this date and radiocarbon dating of its mortar indicated a seventh- to tenth-century date bracket (R. Berger, 1995: 164).

Related to St Columba's House is the more complex building known as St Kevin's Church at Glendalough, frequently called St Kevin's Kitchen (Leask, 1955: 34–5). A chancel and sacristy with stone roofs were added to the original unicameral structure. The chancel was then demolished and a round tower was added to the west gable, giving the building a very distinctive appearance.

The most developed Irish stone-roofed church can be seen in Cormac's Chapel at Cashel (Leask, 1955: 113–20). Architecturally this is a remarkable product of the Irish Romanesque. The roof is very steeply pitched, and changes angle slightly at about half its height. It too has a croft, of which the outer face is made to look like a corbelled structure, but which has very little structural value since the support depends on the inner facing of light calcareous tufa which is neither a true corbelled arch nor a true arch. A system of bonding timbers at the base of the vault was an added precaution for the structure. It dates from the twelfth century.

Stone churches outside Ireland

There is very little evidence for ecclesiastical stone building before the twelfth century in the areas of Scotland not dominated by the Angles of Northumbria (Fernie, 1986). Stone structures at Traprain (p. 297) and the

Dod, and the early structures at Whithorn and Hoddom (p. 305) may be ecclesiastical and there were stone buildings in the Pictish monastery at Portmahomack from the eighth century. There, the alignment of the east wall of the crypt suggested it belonged to an earlier church. A structure with antae at Chapel Finian (Radford, 1951) may be of the tenth or eleventh century. A rectangular stone church at Barhobble (Cormack et al., 1995), which had three bays divided by pairs of crucks and an altar at its east end, was dated to the eleventh or twelfth centuries. Of probable tenth-century date is the earliest (unmortared) church on the Isle of May in the Firth of Forth (Yeoman and James, 1999: 196).

Fragments of stonework suggest that churches existed at Forteviot (Alcock and Alcock, 1992) and Meigle in southern Pictland (I. Smith, 1996: 32). A much-debated Church, St Rule's, St Andrews, may date to the end of the period under review (Fernie, 1986; Fawcett, 1991; Cameron, 1996). The round tower at Brechin may be late tenth century, since documentary sources state that when the Danes sacked Brechin c. 1017 they left only a round tower standing (Cameron, 1996: 44). However, a twelfth-century date for this and the tower at Abernethy is generally preferred.

Pre-Romanesque stone building is absent in Wales (if the Anglo-Saxon Church at Presteigne, Radnor,[14] is discounted), Cornwall and the Isle of Man, where keeills (the term used there for chapel sites), though originating earlier, have stone structures that are unlikely to pre-date the twelfth century (p. 290).

Clocháns

Stone was also employed in the construction of *clocháns* (Henry, 1957). These are generally circular beehive-shaped living cells with corbelled roofs, which had a single entrance and were built without mortar. There can be little doubt that these buildings belong to a long-established Celtic tradition, though there is at present no evidence to date the surviving examples before c. AD 700. They are concentrated mainly in the south-west mountainous area of Co. Kerry, where a shortage of timber probably necessitated the use of stone for building at a relatively early date. The *clochán* is found widely in both ecclesiastical and secular contexts. Some associated with ecclesiastical sites may pre-date the twelfth century (pre-Romanesque), though most appear to be later. On the evidence provided by secular beehive constructions (as at Leacanabuaile) the domestic sites are also apparently of similar date. It is not unlikely that such buildings were constructed by shepherds in Ireland as late as the eighteenth or nineteenth centuries. The classic site for the beehive type of cell is the monastery of Skellig Michael, where there are also two oratories (De Paor 1955; Horn et al., 1990).

Round towers[15]

A characteristic Irish monument is the round tower. It has been suggested that most were built in the twelfth century to symbolize reforms within the Irish Church, and to celebrate the revival of the Golden Age (Corlett, 1998: 27; Fig. 98). They are normally c. 10–13 m high, and c. 5–6 m in diameter with walls c. 1.2 m thick. The towers taper towards the top, and have conical stone roofs. The doorways are several feet above ground level, and were originally approached by a wooden ladder.

Inside a round tower was a series of wooden floors (usually five, six or seven), each storey having a window facing a different way from the others. The top storey had windows facing the four compass points. The windows were narrow, with triangular or lintel heads. There are two examples known of stone floors. The towers were built at a distance from the associated churches, never attached to them (except for one projecting from the roof at St Kevin's Kitchen in Glendalough). Round towers were built first as bell towers, and were used as watchtowers in times of emergency and possibly as treasuries. While their shape and design made them impregnable against normal siege techniques they would have been vulnerable to fire, acting as chimneys once the ground floor was ignited. This probably explains the accounts of important personages being burned in them. Human bones and charcoal were found in the Kilkenny round tower in 1847. Their defensive function however should not be over-estimated – only seven round towers were deliberately fired, and only two (at Slane and Armagh) were due to Viking attacks (Corlett, 1998: 26).

The earliest documentary evidence for the building of a round tower (no longer surviving) is from Slane in 950 (Corlett, 1998). Other references appear in the Annals for the years 964, 981 and 994–6. Such references continue through the eleventh and twelfth centuries, so it may be assumed that the structures were first constructed in the tenth century. Timber prototypes probably preceded the stone versions. Like the East Anglian series of Anglo-Saxon towers, they were probably imitations of Continental prototypes (which first appeared in northern Italy in the ninth century). The best preserved examples are those at Kilkenny, Monasterboice, Clondalkin and Kinneigh. Outside Ireland there are examples on St Patrick's Isle, in the Isle of Man, Abernethy and Brechin.

Cemeteries

Cemeteries range from simple burial grounds without associated features (such as chapels or founders' tombs), to sites where the burials are subordinate to the associated structures (such as oratories or chapels). While some

Fig. 98 Round tower, Abernethy.

cemetery sites may have developed from simple graveyards with the secondary construction of dedicated above-ground features, many were undoubtedly intended as places of religious observance from the outset. There is some evidence of continuity of burial site from pagan to Christian times. In some cases burials adjoin a Bronze Age barrow and in a few cases Christian burials have been dug into the barrow itself. This could be explained by a sense of using ancestral burial places, or simply because barrows were distinctive markers (H. James, 1992: 93).

Burial rites

The (fourth-century Christian Roman) practice of inhumation continued into the post-Roman/early medieval period. In the areas within former Britannia, there is evidence for continuing use of extended supine inhumation with the head to the west without gravegoods from the fourth century through to the pagan Anglo-Saxon advance, though north–south burials also occurred in more rural districts (E. O'Brien, 1999: 185). Although there is little evidence for burial practice in the Roman period outside Britannia, there are signs that the Roman burial practice had spread to the west and north and across to Ireland by the fifth centuries.

Whether this was due to an extension from the Romanized areas of Britain, or more probably the result of contact with the Continent where similar burial rites were practised in the period, has been debated (Petts, 2003: 85). There is evidence for the continuity of use of some cemeteries from the fourth century into the seventh and later, for example at Mary Major, near Exeter, where burials in slab-lined and unprotected graves were radiocarbon dated to this period, or Brean Down and Lamyat Beacon where radiocarbon dates indicate even longer usage (O'Brien, 1999: 32–3). At Llandough in south Wales where there were Iron Age burials and a Roman villa, a cemetery was in used from the fourth to the eleventh or twelfth centuries.

Bodies in the early medieval period were normally laid in the ground or in a hollow worked out of bedrock (dug graves); in tree-trunk coffins; in stone-lined boxes (cist graves); or in stone cists with a capping of stones (lintel graves) (classification in Thomas, 1971: 49).

These burials were normally oriented west–east. The belief that the body needed to be protected for resurrection on Judgement Day probably explains the careful orientation which would permit the resurrected to face Christ. Cemeteries were generally relatively small – assemblages of over 100 burials are rare. It is likely that cemeteries were graded according to the social status of those interred.

Enclosed and unenclosed cemeteries

Many of the earliest known Christian cemeteries comprise unenclosed groups of burials, as at the long-cist cemetery at Parkburn (Henshall, 1955–6). Many cemeteries were enclosed, normally by a curvilinear or partially curvilinear vallum or ditch which symbolically separated the sacred from the profane and the dead from the living. A few rectilinear enclosures are known, for example in Cornwall, where it has been argued that they are relatively late (i.e., immediately pre-Norman: Preston-Jones, 1992: 111–13; Fig. 99).

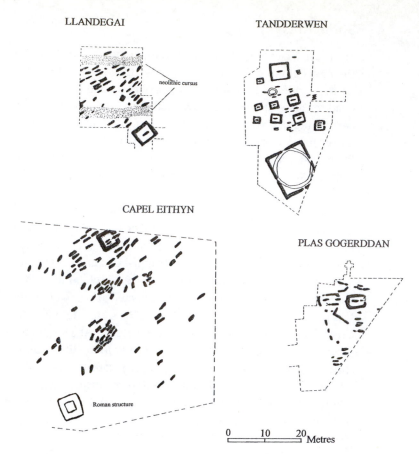

Fig. 99 Welsh cemetery plans, with special graves: Llandegai; Tandderwen; Capel Eithyn; Plas Gogerddan.

Graves

A variety of grave types were used.

Dug graves   Simple, extended burials in an unlined hole in the ground, which are widespread. They may or may not have had wooden coffins.

Tree trunk coffin burial   A particular type of ritual found at Whithorn in the first phase of the monastery, which is a specialized form of dug grave (Hill et al., 1997: 73).

Cist graves   Composed of burials laid in graves lined with slabs of stone forming a coffin or cist, are found widespread in Scotland, the Isle of Man, Wales, Ireland and south-west England. The skeletons are normally extended and supine, with the arms at the sides, though there are some instances of arms crossed on the pelvis. They are generally oriented east–west. There was usually only one body in each grave, but there are exceptions, such as the female burial with a baby on her chest at Knockea (O'Kelly, 1967: 77). Additional skulls have been noted (Mytum, 1992: 95).

Slab-lined isolated graves   In Ireland, inhumation burial seems to have been introduced through contact with Roman Britain. Slab-lined cists with the body laid with the arms loose or hands on the pubic area, without evidence for the compression caused by a winding sheet, have been dated in the fifth century. They occur inserted into or disposed around prehistoric burial monuments, and may have been élite burials (E. O'Brien, 2003: 66).

Lintel graves   Although exhibiting lining stones, these differ from long-cist graves in that they have side slabs but no floors, and are tapered. They have lintel-type covering slabs and show signs that the dead were wrapped in a winding sheet. They usually date from the seventh century or later (E. O'Brien, 2003: 67). Lintel graves were sometimes not totally covered by slabs, and in a few instances slabs were laid directly on the bodies rather than resting on side slabs.

Square-ditch enclosed burials   These burials are sometimes covered by barrows. At least thirty cemeteries of burials enclosed by square ditches have been found in Pictland (Close-Brooks, 1984; E. Alcock, 1992; Fig. 100). They also occur in south-west Scotland and in Wales. At Garbeg the ditches had causeways at the corners, and the cemetery contained low round barrows (sometimes with a large berm), long cists and dug graves (Wedderburn and Grime, 1984).

Some features associated with burials

In north-west Wales, some burials appear to have been oriented according to the sun's position in the spring and summer, particularly the rising of the sun during mid- to late April, the period in which Easter fell (Longley, 2002). In some graveyards (such as Kingarth, Bute, and Iona) the sexes were separated. A burial ground for women only was noted at Carrickmore, though this seems to have been a late phenomenon associated with the Culdees (Hamlin and Foley, 1983). Special areas at the north side of the church seem to have been reserved for those murdered or killed in battle who had not received the last rites (Hamlin and Foley, 1983).

White quartz pebbles are associated with some burials, and with lechta (p. 229), wells and (in some cases) churches, where they are found in the floor. They appear to indicate either that a prayer has been said, or to have been tokens for entry to heaven (Yeoman and James, 1999). They are found in the keeills in the Isle of Man, where up to eighty pebbles were found in graves at

GARBEG

Fig. 100 Square barrow cemetery, Garbeg.

0   10   30 Metres

Ballavarkish and Sulbrick, at Church Island, where they were associated with a shrine tomb as well as in the floor of the church, and at Inishmurray, where speckled water-worn pebbles (in this case not white) are found on the top of lechta. They are also known at Ruthwell, the Isle of May and Cartmel (Crowe, 1982; 1984).

Special graves

Some interments were grouped around special burials, which are usually presumed to be that of a local saint or a founder. Special burials could have round or rectangular enclosures, and are well exemplified in Wales, Ireland and south-west England. The custom of marking special burials with an enclosure, round or rectilinear, was first apparent in Britain in the Iron Age, and persisted through the Roman period (E. O'Brien, 1999: 185). They did not necessarily have substantial above-ground features, if any. A special type were lechta (which may however, not necessarily have been funereal).

Wales

A key site in Wales is Plas Gogerddan, where twenty-two burials, apparently in wooden coffins, were grouped with three rectangular special graves. One of the special graves measured 5.5 × 3.8 m, with an entrance in the east marked by two post-holes. It had slightly bowed walls, and appears to have been a 'mortuary house', containing an oriented burial with a stone-lined pit at its entrance which may have contained a wooden box. There was no date for this feature, but a burial in the cemetery provided a radiocarbon date of AD 263–636 (Murphy, 1992; H. James, 1992: 90–1). This was presumably a shrine house (Totenmemoria), which are attested in Germany (Thomas, 1971: 147–9).

Other sites with special graves in Wales include Tanderderwen (H. James, 1992: 92–3); Llandegai (Houlder, 1968); Capel Maelog (Britnell, 1990), and Capel Eithin (White, 1982).

Ireland

In Ireland there are five examples of penannular (shaped like a broken circle) burial enclosures. These are mostly in the east, which has led to the suggestion that they may reflect Anglo-Saxon influence, though a western British influence seems equally probable (E. O'Brien, 2003: 69). Over thirty sites have special graves identified as those of the founder, and on other sites can be found burials designated 'the priest's grave' or the 'saint's grave' (Herity, 1995: 26). Many of these have no special indicators, except perhaps for a grave-slab, but a more ornate special grave was noted at Reask (Fanning, 1981).

South-west England

Special graves of the fifth to seventh centuries are documented near Kenn (Weddell, 2000), Westhampnett, near Chichester (Fitzpatrick, 1992), and on Lundy, at Beacon Hill, where thirty cist graves were focused on a special burial (Thomas, 1969; 1994: ch. 5).

Scotland

A special grave excavated at Whithorn had been the focus for the subsequent development of a shrine (Hill et al., 1997: 91–5).

Lechta

The idea of a superstructure above a saint's tomb appears to have come to Britain from the Mediterranean. In Ireland a lecht is a small rectangular construction of stones or slabs, or sometimes a single block, with a flat top on which stones may be laid (Thomas, 1971: 169). It is unknown whether all lechta covered burials in Ireland – there were burials in the lecht-like structures at Ronaldsway, Isle of Man (p. 289) – but they show such features as surrounds which are comparable to those round important graves, and the name itself (which is derived from Latin *lectus*, a bed) implies funerary connections.

However, the other features of lechta have more in common with altars: they stand to the average altar height (about 1–1.5 m) and the stones set in them have a central cross flanked by four smaller ones, as on an altar table. The most famous collection is on Inishmurray, where they are spaced out round the perimeter of the island and were used until recently as processional stations (Thomas, 1971: 169–70). Nine of the eleven lechta have specific names. The best-known is Altoir Beag ('little altar') which has pebbles on top of it of a type found elsewhere, for instance on Islay, associated with votive custom and prayer, the pebbles sometimes being turned as prayers were said.

Shrines

The custom of venerating relics seems to have reached Britain from the Mediterranean in the fifth century. It has been suggested that relics of Sts Peter and Paul, for instance, were brought to Ireland by Palladius and that a few early church sites in Ireland with the name basilica held relics in the fifth century (Doherty, 1984). The importance of relics became greater from the end of the eighth century. From this time onwards a variety of structures is recognizable in cemeteries that were designed to hold the relics of saints (Fig. 101).[16]

The recently excavated site at Caherlehillan demonstrates the complexity of early ecclesiastical sites in which shrines were built. Radiocarbon dating of a drainage ditch associated with the earliest use of the site lay in the late fifth to early sixth centuries. The site included a developed cemetery with an enclosure, a timber chapel and a corner-post shrine (one post of which was marked with a cross). A long-cist burial under the shrine was one of the two earliest in the cemetery and was associated with E Ware (seventh century). A figure-of-eight house and a rectilinear house were associated with B Ware and E Ware as well as glass of the seventh century. An inscribed stone was carved with peacock and flabellum (a processional fan).

The site appears to have been abandoned in the late eighth century and may have been associated with an adjacent cashel from which it gets its name.[17]

Slab shrines

A group of structures, named slab shrines, probably dating from the early seventh century, occurs in south-west Ireland, where they are found associated with surrounds of rectilinear plan. They consist of a hollow dug into the ground roofed with two sloping stones and two triangular end gables. The overall appearance is of a ridge tent. One of the finest examples is at Killabuonia, where the gable stone is furnished with a porthole to enable the relics to be touched (Thomas, 1971: 141–4).

Corner-post shrines

Many corner-post shrines have four stone pillars with grooves on two faces, into which end slabs are slotted (Thomas, 1971: 150–5). The more elaborate stone shrines have either eight or thirteen pieces, excluding the roof

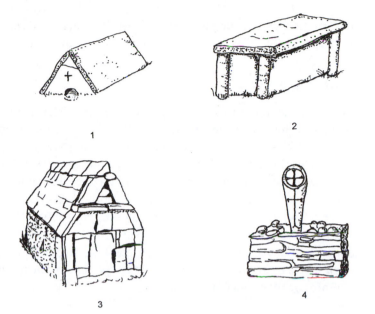

Fig. 101
Shrines: 1. slab shrine, Killabuonia; 2. St Ninian's Isle, shrine A; 3. Banagher; 4. Inishmurray.

slabs. The lid is either flat or the two end slabs rise into gables, to support two roof slabs. Frequently one slab could be removed to allow the relics within to be touched. The distribution of corner-post shrines appears to be mostly north British. The norm is the single shrine, but there are a few double shrines, possibly of Northumbrian origin, such as one from St Ninian's Isle, Shetland.

Corner-block shrines

A slightly more sophisticated variant of the corner-post shrine is the corner-block shrine, which has neatly made large rectangular blocks at the corners. Good examples are that from Monifieth (Thomas, 1971: 152–3), and the St Andrews Shrine (Foster, 1998).

Solid shrines

The final stage in the development of stone shrines is the solid shrine which consists of a solid house-shaped piece of stone, placed over a grave. An example from Clones is an exact copy of a timber prototype, including imitation locks and hasps (De Paor and De Paor, 1958: 60).

Memorial stones

One of the most valuable resources for studying early Christianity in Britain and Ireland is the body of inscribed memorial stones which provide information about language and society. The material comprises ogham stones and memorials with Latin, Irish and Welsh inscriptions.

Ogham stones

The ogham alphabet was a method of conveying the Irish language as it was spoken in the fourth century, incised in stone and other materials (p. 325; Fig. 102). The stones on which the inscriptions appear are memorials to the dead (reflecting Roman tradition), but were sometimes also boundary markers (Charles-Edwards, 2000: 173). The formula gave the name of the deceased and usually that of his father, as in 'A Maqqi B', Maqqi meaning 'son of'. Ogham stones are also found in Dumnonia (p. 246), Wales (p. 257) and in Scotland (p. 311). An ogham inscribed stone from the Romano-British town of Silchester has been argued as having been set up to mark the ownership of a town house by an Irishman, some time in the fourth or early fifth centuries (Fulford, Handley and Clark, 2000).

Latin-inscribed stones

The second main series of memorial stones is those with Latin inscriptions in the Latin alphabet, which are found in Scotland, Wales and south-west England, but not Ireland (Fig. 103). Bilingual inscriptions rendered in both Irish ogham and Latin are found in Wales and Dumnonia.

There are about twenty in north Britain, spanning the period from the late fifth to the early eighth centuries. Their distribution extends from Vindolanda just south of Hadrian's Wall to the Catstane near Edinburgh, and they are memorials to individuals with names which are either Roman or late British (Thomas, 1992). They represent nobility, clerics and landowners and relate to a Roman Church the followers of which continued to speak, read and probably write Latin (Thomas, 1992: 3). They indicate the spread of Christianity northwards from the area of Hadrian's Wall, a process which probably began within the Roman period (p. 103).

The Welsh series is the most extensive. The Latin- and ogham-inscribed stones were termed Class 1 in the classic survey of the Welsh monuments (Nash-Williams, 1950). A few stones probably represent the continuation of late Roman memorial tradition and can be classed along with late Roman gravestones – they have the inscriptions set in parallel lines on the stones, horizontally, in Roman capitals. These are found in north-west Wales, such as those from Aberdaron (Gwynedd), or in Scotland, such as the Latinus stone at Whithorn (p. 304).

There has been some debate about the date of the inscriptions, which are

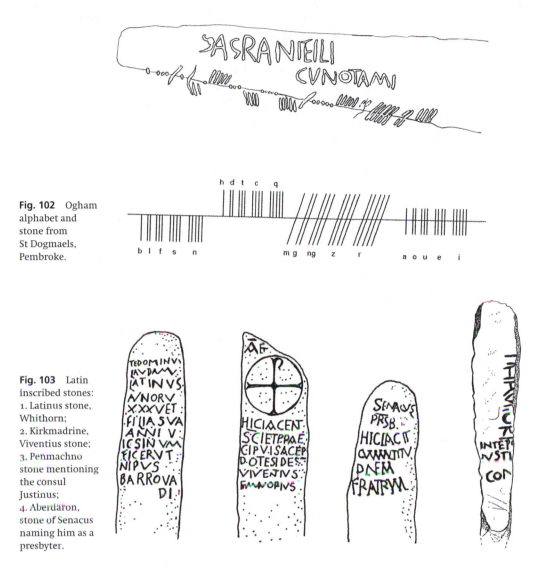

Fig. 102 Ogham alphabet and stone from St Dogmaels, Pembroke.

Fig. 103 Latin inscribed stones:
1. Latinus stone, Whithorn;
2. Kirkmadrine, Viventius stone;
3. Penmachno stone mentioning the consul Justinus;
4. Aberdaron, stone of Senacus naming him as a presbyter.

assumed to be, but need not all have been, Christian. Many were apparently set up in isolation. The most widely accepted view is that the earliest are mid- to late fifth century. Conversely, it has been suggested that they originate in the late fourth century, and were part of a wider trend that extended to Spain, Italy, Gaul and North Africa (Dark, 1992; Handley, 2001).

There has been considerable discussion about whether some of the inscriptions contain encrypted messages revealed through numerology. The stones concerned are in Biblical style, and set out for public display. It has been argued that the letters are arranged to form patterns that can reveal hidden divine names, words, Biblical allusions and (in some cases) absolute dates. They display a knowledge of geometry and arithmetic. Some, it has been suggested, can be used to generate pictures or images. Since it is well known that the Romans were fond of word and letter games, the tradition has been seen as of Classical derivation.[18] Some of the inferences claimed are debatable (McKee and McKee, 2002), but on the simplest level there is no reason to reject the use of numerology and a kind of cryptology in the arrangement of some inscriptions.

There are nine certain inscriptions of the fifth to sixth centuries in Cornwall, with a further five more dubious and fragmentary examples. In general, they are similar to the Welsh monuments. Six stones carry ogham inscriptions.

Apart from these early stones, there are various later groups of inscribed stones, not all of which are memorials to the dead. Plain inscribed crosses (Group 2) and various classes of stones with simple inscribed crosses are widespread in the Celtic world and seem to span a long period from the sixth or seventh centuries to the twelfth and probably later. A few are datable on the basis of the form of the cross. From the seventh century onwards there are a considerable number of different types of inscribed stones including cross slabs and high crosses (p. 193).

10 South-western Britain

What is now south-west England, fell into two distinct sections in the post-Roman/early medieval period. The former territories of the Iron Age tribes of the Durotriges and Dobunni covered roughly what is now called the West Country (Dorset, Somerset and Gloucestershire) and Dumnonia the former territory of the Dumnonii, covered modern Cornwall and Devon (Thomas, 1966: 83–4; 1976: 199; Dark, 2000: 150–1). The West Country was the first area of south-western Britain to have contact with the Anglo-Saxons, and it is from this region that the legends of King Arthur's struggles against the incoming pagan Saxons can be traced (p. 257). The boundary between Celt and Saxon fluctuated until the entire area was absorbed into the mainstream of English cultural developments in the ninth century.

Dumnonia retained a strongly British/Celtic culture throughout the Roman period, though it is notable that it was literate in post-Roman/early medieval times and, unlike Anglo-Saxon dominated areas further east, has yielded a number of inscriptions of the period. Dumnonia was traditionally and culturally close to Brittany and during the late- and post-Roman period migrations from Britain are recorded in the written sources (p. 244). There were also immigrations of Irish into the region, probably from south Wales.

The Romans in the West Country

When the south fell to the Roman forces in the early months of conquest in AD 43, the Iron Age hillforts were evacuated to newly established towns nearby. The widespread adoption of a Roman lifestyle is very evident, with, by the fourth century, a concentration of rich villas, estates and towns, including the spa at Bath. Mosaics, wall paintings, wine and many luxury goods imported from the Continent were part of life for the Romano-Britons who have left abundant evidence of their lifestyles. When Rome was unable to maintain the province (in the early fifth century) the area has been traditionally seen as reverting to an Iron Age 'Celtic' lifestyle whilst holding out against incoming Germanic peoples. Since the 1970s this view has been regarded as misleading: it is more likely that an increasingly diluted Romano-British lifestyle survived until absorbed by the Saxons during the late sixth/early seventh centuries. The relationship between the Saxons and the post-Roman Britons in the area is still imperfectly understood.

Fig. 104 Map of Dumnonia in the early medieval period.

The evidence suggests that people continued to live in the towns into the fifth century, though ruined stone buildings were replaced with timber, presumably because the stone industry had collapsed. Such is the case in Cirencester (Holbrook, 1998), Gloucester (Darvill, 1988: 9–11; Dark, 2000: 106) and Dorchester (Dark, 2000: 107–8).

There seems to have been continuing manufacture of Roman black-burnished pottery at Ower (outside Dorchester), where production began in the fourth and probably continued into the sixth century (Sunter and Woodward, 1987; Gerrard, 2004). In the smaller towns, notably at Bourton-on-the-Water, Bath and Ilchester, the evidence is similar (Dark, 2000: 110–11).

In the countryside there is evidence that Roman-style life continued. At the classic site of Poundbury a fourth-century Roman cemetery with mausolea was succeeded by a settlement with rectangular timber buildings and sunken-floor features (Sparey-Green, 1982; 1987; 2004).

Villa sites show continuing use during the fifth century (though without new building or maintenance). At Barnsley Park, Cirencester, a platform was built in the final phase for a meeting place, or to take a timber building. A Merovingian ring ornament from the site implies occupation in the late fifth to seventh centuries (Webster and Smith, 1982: 121; wider discussion of this type of ornament in south-west England in Dark, 1994b: 80–1). At Frocester, there is evidence for the continuing use of the villa into the fifth and probably the sixth centuries (E. Price, 2003). At villas such as Lufton, Box, Low Ham, Dewlish (Branigan, 1976: ch. 8) and at Wortley (Wilson, 1993: 1995) there was stone building after the fourth century.

In the vicinity of the hillfort at Cadbury Castle survey has shown that strong agricultural development continued from the third century (when the agrarian landscape was resturctured with new field boundaries) into the fifth and sixth, though some marginal land reverted to wood, marsh or downland (Davey, 2004: 52). In the mid-fifth century the focus of settlement moved from Ilchester to Cadbury Castle, but agriculture continued until there was a mixture of Romano-British and Anglo-Saxon traits discernible in the seventh century (Davey, 2004: 53).

The Anglo-Saxons in the south-west

Within the Roman province of Britannia, the structure of society was already undergoing modification when in the early fifth century Germanic settlers arrived. To judge from both the archaeological material and the written records, the first incomers were almost certainly recruited to replace or augment the regular troops against other settlers or raiders.

A British leader, Vortigern, is identified in written sources (of debatable reliability, but see Chadwick, 1959; J. R. Morris, 1973: 55–6) as inviting the Saxons Hengist and Horsa and their followers to settle in Britannia during the mid-fifth century. The policy went very wrong, and the incomers took power for themselves.

There were a number of distinct Germanic peoples involved in the settlement of what became England. Since the time of Bede in the eighth century, historians tried to rationalize the picture by maintaining that the Angles settled mainly in eastern England, the Saxons south of the Thames (with the Jutes in Kent and the Isle of Wight). Although very simplistic, this probably has some basis in fact.

By around AD 500, eastern England south of a line from roughly the Isle of Wight to the Tees and Tyne, was settled by Anglo-Saxons. The scale of the settlement has been vigorously debated. The minimalist view argues that as few as 10,000 to 20,000 incomers were involved with a take-over at the top (M. E. Jones, 1996: 27). The opposite view argues that settlement was on a large scale and that the population of Romano-Britons in the fifth century was much depleted (Snyder, 2003: 88–9). Prominent in the struggles against the Saxons and in later fiction (especially that of the fifteenth-century Malory),[1] was the legendary figure of King Arthur. Current thinking sees him more as a latter-day Romano-Briton rather than a 'true' Celt, operating from somewhere in the West Country (though in legend he is associated with many locations including Scotland). Vigorous debate surrounds him, though it is generally agreed that the sources indicate a leader in the early sixth century.[2] His possible historicity lies with a set of Welsh Annals (*Annales Cambriae*, BL, MS Harley 3859), which has an entry for AD 518 referring to Arthur's victory over the Anglo-Saxons at Mons Badonicus. A subsequent entry for 539 alludes to the death of Arthur at the battle of Camlann.

Gildas did not mention Arthur by name, but does allude to Mons Badonicus, as fought in c. 500, which he asserted halted the Anglo-Saxon advance for forty-four years. An entry in the *Anglo-Saxon Chronicle* for the year 567/8 noted that Gloucester, Cirencester and Bath fell to Ceawlin of the West Saxons in the battle of Dyrrham. The historicity of this event has been questioned but it would fit with the archaeological evidence for the spread of Anglo-Saxon material, even though it seems that the creation of a large Anglo-Saxon kingdom at this date was unlikely (Snyder, 2003: 159).

As archaeological studies stand at present, there is some evidence to support the view that the late Roman population resisted the Saxon advance, but there could be other factors involved. If there were a stand against the incomers, it seems logical that the hillforts of the Iron Age (which had made the futile stand against the Roman four centuries earlier) might be pressed into service once more. This could be seen as the centres of power moving from the towns to traditional Iron Age hillforts, which (whether this was a prime motive or not), would have been easily defendable. However, the re-occupation could also be explained by more local struggles, or other, unrelated factors. They may have been new power centres rather than military in function.

Re-occupied hillforts

Several hillforts were refurbished and re-occupied in the post-Roman period, some clearly housing occupants of high status.

Cadbury Congresbury   had extensive post-Roman defences (Rahtz et al., 1992). A rock-cut ditch was dug with an associated flat-topped platform with a timber or turf façade, probably in the fifth century. The existing defences gradually decayed during occupation, but concurrently some time after the end of the fifth century, imported pottery appeared on the site. Subsequently, the fifth-century bank may have been refurbished with D-shaped annexes or bastions. Within the fort rectilinear and circular structures were built.

Cadbury Castle,   though producing less imported pottery than Cadbury Congresbury, had more extensive evidence of re-occupation, which possibly began after 470 (L. Alcock, 1995). There was Roman-period occupation within the Iron Age hillfort, probably with a temple which may still have been visited in the fifth century. At this time the fortifications were totally refurbished with a drystone rampart incorporating Roman masonry (p. 37). The road through the gateway was repaired, and it seems to have been built in the late fifth or early sixth century – a late sixth-century Anglo-Saxon buckle was found below the upper surface. Within the fort a large timber building or hall (p. 52), stood near a smaller structure which may have been a kitchen.

Since the sixteenth century, this site has been associated in popular tradition with King Arthur, but no direct archaeological evidence has so far confirmed this.

Crickley Hill had Neolithic, Iron Age and later occupation (Dixon, 1988). There was no evidence for re-fortification, but there were two areas of late and post-Roman occupation within it. Inside one palisaded enclosure were rectilinear timber buildings, while a separate area had scooped huts. It has been suggested that the two areas represent social stratification among the residents.

Glastonbury Tor has been variously interpreted as a monastery and a princely stronghold (though it had no fortifications apart from its elevated commanding situation), and was certainly used for industrial activity (Rahtz, 1971).

There is evidence for occupation in the late Roman period at Cannington Hillfort (Rahtz et al., 1992: 225–3), and Ham Hill (Burrow, 1981: 268–77).

A number of hillforts have produced Anglo-Saxon material: Hod Hill, Dorset, Cadbury Congresbury, Badbury Regis, Dolebury, Worlebury, South Cadbury, Ham Hill and Hod Hill. The significance of this is under debate: one suggestion being that it was brought there by Anglo-Saxon mercenaries employed by the British leaders, a situation graphically (and possibly exaggeratedly) described by Gildas (Pearce, 2004: 229).

Dumnonia

Dumnonia roughly corresponded to modern Cornwall and Devon, with the Roman town of Isca (Exeter) on its easterly edge. Bounded by water on three sides, with rivers running north–south, access to it was impeded from the east, but easy by boat from the Continent, Wales and Ireland. The area therefore retained many Iron Age features through the Roman into the post-Roman periods. Although it had good metal resources, it remained more culturally impoverished than the rest of southern England, though there is evidence of growing wealth and social differentiation which may have been attendant on the development of tin mines. Coin hoards in the area represent new-found wealth in the period 250–340 (P. Isaac, 1976: 62), though possibly as bullion rather than currency. The process seems to have continued into the fifth-century period, since silver coin hoards are documented from this period in Cornwall and the Scillies (Archer, 1979: 31).

Ptolemy lists three *poleis* (communities – probably native settlements). In Cornwall, placenames including the element *lys*, are associated with many ancient sites, for example, Leswidden, Lestowder (which also contains the personal name Teudar) and the town name, Liskeard. Lys means 'court' and may relate to administrative divisions of the Roman period (Thomas, 1976: 201–3).

In the Roman period the dominant settlement type was the round, an embanked farmstead with ditch and enclosing round houses (p. 43). In addition, there are a number of undefended coastal settlements.

There are indications of increasing social differentiation among the owners of the rounds by the late first or second centuries AD. This is manifested by the appearance of high-status goods in contrast to the more Romanized areas further east where new houses (villas) were built along Roman lines. Some rounds were rectilinear – a sign of Romanization which is not seen in for example Irish ringforts (Chapter 2). The excavated round at Carvossa produced a range of Roman imports and shows rectilinear planning (Douch and Beard, 1970). Evidence for fifth- or sixth-century occupation has also been found at, for example, Castle Gotha (Saunders and Harris, 1982) and Grambla (Saunders, 1972) which is a rectilinear round with Roman material of the second century.

Kings and high kings in Dumnonia

Traditional tribal leadership seems to have developed in the early medieval period, through a fluctuating hierarchy dominated by overlords who later became kings. The word used by Gildas is *tyranni* (literally, tyrants). These were leaders who built up a client relationship with a group of followers, and wielded regional power (Snyder, 1998: 16). The word does not carry modern connotations of despotism.

Gildas states that Dumnonia was ruled in the early sixth century by the tyrant Constantine.[3] From the same century, the name of Cynfawr (Cunomorus) appears on the 'Tristan Stone' near Castle Dore (Fig. 105). The inscription on this reads DRUSTANUS HIC IACIT CUNOMORI FILIUS ('Here lies Drustanus, son of Cunomorus'). The name Drustanus (i.e., Tristan) is Pictish, though what can be inferred from this is uncertain. A man named Cunomorus also seems to have ruled in Brittany (Snyder, 2003: 166–7).

Fig. 105 Tristan stone.

In the later seventh and early eighth centuries a king called Geraint is recorded in the *Anglo-Saxon Chronicle* as fighting against Ine and Nunna of the West Saxons in 710. These rulers may have been overkings, and there is evidence from memorial stones for rulers described as *principi* and *cumregni* (both, significantly, Latin-derived words), roughly translatable as 'minor kings' and 'co-rulers'.

Excavated settlements in Dumnonia

The wealth of folklore and myth about the period has led to discrepancies between popular belief and archaeological finds and sites. Several (Tintagel, Bantham, Gwithian and Mawgan Porth) have produced a considerable amount of information.

Tintagel was for long erroneously believed to have been an early medieval period monastery, with the ruins of a later medieval castle.

Originally excavated before the Second World War (Radford, 1935), and more recently intensively investigated,[4] it seems to have begun as a Roman-period settlement of indeterminate nature. It became a major centre in the fifth to sixth centuries, the recipient of masses of imported pottery and glass. It may also have been the seat of a major local ruler in Dumnonia.

It occupies a commanding position on a headland which was cut off by a substantial bank and ditch that protected a small stone-built citadel of uncertain date. Within the enclosure over 100 rectilinear buildings (some on artificial platforms) were distributed in a series of zones. The structures are stone-built, lined with slate benches the tops of which have slots for timber posts. An elaborate structure dominated site A – which might have been a residential centre for the leader (p. 327).

Finds from Tintagel include slates with graffiti, including one drawing of a warrior holding a round shield, one of a ship, and one of a stag, though these may all be as late as the twelfth century (Laing, 1996: 134).

One re-used slab bears Latin inscriptions, which include the personal name 'Artognou',which led to identification in the media with 'Arthur', but with little probability. It may be a Roman-style building inscription, and indicates a level of literacy in sixth-century Dumnonia. In addition, a rock-cut footprint may, like that at Dunadd (p. 327) have been for the ordination of kings. Whether the site was continuously occupied, or only seasonally (possibly by a king making his rounds), has been debated.

Bantham, near Thurlestone, has been shown to have had extensive middens with associated hearths and hollows and stake holes (possibly for tents) (A. Fox, 1955; Silvester, 1981; May and Weddell, 2002). The site lies at the end of a promontory with a sheltered harbour, where there are good lines of communication across a series of natural ridges. The finds included imported pottery (one sherd with an inscription), and native gabbro-filled coarse wares, and it has been suggested that it was a trading post at which imported pottery first arrived. This theory was more probable when it was published in the 1950s than today, since very little imported pottery from other sites had then been recognized. Another similar site lies a few miles away to the west, at Mothecombe, on the mouth of the Fine.

Gwithian is a complex of many archaeological sites that had fifth to ninth-century (and later) occupation (Thomas, 1958). The stone-built houses are notable for their level of preservation which has enabled definite plans to be made (p. 51). A notable feature of phase B at Gwithian was an arable field (Site XX) contemporary with it (p. 73) and datable from pottery.

Mawgan Porth (near St Mawgan-in-Pyder), was a village of stone-built rectilinear houses (p. 73) and associated cemetery which flourished between c. 850–c. 1050 (Bruce-Mitford, 1956; 1997). A coin of Aethelred II implies that the vilagers had contacts with the Anglo-Saxons. The finds from Mawgan Porth show that the inhabitants were essentially pastoralists, shell-gatherers and fishermen. A notable feature is the virtual absence of metal: implements were made of stone and bone. The sole evidence for agriculture was a granite quern built into one of the walls. The cemetery consisted of slate cist burials, which displayed the Christian feature of east–west orientation. There was a very large proportion of child burials, which seem to have been grouped together to the west of the main burial area.

Minor royal sites in Dumnonia

In addition to Tintagel, some sites may have been the seats of under-kings. They include include Killibury (Miles, 1977), Chun Castle, Trethurgy and High Peak. The diversity of these alone implies the complexity of lifestyle and society during the period, but also illustrates how, on such a small sample, no generalizations can be made.

Chun Castle is an Iron Age fort on open moorland, which consists of two concentric stone walls. After a period of abandonment in the Roman period it was re-occupied (Thomas, 1956). The inner wall encloses an area almost 55 m in diameter. It is 3.65 m wide, and still stood 4.5 m high in the seventeenth century. The Iron Age entrances consisted of two straight passageways, that were altered (probably at the time of the re-occupation), to give a narrow twisting approach; a feature which implies the need for improved defence. The interior of the fort was divided into compartments in which houses were erected in the sixth century – finds included a grass-marked pot and sherds of Class B Ware (p. 139), as well as a lump of tin ore and a smelting furnace.

Trethurgy was a high-status round (Miles and Miles, 1973; Quinnell, 2005) which measured 55 × 48 m internally, and was bounded by a bank up to 6 m wide at its base, with a single entrance. The ditch was relatively insubstantial. The site was occupied between the third and sixth centuries, and contained four or five frequently rebuilt circular structures with outer walls of stone, and a putative shrine or four-post store. Imported pottery included both A and B Wares and a solitary sherd of E Ware. Of particular note was the discovery of an ingot of tin.

High Peak seems to be entirely the work of the post-Roman/early medieval period (Pollard, 1966). The fort appeared to have some Neolithic pre-fort occupation, followed by a long period of abandonment after which a ditch was dug, which was dated by Class B amphorae to the fifth century.

The Irish in the south-west

There is limited evidence that people of Irish origin settled in the south-west, particularly in Dumnonia. Although the evidence is somewhat tenuous, the arguments are becoming increasingly persuasive (Thomas, 1972b; Thomas, 1973).

Some may have arrived from the settlements of Irish in south Wales, especially near Carmarthen. The evidence is primarily ogham stones (p. 232) which suggest that the migration took place at some point in the fifth century.

Ogham-inscribed stones in the south-west appear almost exclusively in north-east Cornwall and south-west Devon. Among the few outliers are a late fifth- to early sixth-century bilingual stone from St Clement, near Truro, and others from Lewannick, Worthydale, St Endellion and St Kew. A group of stones with Latin inscriptions but Goidelic/Gaelic Celtic names are found in the same area, with only one outlier (from Gulval near Penzance), which is dated to the mid- to late sixth century. The name SAGRANUS was added in the late seventh century to an already standing memorial stone at Fardel, Ivybridge, indicating Irish traditions. A few Cornish stones have personal names which also appear in Welsh inscriptions.

The presence of grass-marked pottery in Cornwall has been explained by a separate migration from Ulster, where souterrain ware displays the same feature (Thomas, 1968a; 1973). However, in the light of more recent study, this is more likely to be a survival from Romano-British potting traditions (p. 88) (Laing and Laing, 1990: 169).

A late ninth-century Irish text, *Cormaic's Glossary*, indicates that the Irish were settled in western Britain and had two fortresses in the lands of the Cornish Britons, *dind map Lethain* and *dun maic Liathan*. These incorporate tribal names found in south Wales, and would further support then idea of secondary colonization from there.

Migrations from Britain to Brittany

There is some evidence that there may have been migrations to Brittany from south-west England and/or south Wales. The Breton language is closely related to Cornish and some placenames, such as Domnonée (from Dumnonia) and Cornuaille (Cornwall), seem to have been borrowed from south-west England (Fleuriot, 1980: ch. 2). There are also a notable number of inscribed stones in Britanny which are related to those found in south-west England.

Settlements of British in Brittany were of a different character from those of the Irish in Britain (Gaillou and Jones, 1991; N. Chadwick, 1969; Snyder, 2003: ch. 7). There may have been three phases: the first (possibly legendary) may have taken place in the time of the Romano-British usurper Magnus Maximus in 383 (Snyder, 2003: 147; J. R. Morris, 1973: 250). The second has been dated to 458–60, and is mentioned in Latin sources, including the writings of the fifth-century Gallic author Sidonius Apollinaris (J. R. Morris, 1973: 251). He refers to the leader as one Riothamus, a figure also mentioned by the Gothic author Jordanes, who calls him leader of 12,000 Bretons who appealed to the Byzantine emperor Anthemius around 470 (Jordanes, *Getica*, 327). The identity of Riothamus is in dispute – one suggestion is that he was a late Roman-style general who left Britain with a military force (Wood, 1987: 261). Gildas implies that there was some reason for forced flight, saying that they 'loudly wailed' and took from Britain those books that were not burnt (Gildas, *De Excidio*, 25.1).

The sixth century apparently saw the most prolonged settlement in Brittany which continued into the seventh (N. Chadwick, 1965; 1969: ch. 6). Traditionally, this migration to Brittany was led by a prince from Gwent in south Wales. The leaders are described as eastern Welsh chieftains, although the majority of the emigrants probably came from Cornwall. The migration was an organized operation, and appears to have met with little resistance. Some of the chiefs held both their estates in Wales and new territory in Brittany, which was partly opened up by the clearance of forest.

Early Christianity in south-west England

It is likely that Christianity spread westwards from the major villa estates in the fourth century and later. A series of cemeteries, most notably at Cannington (Rahtz and Hirst, 2000), and Poundbury (Sparey-Green, 1996), are characterized by the typically Christian east–west orientation of graves and general lack of gravegoods. Burial was in rows in long-cists or wooden-lined pits. Cemeteries of this type extend northwards as far as Wroxeter.

In addition, smaller graveyards are known from, for example, Brean Down, Lamyatt Beacon and Henley Wood. These Christian communities presumably had bishops based on urban sees. Romano-British pagan temples seem to have ceased to be in use after c. AD 400, and several show signs of conversion to Christian use. At Uley, for instance, an enclosed settlement was established, probably with an associated church (Woodward and Leach, 1993), and at Nettleton there was a (probably enclosed) Christian cemetery (Wedlake, 1982). The settlement on Glastonbury Tor may have been monastic. There, small post-built rectilinear buildings were associated with a grave-shaped cairn (possibly a shrine). Associated finds included imported Class B Ware and a small copper-alloy human head, which could have had an ecclesiastical origin (Rahtz, 1970; 1993: 54–60).

At Wareham a group of post-Roman memorial stones has been seen as indicating an élite community in the fifth–sixth centuries, pre-dating the later Saxon burh (town) (Radford, 1975).

Early Christianity in Dumnonia

The most likely starting point for the spread of Christianity to Dumnonia was Exeter, where Roman-period Christianity is attested by a Chi-Rho scratched on a potsherd (A. Fox, 1952: pl. Xa). Chi and Rho, the first two letters of the word Christ in the Greek alphabet, are invariably accepted as definitive proof of Christianity. The town may have been the centre of a late Roman diocese embracing Dumnonia.

The late seventh-century *Life of St Samson*, compiled by a monk in Brittany, describes the saint as crossing over to Cornwall from south Wales, where he went to the monastery at Docco, identifiable as St Kew (Orme, 2000: 257).

In Dumnonia Christian-style long-cist cemeteries are distributed in both Devon and Cornwall, as well as in the Scillies (Okasha, 1993).

Memorial stones

The most prolific and persuasive evidence for the early Church in Dumnonia comprises memorial stones. There are seventy-nine documented, starting within the fifth century, perhaps around 475, and extending to 1100 (Okasha, 1993: 3). Most of the inscriptions are in Latin, but eight are bilinguals in ogham. Of the sixteen stones in Devon, four bear Irish names. Although none is definitely in its original position, many (such as the group at Beacon Hill, Lundy, and that at Lewannick), are in churchyards.

The Cunaide stone bears a fifth-century inscription and was erected over a burial in an abandoned round at Carnsew. Others such as the Tristan stone (p. 240) (on a track from Fowey to Padstow) and the Enarbarrus stone (on a track from the Tavy valley in Dartmoor), were located on roads, while some seem to have been totally isolated, such as the Men Scyfes stone in West Penwith (Todd, 1987: 251–2).

A recent re-appraisal of the stones in the south-west suggests that previous dating schemes have often been too precise. It has been argued that while stones with ogham inscriptions or primitive Irish personal names may date from the fifth to the eighth centuries, those with a Latin name or a Chi-Rho are likely to date to no earlier than the sixth century and can cover a correspondingly wide date bracket (Okasha, 1993: 55–6). It has been suggested that the language of the stones shows no direct link with Roman Britain, and that although there may have been some influence from Gaul, the direct influence of ogham stones and similar stones in Wales is more likely to have operated (Okasha, 1993: 41–2).

A group of four stones from Beacon Hill cemetery on the island of Lundy appear to be in their original setting, though not necessarily their original positions (Thomas, 1985; 1994). The cemetery itself is a polygonal enclosure around a twelfth- or thirteenth-century church. The four stones range in date from the fifth to the seventh centuries. They are associated with a series of cist graves, of which the focus seems to have been a type of shrine (*cella memoria*), comprising a small enclosure, 2.28 m inches from east to west and c. 5.2 m from north to south, formed of upright slabs. Within this enclosure three graves were covered by a low cairn of granite stones.

Church sites

Many medieval parish churches often appear to have been sited over or near earlier cemeteries. However, it is notoriously difficult to prove the date of material in churchyards due to ethical and other issues over intrusive methods of archaeological investigation, so reliance must remain largely with other evidence.

In Cornwall, for instance, the presence of the placename element *lann-* (combined with a personal name, usually that of the saint to whom the church was dedicated), may be an indicator of a pre-eleventh-century cemetery (Padel, 1985; see also Preston-Jones, 1992, for the relationship of these to ecclesiastical sites). Placenames with *eglos-* (from *ecclesia*, a church), combined with personal names, indicate the presence of a church. Cornwall is notable for its variety of specialized chapel sites which include hermitage chapels, of which the most noteworthy is that excavated on St Helens in the Scilly Isles (O'Neill, 1964; Thomas, 1985: 181). The complex comprised a round hut, an oratory, a chapel and three rectangular huts enclosed by a precinct wall. The earliest structure was the round hut, which measured just under 3.65 m in diameter. The roof may have been of beehive form.

The associated oratory, which was of more primitive 'megalithic' appearance, measured 4.5 × 2.43 m and contained an altar with a relic cavity.

The chapel had three phases of construction, of which the first seems to have been built round a founder's grave. In the absence of firm evidence, an eighth-century date has been argued for the complex, but there is some evidence that the site remained in use into the sixteenth century.

Some masonry chapels datable to before c. 1200 have survived, at least in a fragmentary state. The double-square plan was favoured in Cornwall in contrast to the 3:2 ratio for the walls in most of Ireland. Also arguably pre-1200, the chapel at Tean lay on top of a cemetery which post-dated a small homestead with pottery of the fifth to seventh centuries (Thomas, 1985: 187).

Monasteries

There is some evidence throughout the south-west that major monasteries were deliberately sited near hillforts. Cadbury Congresbury is adjacent to a putative monastic site associated with St Congar; Glastonbury Tor (if it is in fact secular: see p. 239) with Glastonbury Abbey; and South Cadbury possibly with Sherborne. Tintagel seems to have been paired with the adjacent church (Pearce, 2004: 243). If so, this would repeat the close association between temporal and ecclesiastical authority found elsewhere in Britain and Ireland.

11 Wales

Although the Romans occupied the whole of Wales, the mountainous terrain meant that overall lifestyle was changed far less than in many parts of England. After the Roman period the area developed into kingdoms, with little apparent outside disturbance. Some Irish settlements probably from the third into the fifth centuries have left scant though credible evidence and Norse raids and limited settlement in the ninth century were of relatively small importance.

The area was closely involved with neighbouring areas until they came under Anglo-Saxon influence: Cumbria for example was connected with Wales until the seventh century. As in Dumnonia (and northern Scotland), Roman influence on the material culture and lifestyles of the general population was minimal. Towns and villas were few and concentrated in the south. While some hillforts were abandoned during the Roman period (though some saw continuing use and a few, such as Tre'er Ceri, saw refurbishment of the defences), non-defensive traditional settlements and everyday objects continued in use.

As in most other areas under Roman control, Roman administration was based on the existing Iron Age tribal structure, which is therefore readily discernible in the kingdoms of the post-Roman period. The increasing pressure from neighbouring (Saxon, eventually English) areas on its western marches, was marked by (still visible) defensive and/or demarcatory earthworks.

Only a few settlements (almost all belonging to the fifth to seventh centuries) have been investigated. It is not known whether this is a true reflection of population pattern; whether sites failed to survive; whether they remain unidentified or simply whether they have been buried under later settlements. The remainder of the archaeological material includes some ecclesiastical sites, a series of later sculptured stones and an outstanding wealth of early Latin epigraphic material, and epigraphic material influenced by Irish inscriptional style, of the fifth to the seventh centuries.

Language

From the third century to the sixth century and beyond, despite the area being part of the Roman Empire, the Brythonic/Brittonic language (p. 10) went through the final stages of its development into primitive Welsh

249

(Ellis Evans, 1990). Part of this process included borrowing from Latin, though as time went on, the borrowings were of a learned nature rather than colloquialisms. This probably shows that Latin gave way to British in everyday use. Latin probably remained the 'upper-class' or possibly the 'educated' language throughout the sixth century with the British Latin pronunciation that had developed in the fifth century. This continued to be the language of the Church. There can be little doubt that the Welsh chieftains and kings of the sixth century maintained some veneer of Romano-British culture.

Wales under the Romans[1]

The Romans advanced into Wales in AD 47, when there were at least six tribal areas; the Cornovii and Dobunni (in the Marches); the Deceangli (in the north-east); the Silures and Demetae (in the south); and the Ordovices (in west central Wales; Fig. 106). Resistance was fierce but short-lived (it was in this period that the British leader Caratacus fled to the Silures). The final stand in Anglesey under druidic leadership was quashed in AD 60 (Arnold and Davies, 2000: 3–5).

Full military control was established by the end of the first century and a series of forts was built. Roman-style settlements included *vici* or *canabae* (civilian settlements outside military installations) which grew up round forts such as Caernarvon, Caerhun, Caer Gai and Cefn Caer. Industrial sites at, for instance, Prestatyn and possibly Tremadoc, towns such as Caerwent and Carmarthen and villas such as those as Ely near Cardiff, Llantwit Major, and in the vale of Glamorgan, appeared.

Romanization was slower than in the south of England, but towards the end of the Roman period in Wales there are archaeological indications of strong pro-Roman lifestyle. The towns in the south showed strong Roman features such as the provision of larger and more sumptuous dwellings – the more élite houses in Caerwent often had a Mediterranean plan based on courtyards. Such adoption of house plans shows a change from an Iron Age style of living to Roman in limited areas.

There is evidence for late Roman Christianity in Caerwent – most notably a pewter bowl with an incised Chi-Rho. It has been suggested that a house (V22.N) served as a church there, raising the possibility of a bishop operating from the town (Boon, 1962; 1992; Knight, 1996b). There is a notable assemblage of late Roman military metalwork from Caerwent, and the additional presence of lead-weighted javelin heads implies a late Roman military unit (Knight, 1996b).

At the end of the fourth century urban life went into decline due to the cessation of communications, administrative structure and trade links.

Fig. 106 Map of tribal areas of Iron Age Wales.

There is some evidence that the towns were still occupied into the seventh century, on a much reduced level (Knight, 1996). In the countryside, villas seem to have been abandoned by the middle of the fourth century (Arnold and Davies, 2000: 87), though there are some indications of later use (Dark, 2000: 115; Edwards and Lane, 1988: 76–8).

Roman troops were withdrawn from Wales during the fourth century – few of the forts in Wales with third-century occupation continued past 330. The exceptions were Caernarvon, Cardiff and Forden Gaer. There is no evidence to prove this was connected with raiding from Ireland but it is generally agreed to be the most likely explanation (Arnold and Davies, 2000: 31), though Caernarvon was probably maintained for tax collection and supervision of the north Welsh mineral resources.

Iron Age style sites in the Roman period

Non-Roman settlements in Roman Wales fall into regional groups, with most evidence coming from the north-west where there was a long tradition of stone-built hut groups (Hogg, 1966). The best examples include those from Hafoty-wern-Las, Din Lligwy and Graeanog (p. 260).

A number of possible explanations have been forwarded; enclosed hut groups could have been the result of deliberate Roman resettlement of a depopulated area, or settlement of an under-populated area, or they could have been a natural evolution under Roman influence, of native Iron Age farms.

Some of the hut group enclosures are polygonal, probably indicating Roman influence.

Early medieval Wales – the fifth and sixth centuries

By the sixth century Wales was divided into a number of small kingdoms, ruled by dynasties rooted in Roman tradition – Gwynedd, Dyfed, Gwent and Glywysing, Builth, Brycheiniog and Powys.

Significantly, some traced their roots to Roman founders. Roman names often appear on Latin memorial stones in the Celtic world (p. 232). The Welsh stones commemorate people called Bona, Nobilis, Paulinus, Martius, Salvianus, Cupetianus, Saturninus, Veracius, Secundus, Turpillius, Justus, Martinus, Eternus, Salvianus, Externalis, Carausius and Paterninus (Nash-Williams, 1950: 8–10). Such a list is a clear indication that Roman values were still held in esteem in Wales into the later fifth and sixth centuries.

Gwynedd

In the Roman period the territory of the Ordovices was controlled from the fort at Segontium, with some administration possibly in the hands of local leaders, whose centres may have included Dinas Emrys and Degannwy (p. 34). The survival of the tribal name can be seen in the use of the personal name Ordous which appears on a stone from Penbryn (Nash-Williams, 1950: no. 126). The name of the Ordovices was replaced by that of Gwynedd by the end of the sixth century at the latest; the latter appears rendered as Venedos on a stone from Penmachno. The change of name may have been attendant on a shift of focus from the mainland to Anglesey in the fifth or early sixth century (Dark, 2000: 178).

A story appears in the ninth-century compilation, *Historia Brittonum* that a northern ruler named Cunedda (p. 298), from the area round the Firth of Forth, migrated to Wales to drive out Irish raiders (*Hist. Britt.* 62). His date is given as 146 years before Maelgwn reigned, which would put it c. 400. The text does not specifically say he migrated to north Wales, but he and some of his sons are also prominent in the north-west Welsh genealogies (L. Alcock, 1971: 125–8).

It has been suggested that this migration was in some way officially encouraged by Roman authorities, in particular, Magnus Maximus (a Romano-British usurper, 383–88; L. Alcock, 1971: 127). This tradition was dismissed by historians in the 1970s as a later fabrication (Dumville, 1977), and unsuccessful attempts have been made to find archaeological support for the legend in recent years (Dark, 1994a: 74–5). Given however the growing support for the

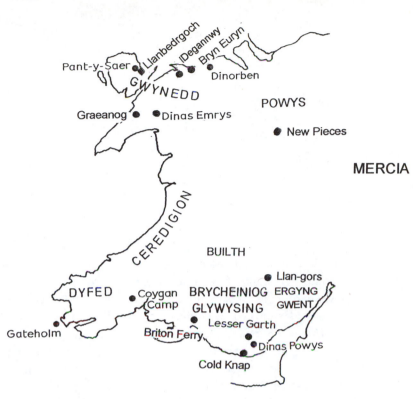

Fig.107 Map of Wales in the early medieval period.

view that Irish settlements were actively encouraged by Roman authorities (below), a similar encouragement for a migration from Scotland seems not impossible.

One of the most prominent kings of Gwynedd was Maelgwn (who, according to the Welsh genealogies, died of the plague around 550 and was vilified by Gildas, who described him as 'the island dragon . . . first in evil': W. Davies, 1982: 92). His capital was claimed in later sources as being Degannwy, though this is not seen as a reliable tradition (Edwards and Lane, 1988: 52).

Dyfed

This kingdom seems to have roughly corresponded with the territory of the Demetae. The Roman focus was Carmarthen, though in the post-Roman period new centres, such as Brawdy or Coygan Camp, are apparent. The tombstone of one king of Dyfed, Vortepor (castigated by Gildas) survives (Fig. 108). An ogham bilingual, it bears the Latin inscription:

MEMORIA VOTEPORIGIS PROTICTORIS
(The memorial of the Protector Vortipor).

Fig.108
Vortepor's stone.

Protector is a technical title, applied to certain categories of officer-cadet in the late Roman army (L. Alcock, 1971: 122). It is probable that this title had become hereditary, from one of his ancestors. The earliest dynastic line describes him as 'Maxen guletic map Protec map Protector', suggesting that Magnus Maximus was regarded as the starting point.

Vortepor's ancestor may have been a hostage at the court of Maximus, following the Roman custom of holding hostage the son of a potential enemy/federate leader. To further underline the Roman military connotations in the dynasty, both Irish and Welsh versions give the name of Vortepor's father as Agricola (a common Roman name but perhaps not fortuitously that of the commander responsible for the Roman conquest of Wales). His grandfather is named as Triphum, which is probably a blundered version of *tribunus*, the commander of a military unit (L. Alcock, 1971: 122–3).

Gwent and Glywysing

These were formed from the tribal territory of the Silures. Gwent took its name from Venta Silurum, the Roman name for Caerwent. Glywysing had as a dynastic name Caradog – the Welsh version of Caratacus. It has been suggested that there was a deliberate effort in the fifth to seventh centuries to glorify the ancestral British in Wales, in a similar way to the antiquarianism found in Ireland in the same period (Koch, 1987).

Brycheiniog

Located in south-central Wales (modern Brecknock) this kingdom had no Roman or Iron Age predecessor: its name comes from an Irish personal one (Brychan) and there are ogham stones from the area (Dark, 1994b: 81–3; 2000: 191).

Builth

This area on the River Wye had a dynasty that claimed descent from Vortigern (p. 237) who was also claimed as the founder of the kingdom of Gwrtheyrnion (the name itself is derived from an archaic form of his name) in central Wales (W. Davies, 1982: 94).

Powys

This area on the Welsh border was focused on the former territory of the Cornovii. Its dynastic origins, however, are confused, though the former Roman town of Wroxeter may have remained an administrative centre (Dark, 1994b: 78–9).

Territory of the former Deceangli

Little is known about the origins of the kingdoms that replaced the old tribal territory of the Deceangli to the east of Gwynedd (Dark, 2000: 181), which included the hillforts at Dinorben (Edwards and Lane, 1988: 65) and Caergwrle (Manley, 1994: 110). At the latter site there is a late-Roman date for the rampart which now encircles the castle. The finds from Dinorben indicate late Roman activity, and there are post-Roman finds including sixth-century Anglo-Saxon metalwork, a Germanic glass bead, and an Irish slotted iron object of the type represented at Lesser Garth Cave (Gardner and Savory, 1964).

The fort at Bryn Euryn, produced no datable evidence in excavation, but is likely to be of early medieval period date.[2] This may have lain in the shadowy kingdom of Rhos, To the south of the territory, the site at New Pieces has produced post-Roman material.

Irish raids and settlements

It is generally accepted that there were raids from Ireland from the later third century onwards, followed by settlements. Evidence is difficult to evaluate, consisting of inconclusive archaeological and written material including ogham stones and placenames (1972b; Thomas, 1973; Fig. 109).

Archaeological evidence for Irish in Wales

Some archaeological features have been seen as indirect evidence of threats from Ireland in the later Roman and early post-Roman period. There is evidence for newly built forts at Cardiff (probably built in the late third

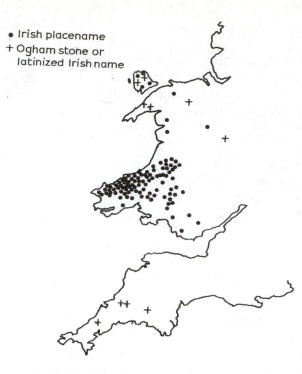

Fig. 109 Map of Irish placenames and ogham stones in Wales.

century); Loughor and Neath (Cardiff: P. Webster, 1990; Loughor and Neath: Arnold and Davies, 2000: 29). Chester was rebuilt. Evidence of late third-century coin hoards may indicate third century 'security alerts', or, conversely reflect internal problems in Roman Wales (Arnold and Davies, 2000: 29).

There are few objects from Wales of definitive Irish type – most are later than the period when historical evidence points to settlement. They have therefore been seen as indications of continuing links between the settlers and their original homelands (Graham-Campbell, 1991a).

While not in itself evidence of Irish settlement, the linear earthwork known as the Clawdd Mawr corroborates the putative boundary of Dyfed in the post-Roman period (Bowen, 1937). This earthwork, similar in some respects to Offa's Dyke and Wat's Dyke (p. 262), consists of a single rampart and ditch running along high ground separating the Teifi and Tywi river valleys. It was probably constructed by the Irish-born inhabitants of Dyfed, as a defence in the eighth century. In this period there was an expansion of Welsh-speaking peoples in the vale of Tywi (Bowen, 1937).

Written evidence for Irish in Wales

The wealth of written evidence for Irish settlement in Wales is persuasive. Ptolemy (in the second century AD) suggested an Irish connection with north

Wales when he called Lleyn the 'Promontory of the Gangani', a tribe which he noted as being in western Ireland (L. Alcock, 1970: 65). There is linguistic evidence to suggest that Irish was a living language in Wales in the fifth and sixth centuries (Ellis Evans, 1999).

A late third-century source (*Panegyric of Constantius*, 11.4) singles out the Irish as a major enemy of the Britons. A late eighth- or ninth-century legend (the 'Expulsion of the Déisi') tells how this group was driven out of Waterford and Tipperary counties. The oldest version states that they settled in the territory of the Demetae, an event also recorded in the *Annals of the Four Masters* for the year 265 (text: Meyer, 1900; dating: Meyer, 1895–6: 58).

The genealogy for the later kings of Dyfed in the account of the Expulsion corresponds closely with that given in Welsh sources. Accordingly it was for long believed that the Expulsion of the Déisi took place c. AD 270, though this date is not accepted by modern historians.

The most recent study of the Irish settlements in Britain has argued that the Déisi were one of several groups of Irish who raided and settled in western Britain from the fourth century onwards. The migrants included the Attacotti (whose name has been seen as a Latin rendering of the Irish *Aithechthúatha*, a term applied to 'rent-giving people') and the Uí Liatháin as well as the Déisi, both of whom were probably regarded as *Aithechthúatha* (Rance, 2001). All have been seen as being tolerated as settlers within Roman Britain, and perhaps officially encouraged as a early instance of the establishment of *foederati* (barbarians employed as Roman federates in buffer areas: Rance, 2001).

A ninth-century Irish document, *Cormaic's Glossary*, refers to the Irish settlements in western Britain – it is a late attempt to explain, either by fact or fiction, the derivation of certain archaic words. It draws on old tradition (Meyer, 1895–6: 59–61).

The *Lives* of Welsh (and less frequently Irish) saints refer to the Irish–Welsh contacts. One *Life of St Carannog* refers to Irish invasions, and another version refers to fighting between Irish and Welsh in Ceredigion (Richards, 1960: 139). In other saints' *Lives* there are references to the rulers of the Irish dynasty in Dyfed, namely Tryffin and Aergol (Richards, 1960: 139). While these references are after the event they describe, they imply traditions about a sixth-century dynasty.

Ogham stones

The most important category of archaeological evidence for the Irish settlements in Wales is memorial stones with ogham inscriptions of which fifty have been noted (Nash-Williams, 1950: 3–8). Ogham stones are most plentiful in southern Ireland, with only five stones being found in the north. Irish settlement in the Lleyn peninsula of north Wales probably came from northern Ireland, which has led to suggestions that ogham was taken up by the descendants of the original settlers, through the influence of the southern Irish who had settled in south Wales.

From the distribution of ogham stones it seems that that the boundary between the Brittonic/Brythonic speaking tribes of north Wales and the Gaelic/Goidelic speaking Irish of south-west Wales lay along a line from the Dee to the Teifi, though the distribution may reflect more the geographical origin of the settlers than an actual linguistic divide. It is possible that inscriptions not in ogham that follow Irish convention in giving a single name arranged vertically, or a name associated with that of the father also vertically, may in fact reflect Irish influence.[3]

Ogham stones are memorials to members of the ruling class. Most of the personal names recorded are Irish (Goidelic), but there are also a few Brittonic/Brythonic. In some cases continual usage of names can be traced in local placenames. A stone from Llartfaelog, Anglesey, bears the name of Cunogusos, which is preserved in the neighbouring placename Pencaernisiog (a corruption of the personal name Conysiog) (Richards, 1960: 145). The *-iog* suffix is territorial and implies that Cunogusos was a ruler in the district.

These stones are often inscribed with explicitly Christian formulae in Latin or Irish ogham, or sometimes both. They are found mostly in the kingdoms of Dyfed and Brycheiniog, where there were ruling Irish dynasties. A few however come from north Wales, where the lineages were British/Welsh.

The ogham inscriptions follow very simple formulae. They usually give the name of the deceased in the genitive, with some introductory word meaning 'the stone' or 'the memorial' understood. In this category falls the stone from Brynkir, Caernarvonshire, with its inscription ICORIGAS, 'The stone of Icorix' (Nash-Williams, 1950: no. 84).

An extension of this formula gives the name of the father of the deceased, usually employing the word *Maqi*, meaning 'son of' with the second name in the genitive. Thus the inscription usually follows the pattern of the example from Nevern, Pembroke, with its inscription reading MAGLICUNAS MAQI CLUTARI, meaning '(the stone) of Maglicu, son of Clutarius' (Nash-Williams, 1950: no. 353). Occasionally instead of *Maqi* are the words *Avi* (grandson or descendant), or *Inigenia* (daughter). A stone from Llangeler, Carmarthen, attempts to render the Latin formula HIC IACET in ogham (Nash-Williams, 1950: no. 160).

Placenames

Irish (Gaelic) was certainly being spoken in south-east Wales until the end of the sixth, and probably into the seventh century (Ellis Evans, 1999).

Placename evidence provides useful corroboration of other sources of information (Richards, 1960: 147).

The name given to Lleyn incorporates the same element as Leinster (one of
the five provinces of Ireland). The district of Gwynedd seems to derive its
name from *Feni*, the name of a group of people who appear to belong to the
Connachta (a ruling dynasty in Ireland, see p. 277).

The root of single names such as Dinllaen and Llyn in Caernarvonshire,
or Mallaen in Carmarthen, was probably derived from the Irish proper
name *Laigain*. Names which describe natural features such as a river,
brook or hill are usually the oldest strata in placenames. Into this category fall names with the Irish suffix -*ach*, which usually appear as river
names, or those incorporating the element -*cnwc* (a hillock), which stems
from the Irish -*cnoc* (Richards, 1960).

The distribution of *cnwc* names is mainly in Pembrokeshire and
Cardiganshire south of the River Ystwyth, extending over to the upper
reaches of the Teifi and Tywi and into Carmarthen, with some outliers. This
distribution corresponds well with the presumed ancient boundaries of the
kingdom of Dyfed.

It is difficult to determine how early these Irish placenames are. Certainly
they do not all date back to the fourth, fifth or sixth centuries, but their
distribution must at least reflect fairly accurately where words borrowed
from the Irish remained current in the sixth and later centuries.

Post-Roman settlement sites

Most of the archaeological evidence for post-Roman Wales comes from a
series of excavations carried out since the mid-1950s on fortified sites that
appear to have been occupied or re-occupied in the late and post-Roman
period. Mostly high-status sites, they are mainly situated on the coast
probably for ease of defence and communications and have been dated to
between the late fifth and seventh centuries.

Hillforts

Dinas Powys   is undoubtedly the most impressive site occupied in post-Roman
Wales (L. Alcock, 1963; 1987a: 3; Edwards and Lane, 1988: 59–61; Laing and
Laing, 1990a: 54–6; Campbell, 1989; Graham-Campbell, 1991a; Dark, 1994a:
67–9). The hilltop was first occupied in the early Iron Age. In the later fifth or
sixth centuries AD the northern end of the hill was defended by insubstantial
earthworks. Two buildings may have been constructed within this area – their
plans were reconstructed from drainage gullies. They consisted of a hall with
bowed-out sides and a smaller building, which appears to have been preceded

by an unfinished timber structure (p. 52). The two were set at angles to one another, forming a courtyard in which a number of hearths were used for a variety of activities, including metalworking.

There was no dating evidence for the buildings themselves. Dating was inferred from associated finds outside, mainly from middens, which produced pottery and glass and, among other scrap metal, a fragment from an Anglo-Saxon bucket. Bronze working seems to have been quite extensive. The site was presumably the stronghold of a local chieftain.

Also noteworthy for producing evidence of occupation in the post-Roman period are Dinas Emrys (Savory, 1960; Edwards and Lane, 1988: 55–7; Laing and Laing, 1990a: 57), Degannwy Castle (L. Alcock, 1967; Edwards and Lane, 1988: 51–3), Dinorben (Gardner and Savory, 1964; Guilbert, 1979; 1980; Edwards and Lane, 1988: 66), Brawdy (Dark, 2000: 185), Drim Camp (Edwards and Lane, 1988: 68–9), and Coygan Camp (G. Wainwright, 1967: 158–60).

Enclosed hut groups

The strongest evidence for continued post-Roman occupation of hut groups comes from Graeanog and Cefn Graeanog 2 in Gwynedd (R. Kelly, 1990; 1998), and Cefn Cwmwd on Anglesey (Dark, 2000: 173). Radiocarbon dating suggests that a hut group at Ty Mawr, on Holyhead Mountain, Anglesey, also saw post-Roman occupation (C. Smith, 1987), and evidence for continuing occupation is accumulating from further recent investigations.

At Pant-y-Saer, Anglesey, an enclosed hut group with pre-Roman and Roman Iron Age occupation was extended by two further rectangular annexes built against the wall of the eastern hut. A brooch (of Class H, see p. 157) was recovered from the floor of one (Phillips, 1934; Edwards and Lane, 1988: 99–101). Finds at Porth Dafarch, Anglesey, included a Class E/F penannular brooch (Kilbride-Jones, 1980: no. 14, where seen as Irish), riveted Roman pottery, and evidence of use of the site for a dug-grave and long-cist cemetery (Dark, 2000: 173).

Open settlements

A number of open settlements have been identified in Wales. They include Longbury Bank (Campbell and Lane, 1993), where occupation extended probably from the fifth to the seventh or eighth centuries and Hen Gastell (Briton Ferry) (Wilkinson, 1995).

Gateholm Island is an enigmatic site. It was once attached to the mainland, and rectangular huts have been noticed both on the mainland and the island itself

(Edwards and Lane, 1988: 73–5). The complex consists of about 130 huts, mostly arranged in rows, end-on around small courtyards. Occupation began in the third century, as evinced by a coin of Carausius and by Roman pottery, and almost certainly continued into the early medieval period, since the finds from the cobbling of the main building investigated included Roman Oxford colour-coated ware, a ringed pin, shale bracelet and whetstone.

Historical outline, seventh–twelfth centuries

During the seventh century there was considerable activity on the eastern frontier of Wales (W. Davies, 1982: 92–4). In the early part of the century the kingdom of Gwynedd seems to have been of considerable importance, and was ruled over by Cadfan, whose memorial stone has been found at Llangadwaladr in Anglesey (Nash-Williams, 1950: no. 13). For a period there were alliances with the Anglo-Saxon border kingdom of Mercia, which by the mid-seventh century had extended its influence to the Upper Severn.

Towards the end of the eighth century, Wales became increasingly opened to external stimuli, including from the Carolingian court. The king, Rhodri Mawr, expanded Gwynedd until it embraced a large part of Wales (W. Davies, 1982: 105–6). Under him there was something of a cultural revival. The oral traditions both of the northern British and of the Welsh were probably set down in writing at his court. There is some circumstantial evidence for the occupation of Degannwy in the eighth century and later, notably references in the Welsh Annals which include the note that in 822 it was besieged and destroyed by Saxons.

He successfully kept the Vikings at bay, killing the Danish leader Horm off Anglesey in 876. Conflict with the Anglo-Saxons however became a major problem, and by the middle of the ninth century the king of Mercia is described as reducing Wales with the help of the king of Wessex. The extent of the Anglo-Saxon conquest of Wales is probably exaggerated in the documentary sources, but there can be no doubt that the conflict was serious. By the time of Rhodri's death, marriage alliances had united all Wales except Dyfed and the south-east under the control of Gwynedd. Following Rhodri's death, a sharp division grew up between those who were violently opposed to union with England (the supporters of this cause being mainly in the north), and those who favoured it (mainly the south, who had allied with the Saxons against Rhodri).

Hywel Dda, Rhodri's grandson, annexed south-west Wales and pacified resistance in Dyfed by marrying the local ruler's daughter (W. Davies, 1982: 106). From 942 he was virtually sole ruler of Wales, and pursued a strong pro-English policy. Coins were struck in his name at Chester in the last years of his reign, though only one coin has survived, which implies a very limited output probably struck by the Anglo-Saxons as a diplomatic gift to him. After Hywel's death in 949 or 950, much of Wales was increasingly pro-English. In the north, however, anti-English feelings lingered on, and flared up throughout the middle ages.

Frontier works in Wales

The frontier between Wales and Mercia was peaceful until the early eighth century, when in 705 and 709 there were Welsh raids on Mercia. The outcome may have been the Mercian construction of the linear earthwork known as **Wat's Dyke** which extended from the southern extremity of the Dee estuary near Basingwerk to just south of the River Morda in Shropshire, a distance of 62.12 km (Fox, 1934). It has been surmised that it was built by King Aethelbald (716–57), and was intended not simply as a boundary line but as a declaration of Mercian conquest, but there is no certain dating evidence for it.[4] Because it follows so closely Offa's Dyke it is likely to be of the same general period (Hill and Worthington, 2003: 163).

Northern Powys suffered repeated Mercian attacks in the later seventh century. This period of Mercian offensive culminated with **Offa's Dyke**, built probably between 784 and 796 and which extended from Treuddyn in Clwyd to Rushock Hill on the Severn estuary, a distance of 103 km (C. Fox, 1955; reappraisal, Hill and Worthington, 2003: esp. ch. 4). It served as a boundary between Mercia and its Welsh neighbours, not as a military frontier.

Sites of the eighth century and later

These include the Anglo-Saxon burh at Rhuddlan, which was founded by Edward the Elder in 921, and apart from late Saxon pottery, has produced bone motif pieces with zoomorphic decoration and evidence for weaving and antler working. Structures were timber-built in Anglo-Saxon style (Quinnell et al., 1994). It has been suggested from documentary sources that certain sites should be seen as royal centres of the later period, notably Cwrt Llechryd, Aberffraw, Degannwy and Mathrafal. Mathrafal has been shown to be entirely of later medieval date, and there is no evidence from Degannwy for occupation at this period. Cwrt Llechryd was a rectilinear moated site dated to the period AD 700–1100 but without diagnostic finds (Musson and Spurgeon, 1988), and the enclosure at Aberffraw is problematic in terms of date and function (Dark, 1994: 35–8).

Llan-Gors crannog is the only example of this type of settlement from early medieval period Wales (Redknap et al., 1989; Campbell and Lane, 1990). It was built in the late ninth or early tenth century as the residence of

Elisedd ap Teuwr, the king of Brycheiniog, and was constructed with a ring of vertical planks (some from oaks felled in the summer of 893) retaining a platform of sandstone, brushwood and timber, which was periodically extended. Finds included textiles, leatherwork, metalworking remains, and a mount from what may have been a shrine of Irish character.

Other sites with evidence for occupation in this period include Cold Knap (E. Evans et al., 1985; Edwards and Lane, 1988: 35–8), where one room in a Roman building saw occupation and a rectangular building with rounded corners was put up in the courtyard. Radiocarbon dating for this phase indicated use between the eighth and eleventh centuries.

At Graeanog the latest phase was an enclosed settlement with associated corn-drying kiln. Dates indicate occupation in the tenth and eleventh centuries (R. Kelly, 1990). The remains from Llanbedrgoch, Anglesey, also belong mostly to the tenth or eleventh centuries. Occupation started perhaps around AD 600 with an enclosure ditch containing a mixture of round and rectangular houses and halls (Redknap, 2000: 69–71). In the ninth century this was refortified with a drystone wall c. 2.2 m wide, possibly in the face of the Viking threat. It was continuously occupied into the Viking period (p. 269).

Christianity in Wales

Christianity was established in south-east Wales within the Roman period. The main evidence for Christianity in post-Roman Wales is an abundance of memorial stones and later ecclesiastical sculpture.[5] A number of important monastic foundations are known from historical sources, but there are few ecclesiastical sites with visible remains before c. AD 1200. Some dubious information is provided by placenames and church dedications. More cemeteries of the period have been identified (and some excavated) in Wales than in any other area covered by this book (pp. 226–7).

Christianity in late Roman Wales

Gildas refers to the martyrdom of Julius and Aaron at Caerleon (Thomas, 1981b: 48), and there is evidence for a Christian community on the Welsh border at the Roman town of Wroxeter continuing into the post-Roman period. A fourth-century lead tablet from Bath seems to be a letter from a cleric at Wroxeter. Excavations on the forum site in 1860 and 1923–7 produced evidence of a post-Roman Christian cemetery, and certainly the town continued in occupation into the fifth century (White and Barker, 1998: ch. 7 and p. 125).

A Latinized memorial stone with an Old Irish inscription CUNORIX MACUS MAQUICOLIN was ploughed up on the site, probably dating to the sixth century (Wright and Jackson, 1968). Significantly, the nearby Church of St Andrew has masonry belonging to the earliest phase of Anglo-Saxon church architecture, demonstrating continuous belief (Taylor and Taylor, 1965: 694).

Christianity in post-Roman Wales

It can be assumed that Christianity survived in south-east Wales at least into the fifth century. There, links with Christian communities in Gaul and later with the Irish Christians in south-west Wales were established. The first to be converted are likely to have been the kings and nobility. By the late fifth or early sixth century it appears that a diocesan system was in operation in Wales (Pryce, 1992: 48–61), a fact which is corroborated by two stones from Aberdaron which refer to Veracius and Senacus, who are each described as a *presbyter* (Nash-Williams, 1950: nos. 77–8). Stones from Bodafon and Llantrisant commemorate *sacerdotes* (priests) (Nash-Williams, 1950: nos. 83 and 33). It should probably however not be seen as a disocesan organization on the Continental model, and the presbyter Senacus from Aberdaron is described on his memorial as being buried '*cum multitudinem fratrum*' ('with a multitude of his brethren'), perhaps implying a monastic foundation.

As elsewhere in the Celtic world, however, from the later sixth century organization was through newly established monasteries. The main churches were probably monastic, and administered large *paruchiae*, presided over by a bishop, within which daughter houses, churches and cemeteries developed (Edwards, 1996: 5).

The evidence includes memorial stones, monasteries and church dedications.

Memorial stones

Memorial stones are of major importance for the study of the Church in Wales (Nash-Williams, 1950; N. Edwards, 2001). In the classic study (Nash-Williams, 1950), the Welsh stones have been grouped into Group 1 (stones with Latin inscriptions), Group 2 (stones with only incised crosses), and Group 3 (relief sculptures, Chapter 8).

Group 1 stones

Apart from a few early stones which may represent the continuing tradition of Roman gravestones, the majority of memorial stones reflect the general situation during the fifth and sixth centuries when similar monuments expanded from the Mediterranean through Gaul and western Europe. The formulae (such as *hic iacit* and *filius*) are mostly of the type found in Gaul (in certain cases, Italy).

The inscriptions on one group suggest direct influence from Gaul. A stone of the late sixth century from Llantrisant, Anglesey, may commemorate a Gaulish immigrant (Nash-Williams, 1950: no. 33), though the stone displays some Iberian features. A stone from Penmachno bears an inscription indicating that it was set up 'in the time of the consul Justinus'. The same name appears in a restricted area round Lyons, and the inscription provides both a date for the stone (540) and evidence for direct contact with the Lyons area (Nash-Williams, 1950: no. 104).

Some Group 1 stones (notably at Pentrefoelas) have been found in association with long-cist burials (a Roman-style grave lined with stone slabs: p. 226), though here (and elsewhere) it was re-used as a slab in a cist. In other instances two or more stones have been found together, which may imply the existence of an early medieval period site. Isolated stones are misleading, since often they are not on their original sites. In most of north Wales, where the evidence is clearest, the distribution of sites with two or more Group 1 stones notably coincides with the distribution of enclosed hut groups, though in Anglesey the memorial stones have been found in the inland forest areas, away from the coastal settlements.

HIC IACIT stones

The distribution of two types of inscription – those with HIC IACIT ('here lies') and those with FILIUS ('son') is important. The HIC IACIT inscription seems to originate in and is found in the Roman provinces of Gallia Belgica and Germania as well as around Vienne – elsewhere in Gaul the common formula is HIC REQUIESCET ('here rests'). They were probably added to the already present tradition of ogham memorial stones, in the mid- to late fifth century (Knight, 1992: 50; 1996a).

The HIC IACIT inscriptions have concentrations in north-west Wales and south-west Wales, which implies that the areas were strongly influenced by Gaulish Christianity. They have been seen as essentially commemorative, and to be tombstones, though none has actually been found associated with a grave. Some may have been boundary markers or indicators of land ownership: the use of the genitive may mean 'the land of' as much as 'the body of', a usage which, it has been suggested, may have come to Wales with the Irish settlers (Handley, 1998: 340; N. Edwards, 2001: 18). Some seem to be associated with prehistoric burial sites, which may have been a deliberate attempt to show a link with the past (N. Edwards, 2001: 23). A few stones seem to have been sited on the line of Roman roads or adjacent to Roman forts. This may be a deliberate echo of the Roman custom of siting burials along roads.

FILIUS

The inscriptions with FILIUS, normally in the form A FILIUS B (A son of B) belong to a different tradition (Thomas, 1971: 110–12). This is a direct translation of the ogham A MAQQI B, and is very rare in Gaul, there being one example at Vienne and another commemorating a member of the royal house of Burgundy. It was frowned on as it seemed to disobey Matthew 23:9, 'Call no man your father upon the earth'. The distribution of stones with FILIUS is concentrated in south-west Wales, and may be the result of the Irish settlements. Irish influence too must be seen behind inscriptions in vertical lines (again following ogham, which could not readily be inscribed horizontally), the use of the genitive '(the stone) of X' being understood, and bilingual ogham–Latin stones.

The dating for the Group 1 memorial stones

A broad date span can be confirmed through comparison with comparable Gaulish monuments which can be closely dated. The classic study attempted to provide a detailed chronology based on the gradual transition from Roman to half-uncial lettering (Nash-Williams, 1950: 11–14). While this transition is largely valid, and can be paralleled in Gaul, the character of the epigraphy of any one stone cannot be used to provide a firm date for it, since there are too few firmly dated inscriptions from Wales. Furthermore it is highly probable that the transition did not proceed everywhere in Wales at the same rate, and archaism in lettering was probably fairly widespread.

Group 2 stones

These stones belong to a general class designated as 'primary cross-marked stones', despite the fact that none has been found associated with a burial (Thomas, 1971: 124–6). Some may also have served other purposes, such as symbols of holy ground (as cemetery markers), markers of land given to the Church, and boundary markers of Church land (Edwards, 2001: 32). In Wales they are concentrated in the north.

The classic study gave a chronological span to them from the seventh to the ninth centuries, which, in spite of efforts to establish a fixed sequence, must remain fluid at the present state of knowledge (Nash-Williams, 1950: 17–20). The use of an incised cross was in use on the Continent prior to the seventh century. Some at least probably date from the sixth century: a cross on the 'Catamanus' stone can be paralleled with one on a Gaulish memorial stone of 503 (Nash-Williams, 1950: no. 13). At the other end of the chronological scale such cross slabs were probably being erected in Scotland well into the middle ages, and there is no reason to suppose that they did not recur later in Wales as well.

Monasteries

The introduction of monasticism in the sixth century from the Continent almost certainly had considerable impact on the Welsh Church (W. Davies, 1982: 141–8). The Welsh saints' *Lives* (notably that of St Samson), taken with the other evidence, point to the growth of monasticism being a fairly prolonged process, though many of the great Welsh monasteries appear to have been founded during the sixth century. The foundations at Bangor, Penmon and Clynnog Fawr seem to have survived the Viking period, whilst those at Bardsey (Enlli), Ynys Seiriol and Beddgelert survived into the twelfth century.

Monastic remains

Almost nothing survives of the major monasteries in Wales. The antiquary William Camden recorded ruins at Bangor-is-y-Coed in the sixteenth century. At Bangor Fawr, modern Bangor, some inconclusive remains were uncovered during building operations for the university (White, 1972; H. Hughes, 1925).

The monastery at Clynnog Fawr may have started in association with a founder's tomb (that of St Beuno) since a structure was found in excavation beneath the floor of an ancillary chapel, on a different axis from the medieval church (Stallybrass, 1914). Long-cist burials were encountered which may have been grouped round the founder's tomb.

Beneath a twelfth-century church at Burry Holms, four corner-post-holes of a timber church were found to be on a slightly different alignment (Hague, 1966). The structure had been standing when the stone church was built – the posts were deliberately removed for its construction. This timber chapel was probably the work of Caradog (d. 1124), and therefore should be assigned to the end of the eleventh century or beginning of the twelfth.

Church dedications and placenames

The interpretation of church dedications has often been stretched beyond the limits of reasonable inference. An attempt was made on the basis of saints' *Lives*, to demonstrate that the areas in which particular saints operated, coincided with the pattern of dedications to them (Bowen, 1954; N. Chadwick, 1961). However, no Welsh dedication is attested before the Norman period, and so at best the distribution is that of medieval dedications. Second, in the fifth and sixth centuries church dedications appear to have been mainly to St

Peter and St Paul, followed by other major Biblical saints and later by ascetics, notably St Martin of Tours.

By far the greatest number of dedications to local saints can be shown to be the result of later (especially twelfth-century) interest in earlier cults. However, the many dedications to St Bueno and St Tysilo have distinct and separate distributions in north Wales, which might point to an earlier origin.

Placenames are more informative, but have to be used with caution (Roberts, 1992). The parish of Basaleg (Gwent) seems to be derived from the Latin word *basilica*, and is deemed to be an early borrowing. Placenames employing the element *merthyr* are derived from Latin *martyrium*, meaning the shrine of a martyr, and probably relate to early burial sites round a special grave. Many placenames that at first sight appear to be early borrowings from Latin are not necessarily so.

The Vikings in Wales[6]

Wales appears to have first been attacked in 852, when the Vikings killed Cyngen of Powys. From 855 Anglesey became a target for attack, and there was a succession of raids intermittently until 919. Rhodri Mawr actively and successfully campaigned against the Norse in the years up to 878, and his successors maintained the resistance in the latter part of the century.

The first phase of Viking activity is attested by two hoards, one from Llanbedrgoch, the other from Minchin Hole, both deposited c. 950. A further five were deposited in the tenth century, and four in the eleventh (Redknap, 2000: 105). According to Asser, in his *Life of Alfred the Great*, a Viking army wintered in Dyfed in 878, where they were slaughtered.

In 893 a Danish army advanced from Mercia up the Severn, and were defeated by the combined forces of English and Welsh at Buttington, near Welshpool. A nineteenth-century find of bones and about 400 skulls in three pits may represent the battle victims (Redknap, 2000: 35). The Danes then retreated to East Anglia.

A group of Norse led by Ingamund were driven out of Ireland and arrived in Anglesey in 903. They were successfully repulsed, and subsequently unsuccessfully laid siege to Chester between 903 and 911. They were allowed to settle near Chester by Aethelflaeda, probably in the north Wirral, where there is a concentration of Norse placenames (Wainwright, 1975: 157). In Chester there is some evidence for a Viking community outside the walls of the Roman fortress. A Viking hoard was deposited around 965 on what is now the Castle Esplanade, and there is a church dedicated to Norse St Olave as well as a major collection of Anglo-Scandinavian sculptures in St John's Church (Bu'lock, 1972).

The 'second Viking age' in Wales followed the death of Hywel Dda, and was heralded by a succession of attacks concomitant with the expulsion of Eric Bloodaxe from York in 964. The raids were focused on the Welsh Lowlands, and were carried out by raiders from Ireland, Man or the Hebrides. In 987 south Wales came under attack from an army which was subsequently bought off in 1002.

A third phase of raiding took place in the eleventh century. The Norse presence in the Severn estuary increased, and Glamorgan was raided by Eilaf (1018–24). During the eleventh century there was an alliance between the kings of Gwynedd and the Norse rulers of Dublin and the Isle of Man: there may even have been a measure of Norse rule in north Wales in the early eleventh century.

Archaeological evidence for Vikings in Wales

Most of the archaeological evidence for Viking activity in Wales comes from Anglesey where the only settlement with Viking-period occupation is known at Llanbedrgoch. Stray finds include the pommels of Viking-period swords from Llan-faes, Anglesey, and from near Milford Haven. There is a spear and battle-axe from Caerwent, and stirrups from St Mary Hill, all of which may have come from Viking burials (Redknap, 2000: 50, 53–4). Of particular note is a sword guard decorated with Urnes style ornament from Smalls, a reef off the western island of Grassholm in the Irish Sea. It is believed to have come from a wreck (Redknap, 2000: 55, 58–9).

The key site for Viking period occupation is Llanbedrgoch on Anglesey, where within the enclosure there were in the tenth century at least three buildings, each constructed with a stone base supporting a timber superstructure (Redknap, 2000: 5–8). Building 1, dated to c. 890–970, was c.11 m long and consisted of a single room with a sunken floor and raised benches round a central hearth. The southern half of the building was flagged, with a stone-lined drain, but there was no evidence that this was used for livestock. Building 2 was similar, 12 m long and dated to c. 855–1000. It is not clear whether these buildings were native, but showing influence from Viking building traditions, or regional versions of Scandinavian houses.

The copious finds from the Viking-period occupation at Llanbedrgoch include Chester Ware imported from Mercia, an enamelled stud of a type associated with harness in Viking burials in Ireland and the Isle of Man, a piece of a Viking tortoise brooch, a strap end of a type found on Viking period sites with Borre-style ornament, and a series of Viking weights. Antler was worked, and there was evidence for smithing. One possible explanation for the site was that it was for a time a trading base under Viking control, similar

Fig.110 Roman silver ingots from the Balline hoard.

to that which existed at Meols in Wirral which is known from stray finds washed up on the beach in the nineteenth century (Bu'lock, 1960b).

There are probable burials at Bellech, Anglesey (Edwards, 1985b), and Talacre (F. Smith, 1931–2). A small coastal promontory fort at Castell, Porth Trefadoch on Anglesey, may have been connected with the ties between the rulers of Dublin and north Wales in the eleventh to twelfth centuries (Longley, 1991).

12 Ireland and the Isle of Man

The Romans never added Ireland or the Isle of Man to their conquests, so both areas fared quite differently from Britain and were able to develop relatively independently until the arrival of the Vikings and later the Normans. A wealth of documentary sources from the seventh century AD onwards sheds light on Ireland's history, social structure, laws and customs (pp. 12–13). Due to climatic and geographical factors, much archaeological evidence survives, though only a minute fraction has been investigated of what may belong to the early medieval period. Settlement types are discussed in Chapter 2.

During especially the past twenty years however, new finds and approaches to the subject have led to a rethink on whether the area was as inward-looking and oblivious of outside events and contacts as previously thought.

Ireland

The Iron Age background

Unlike almost all the rest of Europe, Ireland was little mentioned in written sources, during the expansion of Rome into Gaul and Britannia. There is a general scarcity of diagnostic types of sites or finds that can be used to establish a framework for study. There is virtually no pottery, few graves and few classes of site which are distinctively Iron Age (B. Raftery, 1984: 335). Some sites may be of any date from Iron Age to medieval. Until the development of modern scientific methods of data retrieval, this situation was more than usually open to theorizing.

Considerable debate has taken place during the past 150 years, over (1) the Iron Age antecedents of the early medieval Celts in Britain and particularly Ireland; and (2) their relations with the Roman world. In particular, virtually all research and discussion revolved around the theory that Ireland nurtured the purest form of Celtic society from the early Iron Age onwards, culminating in a blossoming of Irish art and learning in the 'Golden Age'. The archaeological arguments for long surviving Celtic culture in Ireland depended on: (1) an equation of an Irish 'Celtic' culture with the Iron Age culture on the Continent named La Tène; (2) this culture being disseminated not merely by trade but by immigrants to Ireland; and (3) there being no Roman influence on Ireland until the adoption of Christianity. New research methods and data bases have, over the past twenty years, changed the overall view almost unrecognizably. None of these three factors can be seen as a constant, and the complexity of the arguments is too great to be discussed in this book.[1]

Despite the lack of evidence for intrusive Celtic settlers in Ireland in the early Iron Age, there is now considerable evidence for a flourishing Iron Age culture in Ireland associated with major ritual centres flourishing from the third to the first century BC (B. Raftery, 1994: chs. 4–5). From the point of view of early medieval society, the most significant sites are a group of ceremonial centres which passed into early medieval mythology.[2] The society mirrored in these archaeological remains has been seen as reflected in later literary tradition. In particular, the ritual centres figure in the collections of stories known as the Ulster Cycle, preserved in later medieval texts, of which the *Táin Bó Cúailnge* (*The Cattle Raid of Cooley*) is the most famous. But the 'archaeology' of the *Táin* is spurious as it was a purely literary construct. It nonetheless must have drawn upon some distant memory of these major Iron Age centres, which we now know were abandoned by the first century AD (Mallory, 1982; McCone, 1990).

This flourishing culture, however, came to an around the first century BC, and the ensuing first five, some might say six, centuries AD, has been termed a 'Dark Age' in Ireland, for which the evidence is particularly tantalizing. There are almost no sites that can be ascribed with any confidence to the period before AD 350. What can be said however is that c. AD 600 there was the proliferation of settlements, both raths and crannogs, and considerable attendant changes in settlement, economy and beliefs. The economic decline which characterized the period up to AD 350 appears to have been dramatically reversed. How did this come about?

One factor may have been the changes that were taking place in farming. The pollen sequences, for instance, show that farming increased from the later third century: at Red Bog this seems to have been happening in the third century (Mitchell, 1976: 159). Elsewhere in Limerick, Tipperary, Meath, Antrim and Tyrone the recovery seems to have taken place c. AD 300 (Mitchell, 1976: 160). This has been accounted for by the possible arrival of the coulter plough from Roman Britain (Mitchell, 1976: 166).

Around AD 600 the weed of cultivation *artemisia* appears for the first time in the pollen record. It too has been matched with the introduction of another new type of plough from Britain, along with perhaps ridge-and-furrow cultivation (Mitchell, 1976: 166).

A strong argument has been advanced that prior to the fourth century dairying was not practised to any extent in Ireland, but that its introduction led to a marked increase in food production (McCormick, 1983; 1995).

Contacts with Roman Britain

There has been considerable interest in the evidence for Roman relations with Ireland, since it came to public attention that Roman material dating from the first and second centuries AD had been found by metal detectorists in a promontory fort at Drumanagh (B. Raftery, 1996; Di Martino, 2003; Warner, 1994a). There has even been some revival of the possibility of an 'invasion' from Roman Britain that was dimly reflected in later literature, and may be alluded to in a satire by Juvenal of the early second century AD which asserted that 'we have extended our arms beyond the shores of Ireland' (Warner, 1994b: 114).

It has been argued that later myths reflect a real event in the first century AD, when an Irish leader (Tuathal Techtmar) went to Roman Britain and subsequently returned, making his base at Tara. Some commentators have seen him as perhaps the exiled Irish chief who met Agricola (Tacitus, *Agricola*, 24; Warner, 1995). Certainly the Greek geographer Ptolemy mapped Ireland, and included in his list of tribes the names of Brigantes and Manapii, names which appear in Britain and Gaul (B. Raftery, 1994: 206; Warner, 1994b: 114).

In the fourth century Roman Britain was an exceptionally rich province, with much wealth being focused on the villa-estates of the south-west near the Bristol Channel region – one of the main points of potential contact with Ireland. It is probable that trading took place, possibly controlled by Romano-Britons in the earlier part of the period. By the mid-fourth century it seems clear that the Irish Sea was largely under the control of Irish rulers (Charles-Edwards, 2000: 157).

By extension, Irish fortunes are likely to have benefited from Roman pay-offs to raiders which are attested in Wales and Scotland (pp. 256 and 294). The archaeological manifestations of such a situation may include the hoards of silver plate and ingots from Balline, Ballinrees and Coleraine (Ó Ríordáin, 1947: 43–53, 77–8; B. Raftery, 1994: 214–6; Fig. 110). Such an increase in wealth and growing awareness of the Roman world may well have led to the growth of new power structures, in much the same way that new political configurations are apparent from the fourth century in northern Europe beyond the Roman frontiers (Hedeager, 1988; Randsborg, 1991).

It may even be possible to discern in Ireland a similar change in society to that which is apparent amongst contemporaneous peoples on the fringes of the Roman Empire. Tribal structure in Germany beyond the Rhine frontier in the time of Tacitus (first century AD) and that of Ammianus Marcellinus (fourth century) were very different. Similarly, the Irish world reflected in Ptolemy's geography is very different from that of the early Irish historical sources.

It has been suggested that the main channel of Roman influence on Ireland came through the Irish colonies in Britain (Mytum, 1992: chs. 2 and 8), though this seems unlikely, as the settlements seem in the main to be later than the beginnings of 'Romanization' in Ireland.

Roman material in Ireland

The material on which the above change in thinking is based, is persuasively wide and substantial. A list of Roman material from Ireland was compiled in the 1940s. It can now be extended, and it is increasingly apparent that it cannot simply be confined to the period of the Irish raids (Ó Ríordáin, 1947; Bateson, 1973; 1976).

Much of the evidence for Roman contact takes the form of metalwork and pottery and it is now clear that Roman objects were brought into Ireland from the first century AD and assimilated by the Irish who developed their own variants of at least some. There was clearly much activity across the Irish Sea, with at least one trading base in the vicinity of Dublin Bay, and with influences spreading inland into the Irish midlands and Munster.

A boat found at Cummerstown on Lough Lene appears to be of a type found in the Mediterranean, and has been dated to AD 180–540 by radiocarbon (Brindley and Lanting, 1990; Ó Heaildhe, 1992). It was a plank-built vessel, and as these did not become a feature of Irish seamanship until the Viking Age, it may well have been used by Roman merchants.

At Freestone Hill, for example, the finds of undoubted Roman origin include a coin of AD 337–40 (B. Raftery, 1969: 62). Roman pottery and other finds including a seal were discovered at the Rath of the Synods at Tara (B. Raftery, 1994: 212) and Roman brooches have been found in the ritual site at Knockaulin and at Cashel (Warner, 1994b: 114). At Rathgall a tag copying a Roman military uniform brooch was found, and another Irish version of a Roman harness mount was found at Feltrim Hill (J. Raftery, 1970). An oculist's stamp for marking eye ointment (a type of object associated with high-status Roman patrons) was discovered at Golden where it may have been associated with a healing well (B. Raftery, 1994: 218).

Finds of Roman material from ritual sites may be significant. Discoveries from the prehistoric tomb at Newgrange, for example, show that it had clearly been visited in the fourth century by Roman pilgrims (Carson and O'Kelly, 1977); they included an already ancient Bronze Age gold torc fragment with an added Roman inscription, and a group of late Roman gold solidi and ornaments, which seem to have been votive offerings. A cremation burial in a glass urn with associated objects suggests a Roman burial at Nore,

Stonyford, around the second century AD (E. Bourke, 1989), and a cemetery of inhumations with Roman coins excavated at Bray may have been of immigrants from Roman Britain.

A site on Lambay Island, Dublin, produced a series of graves with Roman and Romano-British objects of the late first century AD, possibly from Brigantia (Yorkshire) (B. Raftery, 1984: 282). The imports include an iron mirror and four bronze brooches. A fifth brooch was a native copy in which the pin and catch plate were cast as one.

Roman influence on Ireland

Roman fashion (reflected in types of dress-fastener), the ogham alphabet and the use of patronyms in ogham inscriptions, loan words borrowed from Latin and the introduction of inhumation burial and Christianity took place before the beginning of the fifth century (Warner, 1994a). The series of Irish brooches shows very clearly the extent of influence on artists and artisans from Roman Britain. The Navan series of brooches appears to have been developed in Ireland in the first century AD and the features of divided bow, openwork pattern and bulbous snout-like foot are derived partly from the Roman divided-bow brooches and openwork mounts (Jope, 1962). The evidence is supported by some of the metalwork from the Somerset (Galway) find, which included thin bronze discs with cut openwork, which may be derived from Roman enamelled disc brooches, or, less certainly, late pre-Roman Iron Age enamelled roundels (B. Raftery, 1984: 244).

Ogham inscriptions

The ogham inscriptions in Ireland enjoy a distribution that coincides with the areas where Iron Age hillforts were most common. The stones on which the inscriptions appear are memorials to the dead (in this reflecting Roman tradition), but were sometimes also boundary markers (Charles-Edwards, 2000: 173). The earliest ogham inscriptions probably date from the fourth if not the third century AD, and thus cannot be ascribed to some post-patrician introduction of Roman literacy.

Loan words

Latin loan words were first borrowed from pagan Roman Britain, and borrowings from Britain continued increasingly with the spread of Christianity in the fifth and sixth centuries (McManus, 1984; Charles-Edwards, 2000: 184). Loan words from pagan Roman Britain include words such as *legion* (*legio*), *trebun* (*tribunus*), *long* (*navis longa*), *Mercuir* (*dies Mercurii*) and *Saturn* (*dies Saturni*).

The last two in particular seem difficult to explain in a Christian context (Carney, 1971: 70).

Inhumation rites

As far as can be established, burial rites in Iron Age Ireland involved crema-tion, and continued to be made intermittently into the early medieval period. Inhumation seems to have been introduced from Britain in the first century AD. It is attested at Lambay, as well as at Bray where extended inhumations in dug graves with a stone at the head and the foot, were accompanied by early second-century coins 'in the chest cavity' (O'Brien, 1992: 132; 1999: 27).

Everyday objects of Roman derivation

Most significant of all, in implying assimilation of Roman attitudes and taste, are the many everyday objects on Irish early medieval period sites that are of Roman derivation. In essence, by the fifth or sixth centuries AD Ireland displayed a Roman-influenced material culture (Laing, 1988).

Lagore crannog, for example, has produced a list of Roman-derived finds that are typical of a pattern repeated on other sites. On present evidence Lagore was first occupied c. AD 600, though it is possible that occupation may have begun in the sixth century.

A series of tools at Lagore were derived from the Roman: axes, adzes, draw knives, forks, socketted pronged tools and certain features of swords. Toilet articles are Roman in inspiration, as are many of the pin types and possibly the bronze bowls. A number of objects – barrel padlocks and keys, rings with sliding knots, twisted-iron bucket handles with a flat grip in the middle, and some bead types – are of Roman origin, but found fairly widely in post-Roman Europe as well.

Some types of spear at Lagore are of purely Roman derivation. Many of these 'Roman' elements probably do belong to the period of activity between Britain and Ireland in the late and post-Roman period; for example dress-fasteners of various types, bronze bowls and possibly, but by no means certainly, weapons.

The early medieval period

Historical outline[3]

Irish history may be said to begin with the arrival in Ireland of the Romano-Briton Patrick (later St Patrick). He was abducted from Britain by raiders as a slave (traditionally c. 396–459, but probably later in the fifth century). He

Fig. 111 Map of secular sites in Ireland in the early medieval period.

was converted to Christianity and later returned to spread the faith in the north of Ireland.

Belonging to the period before this, however, is a considerable body of myth and quasi-history, set down by the monks in later centuries.

Ireland was traditionally divided into four provinces: Ulster in the north, Connaught in the west, with Munster and Leinster to the south (Fig. 111). According to legend preserved in the *Lebor Gabhála*, the four later became five provinces, with the formation of Meath which had originally been part of Leinster. In the period of the legends the beginning of the struggle between Leinster and central Ireland can be discerned; in the fourth century the largely mythical Cormac mac Airt, who ruled at Tara, supposedly exacted a tribute from Leinster.

With the fifth century came the rise of the largely legendary Niall (Noigiallach) of the Nine Hostages (Byrne, 1973: ch. 5), who ruled from Tara. He is credited with raiding in the Western Isles of Scotland, and traditionally gained virtual control over Ireland. Under him and his sons Ireland allegedly was split in two; his sons conquered Meath.

Northern Ireland was ruled over by Niall's family (the Uí Neill), while southern Ireland was dominated by the ruling family of Munster. It is from this time that the development of Tara as the seat of the north and Cashel of the south can be recognized. Eventually Tara became pre-eminent. There were two branches of the Uí Neill, the eldest sons became the southern Uí Neill and were based on Tara, while the younger sons comprised the northern Uí Neill (which remained unified until the eighth century). However, the history is largely mythological, the construction of later Uí Neill propagandists.

The north was the best-represented area of Ireland in the period preceding the Viking raids. The main source for its history is the *Annals of Ulster*. The history of southern Ireland is less well documented until the time of the Vikings and the rise of Brian Boru. There were some disputes between Munster and Leinster, but Munster tended to be oriented towards the Continent and was culturally more progressive. For the history of the south, the *Annals of Innisfallen* is one of the most useful sources.

Contacts with the Anglo-Saxons

Despite its proximity to England, there is comparatively little evidence for Anglo-Saxon influence in Ireland, except in art and ecclesiastical affairs. Documentary sources indicate there were Anglo-Saxons present in Ireland from at least as early as the sixth century, and there is plenty of evidence for ecclesiastical links, including the presence of Anglo-Saxons in Irish monasteries in the seventh and eighth centuries (O'Brien, 1993; 1999: 179–86). The impact of Anglo-Saxon art on Irish art should not be under-estimated.

Very few objects of Anglo-Saxon origin can be identified in Ireland, but there is a limited amount of evidence for settlement from a group of burials displaying Anglo-Saxon characteristics. At Betaghstown a female crouched burial (dated by radiocarbon to the fourth to seventh centuries) contained a pair of Anglo-Saxon penannular brooches, worn Anglo-Saxon fashion at the shoulder, among other artifacts. There is also evidence for Anglo-Saxon burial customs at a number of other sites in the Brega region and near monasteries where higher status Anglo-Saxon incomers are attested in literary sources. Burials seem to belong for the most part to the sixth to seventh centuries (O'Brien, 1993).

Early medieval settlements

Around AD 600 settlements proliferated, both raths and crannogs, and there were considerable attendant changes in settlement, economy and beliefs (Fig. 111).

Fig. 112
Cahercommaun.

As was seen under settlements (Chapter 2), many sites have been imperfectly investigated (if at all), leaving room for much argument about chronology. A major difficulty is that, given the lack of diagnostic or securely datable material and the overwhelming numbers of sites, it is excessively difficult to recognize an early medieval site in the first place.

Much interest was created in the 1970s and 1980s when it was argued that some key sites in Ireland had been wrongly dated, and were Iron Age rather than early medieval. The starting point for this chronological review was a re-appraisal of the stone fort at Cahercommaun, which had been dated at the time of its excavation to the ninth century (original dating: Hencken, 1938: 2; re-appraisal: B. Raftery, 1972: 51–3; Fig. 112). The revised dating was disputed in the first edition of this book, and a case set out for seeing Cahercommaun as more or less correctly dated by the excavator.[4]

Other sites that were subject to chronological re-appraisal included Carraíg Aille, dated by the excavator to the eighth or ninth centuries (Ó Ríordáin, 1949), but later argued as mostly of the Iron Age. Raheenamadra and Cush were considered in the same study (Caulfield, 1981: 207, 209), but although some activity on the sites might go back to the fourth century, the main occupation phases on these sites is fairly clearly post-400 (Laing and Laing, 1990: 50–1). Radiocarbon and recent dendrochronological dating for a number of Irish early medieval sites has shown very clearly that the vast majority of ringforts and crannogs are early medieval, not Iron Age (Lynn, 1983), and the following seem now reasonable dating brackets for some key Irish sites (which are also discussed in Chapter 2):

Garranes   c. 500 (or earlier) – 600+ (Ó Ríordáin, 1942; re-appraisal in Laing and Laing, 1990: 53–4)
Garryduff 1   c. 650 (O'Kelly, 1962)
Ballinderry 2   c. 600–750+ (Hencken, 1942; re-appraisal O'Sullivan, 1998: 111)
Lagore   c. 600 or possibly slightly earlier – 1000 (Hencken, 1942; re-appraisal Warner, 1986; O'Sullivan, 1998: 111)
Moynagh Lough   c. 625–750 (Bradley, 1991)
Carraíg Aille 1   c. 500 (or earlier) – 950 (Ó Ríordáin, 1949; re-appraisal Caulfield, 1981: 208–9; Laing and Laing, 1990: 50–1)
Carraíg Aille 2   c. 450 (or earlier) – 1000 (or later) (sources as for Carraíg Aille 1, above)
Ballinderry 1[5]   c. 900–1100 (with a possible pre-crannog occupation)

Key sites

A few key sites (outlined below) have played an important role in understanding early medieval Ireland.

Ulster

The dominant settlement type in Ulster was the rath, platform raths representing a fairly localized type. There are a number of major crannogs, and souterrains are commoner in this province than elsewhere in the country. Key sites include:

Deer Park Farms   At this platform rath, five contemporary wicker houses, datable to c. AD 700 were identified (Lynn, 1989; 1994). The wickerwork of the walls was preserved through waterlogging. All the houses were double-walled, ranging from 4 to 7 m in diameter, made almost entirely of hazel. Grass was used for 'cavity wall insulation'. They were constructed with basket weaving technique. The walls were at least 2.5 m high. Finds included a complete door frame, dendro dated to AD 648. A total of thirty houses were recognized in the upper levels, though poorly preserved. The site produced evidence for wooden vessels, textiles, ironwork, glass beads and copper alloy objects, along with such things as fish fins, woadpods and puff balls.

Lough Faughan   This crannog is now in a reed swamp, but once stood in open water (A. Collins, 1955). The crannog was c. 35.05 m in diameter, and consisted of layers of brushwood and peat. On the natural marsh deposits of peat, and 4.27 m thick, the upper surface of the crannog was covered by woven wicker matting; but there was no evidence for a house, though several hearths were found. It seems to have been occupied in the period between the seventh and the tenth centuries with an additional later occupation.

Other raths and cashels that have provided extensive information about settlements in Ulster include Rathmullan (Lynn, 1982), Gransha (Lynn, 1985), Lissue (Bersu, 1947), Boho (V. Proudfoot, 1953), Ballyfounder (Waterman, 1958), The White Fort, Drumaroad (Waterman, 1956), and Dressogagh (A. Collins, 1966).

Leinster and Meath

Several major crannogs are found in this area.

Lagore   This site is exceptional in that it was a royal residence, and without doubt is the richest early medieval period site so far excavated (Hencken, 1950; Warner, 1986). Its occupation started c. 600, and its destruction is recorded in 934. On a foundation of animal bones the artificial island was built up to a height of almost 3 m. Pieces sliced off the backs of skulls attested a massacre during the construction. There were three circles of palisades made of piles, posts and planks, which represent three periods of occupation. The last two were refortifications and large numbers of piles found outside the crannog may have served as *chevaux de frise*. No information about the structures that stood on the island was available due to extensive disturbance.

Ballinderry 1   There are two crannogs in the same lough (lake), known as Ballinderry 1 and 2 (below). Ballinderry 1 was built in a swampy shallow in the tenth century, when a large round wooden building was constructed occupying almost the whole area of the island (Hencken, 1936; Johnson, 1999) where a Viking construction was suggested. The floor of this house was roughly horseshoe-shaped, measuring 17 m in diameter at its greatest extent. Around AD 1000 a second house was built over the first, which was in turn replaced by a third, post-1200. The site was occupied intermittently into the nineteenth century. Prior to excavation it appeared as a hillock 1.37 m high, 30.48 m long and 18.29 m wide. The platform was surrounded by a palisade of piles inside which was a partial palisade of planks. An entrance through the pile palisade was later abandoned – the plank palisade continued across it. A raft in the centre of the island had held a hearth and the main support of the building.

Ballinderry 2   This began as a late Bronze Age settlement of wicker huts and a larger structure (Hencken, 1942). The site was swamped by a rise in lake level and not reoccupied until the early medieval period when the crannog was built as an extension of a natural island. Occupation of the crannog extended from the sixth to the eighth centuries.

Moynagh Lough   This site was first used in the Mesolithic and Bronze Age, when it was a fishing or fowling platform. Subsequently an early medieval crannog was built, which has produced evidence for industrial activity (Bradley, 1991; 1993). In Phase 10 (AD 720–c. 748), there was a round house, two metalworking areas, an entrance path and a group of cess pits. Associated with this phase was crude coil-built pottery, crucible sherds, moulds and motif pieces as well as numerous moulds, some with interlace decoration. In the eighth century there were two round houses and a furnace, with a palisade around the crannog. The palisade was gapped, indicating a post-and-panel construction. The large house was 11.2 m externally in diameter, the smaller had a diameter of 5.2 m. Associated were crucibles, heating trays, a mould, tuyères, ironwork and a pseudo-penannular brooch. The houses employed double walling (as at Deer Park Farms, above). The site is important for being a crannog largely devoted to metalworking, with activity dated by dendrochronology.

Coolure Demesne, Lough Derravarragh[6]   This recently investigated site seems to have been founded at the beginning of the fifth century, and would appear to have been been a royal centre associated with an adjacent rath. The main occupation extended from the seventh to the eleventh centuries, with increased use in the ninth to tenth centuries, and some later medieval use. The finds included a hanging-bowl hook, enamelled handpin, Viking hack-silver, a series of ringed and stick pins, and eighth–ninth-century drinking horn terminal. Iron leg shackles similar to that found at Lagore might support the idea that prisoners were kept here.

Connaught

Although there is quite a high density of ringforts in south-east Connaught, including a number of multi-ramparted examples (Stout, 1997: 81–2), relatively few sites of the period of any type have been excavated in the region. The most notable sites are Ardcloon (Rynne, 1956) and Letterkeen, a rath with evidence of cereal processing (Ó Ríordain and MacDermott, 1952). Of the crannogs, that at Rathtinaun, Lough Gara, has produced notable finds but remains still unpublished.

Munster

Munster is noteworthy for a series of stone-walled forts, most of which are probably of Iron Age construction. There are also a considerable number of ringforts, and a few open settlements.

Cahercommaun (p. 279)   The fort consisted of three limestone walls without ditches, the two outer enclosures being used as cattle kraals. A few huts in the outer enclosure probably belonged to herdsmen (Hencken, 1938). Only the inner wall was defensive, and within it were a dozen small irregularly built structures, including a guard house, a sentry post and a major dwelling with two souterrains. There was some evidence for two phases of occupation but without a substantial break.

Garryduff   The site comprises two ringforts (O'Kelly, 1962b). At Garryduff 1 two flimsy houses of timber were excavated. Elsewhere in the fort were other hearths, paved areas and a pit. The entrance passage was gravelled and it had a timber gateway. Garryduff 2 had no habitation and may have been a farmyard. It had an unusual gateway with a palisade set into the walling.

Lough Gur – Carraíg Aille   The two forts at Lough Gur known as Carraíg Aille 1 and Carraíg Aille 2 are particularly informative (Ó Ríordáin, 1949). At Carraíg Aille 1 the houses were stone-built and associated with areas of paving, but the walling was badly preserved. Most of the structures seem to have butted on to the rampart. Nearby was a group of rectilinear stone-walled structures which produced no dating evidence but were interpreted as animal shelters contemporaneous with the rath. At Carraíg Aille 2 the earliest phase of occupation was associated with stone-built huts with curvilinear plans. In the second phase the structures appear to have been rectilinear. Evidence points to continuing occupation after the abandonment of the fort, as some of the adjoining house sites were butted onto the fort wall and one was built over it. In character these rough rectilinear structures with yard walls were similar to those inside the fort. At both Carraíg Aille 1 and 2 the fort walls were provided with substantial gateways and steps in the ramparts.

Among other sites in the region, Lisleagh has two adjacent ringforts, which are currently being excavated to study the relationship between the settlements and their wider context in the area (Monk, 1988). Other important sites include Beal Boru (O'Kelly, 1962a), Dunbeg (Barry, 1981) and Beginish (O'Kelly, 1956).

The introduction of Christianity to Ireland

Archaeological and historical sources shed little light on the development of the Church in Ireland in the fifth century. By the sixth century it was organized on diocesan lines, each bishop having authority over his own *paruchia*, which at this period can be translated as 'diocese' but which was based on the tribe.

The wealth of memorial stones available from Wales and Cornwall does not exist in fifth- or early sixth-century Ireland. A series of ogham inscriptions give early formulae of the type 'of A of the son of B', the genitive being used for all three words. There are more than thirty ogham stones in Ireland, concentrated in the south-west, in counties Kerry, Cork and Waterford, with outliers in Kilkenny, Carlow, Wicklow and Kildare (N. Edwards, 1990: 103).

The range of bilingual inscriptions in Latin and ogham found in Britain are absent from Ireland. The ogham stones may not be necessarily Christian, though a few seem to commemorate clerics, and over 34% are associated with ecclesiastical sites.

Additionally, there are many stones with inscriptions in the Irish alphabet, of which the collection from Clonmacnoise is notable (p. 193). The extent of influence of the Continental Church at this early period can only be surmised. A series of stones displaying Chi-Rhos have been seen as demonstrating a spread of influence from Gaul in the sixth century (Hamlin, 1972), though the early dating of these has been disputed. A Chi-Rho inscribed stone from Ardmoneel has been seen as representing a combination of Merovingian and local motifs in the seventh century (Sheehan, 1994). Other early indicators of external influences include a cross with pendant alpha and omega at Loher, and representations of the flabellum or liturgical fan, notably at Reask (Fanning, 1981: 139–41). There is ample evidence for Continental influence later, however. Certainly, the trade which brought it to western Britain, as shown by imported pottery, affected Ireland.

The Church in early Ireland

The early diocesan organization (*paruchia*) of the Irish Church under bishops was gradually replaced by one in which the main element was the monastic *familia* (the 'family') of the founding saint under an abbot (*comarba*). Frequently the abbacy passed within families, father to son, and the abbots could be laymen or monks in minor orders. The bishops ceased to have an administrative function. In the early Irish monasteries there was no adherence to a rule comparable with that of the later medieval monasteries – each monastery followed the rule of its founder (Fig. 113).

By the end of the sixth century a number of major *paruchiae* were established. Armagh claimed pre-eminence because it was founded by St Patrick. Clonard, founded by Finian, was established by the early sixth century, and during that century monasteries grew up at Clonmacnoise (founder Ciaran), Clonfert (Brendan), Bangor (Comgall), Ferns (Maedoc) and Aran (Enda). Columba's foundation at Iona had daughter houses at Durrow and Kells (Swan, 1994: 137). Visible remains are often of a very much later date than the foundation period.

Fig. 113 Map of ecclesiastical sites in Ireland.

Ecclesiastical sites

It has been estimated that there are at least 2,000 early ecclesiastical sites in Ireland (Swan, 1994: 139). The distribution of monasteries in Ireland is most dense in the central plain. They are often near rivers and seldom above the 120 m contour. This is generally in contrast to the distribution of secular settlement, which is on higher ground (Stout, 2000: 99). It has been suggested that political factors involving the rivalry between groups dictated location. Studies centred on Co. Offaly suggested that churches were patronized by rival kings and were involved in disputes over territory (Fitzpatrick, 1998; Fitzpatrick and O'Brien, 1998). Churches in general seem to have been located on territorial boundaries (where royal centres were also found), perhaps preserving in some instances the continuity of pagan religious sites (N. Edwards, 1990: 105).

Aerial photography has identified the layouts of a number of early monasteries – the concentric planning of modern streets reflect the monastic layout at such sites as Duleek, Armagh, Lusk, Clondalkin and Kells (Swan, 1983;

1985; 1994). At Armagh rescue excavation revealed a huge ditch which was used subsequently to dump debris from a metalworkshop which presumably belonged to the monastery and was datable to the fifth to ninth centuries (Gaskell-Brown and Harper, 1984). In the countryside aerial photography has been used to define the original enclosures at Monasterboice, Durrow and Clonmacnoise, Ardpatrick and Glendalough.

Comparatively few monasteries have been archaeologically investigated. Apart from the early work at Nendrum (Lawlor, 1925), and the extensive work at Clonmacnoise (p. 215), the most extensively investigated sites are on islands, such as High Island (also known as Ardoileán: Herity, 1990; White Marshall and Rourke, 2000a), Tullylish (Ivens, 1987), Lackenavorna (Manning, 1984), Millockstown (Manning, 1986), Inishmurray (Wakeman, 1893), Illaunloughan (White Marshall and Walsh; 1994; 2005) and Skellig Michael (De Paor, 1955; Horn et al., 1990).

Recent survey suggests that Skellig Michael (which is situated on a craggy rock stack) was in use from the sixth to the eighth centuries. A hermitage was constructed at the highest point of the rock, probably in the ninth century.

A classic example of a smaller, probably monastic site that has undergone investigation, is Reask (Fanning, 1981). Others include Church Island (O'Kelly, 1958), Killylane (Williams and Yates, 1984) and Rathlin O'Birne Island (Walsh, 1983). The site of Kilpatrick was first identified through aerial photography, but subsequent excavation showed it to have had a flourishing workshop producing ornamental metalwork (Swan, 1976; 1995).

Ecclesiastical architecture in Ireland has been discussed elsewhere (pp. 216–21).

The Vikings in Ireland

The Vikings are first documented as raiding Lambay, off the coast near modern Dublin, in 795. The Viking impact began with plundering raids which lasted until the 830s.[7] Monasteries were particular targets due to the amount of treasure amassed by the church which was easily taken from the non-combative clerics. In the 830s several monasteries were subject to repeated attacks, including among them Armagh.

From the 830s to c. 845 plundering increased, with fleets of more than 100 ships sailing up the main rivers and homing in on rich monasteries such as Clonmacnoise and Armagh. In 840–1 the Norse wintered in Ireland and established fortifications at Dublin and Annagassan. Between 873 and 912 was the 'forty-year peace', when there were fewer raids and Irish counter-attacks on Viking settlements met with varying degrees of success.

The Vikings made military and marriage alliances with the Irish and established small independent kingdoms in Ireland. In 902 they were driven out of Dublin. They took advantage of an internal power-struggle between the Eóganacht rulers and the dynasties of Leinster and Uí Neill, and returned in 912, when they established Dublin as the key centre of Viking activity in Ireland. Other towns also grew up, notably at Waterford, Limerick, Wexford and Cork.

Political factors led to the Viking towns with their associated kingdoms coming under the control of Irish kings, and at Tara the Viking king Olav was defeated by Maél Sechnaill II, king of Meath in 980, with the result that the Vikings paid tribute to Irish kings. From this period until the arrival of the Normans, the Vikings seem to have been peacefully integrated into Irish society.

Archaeological evidence for the Vikings in Ireland

The archaeological evidence for the Viking presence in Ireland is varied. It includes burials, most notably from the cemeteries at Kilmainham and Islandbridge in Dublin (O'Brien, 1998; Harrison, 2001); hoards of silverwork (Sheehan, 1998); stray finds; and the major settlements at Dublin, Waterford and Wexford (Wallace, 2002a). As yet settlement at Cork is known only historically.

Interaction between the Irish and the Vikings

The long-established view has been that the Vikings brought about great changes in Ireland, acting as a catalyst in transforming native institutions (Binchy, 1962b: 131). This view is disputed by those who see both Irish and Viking society as undergoing change during the period of Viking raids and settlements, and the Viking impact more as a catalyst working on a society that was already changing (Doherty, 1998; 2000; 2001). With the establishment of Viking towns, new wealth through trade with a wider network reached Ireland. Irish kings grew prosperous through the acquisition of silver through selling slaves to the Vikings. Under this view, society became more militaristic, and major kingships became more powerful. Warfare changed, with new types of sword and the use of the battle-axe both being significant (E. Rynne, 1966; Walsh, 1996). The independent farmers became rent-paying peasants, and there are signs that they increasingly abandoned the ringforts (which could be seen as their declaration of status) for undefended, open settlements.

The general scarcity of burials, and the relative dearth of Scandinavian loan words and placenames in Irish, suggest that there was no major population influx of Vikings, and comparatively little verbal communication between the two peoples (Fellows-Jensen, 2001).

Materially, however, the Norse impact was significant. Apart from the revitalization of art (in particular with the development of the Irish version of the Norse Ringerike and subsequently Urnes styles (ÓFloinn, 2001a), new types of dress-fastener can be identified. In particular, new types of ringed pin, silver penannular brooches and armlets of jet and lignite were part of a hybrid Celto-Scandinavian cultural milieu (Larsen and Hansen, 2001). Coinage was issued, modelled on Anglo-Saxon proto-types (W. O'Sullivan, 1961).

The Isle of Man

There are insufficient excavated sites to provide a framework for adequate study of the Iron Age background to later settlement in the Isle of Man. The island was virtually aceramic for most of the Iron Age, which lasted through the Roman period and into the early medieval period without break. Hillforts in Man are relatively rare, partly due to the terrain. The two classic sites are South Barrule, which radiocarbon has suggested was occupied around the sixth century BC, and Cronk Sumark, which may be entirely of early medieval period date (Gelling, 1978). There was no Roman occupation of the island, and evidence for contact with Britannia is scant (Kinvig, 1975: 32).

The remaining Iron Age sites in Man fall into two general categories: promontory forts and a type of monument usually called after their excavator 'Bersu hut sites'. Three 'Bersu hut sites' were excavated; two at Ballacaggan and a third a mile away at Ballanorris (Bersu, 1941–6).

Much of the evidence for the Irish settlements in the Isle of Man has been obliterated by centuries of Norse cultural overlay. It would appear, however, that the first recognized dynasty of kings in Man had Brythonic names such as Tudwal (*Toutovalos). Manx, however, is a Goidelic/Gaelic Celtic language and from placenames and personal names it seems that Man changed its language from Brythonic/Brittonic as a result of the Irish settlements. By the sixth century it is quite clear that the Irish language was being estab-lished in Man.

There are five ogham stones from Man, one a bilingual with Latin inscrip-tion which notes that *Ammecati filius Rocatt hic iacit*. The later names Imchadh and Rochadh occur as Irish names, but the form they take in the Latin inscription shows signs of being British, and suggests both languages were being spoken by people in contact with each other (Jackson, 1953: 173).

Man was not thickly populated at the time of the Irish settlements, and could readily absorb immigrants. A connection between Man and south-west Scotland, where there also appears to have been some Irish settlement, is suggested by the Brythonic tradition of early rulers associated with both, and on Man there are a number of dedications to Ninian (Trinian in the Manx form).

The only secular sites ascribable to the early medieval period in Man are the complex site at Ronaldsway and Kiondroghad.

Ronaldsway Now largely destroyed by an extension to the runway at the airport, this site stands amid crop marks of many periods (Megaw, 1938–40; Neely, 1940; Laing and Laing, 1990b; Higgins, 1999). Late Bronze Age and some indeterminate Iron Age activity preceded the early medieval period occupation, which continued through to the Viking Age and later. An Irish community, or one which enjoyed strong contacts with Ireland, occupied the site from the sixth or seventh century, if not earlier. Some of the finds were characteristically Irish (such as an Irish penannular brooch and a ring brooch), and the others were types which would not be out of place in an Irish context. The indications are that the site was ecclesiastical in its later pre-Viking stages, perhaps preceded by a secular settlement with circular stone huts, associated with industrial activity including metalworking (attested by a crucible) and the manufacture of lignite armlets. Notable finds were a balance beam and a small mount modelled on a Frankish or possibly Anglo-Saxon S-brooch.

The later activity involved the use of the site as a cemetery, and the construction of two probable *lechta*, each containing a body and associated with quartz pebbles. Use of the site continued in the Viking period, when at a higher level areas of paving (and more huts?) were associated with later burials.

Kiondroghad The settlement here was secular (Gelling, 1969). A rectilinear hut was associated with metalworking: the finds included motif pieces, ingot moulds and an enamelled bronze roundel. An Irish connection was suggested by the excavator, on account of the possibility that one of the finds was possibly the head of a latchet brooch, but that identification seems very unlikely.

Manx ecclesiastical remains

There are more ecclesiastical remains than secular.

There are some sixty-five pre-Norse stones from Man, twenty-five of which have come from Maughold, which may have been an Irish monastic foundation of the seventh century. The earliest stone from there (of the late seventh century) is Irneit's Cross. It bears a marigold surrounded by an inscription above a Chi-Rho and similar plain cross on each side of an inscription beneath. Another stone, datable to the early ninth century, notes that Branhui 'led off water to this place', while a third has the (Anglo-Saxon) name Blakman, in Anglo-Saxon runes (Kinvig, 1975: 48).

The monumental stone known as the Crux Guriat found near Maughold commemorates Gwriad, who may have been the Welsh prince mentioned in documentary sources as having retreated to Man before 825.

Keeills are a familiar feature of the Manx landscape. About 170 are known, of which about 35 still exist. They were small rectilinear chapels, ranging in size from 8.86 sq m to 33.58 sq m, though most are around 16–19 sq m. They were surveyed first in the early twentieth century. Dating is problematic since some (for example, Lag ny Keeilly) may be as late as the thirteenth or fourteenth century.

Their location relates to treens (land divisions, which preceded the later parishes) which implies that keeills are generally pre-twelfth century in origin. No dating evidence was forthcoming from Keeill Vael, Druidale, when it was excavated in 1979–80, though it was clear that the enclosure wall pre-dated the construction of the keeill (C. Morris, 1983).

At Peel activity on the island extended from 650 to 950. A long-cist cemetery with a keeill was dated to the tenth century and was subsequently destroyed in the eleventh (Freke, 2002).

Long-cist cemeteries and lintel graves are widespread on Man. At Ballaquayle the lintel graves were associated with markers, and the possible post-holes of a timber chapel.

The Vikings in Man

Viking settlement on Man began c. AD 900. A site at the Vowlan, north of Ramsey, may have been a wintering base used in the earliest stage of the raids and settlement (Bersu, 1949). The Norse incomers seem to have settled particularly intensely in the north of the island, where the greatest concentration of burial mounds, Norse placenames, and tenth to eleventh-century Norse cross slabs are found (Cubbon, 1983: 13). Placename evidence suggests that the settlers were predominantly Norwegian in origin and are likely to have been colonists from Scotland, of mixed Gaelic-Norse origins (Fellows-Jensen, 1983: 45). The Viking presence is attested by burials, including the ship burials at Knock-y-Doonee and Balladoole (Kermode, 1930; Bersu and Wilson, 1966). Other evidence includes burials at Ballateare and Peel, hoards of silverwork (notably that from Douglas); and a number of stray finds, including of swords.

The first settlers were probably male, and took Manx wives. Most female names on the Manx runic inscriptions are Goidelic rather than Norse (Cubbon, 1983: 19). With the exception of the rich female burial at Peel and the sacrificed woman found accompanying a man at Ballateare, there are no pagan female burials on Man.

There is some evidence that the settlement pattern remained undisturbed, a fact reflected in the survival of Gaelic placenames (Fellows-Jensen, 1983: 42–3).

The most noteworthy finds of the Viking period are sculptured slabs, often with scenes from Norse mythology and sometimes with Viking runic inscriptions.

13 Southern Scotland and northern England

It took the Romans some thirty years after AD 43 to consolidate their position in Wales and most of what is now England and to push northwards into Scotland. Aerial photographic evidence of marching camps shows the extent of their reconnaisance sorties. However, they were unable to subdue or keep control over the Highlands. They defined the northern frontier of Britannia both symbolically and physically by building two successive barriers – Hadrian's Wall and the Antonine Wall – between the estuaries of the rivers Solway and Tyne, and Clyde and Forth respectively (Maxwell, 1989; D. Breeze, 1996). The local Lowland tribes between these two frontier works and immediately south of Hadrian's Wall acted as 'buffers' between the Romans and the more hostile tribes north of the Antonine Wall (Chapter 14).

By analogy with other frontier areas for which there is copious and reliable written evidence, Roman influence would have been a mixture of material inducements and the bestowing of local power to tribal allies as well as the constant threat of military action.The evidence supports such a situation, since the area has produced an array of Roman finds but no villas or towns, evidence of uprisings and destruction, yet also of the widespread use of Latin.

As a result, there are many unanswered questions about the social and political milieu of the period.

One probable reason why the frontiers were so inadequate was that they followed logic to run between geographical features, so that tribal territories would have been bisected. This would clearly have been an unacceptable situation not only for tribal stability but also because Roman troops along the Walls would have been 'sandwiched' between potential enemies. Tribes would have gained new political viewpoints dependent upon their reaction to the close presence of Roman power. Differing inter-tribal relationships would have resulted in the formation of new power bases, from which the post-Roman kingdoms grew.

The Roman period

Before and during the Roman period very little was written about Scotland, except in passing. The Romans and tribes in Scotland were aware of each other even as early as the conquest under the emperor Claudius, when the Orkneys sent diplomatic emmisaries.

Fig. 114 Map of tribal areas of Iron Age Scotland.

The *Geography of Ptolemy*[1] (compiled in the mid-second century AD, but drawing on material collected in the late first century AD) refers to the tribes in Scotland (D. Breeze, 1982: 28–30; Strang, 1998; Fig. 114). Those in southern Scotland include the Votadini, the Selgovae, the Novantae, the Damnonii and the Brigantes. North of them were two confederations of tribes – the Caledonians in the far north and the Maeatae south of them. During the Roman period these two tribes developed into the northern and southern Picts (Chapter 14).

The Roman advance into Scotland began in AD 79 after which military installations were built, including the legionary fortress at Inchtuthill (north of the Forth–Clyde). By 83 the local Caledonians had made a spectacular stand in which 30,000 of their warriors were slaughtered at the battle of Mons Graupius. By 86 the Romans were failing to maintain authority and within fifty years the situation was volatile enough for them to build Hadrian's Wall (started in 122 or 123, and under modification until at least 138) (Bidwell, 1999: 17–21; Breeze and Dobson, 2000: ch. 2). From this base, further advances north were made and the Antonine Wall (begun c. 142) became the northern frontier. Clearly still unable to hold the area, the troops once more returned soon after AD 161 to Hadrian's Wall (Ritchie and Breeze, 1991: 21). Part of this may have been damaged around 197 by the Maeatae; certainly by 208 the situation was seen as sufficiently serious for the emperor Septimius Severus personally to come to Britain to establish order.

Although there were no major garrisons north of Hadrian's Wall after the time of Severus, there is increasing evidence that some Roman presence was maintained. For example, the fort at Cramond (on the Firth of Forth), which was largely dismantled after 211, continued to be manned.[2] Activity continued at Birrens into the third and possibly fourth centuries.[3] It is possible that some new outposts were built, to judge from a fragmentary Roman inscription from a site near Jedburgh (D. Breeze, 1996: 107), and Roman masonry (probably from a demolished signal post) which was amongst the rampart material at Ruberslaw (L. Alcock, 1979: 134; A. Curle, 1905).

The most likely explanation for such activity is that Roman patrols continued to maintain a presence in southern Scotland through the third century, presumably because they were tolerated, possibly even welcomed, by the local tribes.

There may have been some official encouragement of farming, since, for example, rectilinear features are found on enclosed hut groups in Northumberland, Durham and the adjoining parts of the Scottish Lowlands, and on a farm at Tamshiel Rig (RCHAMS, 1956: 426–7; Halliday, 1982: 79). Such features are generally taken as evidence of Roman architectural influence in Britain (Jobey, 1966: 105–6).

Relations between Britons and Romans are also reflected by Roman material on native sites. This is mostly of high quality – for example, pottery and glass – which suggests that local leaders wanted it for conspicuous display at feasts (Holmes and Hunter, 2001: 174). Some Roman material may have reached the area as subsidies and diplomatic gifts. Such action would explain a large hoard from Falkirk (on the line of the Antonine Wall itself), which ends with a coin of 235 (Todd, 1985). It might also be the explanation for some of the high-quality late Roman glass from Traprain Law (a major hillfort in Votadinian territory, p. 297) (D. Breeze, 1996: 112–13).

The pattern of contact and trade continued through the third and fourth centuries. Over 200 coins mostly of this period have been found at Springwood, Kelso. Perhaps even more significantly, a forger set up a workshop at Brighouse Bay, making coins based on those of the 220s (Bateson and Holmes, 1997: 554–5). At Newstead a third-century counterfeiter's mould and coin of the late fourth century have been recorded (Bateson and Holmes, 1997: 555; coin mould in Holmes and Hunter, 2001).

As happened in other frontier areas, it is probable that the tribes outside the Roman-held areas were not satisfied with being excluded from the advantages within the Roman world. Certainly there was a serious disturbance in north Britain c. AD 342 when the Picts from northern Scotland devastated the territory north of Hadrian's Wall. In 360 a further attack by the Picts, in conjunction with the Scots of northern Ireland, was followed in 367 by successful attacks on Britannia by a consortium of Picts, Scots and Attacotti (Chapter 11).[4] It is notable that the timing of the attacks coincided with political problems on the Continent and were clearly orchestrated to take advantage of Roman military weaknesses.

In 368 the defences were once more reorganized and Hadrian's Wall refortified. By the early fifth century all regular Roman troops had been withdrawn from Britannia to deal with continued civil unrest as well as attacks from the barbarian tribes such as the Huns, Vandals and Goths. Scotland ceased to be of interest to the Roman world and researchers must rely almost exclusively on archaeology until the king-lists give glimpses of political history.

The origins of the post-Roman British kingdoms

The tribal areas that were discernible during the Roman period were after the early fifth century slowly transformed into the early medieval period British kingdoms of Rheged, Aeron, Strathclyde and Gododdin (Fig. 115). Much of the written evidence for post-Roman kingdoms comes from king-lists (p. 14). Recent archaeological research has produced evidence that points to ways in which the transition may have been effected.

By the late sixth century the former Roman Britannia had similarly become organized into (Anglo-Saxon) kingdoms, from which the Angles in the Northumbrian kingdom of Bernicia advanced aggressively northwards. A few settlers from Ireland are also traceable in the archaeological record and there is evidence that Picts briefly extended their territories into the area.

Frontier areas after Rome

Although the regular garrisoning of Hadrian's Wall definitely ended when Roman troops were withdrawn from Britannia, there is growing evidence for continuing activity in the Roman forts on or adjacent to Hadrian's Wall in the fifth and even the sixth centuries. Since this was certainly not officially organized from Rome, its nature is of considerable pertinence to the post-Roman/early medieval period in Scotland. It has raised considerable debate. Some commentators view it as essentially military under local command (Wilmott, 2000: 17), others see it as the result of local leaders in occupation with their war bands (Dark and Dark, 1996: 68).

In this context, a text in the compilation known as 'Nennius' (*Historia Brittonum*, 37) assumes a certain significance. This states that the Anglo-Saxon Hengist encouraged Vortigern to settle Hengist's sons in the neighbourhood of Hadrian's Wall 'as far as the borders of the Picts'. While the historicity of

Fig. 115 Map of southern Scotland in the early medieval period.

the *Historia Brittonum* has been seriously questioned, there is some reason for believing this section was based on an old tradition (J. Morris, 1980: 4).

At the fort of Birdoswald on Hadrian's Wall, a revetted defensive bank and new timber buildings were erected sometime in the late fifth century. These included a gateway which continued in use into the sixth century (Willmott, 1997; 2000: 14), and a structure similar to a hall which was built on the ruins of a granary.

The defences at South Shields (a former supply base at the east end of the Wall), were maintained after AD 400 (Bidwell and Speak, 1994: 46). The gateway was refurbished and radiocarbon dates for inhumation burials which lined an approach road (a Roman custom) provided dates of the fifth century. Two skeletons were buried in a courtyard house in the first half of the fifth century (Bidwell and Speak, 1994: 46). Since burial of the adult dead within houses was not a Roman custom, this gives rise to speculation about the use of the base.

The evidence from the supply base of Vindolanda and the fort at Housesteads both indicate strengthening of the defences in the late fourth or early fifth century.

Timber structures at Stanwix are similar to those at Birdoswald (Willmott, 2000: 15) and the town of Carlisle at the western end of Hadrian's Wall shows sign of continued occupation (Willmott, 2000: 15). There is growing evidence (including an unusual type of penannular brooch), which suggests that the type of material goods in use changed in the late fourth and fifth centuries.

This may be due to a change in economics, fashion and/or socio-political environment (Cool, 2000).

Iron Age sites with special status

Occupation of Iron Age hillforts in strongly held Roman areas was not tolerated. The strongholds in southern England, for example, were evacuated in favour of nearby towns where Romanization of the inhabitants was inevitable. It is therefore of considerable significance when locals were able to continue living in traditional settlements. They were able to perpetuate their traditional, non-Roman lifestyle and retain potentially defensive environments. In southern Scotland, a few hillforts definitely remained in occupation during the Roman period, leading to the conclusion that the inhabitants held special status from the outset. Privileges may have been enjoyed by the Damnonii, in whose territory lay Castlehill, Dalry (a hillfort with both Roman and later finds: J. Smith, 1919), and the Votadini, with evidence coming from both Traprain Law and Edinburgh.

Traprain Law is a major hillfort in Votadinian territory which has yielded Roman material from the first century onwards, including coins of AD 395–423 (Honorius). During the late first and second centuries Traprain may well have been both a trading and manufacturing base since there is abundant evidence of metalworking. The type of finds point to direct connections with the Roman military and its supply lines (Erdrich et al., 2000: 453).

By the fourth century, the nature of the occupation had changed;[5] not only was there a stone rectangular building (presumably due to Roman architectural influence), but the use of keys and locks. At some point in the Roman period at least one of the occupants was literate – a piece of mudstone was found with ABCD scratched on it (D. Breeze, 1982: 152).

Edinburgh is usually identified with the *Din Eidyn* of the *Gododdin* poem, and therefore seen as the stronghold of the kingdom of the same name. Excavations of a midden at Castle Rock produced some evidence of continuing occupation during and after the Roman period (Driscoll and Yeoman, 1997: 146–8 (combs) and 226–9 (general discussion)).

The king-lists

The genealogies show the legacy of the Roman past. Those for the dynastic lines of Strathclyde, Gododdin and Manau (p. 302) notably trace the ancestry of the kings back to a Romano-British usurper Magnus Maximus (383–88)

(Higham and Jones, 1991: 126), who was also important in Welsh genealogies and later legend. The genealogies for Manau traced the line of their king Cunedda to men with Roman names: he was 'son of Aeternus, son of Paternus, son of Tacitus'. Cunedda also figures prominently in a legend that alleged he migrated to Wales (p. 252).

The early sections of these genealogies are beset with pseudo-ancestries and are difficult to corroborate (Chadwick, 1949: 142–9; K. Jackson, 1969; Miller, 1975; Dumville, 1977; 1989). Since the earliest names are Roman in character, much debate surrounds whether this implies that they originated in the Roman period and reflect Roman influence in the establishment of post-Roman administrations (Chadwick, 1949: 150–1). Objectors argue that a Roman name need only reflect reverence for the Roman past, which in turn may have been superimposed through the widespread adoption of Christianity (Smyth, 1984: 16–18).

The kingdoms

Strathclyde

The kingdom of Strathclyde grew up on the Firth of Forth, its principal seat being Dumbarton Rock (originally the centre of its predecessor, Alclut). A genealogy provides Roman names for its early rulers. For example, Coroticus (whose soldiers were attacked by St Patrick for their apostacy), had a grandfather who is named as 'Quintilus, son of Clemens'. Strathclyde does not appear by name until after the Bernicians arrived in southwest Scotland: it was first mentioned in the *Annals of Ulster* in an entry for AD 872.

Documentary evidence for Alclut comes from both Irish and Welsh literary traditions. The Welsh sources mostly owe their preservation to the interest shown in the Britons of the Solway–Clyde by Owain ap Hywel Dda of Dyfed in the tenth century. A copy of the Strathclyde genealogy has survived in Wales, for which a relative chronology has been established through cross-references from annals and other sources (Chadwick, 1949: 142–6).

Rhydderch Hael is the best known and last of its kings of note; after his rule the kingdom was annexed by Bernicia, probably before 685.

Dumbarton Rock, a volcanic plug of basalt, is the key site in this area (Fig. 116). Bede described it as 'a well-fortified city of the Britons', and the summit seems to have been a citadel, fortified on its eastern side with a rampart of rubble, earth and timber (L. Alcock, 1975–6; Alcock and Alcock, 1990). Radiocarbon dates were compatible with its construction between the late sixth and the ninth centuries, and its destruction by fire may have been

Fig. 116
Dumbarton Rock.

as a result of an attack by the Norse in 870. The finds from the site included imported glass, Bii and E Ware, two heating trays, and a glass inlay.

Aeron

Aeron was centred on the Ayr valley and is known chiefly from placename evidence, notably the occurrence of the name Coylton (probably a reference to Coel Hen, to whom many of the genealogies in Strathclyde and of Aeron traced their ancestry, and who may be the Old King Cole of folklore). A fleet of Aeron is mentioned in the *Gododdin* poem. In Ayrshire there is evidence for post-Roman occupation of a few crannogs (notably Buiston and Lochlee) and some hillforts (such as Dundonald and Castlehill in Dalry).

Buiston   began with a phase in which the crannog was composed of alternating layers of turves and brushwood, within a circle of oak stakes (Munro, 1882: 190–239; Crone, 2000). Three superimposed floors were laid on this, but its date is unknown. Around the fourth century AD the crannog was extended and a circular house built over the extension, with a central stone hearth. This was rebuilt three times, but the primary crannog then slumped forwards, collapsing the house. The site was abandoned until the sixth century, when a substantial timber framework was constructed creating a palisade and inner walkway over the lake mud.

The finds from Buiston include two fine composite bone combs with ring-and-dot decoration; horn points; a knife handle; five iron knives; an iron axehead; iron punch, awl, spearhead and arrows; two gold spiral finger rings; two bronze pins (one with a blue glass bead inset in its head); an annular brooch; a cylindrical bead with trailed red and yellow glass decoration; a jet slider; flints; spindle whorls; polishers and whetstones; and four curious iron objects, two with spiral heads and one with a spring which is probably from a barrel padlock, the fourth being fish-tailed and possibly being used as compasses. There is also a crossbow nut from the site. Other finds from the recent excavations include a hanging-bowl and E Ware. A contemporaneous forgery of a seventh-century Anglo-Saxon gold 'thrymsa' or tremissis points to connections with the advancing Bernicians.

Lochlee is a crannog with occupation in the Roman period, attested by Roman fibulae, a dress-fastener and a Roman melon bead (Munro, 1882). The site was re-occupied in the early medieval period and produced a fine ringed pin with decorated head, probably of ninth-century date. A number of other finds, such as a wooden trough and possibly some of the ironwork, belong to the period.

Dundonald is a thirteenth- and fourteenth-century royal castle which stands within an earthwork which follows the contours of the hill. A series of timber round houses were located within a timber-laced rampart, radiocarbon dated to the fourth or fifth century. The site has also produced E Ware (Dark, 2000: 210).

Castlehill, Dalry, is a small stone-walled fort, which had two periods of occupation, one within the Roman Iron Age and a second phase represented by a penannular brooch, imported Frankish glass, glass canes for making inlays, a cannel coal armlet (there was evidence for their production), and a series of socketted iron spearheads, two with Anglo-Saxon affinities (J. Smith, 1918–19). There were also stone-built structures within the fort, which may relate to the later phase.

Rheged

The extent of the kingdom of Rheged is unknown: it probably extended beyond the south-west of Hadrian's Wall and into former Novantae territory, although a recent case has been made that it was centred on the Rhinns of Galloway, and did not extend into Cumbria (McCarthy, 2002). It flourished mainly in the later sixth century: its king, Urien allied with Rhydderch Hael against the Angles of Bernicia about AD 580. References to Urien's activities indicate the extent of his kingdom, which appears to have included Carlisle and (as the placename Dunragit, the 'fort of Rheged') suggests part of Wigtownshire. The poems of Taliesin support the assumption that Urien's influence reached the Eden Vale, Westmorland and Ayrshire. Evidence points to Rheged being gradually absorbed into Bernicia by 638.

Three forts in this region are known to have occupation in the post-Roman period.

Fig. 117 The
Mote of Mark.

The Mote of Mark is the most prominent site in the south-west (Fig. 117).
Excavated in 1913, 1973 and 1979, it seems likely from small quantities of
pottery that the hill was occupied in the first half of the sixth century.[6]
Before the rampart was built or perhaps while it was being built, there was
industrial activity which included metalworking. The evidence was sealed
by a rampart constructed c. 550–600, at a time when E Ware and Frankish
glass were already being imported to the site. Metalworking continued
within the defences until the middle of the seventh century and possibly
later. Within the rampart in the central hollow on the hill was a three-sided
stone structure, perhaps a bench or shelter for smithing and non-ferrrous
metalworking, or for a hearth round which a midden subsequently grew up.
A putative rectangular building constructed against the north rampart was
evidenced by padstones. Iron, copper alloy, gold and silver were worked on
the site.

The finds include ironwork, evidence for jet-working, a bone with an
Anglian runic inscription, a runic inscription on stone, a cross-incised stone,
beads and some bonework.

It seems probable that the site was the residence of an important smith,
who was operating in a millieu in which relations between the Britons and
neighbouring Angles were sufficiently cordial for the borrowing of ideas.

Trusty's Hill is a small knoll near Gatehouse-of-Fleet, fortified on its southern and north-eastern sides (Thomas, 1961a). The archaeological evidence for
the date of its occupation is inconclusive: it may be entirely Iron Age, or

entirely re-occupied in the post-Roman period. Some markings carved on a rock face have led to the suggestion that Trusty's Hill was sacked by Pictish raiders (p. 318).

Tynron Doon   is a well-preserved multivallate hillfort (S. Williams, 1971). The fort defences may belong exclusively to the Iron Age, but were modified with the addition of a courtyard on the north-eastern side, which was later converted to a motte. Excavation of a midden on the steep slope on the south side produced evidence of early medieval occupation.

Less important sites include **Castle Haven**, Kirkandrews, a stone fort, built like a dun, with intramural galleries (Barbour, 1906–7; Stell, 1990: 121–2). The plan is sub-rectangular, and except on the west, where it is defended by a rock face, the fort has an outer courtyard. The finds point to a Roman Iron Age construction, with later use in the early medieval and later periods.

Also possibly of this date is the crannog at Dowalton Loch, though a group of bronze vessels (one radiocarbon dated from soot to the period) may have been the latest in a series of votive deposits in the loch (F. Hunter, 1994).

It has been suggested that there were Irish settlements in Rheged, the possible historical evidence for which begins in AD 81–2, when the Roman general Agricola met an Irish 'prince' who was in exile in southern Scotland (p. 273). The evidence of placenames, notably those with the Gaelic *sliabh* element, has led to the suggestion that there was a dense concentration of Irish settlement in the Rhinns (Nicolaisen, 1976: 39–46). There is, as yet, no corroborative evidence, except for claims that the church at Ardwall was an Irish foundation (Thomas, 1967: 182: but see *contra* Laing and Laing, 1990: 162–3).

Gododdin and Manau

Gododdin (part of which was known as Manau), incorporated former Votadinian territory. There are no sites with substantial evidence for occupation in the early medieval period in the area. The only sites which can be placed in this period are Crock Cleugh (Steer and Keeney, 1947), Hownam Law (C. Piggott, 1947–8), Ruberslaw (RCHAMS Roxburghshire, 1956: 102–5; L. Alcock, 1979), and possibly Whiteside Rig and Shaw Craig (Feachem, 1966: 84). A few further putatively post-Roman hillforts may be noted from eastern Scotland, notably Bonchester Hill (RCHAMS, 1956: 277), Peniel Heugh (RCHAMS, 1956: no. 201), Woden Law (RCHAMS, 1956: no. 308) and Chatto Craig (RCHAMS, 1956: no. 305).

Gododdin was bordered to the north by the Picts, and Class 1 symbol stones from Edinburgh and Borthwick suggest that Pictland extended for a time south of the Forth. Pictish placenames (those including the element *-pit*) are found in the Lothians, namely Pitcox and Pittendreich. One 'preas' name (Pressmennan), is also likely to be Pictish (Nicolaisen, 1976: 152). It has been suggested that Traprain Law was occupied by the Picts (I. Smith, 1990: ch. 5, esp. 148–53).

At the Dod five prehistoric phases of timber and stone round houses were followed by twelve sub-rectangular buildings (including a putative church), associated with Roman glass. These were likely to be post-Roman as they are similar to the earliest buildings encountered on the Northumbrian site at Yeavering (I. Smith, 1990: 84).

Christianity

Since Christianity was the official Roman religion from 395 onwards, its adoption in Celtic border areas is further evidence of close ties with the Roman world – political, economic and intellectual as well as spiritual. The evidence is diverse.

The Traprain Treasure is a huge hoard of silverwork deposited around the beginning of the fifth century, which contained items of specifically Christian interest (J. Curle, 1923). It is impossible to know whether this was acquired because of its religious significance or for its bullion or barter value. It is possible that there was a stone-built church with D-shaped end at Traprain in the late Roman period (I. Smith, 1996: 26).

Christian activity is also hinted at on Hadrian's Wall, since putative churches have been found at the supply base of Vindolanda, and the Wall forts of South Shields and Housesteads. At Vindolanda the finds include a Chi-Rho inscribed stone, some late metalwork and a sixth-century memorial stone.

Long-cist cemeteries (p. 226), which are assumed to be Christian, near the Firth of Forth at the Catstane, and at Four Winds, Longniddry, have radiocarbon dates within the fifth to the seventh centuries (Dalland, 1992: 204). In Galloway a Christian community was possibly established at Whithorn at least as early as the early fifth century (Hill et al., 1997: 26).

The primary archaeological evidence for early Christianity in southern Scotland and northern England is memorial stones of the fifth and sixth centuries. About twenty, spanning the period from the fifth to the early eighth centuries, are distributed from Vindolanda, just south of Hadrian's Wall, to the Catstane near Edinburgh. They are memorials to individuals with names which represent aristocrats, priests and land-holders and relate to a Latin-speaking Roman Church (Thomas, 1992: 3).

Supporting evidence is provided by the occurrence in southern Scotland of placenames that include the element, *eccles* (which are derived from Latin *ecclesia*, a church) (Cameron, 1968).

Christianity in Rheged

A group of six stones in Galloway display intrusive features in the formulae which point to links with southern Gaulish Christianity. These are from Whithorn, Kirkmadrine and Curghie, and may not all necessarily be memorials. It has been suggested that they are connected with émigré Gaulish clerics (Hill et al., 1997: 19–20). The dating of the stones is debated. The earliest – the Latinus stone from Whithorn – is usually ascribed to the late fifth century, but could be earlier. This has been assumed to be a memorial to a man called Latinus and his daughter, set up by his grandson, Barrovadus. An alternative explanation is that it was set up at the entrance or west front of a church in commemoration of a recent benefactor (Thomas, 1992: 6).

At Ardwall a cemetery was given a timber oratory and subsequently a stone chapel, the latter probably Anglian.[7] The site at Kirkbryde (Crowe, 1987) may be of this period, while that at Chapel Finian is probably of the tenth to twelfth centuries (Radford, 1967: 119). In the south-west, Eccles (near Penpont) and Ecclefechan (near Hoddom), are likely to represent Roman-period church foundations.

Christianity in Gododdin

The Gododdin area has no early memorial stones except the Catstane from the cemetery at Kirkliston (Rutherford and Ritchie, 1975). There is slight evidence for a church and Christian community at Traprain Law and a concentration of long-cist cemeteries (such as that at Parkburn: Henshall, 1955–6; and that at Hallowhill, St Andrews: E. Proudfoot, 1996) on both sides of the Forth, which are usually accepted as being Christian.

The placename *Eglesnamin* associated with Hallowhill, St Andrews, is one of the *eccles* names in Scotland (Proudfoot, 1996: 396).

Christianity need not have reached any but the ruling sector of the community, and the date of the earliest memorial stones indicates its extension from the extreme south to the rest of Lowland Scotland. An inscribed stone from Manorwater belongs to the late sixth century and the Yarrow stone is inscribed to Nudus and Dumnogenus, the sons of Liberalis. A further stone, now lost, is recorded from Peebles, while a sixth-century stone from Over Kirkhope depicts what has been interpreted as an *orans* (praying) figure (Thomas, 1968b: 103; 1993: 3).

Christianity in Strathclyde

Documentary sources point to Christianity in the area by the sixth century, possibly as a result of the extension of the activities from the monastery at

Whithorn. The earliest Christian remains are possibly the chapel and cemetery at St Ninian's Point on Bute (Aitken, 1955).

Monasteries

Amongst evidence for monasteries, are the surviving remains at Whithorn,
Hoddom and Kingarth. The lost stone from Curghie names Ventidius, a *subdi-
aconus* (sub-deacon) and may attest a monastic foundation (Hill et al., 1997:
12). Nothing is known of the monastery at Govan, except from its surviving
sculpture (p. 206).

There was a major monastery at **Whithorn** in the early medieval period.
There is some evidence for a pre-monastic Christian community, probably
with origins within the Roman period.[8] There is a considerable quantity of
Roman material from the site in later contexts, including fourth-century
coins in ninth-century debris in the church (Hill et al., 1997: 292f.).

The first phase recognized in excavations was of insubstantial sub-
rectangular timber structures and the smelting of iron. Soon after the initial
construction phase, imported Mediterranean pottery and glass arrived on
the site. The origins of the monastery have been disputed, but a date at
the beginning of the sixth century would fit the available evidence. The
developed monastery seems to have been zoned, with an outer area demarcated from the inner by a ditch which enclosed timber domestic buildings,
and evidence for industrial activity. Inside was an inner sanctuary which
contained a shrine, a cemetery of lintel graves and log coffins, a founder's
tomb and a church (Hill et al., 1997: ch. 2). At some stage the monastery
acquired a relic of St Peter, commemorated on the St Peter Stone. This
monastery continued until the area was taken over by the Anglo-Saxons
around 730.

At **Hoddom** the main Christian activity was connected with the establishment of a Anglian monastery, but there was a British antecedent (Lowe, 1999:
43). Under the Anglian vallum, excavations uncovered remains of a rectangular stone-built structure, oriented east–west, which was interpreted as a
baptistry. The building was constructed with re-used Roman stones, probably
from the nearby Roman fort at Birrens. Two fragmentary Roman inscriptions
were found adjacent to the structure. The superstructure was a clay and
timber building, on oak sill beams, which was radiocarbon dated to c. AD 600
(Lowe, 1993).

The Anglian settlement of Scotland

The late sixth century in south-east Scotland was dominated by the rise of
the Anglian kingdom of Bernicia and its northerly advance. Documentary

evidence for it is sparse. It has been suggested that the take-over was fairly peaceful (I. Smith, 1983), though this has been disputed (Smyth, 1984: 23). Before the Bernicians advanced they had contacts with their neighbours in southern Scotland (Proudfoot and Aliaga-Kelly, 1996: 3; Cessford, 1999a; Cramp, 1995).

The occupation of southern Scotland was almost certainly represented by overlords rather than immigrants (Duncan, 1975: 65; Smyth, 1984: 23–4). Placenames may provide some evidence of the advance. Names of Anglian origin are confined to the area south of the Forth, and are found particularly in the Lothians west of Edinburgh (Proudfoot and Aliaga-Kelly, 1996: 7 and 9). It has been suggested that the placenames clustered in three 'shires' relate to church dedications and a pattern of tribute exacted by Anglian overlords from British subjects (Brooke, 1991).

There is growing archaeological evidence for Anglian settlement in south-east Scotland. Finds from Traprain Law include two spearheads of Anglian type dated to the fifth to sixth centuries (Proudfoot and Aliaga-Kelly, 1996: 2). Early Anglian material from Scotland also includes a spearhead from Castlehill, Dalry, which is of a type that went out of use by the mid-sixth century (Swanton, 1974: 15–16; Proudfoot and Aliaga-Kelly, 1996: 3).

At Castle Park (Perry, 2000; Lowe, 1999: 21–3), and the Captain's Cabin (Moloney, 2001), both in Dunbar, the archaeological evidence for the Anglian presence is extensive. An Anglian hall at Doon Hill near Dunbar replaced a British hall (Hope-Taylor, 1980). A timber hall of the type represented at Doon Hill is known from Kirk Hill, near St Abb's Head.

Other settlements are known from aerial photography at Sprouston, where grubenhäuser (sunken-floor huts of Anglo-Saxon type) appear to be associated with rectangular timber halls and a cemetery (I. Smith, 1991), Hogbridge, East Lothian (plan in Lowe, 1999: 32) and near Tyninghame (plan in Lowe, 1999: 32). Apart from an Anglian grubenhaus at Dunbar, others have been identified elsewhere in Scotland, most notably at Ratho (associated with loomweights and a copper pin) (I. Smith, 1993), and from the monastic site at Hoddom (Lowe, 1999: 20–1).

The solitary pagan Anglian grave from Scotland, at Dalmeny, contained a necklace of beads of a type associated with the latest pagan Saxon cemeteries in southern England, suggesting a mid-seventh-century date (Baldwin Brown, 1914–15).

The archaeological evidence for the Anglo-Saxon presence in south-west Scotland is largely derived from the ecclesiastical sites of Whithorn and Hoddom. Secular evidence comes mostly from the Mote of Mark. The timber hall at Kirkconnel (p. 53) and another at Cruggleton (p. 53) may also be Anglian.

Other finds of Anglian material include a sixth-century brooch from Botel (Penman, 1998: 475), a fine gilt mount probably of the early eighth century from Rerrick, Dundrennan (Whitfield and Graham-Campbell, 1992), some Northumbrian copper coins of the period 789–849, most of which were found at Luce Sands, and a number of strap ends of the ninth century.

The fragmentary whetstone with facing human head from Collin may belong to the period of Anglian domination. Stylistically it is similar to the whetstone from the seventh-century Lincolnshire cemetery at Hough-on-the-Hill, and the earlier ceremonial whetstone from Sutton Hoo.

The most important group of archaeological remains of the Anglian period are sculptures, which span the period from the eighth century and include some of the finest Northumbrian sculptures known, such as the Ruthwell Cross (Cassidy, 1992), the shaft from Jedburgh (Webster and Backhouse, 1991: no. 114), a late seventh/early eighth-century slab from Wamphray (Bailey, 1996b), and a group from Hoddom (Radford, 1954).

The Vikings

There is very little evidence for the Viking presence in Galloway, despite the fact that the Isle of Man and Cumbria (areas settled by the Vikings), are both visible from there on a clear day. The placenames which seem to combine Norse personal names and Gaelic or English elements, are post-ninth century. A small group of names ending with -by or -bie, from the Danish word for farm-stead, seem to represent an extension of settlement round the Solway Firth. Elsewhere in southern Scotland placenames of Norse origin are very scattered, and probably represent traders rather than settlers (Ritchie, 1993: 95).

The archaeological evidence for Viking influence on southern Scotland takes the form of hogback monuments, a type of Christian grave monument named after its resemblance to a pig's back. These seem to have originated in the Viking settlements in northern England, and are found in monastic contexts at places such as Govan, and Kingarth, Bute (Lang, 1972–4).

From early in the eleventh century, the monastery at Whithorn (which seems to have had some contact with the Vikings in the later ninth and tenth centuries), took on the character of an Irish–Norse trading post. The buildings were smaller than those of the preceding period, and were sub-rectangular, of wattle or wicker, not unlike the Norse houses in Dublin. They may have been built by settlers from Viking towns in Ireland. New types of pins and combs, most readily matched in Viking assemblages in Ireland appeared (Hill et al., 1997: 55–6). There is no archaeological evidence for a church of this period, but the Christian community is likely to have continued (Ritchie, 1993: 99–101).

Northern Scotland

The largest group of people in Scotland north of the Forth–Clyde line during the Roman and early medieval period, were the Picts. Pictland (also later called Pictavia) probably extended to the Northern and Western Isles, from the sixth to the ninth centuries at least. An account set down around 1200 by a Norse writer states that the Orkneys were first inhabited by the Picts (Peti) and Papae who were Scottic/Irish priests (in the *Historia Norwegiae*: Macdonald, 2002: 13). This much quoted source also states that the Picts were little more than pygmies who 'did wonders in the morning and evening, building towns, and at midday completely lost their strength and hid themselves in underground houses'. Such a whimsical description, whether based on any reality such as a liking for taking siestas in earthhouses (below), has without a doubt added to the romantic allure of these people in later centuries.

Some Pictish territory was either settled or subject to overlordship by the Scots who originated in Ireland and traditionally founded the kingdom of Dál Riata (centred on Argyll), in the later fifth century. The Picts and Scots amalgamated in the ninth century to form Scotland (Alba).

Prior to this, both groups were frequently in conflict, though they had allied on three recorded occasions against the Romans. The Picts also came into hostile contact with their southern neighbours, the Britons of Strathclyde (p. 298) and the Angles of Bernicia/Northumbria (p. 305).

Picts and Scots are attested by documentary evidence, inscriptions, settlements, placenames and ecclesiastical sites (Fig. 118). Archaeologically, the two areas show regional differences, and Pictland additionally has distinctive placenames and monumental 'symbol' stones, the meaning of which has been hotly debated.

The Picts

The ancestors of the Picts in the early centuries AD were probably four tribes mentioned in Classical sources in the area bounded by the Moray Firth, the Great Glen and the Forth–Clyde divide (Richmond, 1958; Maxwell, 1987: 31–2; Strang, 1998). By the early third century two confederacies had formed: the Caledonians and the Maeatae. A distinction between the northern and southern Picts (respectively) is assumed to reflect this ancestry (Maxwell, 1987: 31–2). The Roman involvement in Scotland

Fig. 118 Map of northern Scotland in the early medieval period.

is outlined in Chapter 13. Roman military installations have been identified in Caledonian/Pictish territory. The Picts, located beyond the 'buffer' tribes, were able to develop along different lines, though the long-term influence of Rome on the area has perhaps been underestimated in the past when less data was available.

The Caledonians were mentioned by the third-century historian Herodian, who stated that when they encountered the Roman emperor Septimius Severus in AD 208, they were 'ignorant of the use of clothes, and only cover their necks and bellies with iron, which they think an ornament and sign of wealth as other barbarians do gold. They tattoo their bodies not only with likenesses of animals of all kinds, but with all sorts of drawings' (Herodian, 3.14.7).

It is notable that although their descendants, the Picts, called themselves the 'Prydyn' (earlier Priteni), the term 'Pict' derives from the Roman and means 'the painted men'. This description has coloured theories about the symbols which occur throughout Pictland on durable objects, particularly monumental stones (below).

Irish sources document the existence of Priteni in Ireland (there termed Cruithni), who appear to have been settled in Leinster. The significance of these sources has been debated, and their presence is without archaeological support (Chadwick, 1949: ch. 8). In the fourth century the Picts are recorded as taking part in major raids and attacks on Roman Britain in 342, 360 and 367 (p. 294), and were capable of allying with both the Scots and the Continental Saxons.

Historical sources

The Picts may not have regarded written history as important. Certainly, native historical sources for the Picts are poor (K. Hughes, 1980: 1–21). Not a single sentence of Pictish has survived in a document, and the sources for the language are a few brief inscriptions, placenames and a number of personal names and other references in late Classical and early medieval period writings. Legend and factual history were intermixed (K. Hughes, 1980: 20).

The first king whose historicity is not in doubt is Bridei mac Maelcon (r. c. 550).[1] His father, Maelcon, may have been Maelgwn of north Wales (p. 252) who in Welsh tradition came from southern Scotland. Bridei won a victory over the Scots of Dál Riata in the second half of the sixth century, which was followed by fifteen years' peace. The full extent of Bridei's kingdom is unknown, but it probably included Orkney, the sub-king of which was at Bridei's court in Columba's time (Smyth, 1984: 107).

Documentary evidence of Pictish development in the first half of the seventh century is virtually confined to king-lists. At some point after 650 the Angles claimed tribute from part of Pictland until their defeat at the battle of Nechtansmere (probably Dunnichen) in 685 (Cruikshank, 1999). More cordial relations were brought about by Nechtan mac Derelei, who succeeded in 706. His successor, Oengus mac Fergus, was one of the most important figures in early Scottish history: he campaigned vigorously in Dál Riata, and briefly took control there, but Dál Riata won back its independence, probably before 778 (Smyth, 1984: 73–5).

Kenneth mac Alpin, the king of the Scots, became king of Pictland in 849 or 850, an important event for which there is little documentary evidence, possibly because the chroniclers were more concerned with the Norse raids (Smyth, 1984: 176–85). Equally probably, since kings of Dál Riata had previously ruled in Pictland and there had been extensive settlement of Gaels in Pictland (attested partly by Gaelic placenames), it was not the major development later historians believed. From this date onwards subsequent kings ruled the Scots as well as the Picts.

The Pictish language

The language was essentially a Brythonic/Brittonic Celtic language, closely related to the Cumbric of north-west England (Forsyth, 1995a). However, some placenames contain Goidelic/Gaelic elements. It is assumed that these reflect contact with the Irish of Dál Riata in the seventh and eighth centuries, when the names seem to have come into existence. Some debate has surrounded the question of whether Pictish also contained an older, non-Celtic (i.e. Bronze Age) element,[2] which would have considerable implications for the development of northern Scotland in prehistory.

Three scripts are found in Pictland.

(1) Ogham. The Picts acquired this script from the Scots of Dál Riata. 29 examples survive, mostly on stones though also on some small personal items. The surviving ogham inscriptions that are legible record Pictish and Irish personal names. The majority of the oghams in Scotland date from the seventh to the tenth centuries. Although the earliest followed Irish convention, later stones have a guideline as a base line, instead of using the edge. Only two ogham inscriptions follow the Irish convention, one being the example at Newton.

(2) Insular script (of which there are eleven surviving inscriptions) used Latin letters and was acquired from Dál Riata.[3]

(3) An otherwise unknown script appears only on a symbol stone at Newton, along with an ogham text which appears to include a personal name Edarrnonn.

Placenames

The Pictish language can be traced in some placenames (especially those which incorporate the element *pit*, which may denote the centre of an estate) (Nicolaisen, 1976; 1996; Whittington, 1974-5; Fig. 119). It has been argued however, that none are earlier than the ninth century (Ralston and Armit, 1997: 219). An almost identical distribution in historical Pictland is shared by placenames of Brythonic/Brittonic derivation (and which are therefore assumed to be Pictish). These names include the elements *carden*, *lanerc*, *pert*, and *pevr* and mostly relate to woodland (Nicolaisen, 1996: 29).

Some Norse placenames in the Northern Isles incorporate elements that imply the presence of Picts: examples include Pettadale (valley of the Picts), Petester (homeland of a Pict), and Pettafell (mountain of the Picts). The Pentland Firth itself may mean 'firth land of the Picts'.

Fig. 119 Map of 'pit' names in Scotland.

Pictish symbols

The most distinctive features of Pictish archaeology are representations of abstract or highly stylized animals and objects which are assumed to be symbols, though what they might symbolize is subject to debate and uncertainty. Usually carved on stone, they are also found on portable objects (p. 318), when they are often used in discussions over dating. When the sculptured stones of Scotland were catalogued (Allen and Anderson, 1903), the undressed stones with incised symbols were classified as Class 1 and the cross slabs (with generally more developed Pictish symbols) as Class 2. The cross slabs without symbols are Class 3 (for Classes 2–3, see pp. 194–99). The symbols appear repeatedly with little variation, in various combinations incised on undressed stones, and with greater variation in relief on cross slabs.

Fig. 120 Symbol stone, Aberlemno Roadside.

Between forty and fifty symbols have been identified, distributed between some 245 stones (Figs. 120–2). A few appear only once, which has led to claims that they are not symbols as such (Forsyth, 1997). The symbols rarely appear singly, and when they do it is possible that associated symbols are missing or the carving was never completed. Normally they appear in combinations of two to four. They do not overlap, they rarely touch, and normally appear in combination – one animal symbol with an abstract symbol.

There are no local distributions or concentrations of any one or any group of symbols in Pictland which implies that their meaning was understood throughout Pictavia.

The symbols fall into two basic groups.

(1)   Animals, executed in a distinctive style and with great economy of line. These consist of the horse, boar, bull, stag, bear, wolf, fish, eagle, goose

Fig. 121 Pictish symbols.

and some representations which seem to be a horse's head. A seal or otter, the head of a hunting dog and an animal called the 'Pictish beast' or 'swimming elephant', have also been identified, as well as a snake and a beast called the 'Pictish S-dragon'. With the exception of the 'Pictish beast' and 'S-dragon', all these animals could have been found in Pictland.

(2)   Abstract symbols, known by various descriptive terms such as 'notched rectangle', 'Z-rod', 'V-rod', 'triple disc', 'crescent and V-rod' or 'mirror and comb case'.

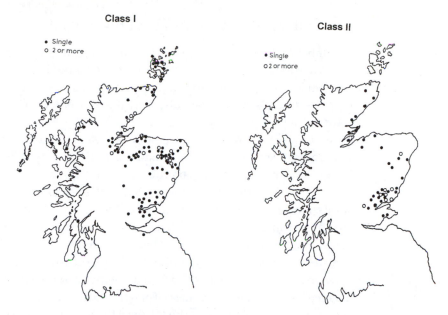

Fig. 122 Map of Pictish symbols.

The function of the symbol stones

The stones are possibly, but not yet provably, tombstones. At Dairy Park, Dunrobin, a stone and grave were found in close proximity in 1977, but the stone was not *in situ* (Close-Brooks, 1978–80). Symbols found on portable objects on settlement sites have no funereal associations (Diack, 1944). The meaning of the symbols might shed light on the function of the stones, but this is a much debated topic.

The meaning of the symbols

No fully satisfactory explanation has yet been advanced to explain the meaning of the symbols, though there has been no dearth of theories (Allen and Anderson, 1903; Diack, 1944; I. Henderson, 1967; 1971; Thomas, 1961a; 1963; A. Jackson, 1984; Laing and Laing, 1984b; Samson, 1992; Forsyth, 1997; Cummins, 1999; Laing and Laing, 2001). The sole 'literary' evidence comes from Herodian and from Isidore of Seville (AD 560–653) who repeated the tradition of tattoos, noting

> The race of the Picts have a name derived from [the appearance of] their bodies. These are played upon with a needle working with small punctures and by the squeezed out sap of a native plant, so that they bear the resultant marks according to the personal rank of the individual, their painted limbs being tattooed to show their high birth (Isidore, *Origines*, 19.23.7).

Some interpretive theories about the symbols

A number of theories have been advanced to explain the use of the symbols.

♦ They were personal indicators, the equivalent of heraldic designs in the later middle ages, or perhaps codified personal names. It has been suggested that the symbols were originally devised as tattoos which proclaimed the status of individuals (Diack, 1944).

Building on this theory, a suggestion was made that the animal symbols were indicative of totemic groups, and the abstract symbols indicated status. Ranks were put forward for particular symbols (Thomas, 1963).

A recent suggestion is that the symbols are hieroglyphs for name combinations. This stems from the argument that aristocratic Celtic personal names are often a combination of two elements, one descriptive, the other an animal name, after the manner of native American names: 'wise eagle', 'fast salmon' and so on (Samson, 1992). Contrary to this is the argument that, since few surviving personal names are, in fact, di-thematic (for whatever reason), they may represent language not ideas (Forsyth, 1997).

Another interpretation has also followed the idea that the symbols represent names, and has used 'bilingual' stones, with names in ogham, to assign name identities to symbol-combinations. According to this, for example, the fish symbol represents 'Nechtan' (Cummins, 1999: 68).

♦ A further suggestion is that the names are to be read from the top downwards, rather than from left to right (Cummins, 1999: 44). The problem with this interpretation lies in the fact that there are too few ogham inscriptions to enable all the 'names' to be read, and in any case some appear to be later additions to the stones, or are unreadable.

♦ An anthropological view has argued that the stones record marriage alliances between dynasties, which required documentation if Bede's statements that the Picts were at least in part matrilineal is accepted (A. Jackson, 1984).

♦ It has been suggested that, because of the similarity between some symbols and Scythian art of the Iron Age, the tradition was transmitted across landmasses through tattoos and other perishable materials that left no archaeological trace (Thomas, 1961b).

The date of the symbols

There are few methods of dating incised marks on stones which may not even be in their original positions and do not belong to a well-documented culture. A symbol is highly unlikely to pre-date the invention of the object it represents (it would have to be a 'blue-print', which is clearly not the case here), but non-pictorial symbols pose greater problems. Comparisons

Fig. 123 Pictish
proto-symbols.

with similar objects or symbols elsewhere have been made and typologies
have been constructed, and have sometimes led to ingenious interpretations
(Samson, 1992; Forsyth, 1997; Laing and Laing, 2001: 106–11).

The discussion over the date of symbols began in 1903, with the view that
the symbols came into widespread use in the seventh century and continued
to be employed until the unification of Picts and Scots around the middle of
the ninth century (Allen and Anderson, 1903). However, excavation at Pool,
Sanday, in Orkney has provided evidence for the use of symbols at least as
early as the sixth century where they are seen as proto-symbols (or 'ur-
symbols') (L. Alcock, 1996; Fig. 123).

The finds from Pool are datable from the following evidence: (1) Alterations
to a building on the site involved the re-use of two stones, one with an ogham
inscription, the other with a double disc, a serpent head and something not
unlike a crescent moon; (2) a bone object shaped like a pin and radiocarbon
dated to (possibly) the fourth century, bore a double-disc and z-rod and part of
another rectangular symbol; (3) a cattle phalanx bone had a crescent-and-v-
rod and some other incised symbols, datable to the fifth to seventh centuries
(J. Hunter, 1997: 32–4).

Some additional evidence suggests that primitive symbols were in use from
at least as early as the fourth century AD. A Pictish imitation of a fourth-
century Roman crossbow brooch from Carn Liath, has a double-disc proto-
symbol incised on it. There are carvings on the cave wall in the Sculptor's
Cave, Covesea, which has produced a series of fourth-century finds but no
later material (Laing, 1994: 29).

Some of the symbols seem to represent objects (such as recognizable types
of comb, or mirrors of Roman type) current in the fifth century or earlier
(Laing and Laing, 1984b), and the style of a number of the symbols appears to
reflect late Roman provincial taste and insignia. The form of the 'spearhead'
on the crescent-and-v-rod symbol recalls the form of the spear carried by
beneficiarii (orderlies to high-ranking Roman officers) with its lateral scrolls,

for example. Design elements in the symbols are also found in Romano-British art – such as the pelta and running leaf pattern.

Pictish symbols are found on hand-pins in a hoard of silverwork from Norrie's Law (Laing, 1994). By association with other items in the hoard, these particular symbols may be argued to be fifth century in date.

Symbols on portable objects

Pictish symbols have occasionally been found on more personal items: a scratched piece of bone from the Broch of Burrian in Orkney; symbols carved on a number of round sandstone discs (Cummins, 1999: 166–76); and a bronze crescent-shaped object, now lost, from Monifieth, which was inscribed with both debased Pictish symbols and (presumably added at a later date), Viking runes (Laing, 1993a: no. 239).

Pictish symbols occur on some silverwork, including on two of twelve chains from southern Scotland, notably outside Pictish territory (I. Henderson, 1979; Cessford, 1994a; Breeze, 1998). The chains are all constructed by the same technique and each has a terminal ring with expanded flanges. They may not have been worn round the neck but across the chest, and two of them, from Parkhill and from Whitecleuch, have Pictish symbols on their terminal rings. They were very probably insignia and could be explained as loot taken from Picts (I. Henderson, 1979), or possibly diplomatic gifts which originated in Gododdin (Cessford, 1994a: 23). Raiders too are probably responsible for the appearance of Pictish symbols in the Lowlands, though the symbols at Trusty's Hill, Anwoth, are probably late and carved by someone who had seen symbols but did not fully understand them (Laing, 2000; Cessford, 1994c).

Settlements

The Picts lived on a variety of sites, the chief settlement types in mainland Scotland including ringforts, hillforts and hierarchically organized forts (Chapter 2). Regional differences in settlement types are closely related to Iron Age precursors, which in turn reflect the available building materials and the lifestyle dictated by the climate and soils. Settlement types found in the Northern and Western Isles therefore differ markedly from those on the mainland. In Orkney, for instance, there was a local resource of sandstone that split readily into building slabs and which had resulted in a tradition of stone building from the Neolithic onwards.

Studies of Pictish settlement patterns in Fife and Angus have attempted to define areas that were favoured, and land-tenure. Placenames which include the element *pit*, have been argued as representing small territorial units.

These have been seen as small dependent estates, though whether the studies have implication for wider geographical areas has been debated.[4] Other settlement studies in southern Pictland have additionally supported the view that the distribution of Class 1 symbol stones and forts are linked, and that Class 2 reflects a different, later pattern with increased nucleation (Cottam and Small, 1974).

Settlement sites on the mainland

Ringforts or duns are particularly common in the valley of the Tay, but they seem to be mostly, if not all, Iron Age constructions in this area, and there is no certain evidence that any were newly built in the post-Roman era.

Most of the settlements are fortified. These include Craig Phadrig (Small and Cottam, 1972; L. Alcock, 2003); Cullykhan (Grieg, 1971; Shepherd, 1983); Burghead (Small, 1969; Shepherd, 1986); Green Castle, Portknockie (Ralston, 1987); Castle Urquhart (Alcock and Alcock, 1992); Clatchard Craig (Close-Brooks, 1986); Moncrieffe Hill (Feachem, 1955; Alcock et al., 1989: 210); and Dumyat (Alcock et al., 1989: 206).

Dundurn may have been the main fort of the Picts of the region (Alcock, Alcock and Driscoll, 1989). Probably the *Dun duirn* mentioned in the *Annals of Ulster* as having been besieged in 683, it is one of the series of hierarchically organized forts which are more abundant in Pictland than elsewhere. The site began as a palisaded enclosure on the uppermost terrace. Constructed somewhere between AD 460 and 665 and later dismantled, it was replaced in the early seventh century with a timber and stone wall, the timbering being laid at right angles and fastened with iron nails. Wickerwork may have been used as infill. It was fired (possibly during the siege of 683), and a new rampart constructed of rubble, probably on the base of the old. A stone building was built, re-using Roman masonry. A further rubble rampart was constructed below the citadel, apparently without timbering. In its final phase it has a roughly oval citadel with a terrace, and four lower terraces delimited by ramparts, with an approach road on the north-west.

Pictish settlements sites in the Northern Isles

The Northern Isles (Orkney and Shetland) appear to have come under Pictish overlordship from the sixth to the ninth centuries. Adomnán, for instance, reported that there was a king from Orkney in the court of Bridei mac Maelchon when St Columba went there in the sixth century (Anderson and Anderson, 1991: 441).

Fig. 124 Post-broch hut, Midhowe, Orkney.

The lack of wood in both Orkney and Shetland led to a tradition of building round houses in stone. This culminated in the building of towers known as brochs, which had single entrances, hollow-wall construction, and internal timber ranges. They remained a feature of the post-Roman period landscape.

From the third century AD new types of settlement became prevalent, with noticeable differences between Orkney and Shetland (Fig. 124). These were undefended sites, often with cellular houses (p. 57) in Orkney and wheelhouses (p. 56) in Shetland. The factors behind this change have not yet been determined.

Orkney

The new types of settlement are exemplified by Buckquoy, Birsay (Ritchie, 1977), Skaill, Deerness (Buteux, 1997), (which continued in occupation until some time after AD 600 when the site was taken over by the Vikings) and Pool, on Sanday (J. Hunter, 1997), (where there were seven Pictish phases). In the seventh and eighth centuries the settlement at Pool contracted, until by the Viking period only one house was still in use.

Shetland

Finds of Roman material suggest that wheelhouses (stone dwellings with radial piers (p. 56)) were first constructed in the later second or third centuries AD. They were replacements for Iron Age brochs. The wheelhouse period is distinguished by a few innovations such as developments in pottery design (p. 89) and notched slate sticks which were used to separate the ear from the corn stalk in harvesting.

Jarlshof was a site with long occupation (Hamilton, 1956: 58). Here, the field system was modified as a result of improved farming techniques. A wheelhouse that was built in the third century AD remained the basic settlement unit on the site until the arrival of the Vikings in the ninth century. During this period the inhabitants became Christian: a rough slab with a cross incised on it was recovered from wheelhouse levels. The final phase before the arrival of the Vikings involved the occupation of a hut and an associated earthhouse (Hamilton, 1956: 90).

At *Clickhimin* a wheelhouse was built within the ruins of a broch (Hamilton, 1968: 125). This continued to be occupied up to the seventh or eighth centuries. The most remarkable feature of the final phase at Clickhimin is a stone in the threshold of the gateway which bears the mark of two 'footprints' with a circular depression at either end, between the toes and between the heels. Similar footprints are known from elsewhere in Scotland (Dunadd, for example), and are traditionally associated with the inauguration of kings (Hamilton, 1968: 151–2). It is unknown what significance this may have for the history of the area, though it suggests that the site held special status.

The Western Isles

Wheelhouses and cellular houses

Brochs were replaced in the Outer Hebrides from the second century AD by wheelhouses at the same time that new types of artefact (notably certain types of bone equipment, especially pins and combs) were introduced. No factors to explain this have been determined.

Wheelhouses include a' Cheardach Mhor, South Uist (Young and Richardson, 1959–60), which had five phases of occupation extending into the sixth century; Bac Mhic Connain (Beveridge and Callander, 1931–2; Hallén, 1994) and Foshigarry (Beveridge, 1930–1; Hallén, 1994) with occupation from the fourth century. Finds include a unique knife handle with an inscription in Pictish ogham.

Hebridean wheelhouses are frequently termed 'earth houses' since they were usually partly dug down into the surrounding sand (Armit, 1997: 41–3). As in the Northern Isles, the wheelhouses of the Hebrides continued in use until the Viking period. They appear in some cases to have been replaced by cellular houses. At Beirgh cellular houses displayed some variety and are dated from the third to sixth centuries AD (Harding, 2004: 265–6).

Coileagan an Udail (The Udal) on North Uist is the most extensive open settlement with cellular houses (Crawford and Switsur, 1977; Crawford and Selkirk, 1996). As at Beirgh, the houses post-date a wheelhouse-building phase, which seems to have ended sometime between the second and fifth centuries. The cellular buildings consisted of a small circular cell leading from a larger ovoid chamber, with one or more turret-like rooms lying along little corridors off the main building. The main room contained slab-lined and floored hearths flanked by low revetments for sleeping platforms. Uprights in the revetting took the roof. Outbuildings were associated with the houses. The finds included elaborate bone combs, gaming pieces, crucibles, clay moulds, bronze pins, decorated bone pins, iron knives, a fish spear, pottery and hand-worked whalebone. The cellular houses continued to be occupied until the arrival of the Vikings.

Open settlements

Isolated open settlements are found on beaches and sand dunes. A considerable quantity of material, including early medieval objects such as bronze pins, is known from casual finds on sand-dune sites in the Hebrides.

Galleried duns

Dun Cuier, Barra (Young, 1955–6), is a galleried dun which utilizes the natural rock surface, and consists of three separate walls (an outer, an inner and a main wall), approached by a paved entrance passage. The majority of the finds were indeterminate. There are a number of similar galleried duns in the Hebrides, which in so far as they can be dated, fall within the early medieval period. They may represent a survival of older forms of developed round house.

Christianity

St Columba undertook a dedicated mission from Iona to northern Pictland at the end of the sixth century. The conversion of the people of the Northern Isles probably followed the visit of Cormac (a follower of Columba) c. 575. By the end of the seventh century, Pictland appears to have been Christian (K. Hughes, 1970).

The conversion of the southern Picts is assumed to have taken place through contacts from south of the Forth since both Rheged and Gododdin were Christian at least as early as the sixth century. The evidence for this assumption is the distribution of long-cist cemeteries, which lie on both sides of the Forth (which by the seventh century was the southern boundary of Pictland). Bede stated that the southern Picts were converted by St Ninian (from Whithorn) in the fifth century. This has caused considerable debate in the past, but is now more universally accepted.

Pictish ecclesiastical remains

The Pictish Church was essentially monastic, though the evidence is sparse and often inconclusive. The bulk of the archaeological evidence comes from the Northern Isles, though there has been important work at, for example, Portmahomack (p. 215). Because of the prominence of St Columba in the conversion of the Picts, and subsequently the work of Irish monks, Christianity in Pictland was strongly influenced by Irish-derived traditions. Christian Irish activity is, for example, well attested in the Northern and Western Isles by placenames which include the element *papar*, which refers to the *papae*, Irish clerics (*papar*: B. Crawford, 2002; placenames: Macdonald, 1977: 2002).

A notable feature of the Pictish Church was square-barrow cemeteries (p. 227) which are found mainly in southern Pictland.

Ecclesiastical sites

Portmahomack, is, to date, the most informative ecclesiastical site in Pictland, after extensive excavations since 1994 (Carver, 2004). Founded in the sixth century, possibly by Columba, it developed by the eighth century into a major monastery. It maintained links with Northumbria and even further afield (finds including a silver coin of c. 715 from the Rhine mouth) until its destruction in the eleventh century, possibly at the hands of the Vikings. Workshops produced a range of ecclesiastical goods, from books through ornamental metalwork and glass to leather. It was also the centre of a major sculptural school.

Applecross was an important monastic foundation, probably founded in the seventh century. Traces of the oval vallum remain (MacLean, 1997). The modern churchyard's wall at Papil, West Burra (Shetland), is built on top of a roughly rectilinear vallum and the present ruined church, built in 1815, is situated on top of an earlier chapel. The site has produced a Pictish cross slab (the Papil stone), a second cross slab and the remains of one single and one double corner-post shrine (site: Macdonald and Laing, 1967–8: 128; sculptures: Laing, 1993b).

Traces of the vallum of the important ecclesiastical site on the Brough of Birsay, Orkney, along with associated burials were found on excavation to pre-date the later Norse graveyard (Cruden, 1965; see also Morris, 1989; 1996b: 48–59; 1996b). At Deerness in Orkney (Morris and Emery, 1986) and in Shetland, small complexes of monastic buildings remain on isolated stacks that were once joined to the mainland by land-bridges (R. Lamb, 1975–6). All however are likely to belong to the Norse period and later, and excavation at Deerness suggested that it may not have been monastic.

The Scots of Dál Riata

The inhabitants of what is now Co. Antrim, Ireland, were known as the Scots, a name they transported to what is now Argyll and the adjacent islands where they established the kingdom of Dál Riata (Ritchie and Breeze, 1991; Laing and Laing, 2001; Foster, 1996; Campbell, 1999).

Although there is doubt over the exact nature of the Scottic influence, there was a definite extension of power into what is now Scotland, from the fifth century onwards into the ninth. Whether this took the form of large-scale migration or merely overlordship is debatable, but the influence was strong enough to give Scotland its name. The name of Argyll appears to be derived from *Airer Gaoidhael*, 'coastland of the Gaels', a reference to Scottic origins in Antrim.

An entry in the *Annals of Tigernach* for c. AD 500 asserts that 'Feargus mor, mac Erc, with the nation of Dál Riata, took part of Britain, and died there'. Current opinion has suggested that the text was taken from a tenth-century 'Chronicle of Clonmacnoise' (Dumville, 1993: 187). A source which survives in a tenth-century version (Bannerman, 1974: 130–3), the *Senchus Fer nAlban* (*Tradition of the Men of Scotland*) relates to the supposed royal line of Dál Riata and provides a genealogy of the kings of Dál Riata from Fergus mac Erc to the mid-seventh century. It additionally gives information on their military and naval strength. Bede noted how under their leader Reuda the Irish came and 'won lands from the Picts . . . they are still called Dalreudini after this leader' (*Historia Ecclesiastica*, 1).

Theories about early Dál Riata

There is so little definitively Irish archaeological evidence for the Scottic kingdom of Dál Riata that some commentators prefer the theory that there was no large-scale immigration and that the story is a later myth created to serve tenth-century political aims (Campbell, 2001). It is likely that there were close links between northern Ireland and western Scotland long before the historic sources indicate – possibly as a result of marriage alliances (Nieke and Duncan, 1988: 8). The name of Dál Riata means 'the portion of Riata' and refers to Reuda or Riata to whom Bede attributes the foundation of the kingdom. Ríata is a genitive of a tribal or deity name. The same man also appears as Cairpre of Riata in another foundation legend which places his rule ten generations before the time of Fergus mac Erc (Duncan, 1975: 41). This suggests a date in the third or even second century AD.

A context for the aristocratic migration and take-over is perhaps provided by the pressure that is known to have been exerted in Ireland by the Uí Néill dynasty (Byrne, 1965).

The *Senchus* gives a muster (list of available man-power) of sea and land in Dál Riata, and a sketch history, which defines a tripartite division of territory according to the ruling families (Cenéla) (Bannerman, 1974: 68–154). The family of Loarn (the Cenél Loairn) occupied northern Argyll (modern Lorn), and were traditionally based on Dunollie, a fort with a medieval castle which stands above Oban. The family of Angus (the Cenél nOengusa) occupied Islay. The Cenél nGabrain had Kintyre and Knapdale, with the stronghold of Dunadd in the Crinan Moss. By the seventh century Dál Riata extended from the Mull of Kintyre north to Ardnamurchan and incopororated the islands off the west coast.

The language of Dál Riata

An important effect of the formation of Dál Riata was the dissemination of Goidelic in Scotland – Scots Gaelic being the result. The language spoken in Ireland and Dál Riata was what is known as 'common Gaelic' (Gillies, 1993: 145). While initially confined to Dál Riata, Gaelic had certainly entered Pictland before its union with the Scottic kingdom in the ninth century. This was probably brought about by ecclesiastical activity from Iona (Gillies, 1993). The main expansion of Gaelic, however, was the result of hybrid Irish–Norse movements in the tenth century (Gillies, 1993). By the eleventh century Gaelic was in use throughout Scotland except for a narrow belt along the English border and in the Norse-speaking areas of the Hebrides and Northern Isles.

There are only a few ogham-inscribed stones from Dál Riata; one from Dunadd, one from the island of Gigha, and a group in Arran. Placenames belonging to the Dalriadic phase are known – it has been suggested that the element *sliabh* meaning a 'hill' is almost entirely confined to Dál Riata but with a scatter in Pictland (Nicolaisen, 1965), though this name element alone is not now regarded as decisive evidence. It is related to the placename element *slew* which has been used as evidence for Irish settlement in the Rinns of Galloway.

The major excavated settlement sites in Dál Riata

Few sites in Dál Riata have produced evidence for occupation during the early medieval period, the most extensively investigated being Dunadd and Dunollie.

Loch Glashan   is a crannog, excavated in 1960, which compares very closely with Irish crannogs such as Ballinderry 2. On the evidence of a brooch and E Ware it has been dated to between the sixth and ninth centuries (J. Scott, 1961: 310).

Fig. 125
Dunadd.

Ugadale Point is a small fort near Kildonan (Fairhurst, 1954–6) which utilized the natural defences of a rock stack. The only excavated structure within the fort was post-medieval, but finds from the site indicate occupation in the seventh to eighth centuries.

Little Dunagoil, Bute, was occupied in the period and has produced E Ware (Marshall, 1964).

Dunadd is the most important site of the period in Dál Riata (Christison and Anderson, 1904–5; Craw, 1929–30; Lane and Campbell, 2000; Fig. 125). It has been extensively excavated and studied. It is also rare among sites of the period in that at least two historical figures are associated with it and at least one dramatic event is known to have happened there. The fort stands on a rocky outcrop in the Crinan Moss, now drained but once a serious barrier to would-be attackers. The first reliable reference to the occupation of the site was in 683, when an Irish annalistic entry refers to a siege of Dunadd. The *Annals of Tigernach* also refer to a further siege and capture of the site in 736 by Oengus mac Fergus, king of the Picts. The archaeological finds from the site attest an earlier occupation.

The excavation at the start of the twentieth century left little undisturbed. The earliest activity involved the construction in the Iron Age of a stone structure, probably a dun, on the summit. The construction of a summit fort enclosed by a drystone wall began in the fourth or fifth century AD. By the seventh century this had been extended with additional enclosures on the lower terraces. The summit fort was later modified to create a pear-shaped layout, the new wall being c. 4 m wide. A substantial outer enclosure wall was built, using the natural rock entrance. The constructional alterations spanned the eighth, ninth, and possibly even the tenth centuries, and some occupation may have continued even later. In one enclosure the excavations produced evidence for an extensive ornamental metalworking workshop, with evidence for the working of gold, silver, copper alloys, lead, tin, iron and glass.

The defences are stone built with traces of stone buildings within; one of which, at least, seems to have been rectilinear. Within the fort is a carving of a boar and an incised footprint, which is similar to other 'inauguration' footprints (such as at Clickhimin, Shetland). The boar is stylistically related to Class 1 Pictish symbol stones, and could be of sixth- or more probably seventh-century date. The pottery consists mainly of E Ware, together with Classes D and F. The absence of A and B Wares, and the presence of certain bronzes and moulds for bronzes (notably penannular brooches), indicates that the site was occupied from the end of the fifth or beginning of the sixth century.

Dunollie, near Oban, is mentioned five times in Irish *Annals* between 686 and 734. An entry for 701 refers to its destruction (Alcock and Alcock, 1987). The first phase of occupation, dated to between the seventh and ninth centuries, may have been unfortified, but occupation material pointed to the presence of a bronze smith and also military activity, attested by weapons. After its destruction it was rebuilt (perhaps in 714); a rubble bank with massive revetment continued in use until the tenth century. Finds included imported pottery of Class E, tools, a rim of a painted Roman glass vessel (possibly part of a buy-off to the Scots) and a gold loop.

Duns

'Duns' (stone-walled forts), were the residences of high-status (but probably not royal) families. At least some were occupied in the early medieval period (p. 39). Recently it has been suggested that they were substantially built as much to resist the climate as hostile neighbours (L. Alcock, 2003: 269–70).

Kildonan Bay seems to have been occupied within the seventh to eighth centuries. A brooch which may belong to either one of the first two phases should probably be assigned to the seventh century rather than later (Fairhurst, 1938–9). In all, the assemblage had much in common with the material from Dunadd. A sherd of Roman samian ware led the excavator to consider whether the fort was occupied or built before the early medieval period. However, samian ware occurs frequently on post-Roman sites and may be of little significance.

Other duns with probable early medieval occupation include Ardifuir, which produced imported pottery of Class E, ingot moulds and a crucible, as well as Roman material (Christison, 1904–5: 269).

Open settlements

Open settlements are known from sand-dune sites. Settlements may also have grown up near duns, as exemplified by the walled terraces below the dun structure at Ardanstur on Loch Melford, where there are two duns in close proximity and oval platforms and scoops which could have been for circular structures (Nieke and Duncan, 1988: 18).

Machrins, on Colonsay, is a sand-dune site where excavation revealed curvilinear house floors, with insubstantial walls composed of slabs backed against the sand. The floor areas were in the region of 15 sq m. A date c. AD 800 was suggested for them, but they could be earlier (J. Ritchie, 1981).

Ecclesiastical remains in Dál Riata

Iona was undoubtedly the most important Irish monastic foundation in Dál Riata, partly because of the personal standing of Columba and his successors (RCHAMS, 1982; Dunbar and Fisher, 1995; Ritchie, 1997). Columba founded the monastery in 567, though there probably already was a community of Christian Irish. Iona's role in the conversion of the northern Picts cannot seriously be doubted, even if the literal truth of Bede's assertion that it held leadership over the monasteries of the Picts is not accepted. Little is known about the early monastery contained within the vallum (p. 213), though it may be inferred that the buildings were of timber. However, the early monastery was probably situated round the rock outcrop known as Torr Abb, where a hut, complete with stone bed, has been excavated.

The attribution of the hut on Torr Abb to the time of Columba must remain speculative. Around Torr Abb, however, were traces of structures possibly connected with the first monastery. Also belonging to the early phase of the monastery were grass-marked pottery, possibly of Irish origin, some early inscribed grave-slabs, which can be paralleled at Clonmacnoise, and a small bronze human head of the seventh or eighth century.

Lismore (Macdonald, 1973b), on the Firth of Lorne, was founded traditionally by St Moluag, whose death is recorded in the Irish annals for 592.

Kingarth (Laing, Laing and Longley, 1998) was traditionally founded by St Blane in the sixth century (Fig. 126). The site is of some complexity, and most of the structural phases visibly post-date the Viking raids. As at Iona, the

Fig. 126
Kingarth.

vallum is not a simple, single-period structure but has subsidiary enclosure walls. A small ringfort associated with the site may be a rath of Irish type, but could be an earlier Iron Age fort, as is the case of Dun Bhuirg, Iona. The monastery is documented in the seventh century, a date which is consistent with the E Ware imported pottery found on the site. The existing stone remains and a series of stone sculptures and motif pieces are probably Norse period and later. The layout seems to follow the type of concentric plan represented at Whithorn.

Inchmarnock, on an island off Bute,[5] is currently under investigation. It was occupied in the seventh to eighth centuries, and a substantial church was built in the twelfth century. In an area to the north a large number of motif pieces and stone gaming boards were found.

Two other early Irish monastic foundations were probably in Pictish territory; that at Eigg, in the Inner Hebrides (Macdonald, 1973b: 57–64), and Applecross (MacLean, 1997), in Wester Ross. The latter was founded by St Maelrubha from Bangor, c. 673, and maintained connections with its parent monastery until the ninth century.

Eileach an Naoimh in the Inner Hebrides has a small monastery with grave-yard, chapel and beehive cells reminiscent of those at Skellig Michael (p. 211). The remains of circular cells are also present at **Annait**, on Skye, which is a small monastic foundation on a promontory. Another eremitic monastery within a stone-built cashel wall of roughly circular shape is situated at **Sgor Nam Ban-Naomha**, on Canna.

Epilogue: The end of Celtic Britain and Ireland

The Normans were the agents of the final absorption of Celtic Britain and Ireland into feudal Europe. The impact of the Norman Conquest of England, following William I's victory in 1066, was fairly rapid. They were the descendants of Viking settlers in Normandy, but the culture introduced to England was feudal, in which land was given in return for military service. The influence of the Normans, in castle building at least, was felt in the Welsh Marches even before 1066, and Norman earls were given holdings in Wales, then Scotland, and finally Ireland.

Scotland

The start of the process of the Anglicization of Scotland can be traced to the foundation of the House of Canmore by Malcolm III (Duncan, 1975: 117–28; Barrow, 1989). The pro-English policy of the House of Canmore developed into pro-Norman in the reign of Malcolm's youngest son, David I, who succeeded to the throne of Scotland in 1124 marking the beginning of feudal Scotland (Duncan, 1975: ch. 7; Barrow, 1989; 1985). David brought many Normans to Scotland, and gave them most of the important offices in the church and state, as well as extensive territorial holdings. The Scottish aristocracy became French-speaking, and Anglo-Norman feudalism became established as the basis of government. Innovations in the twelfth century were many: coinage as a regular means of trade was introduced (Stewart, 1968: 190), many of the important royal burghs were founded (Yeoman, 1995: 54), castle architecture developed (Cruden, 1960a: 22–3; Tabraham, 1986: 29–33) and regular monasticism also flourished (Cruden, 1960b: 48–9). Another innovation was the spread of villages (Laing, 1969: 71–2). They were similar to the English, with stone longhouses or smaller buildings on one or both sides of a road or street.

The changeover to Norman feudalism was probably a gradual process, however, and there would have been a certain degree of compromise. The twelfth and thirteenth centuries witnessed a few Celtic uprisings (Duncan, 1975: 194), but politically the end of Celtic rule in Scotland came with the death of Alexander III in 1286, leaving Scotland open to the invasion of Edward I and the events surrounding the competition for the Scottish crown.

Although there were some obvious differences between the feudal Scottish nobility and its English counterpart, there was no essential difference in the material culture available in a Scottish or an English castle between the thirteenth and sixteenth centuries, and excavations in towns in recent years has shown them very comparable to their English counterparts (Yeoman, 1995: chs. 4–5).

There is some evidence however for early medieval settlement types surviving into the middle ages and beyond. Crannogs certainly continued in use in the middle ages, and several of Iron Age date appear to have been re-occupied, for example Hyndford and Lochspouts. A few appear to have been built in the middle ages or later; as late as 1608 an act was passed by the Scottish parliament forbidding the building of 'crannaks' (I. Crawford, 1967: 88). Similarly, duns appear to have been occupied, if not actually built, in medieval Scotland. A few sites may have been occupied as late as the eighteenth and nineteenth centuries, as suggested by the finds from Ugadale Point (Morrison, 1977).

The continuing occupation of crannogs and duns in western Scotland raises the question of the nature of the territory of the Lordship of the Isles. Ultimately in the period of its greatest power, the fourteenth and fifteenth centuries, the Lordship of the Isles controlled the whole of the west of Scotland north of Kintyre, and much of the east between Inverness and Kincardine. It was a militant state, constantly at war with the Scotto-Norman feudal kingdom based on Stirling, Fife and the Lothians.

Its capital was Finlaggan, which has been excavated (Yeoman, 1995: 116–18). It maintained a fleet and had strong Ulster connections, and within its bounds traditions died hard – the bow and arrow still seem to have been used as weapons in the seventeenth century. Local traditions of sculpture, stemming ultimately from Iona, were kept alive until the sixteenth century in the rich and long-lived school of west Highland grave-slabs, which by their iconographic riches provide an interesting sidelight on life in the medieval Western Isles (Steer and Bannerman, 1997; Fig. 127).

Wales and the Isle of Man

In Wales a situation similar to that in Scotland can be observed, if the changes were not as dramatic (J. Davies, 1990: 103–14; Walker, 1990: chs. 2–3). The process of English annexation began as early as the time of William I who established Norman lords at Chester and Shrewsbury to control the March. The Norman settlement of Wales extended along the coast of south Wales to the mouth of the Teifi and along the north Welsh coast to Rhuddlan. On the lowest-lying part of the coastal belt, especially in south Wales, a pattern of villages of English type grew up, many of them named after Norman founders or owners (Butler, 1971: 24). The coastal settlement was followed by the gradual penetration of the river valleys of central Wales, with the establishment of lordships and the construction of a rash of mottes, mounds crowned by

Fig. 127 Head of Kilchoman cross, Islay, a fifteenth-century echo of earlier sculpture.

timber towers. In north Wales the Norman advance was slower, though some castles were established even in the mountainous regions.

As in Scotland, towns were an innovation in Wales: in the period 1070–1300 some eighty towns were founded, most of them small (J. Davies, 1990: 114). Coins were struck by the Normans (North, 1963: 164–5), though it seems unlikely that coinage as a regular means of trade was early accepted by the Welsh. Benedictine houses were rapidly established. From the 1130s onwards Cistercian monasteries were being built either in Norman territory or at the request of native Welsh chiefs (Walker, 1990: 82–3).

In view of the lack of archaeological evidence in Wales for the later part of the early Christian period it is difficult to assess the extent of native Celtic survival of settlement types or material culture. Certainly, as in Scotland, the homes of the nobility were as well equipped as those in England with the same types of objects. Architecture was innovative, structures, manor houses and even rural longhouses were all introduced from outside.

Documentary evidence indicates that in the later pre-Norman period the basis of Welsh settlement patterns was the *tref*, a township or hamlet, and Welsh society was founded on the bond hamlet with the superimposition of princely and free families, with permanent lowland settlements and temporary summer shelters like the Scottish shielings. From the twelfth century onwards this was replaced by the *gwely*, which was an area of cleared land associated with a single steading occupied by one family, and in its development the bond vill was an important factor. Essentially, the pattern was of gradual change (Butler, 1971: 250; 1977).

In the Isle of Man, as in the Northern Isles of Scotland, Norse occupation was long lived (Kinvig, 1975: ch. 4). The Norse character of the Isle of Man lasted into the thirteenth or fourteenth centuries. By this time the settlement pattern in Man on a peasant level appears to have been changing to one of transhumance from winter lowland to summer highland pastures, and medieval shielings of a type current throughout the Highland zone have been excavated at Block Eary and Injebreck (Gelling, 1962–3). There is little 'Celtic' continuity apparent in Man in the later middle ages, and the Manx castles such as Castle Rushen attest strong feudal influence.

Ireland

The Normans landed in Co. Wexford in 1169, and by 1200 had captured most of the south and east of the country. The first, military phase resulted in the construction of mottes and subsequently, between 1200 and 1220, stone castles, which were put up in the centre of lordships and at strategic river crossings, as well as round the coast. A number of mottes seem to have been sited on pre-existing raths (Barry, 1987: ch. 3; O'Keefe, 2000: ch. 1).

Between 1170 and 1300 there were successive English settlements in Ireland. The area of Anglo-Norman occupation, approximately two thirds of the country, was divided up on an English manorial basis (J. Phillips, 1984). The pre-existing Scandinavian towns of Dublin, Cork and Limerick were developed and inland towns and villages were founded, the former with borough status in many cases. Excavations at Dublin show that materially the larger Irish towns were abreast of those in Britain, and the list of imports from Dublin suggests a considerable trade (Barry, 1987: 118–25; O'Keefe, 2000: ch. 4).

As in Scotland and Wales ecclesiastical foundations were established in Ireland, and there are many fine examples of both Romanesque and Gothic architecture. The Irish Romanesque, however, had a certain character of its own, and in its sculptural adornment at any rate shows some echoes from a Celtic past (Leask, 1955: ch. 8; O'Keefe, 2000: ch. 6 for medieval churches in Ireland generally). Coinage, introduced by the Vikings, continued from around 1182 with the issues of John de Courcy (W. O'Sullivan, 1964). Despite the major changes, however, there were elements of Celtic survival in later medieval Ireland, both in terms of social organization and in economy (history: Nicholls, 1972; archaeology: V. Proudfoot, 1977).

The twelfth century, then, marks a convenient divide in the Celtic-speaking areas of Britain and Ireland. The Norman advance effectively brought late

Celtic Britain and Ireland culturally in line with England and Europe, and though it is unlikely that the Anglo-Norman penetration had any profound effect on basic patterns of settlement or peasant economy, feudalization brought about certain social changes. Archaeology, of course, tells nothing about customs, folk traditions and ideas, but these certainly had a much longer survival than the purely material aspects of Celtic culture. On that level the Celts retained a clear identity.

Groups of people mentioned in the book

Appendix
1

BRITONS   This term is used interchangeably in Britain for the pre- and post-Roman population but also used during the Roman period instead of Romano-Briton for those with less Romanized lifestyle. They spoke a Brythonic Celtic language, usually termed British, out of which emerged Welsh, Cornish and Cumbric.

WELSH   The Britons in Wales during the entire period. The Welsh saw themselves as related to the people of Cumbria.

PICTS   The people in Scotland north of the Forth–Clyde line. They spoke another Brythonic (i.e., British) language (see p. 311). They are first mentioned as a people by Classical writers from the end of the third century AD, and seem to have formed new kingdoms out of older tribal groups. They amalgamated with the Scots in the ninth century under a Scottish ruler and the united kingdom became known subsequently as Alba.

SCOTS   Irish who migrated to western Scotland to form the Scottic kingdom of Dál Riata, which took the same name as their territory in Ulster. They spoke Goidelic Celtic (i.e., Irish), and subsequently when the Scots took over Pictland, their language was spread and developed into Scots Gaelic.

MANX   Originally occupied by Brythonic Celtic speakers (i.e., British), the Isle of Man was settled by Irish and the original language was replaced by Goedelic (i.e., Irish), where a local dialect (Manx) evolved.

ANGLO-SAXONS   Many groups of Germanic people (i.e., non-Celtic, but with a generally similar lifestyle) who emigrated from the Continent in the fifth–sixth centuries AD and who by the seventh century had formed kingdoms in what had been the most Romanized parts of Roman Britain.

THE VIKINGS   Groups from Scandinavia, mainly from Norway (the Norse), who first raided and then settled in northern Britain, the Isle of Man, Wales and Ireland from c. 800 onwards.

THE IRISH   The native inhabitants of Ireland, who spoke Goidelic Celtic, which they introduced into the areas in which they settled in Scotland, the Isle of Man and Wales.

Appendix **2**

Some important people mentioned in the book

AEDAN MAC GABRAIN (d. c. 558)   King of the Dalriadic Scots, the first to campaign outside Dál Riata, who may have been in conflict with the Britons as far east as the Forth, and who was also active against the Picts.

ADOMNÁN (d. 704)   Ninth abbot of Iona, author of the *Life of St Columba*, a major account of monastic life in the seventh century, and *De Locis Sanctis*, on the holy places in Palestine and Constantinople. He was distantly related to Columba, and used first-hand accounts of the saint. He may have met Bede.

ANEIRIN (?late sixth century)   Bard attached to the court of Mynyddawg Mwynfawr near Edinburgh who wrote in Brittonic Celtic *Y Gododdin*, an account of a disastrous raid from the Gododdin area near Edinburgh to Yorkshire in which he took part. The earliest surviving text is thirteenth-century, but it incorporates early if not original material.

ARTHUR (?late fifth/early sixth century)   Legendary war leader, first named in the ninth-century *Historia Brittonum* (q.v.), who also figures in the Welsh Annals. Regarded as the leader of resistance against the Anglo-Saxon advance.

BEDE (c. 673–735)   Monk in the twin monasteries of Monkwearmouth and Jarrow near modern Newcastle in Northumbria. He wrote more than thirty works, of which his *Historia Ecclesiastica Gentis Anglorum* is one of the main historical sources for Anglo-Saxon history up to his time, and which discusses where relevant to his purpose the adjacent Celtic lands.

BRIAN BORU (r. c. 940–1014) (a.k.a. Brian Bórama)   Irish king of the Dál Cais, later High King, who fought the Vikings and finally triumphed at the battle of Clontarf, 1014, in which he was killed.

BRIDEI, son of MAELCHU (late sixth century) (a.k.a. Bridei mac Maelchon, Brude)   King of the Picts, who met St Columba.

CADWALLON (d. 634)   Welsh king of Gwynedd who, having been driven out by the Anglo-Saxon Edwin of Bernicia, joined forces with Penda of Mercia to invade Northumbria, where Edwin was killed at Heathfield. Cadwallon however was killed by Oswald at Heavenfield.

ST BRIGIT (c. 480–525)   Irish saint whose life was chronicled by Cogitosus. Associated with Kildare.

ST COLUMBA (d. 597) (a.k.a. in Ireland as Columb Cille)   Scottish saint (b. c. 521) who left Ireland in 563 and was given the island of Iona to found a monastery by Conall, king of Dál Riata. Reputedly consecrated Aedan Mac Gabrain (q.v.) and was active as a missionary among the Picts.

COLUMBANUS (543–615) (a.k.a. Columba the Younger) Irish monk, initially at Bangor, who travelled extensively in Europe, becoming abbot of Luxeuil (which he founded) in France and Bobbio in Italy.

CUNEDDA (? early fifth century) (a.k.a. Cunedag) Legendary king, probably of Gododdin, in south-east Scotland, who traditionally migrated to north Wales with most of his sons, where he traditionally was the founder of several Welsh dynasties.

ST DAVID (c. 550–589) (a.k.a. Dewi) The traditional founder of Christianity in Wales. Associated particularly with the south, and St Davids.

ST NINIAN (early fifth century?/ sixth century?) (known as Bishop Nynia, and in the Isle of Man as Trinian) Traditional founder of the monastery of Whithorn in Galloway, who according to the eighth-century *Miracles of Bishop Nynia* was active in the conversion of the southern Picts. There is a possibility that there were two Nynians, one in the fifth century, the other in the early sixth.

GILDAS (fl. early sixth century) Writer known mainly for the *De Excidio Britanniae* (often called *The Ruin of Britain*) compiled c. AD 540, which gives a highly literate account of the Anglo-Saxon settlement and was extensively drawn upon by Bede (q.v.). An Irish collection also includes a *Penitential* attributed to him.

HYWEL DDA (r. c. 930–949/50) (a.k.a. Hywel ap Cadell) Grandson of Rhodri Mawr (q.v.) Welsh king. Annexed Gwynedd and Powys to rule a largely united Wales. Pursued a pro-English policy.

KENNETH MAC ALPIN (843–58) (a.k.a. Cinaed mac Ailpin) Scottish king who united Picts and Scots, c. 843, into a unified kingdom, later known as Alba.

MAELGWN (c. 520–551) Welsh King of Gwynedd, attacked by Gildas (q.v.). His seat was traditionally Degannwy, Clwyd.

MAÉL SECHNAILL MAC DOMNAILL (late tenth century) (a.k.a. Maelsechnaill II) High king of the Uí Neill, who successfully defeated the Vikings in 980 and captured Viking Dublin three times.

NECHTAN MAC DERELEI (r. c. 706–724) Pictish king who activated Anglo-Saxon influence in the Pictish Church. Abdicated and went into a monastery.

'NENNIUS' Name sometimes given to the anonymous compiler of the *Historia Brittonum*, who was writing somewhere in Wales in 829 or 830. (A later copy of the text attributes it to someone of this name.) This compilation draws on many different sources including Anglo-Saxon in providing historical information.

NIALL NOIGIALLACH (c. early fifth century) Legendary Irish leader Niall of the Nine Hostages, founder of the Southern Uí Neill. Conquered Meath and ruled from Tara. Allegedly raided in the Western Isles of Scotland.

OENGUS MAC FERGUSA (r. 729–61) (a.k.a. Angus mac Fergus) King of the Picts, who captured Dunadd and was over-king in Dál Riata.

ST PALLADIUS (fl. c. 431) Bishop sent by Pope Celestine to minister to the Christian Irish in 431, according to Prosper of Aquitaine. Active in the east of the country.

ST PATRICK (traditionally c. 396–459, but probably later in the fifth century) Romano-Briton taken by Irish raiders to Ireland, where he was gradually converted to Christianity. A dream directed him to escape, which he did to Britain. Later he returned to Ireland, and spread the faith in the north. His work includes his auto-biographical *Confession*, and his *Letter to the Soldiers of Coroticus*, an apostate ruler in south-west Scotland. Asssociated especially with Armagh.

RHODRI MAWR (r. 844–78) (a.k.a. Rhodri ap Merfyn)   Welsh king of Gwynedd, who expanded the kingdom to embrace much of Wales. Defeated Viking Horm, 856, subsequently driven out by Vikings and died fighting the Anglo-Saxons.

TALIESIN (late sixth century)   Bard who, if the poems attributed to him were actually all his work, was attached to the courts of Elmet, Powys and Rheged. He gave an account of the exploits of Cynan Garwyn, Urien and his son Owain and Gwallawg.

URIEN (fl. late sixth century)   King of Rheged. Fought against the Angles of Bernicia, c. 580, in alliance with Rhydderch Hael of the Strathclyde Britons.

Date brackets

Many different terms have been used for the period c. AD 400–c. 1200, with marked differences notable between archaeologically based or historically based studies, and between the different regions.

In the past the period has been summarily cut into several divisions: the fifth–sixth centuries (traditionally called the Dark Ages, more recently known as the sub-Roman or post-Roman period in those areas of the British Isles ruled by Rome until the early fifth century, or the pagan Saxon period); the seventh century (roughly corresponding to the early Christian period in Celtic areas, but known as the Heptarchy in Saxon areas); the Viking Age (post 800, but also seen as the beginnings of England which developed out of the Anglo-Saxon kingdoms). The period in England from 1066 to the twelfth century was traditionally the early middle ages, the period from then until 1485 being regarded as the high middle ages.

In addition, since in many areas there was no discernible change in lifestyle or beliefs from the Iron Age typical of (say) the first century BC and (say) the sixth century AD, many researchers referred to the entire span in areas such as Scotland in particular as the Iron Age. This is often divided into the pre-Roman, the Roman or the post-Roman Iron Age.

Such terminology becomes untenable when discussing wide issues such as trade. It would be theoretically possible for a 'sub-Roman object' to be taken from a post-Roman town to a pagan Saxon village, thence to an early Christian site in Wales and subsequently to a late/post-Roman Iron Age site in Scotland in the space of a few weeks chronologically.

To obviate such problems some scholars have decided to opt for the all-embracing term medieval (meaning age between the Classical and the Renaissance), from the final abandonment of Roman Britannia by Rome in 409 onwards. Under this scheme early medieval is interchangeable with Dark Age, pagan Saxon etc., but causes difficulties in England in particular where the term has been used for the period from 800 (Alfred the Great) or even 1066 (the Norman Conquest) onwards.

Notes

Introduction

1 The literature dealing with the question of the extent of Romano-British survival and the Anglo-Saxon settlements is considerable. For the arguments relating to the survival of Romano-British culture within former Britannia: Dark, 1994a; Snyder, 1998 and Dark, 2000, may be consulted. For the view that Roman Britain ended fairly abruptly, Faulkner, 2000 and Faulkner, 2004 provide a clear argument. For the arguments favouring a 'small scale' Anglo-Saxon invasion and a take-over at the top, Higham, 1992, and Jones, 1996, provide cogent discussions. For the Anglo-Saxon settlements, Hines, 1990; 1994.

2 The debate was started by Chapman, 1992, and furthered, as far as Britain and Ireland were concerned, by James, 1999. The entrenched opposing views are clearly set out in Collis, 2003 (arguing against Celtic ethnicity) and Megaw and Megaw, 1999 (arguing for it).

3 There are many accessible accounts of Hallstatt and La Tène cultures. Excellent overviews can be found in Moscati et al., 1991; Green, 1995; Cunliffe, 1997.

1 The Celtic world

1 Koch, 1991, argues that proto-Celtic developed in the late Bronze Age (c. 1300–600 BC), spreading from the culture areas in Europe known as Urnfield/Hallstatt C to the Atlantic zone, including south-east England, south Wales, Armorica and Ireland.

2 Useful surveys of Celtic social structure in Dillon, 1954; Mac Niocaill, 1972: ch. 3; Richter, 1988: 16–23; N. Patterson, 1991; Ó Cróinín, 1995: chs. 3, 5.

3 The 'heroic' model has been particularly taken up in L. Alcock, 1987a and 2003, and in S. Evans, 1997.

4 General discussions of women in Celtic society in Bitel, 1996; W. Davies, 1983.

5 This number in Ireland has been projected on the basis of the number of known raths (c. 45,000) and the number of crannogs (c. 1,200), each of which probably had 6–12 occupants, possibly more. However, only some of the raths and crannogs would have been occupied at the same time, and the figure does not take into account open settlements, forts, or sites destroyed or not yet located. This might give us about 50,000–80,000 settlements.

6 L. Alcock, 2003: 115. The figure is based on figures for Argyll in the fourteenth century. See also L. Alcock, 1997, for the methods of calculation.

7 The relatively short life-expectancy echoes populations in the early medieval period generally, but pagan Saxon cemeteries show a rather longer life span, averaging thirty-five years.

8 Surveys of the literature include Dillon, 1948, and Parry, 1955. Collections of translations include Cross and Slover, 1937; Kinsella, 1969; Gantz, 1981 and K. Jackson, 1971. For a recent collection of translations, Koch, 1997.

9 Surviving cult practice in Glen Lyon in Anon, 1977: 440; Fortingall: Anon, 1977: 338. For other examples of pagan Celtic survival, Ross, 1967.

2 Settlements

1 N. Patterson, 1991: 363–4.
2 Stout, 1997: 106–7.
3 Stout, 1997: 107.
4 Dark, and Dark 1996; 1997: 143–4.
5 For prehistoric hillforts in Britain generally, Cunliffe, 1991: ch. 14 and D. Harding, 2004: passim. Irish hillforts in Raftery, 1994: ch. 3
6 L. Alcock et al., 1989: 206–14 reviewed the earlier classification of 'nuclear forts'. He subsequently coined the term used here: L. Alcock, 2003: 190.
7 Stout, 1997: 16–17. The classic sites are Rathmullan, Co. Down: Lynn, 1981–2; and Deer Park Farms: Lynn, 1989.
8 This was the interpretation at Shannon airport: E. Rynne, 1964.
9 Limbert, 1996, argues for this. For cashels, see also Jon Henderson, 2000a: 128.
10 A. O'Sullivan, E. Kelly and R. Sands, *Investigating an early medieval crannog at Coolure Demesne, CoWestmeath* (2004) 27. *http:www.ucd.ie/archdata/external/research/coolure_demesne/2004/COOLURE_DEMESNE_2004_REPORT.pdf*
11 Warner, 1994a, argued strongly for a 'high status' interpretation.

3 Farming

1 Entries in the Annals of Ulster: Mac Airt and MacNiocaill, 1983.
2 *www.ehsni.gov.uk/built/monuments/Chapter15.shtml*.
3 There is an Irish poem about a cat called Pangur Bán: De Paor and De Paor, 1958: 88.
4 For raised beds, F. Kelly, 1997: 233, though not for this interpretation of them.

4 Everyday objects and equipment

1 For example from Loch an Duin, South Uist: Close-Brooks, 1984.
2 Review of types and technology in Macgregor, 1985.
3 The type has three variants. A1 is of the Iron Age, A2 of the early medieval period and A3 is a type of small comb for personal use known from Lagore and Carrickfergus in Ireland.
4 MacGregor, 1985: 85, discusses English examples and their Continental proto- types, ard argues that in England they belong to the late fourth and early fifth centuries. He sees the 'Celtic' examples as a different tradition, but see A. Smith, 2000.
5 Dunlevy has sub-divided the type into three varieties, of which her D1 (straight ends and thick sideplates usually trapezoidal in cross-section) she has seen as dating from the fifth to the tenth centuries, D2 (C-shaped sideplates and shaped end-teeth) to the eighth to tenth centuries, and D3 (elongated ornate combs with highly decorated endplates and the use of copper rivets) from the eleventh century onwards.

6 Hutchinson, 1979. But see also Pearce, 2004: 260, supporting a north Germanic influence.

5 Industry and technology

1 I am indebted to the excavator of Ross Island, Billy O Brien, for information about his discoveries. He has pointed out that they might seem to support the reference to the mineral wealth of Killarney, alluded to in the *Historia Brittonum*, and to the mythology of Lein, the metalworking god, whose name was given to the largest of the Killarney lakes.
2 Laing and Longley, forthcoming. Prehistoric mining at the Great Orme in E. Roberts, 2002.
3 Dolley, 1976, discusses the few imported coins in Ireland in the period, arguing that more must have been imported but melted down.
4 This type may be divided into the following classes: 1A, those tapering to a circular horizontal cross-section, with rounded or pointed base (the commonest type at the Mote of Mark); 1B, general type as 1A but with fixed lids; 1C, as 1A but shallower and with a flat base. Types 1B and 1C occur only at Garryduff: O'Kelly, 1962: fig. 21. Crucibles were current throughout the early medieval period, though some may have a more restricted chronology which can only be proved by further finds.
5 The basic type, 3A, is circular at the mouth with a rounded base, and bulges out from the mouth, reaching the greatest diameter lower down the vessel. The clay is thickest towards the base, and the rim is characteristically 'horn-shaped' in section. At Dunadd it was designated Type E. Examples include substantial vessels from Garranes (Ó Ríordáin, 1942: fig. 24). In Type 3B the base is flat. With the exception of some dubious examples from Garryduff, this type is known from two adjacent sites in Argyll – Kildonan and Ugadale Point – and may be a local variant. Type 3C is similar to 3A but made of stone, and is rounded in cross-section. It occurs at Garryduff and is almost indistinguishable from a stone mortar.
6 These have been catalogued for Ireland in O'Meadhra, 1979; 1987a; 1987b and 1993; the Dalriadic examples, most of which come from Kingarth, Bute, are discussed in Laing, 1996. The most recent group, not yet published, are from Inchmarnock, Bute.

6 Trade and communications

1 Some block wheels are also known: Lucas, 1952.
2 Hamilton, 1956: pl. xxi, 4; ships: pls. xxi, nos. 1–2. The treatment of the dragon prow, however, is reminiscent of Pictish art: for example, the monster on the terminal of one of the St Ninian's Isle brooches. See also discussion in Ritchie, 1989: 50.
3 Argued as from a sixth-century spangenhelm by De Paor, 1960–1, as from eighth-century Anglo-Saxon shrines by Webster and Backhouse, 1991: 174, and as an eighth-century helmet by Cessford, 1994: 77.
4 Campbell, 1996b: 92 notes analyses of madder on sherds of E Ware.
5 Thomas, 1959, was the key pioneer study, which defined D and E Ware; Thomas, 1981a, provided an update; Campbell in Edwards and Lane, 1988, has a useful summary (though mostly about Wales); Lane, 1994; Campbell, 1996b.

6 B1 amphorae are in a pinkish ware with yellow inclusions, and are distinguished by having deep grooves closely set together round the upper part of the vessel. They were produced in southern Greece. Dating is probably the same as *PRS*, i.e., late fifth or early sixth century.

B2 consists of jars in a buff ware with very globular profiles and irregularly spaced ridges and fluting. It came from the same general area as B1, and was imported around the same time.

B3 comprises sherds of undecorated amphorae. A nearly complete profile of one was established at Gwithian, Cornwall.

B4 comes from western Asia Minor, and consists of small lagenae (jugs) with a reddish fabric and the inclusion of mica. B4 vessels are fairly small with stubby bases, globular bodies and a high constricted bottle neck with two strap handles from neck to shoulder. The grooving on these vessels is confined to broad, shallow fluting. It occurs at Constantinople, and can be dated to the fifth and first half of the sixth centuries. It is not always easy to recognize, as one-handled versions were produced in the late Roman period.

B5 is now usually termed *Keay* 7, the term given to it in the Mediterranean (Keay, 1984).

B6 is now similarly usually named *Almagro 54*. Both these types of amphora were imported in the latest period of town life in Roman Britain, and occur at Exeter, Gloucester, York, London and Caistor-by-Norwich, as well as at Tintagel.

7 Clothes and jewellery

1 E. R. Heckett in the on-line report: *www.ehsni.gov.uk/built/monuments/ Chapter* 15, for this and other references to Deer Park Farms fabrics.

2 *Med. Arch.* 5 (1961): 310–11.

3 Briggs, 1985: 103–4. There is also amber from Lagore, Garranes (Ó Ríordáin, 1942: 121), Ronaldsway, Isle of Man (Laing and Laing, 1988: 409).

4 See the series of representations in Trench-Jellicoe, 1999.

5 Etchingham and Swift, 2004: 47. This reference seems to have been a later eleventh–twelfth-century addition to the original text, but it is clear that some brooches were regarded of great value and suitable for pledging. For further discussion of the way brooches were worn and were associated with rank, Whitfield, 2004.

6 For the zoomorphic types (E and F), the former of which he termed 'proto-zoomorphic', Kilbride-Jones, 1980 devised a scheme elaborating upon Kilbride-Jones, 1935–6 and 1937. Simplification of the zoomorphic types was proposed by Graham-Campbell, 1991a. Type G brooches were re-defined by Graham-Campbell, 1976, and Dickinson, 1982. See also Campbell and Lane, 2000: 106–14. Class F3 was re-examined in Newman, 1989; 1990.

7 They include a separate series of bossed penannular brooches, which belong to the Viking Age and which may have evolved in Ireland in the ninth century: Graham-Campbell, 1972; 1975.

8 1a: These have a U-shaped plate beneath an arc of beads or pellets, such as the Oldcroft pin. 1b: Pins with U-shaped plate and horizontal capping of fingers, such as the Gaulcross pin.

9 Cool, 1990, seems to regard all Romano-British pins as hair pins, but it is probable that some of the long-shanked zoomorphic pins that were coming into fashion in the fourth century were dress-fasteners, as possibly were others.

10 I am indebted to Jim Boyle for letting me refer to his unpublished work here.

11 It is possible to distinguish between those with some features of the zoomorphic pins, namely a 'beak' below the head (2a), and those without (2b). A version, 2c, represented at Skaill, Orkney, has a loop on the head to take a ring: J. Hunter, 1997: fig. 10, SF118.

12 This is a specialized variant of (10). They are normally hipped and have a simple triskele on the head. Probably in origin a sixth-century type, which continues into the Viking Age, when it is represented in Dublin and Whithorn: Hill et al., 1997: 368, no. 44.

13 Cool, 1990: fig. 8, no. 13.

14 Pins of this type fall into two groups: those which have solid wheel heads, often inlaid or otherwise decorated, with the fillet integrated with the head; and those which have flatter heads, in which the fillet becomes a projection on either side of the shank below the head, and in which the decoration where present is confined to engraving. The earliest are probably of the eighth to ninth centuries; the developed examples may be later.

15 This very rare type, represented at Lagore, is probably derived from a Roman type of pin. The Lagore pin was unstratified but stylistically is in accordance with a seventh- or eighth-century date. There is a Pictish example from Golspie: Close-Brooks, 1974–5.

8   Art and ornament

1 General surveys of Celtic art in the early medieval period in Laing and Laing, 1992 and 1995, and Laing, 1997; for the earlier part of the period Megaw and Megaw, 1989. Irish art in the period is dealt with in F. Henry, 1965; 1967; and 1970. Major survey of metalwork in Youngs 1989 (exhibition catalogue).

2 For recurrence of the Durrow lion in sculpture, Laing, 2000b: 110, n. 119. For the problems of other long survivals, Lang, 1991.

3 For their use in Anglo-Saxon burials, Geake, 1999. The Romano-British origin is argued in a number of studies, and summarized in Laing, 1993a: 22–5. The view that they are all post-Roman was followed in Brenan, 1991.

4 They may have been decorative hanging vases, lamps, hand basins, or votive chalices. A bowl found in a cist burial from St Paul-in-the-Bail in Lincoln (within the Anglo-Saxon church) points to an ecclesiastical association of some bowls, as indeed does the series of escutcheons from the Anglo-Saxon monastery of Whitby, Yorks. A text from Bede implies that the bowls were secular vessels for washing hands. It has been suggested that the bowls were not suspended from a height, which would have put too much strain on the relatively weak escutcheon loops, but were supported from a tripod.

5 The literature is considerable, but note Whitfield, 1976; 1974; 2001b and the description with references in Ryan, 1983b: no. 48. It was not found at Tara but at Bettystown, but was so named to give it a romantic association by a Dublin jeweller selling replicas of it.

6 Mahr and Raftery, 1932–41: 145–6, where a late tenth-century date was suggested. Bourke, 1987: 166 favoured the ninth. Johnson, 2000: 157, has suggested the possibility of a later date.

7 MacDermott, 1955 and 1957, suggested a tenth-century date for this group; Bourke, 1987, considered them to belong to the late ninth. Michelli (1986; 1996) has compared them with a group of Scottish croziers, suggesting a date in the tenth–eleventh centuries for them. Johnson, 2000, settles for the second half of the tenth century, on the evidence provided by motif pieces from Dublin.

8 Manuscript art generally in F. Henry, 1965; 1967; and 1970. Catalogue of manuscripts, including Anglo-Saxon, in Alexander, 1978. Good introduction in Nordenfalk, 1977.

9 Useful short surveys in Harbison, 1999; Edwards, 1990: 155–61.

10 Many surveys, starting with Allen and Anderson, 1903. Notable are Curle, 1939–40; R. Stevenson, 1955a; I. Henderson, 1967; and Henderson and Henderson, 2004.

11 The prototypes of the free-standing crosses have been discussed extensively, most recently by MacLean, 1995a, who has argued in favour of the carpentry techniques employed in the construction of the Iona crosses, and by N. Edwards, 1985a, who has seen the development as more directly inspired by Northumbrian models.

12 Fisher, 2001: 15–16. The pre-eminence of Iona in the development of free-standing crosses was first advanced by Stevenson, 1956, and has been followed in most recent discussions which have considered the relationship of the Scottish and Irish crosses, see D. Kelly, 1993.

13 General surveys in Henry, 1964; Harbison, 1992; 1994; Stalley, 1996. Useful summary account in Edwards, 1990: 163–71.

14 Harbison, 1979 and the rejoinder by Henry, 1980 on the dating of the inscription; Edwards, 1986.

9 The church

1 For a useful survey of the problems with the evidence in Ireland: Hamlin, 1992.

2 Thomas, 1981b, reviews the evidence to that date; see also Watts, 1991; both authors suggest that Christianity was better established in the Romano-British countryside than elsewhere in the eastern provinces.

3 Thomas, 1981b: ch. 7; Higham, 1992: 99; Redknap, 1995; Blair and Pyrah, 1996.

4 On Palladius and Patrick the literature is extensive. Palladius is historically documented as reaching Ireland in 431 – this is attested by Prosper of Aquitaine, who reported that he was sent by Pope Celestine. The date of Patrick is more controversial, but he seems to have been flourishing in the mid-fifth century. Recent clear surveys of the evidence include Ó Cróinín, 1995: 23–7; Snyder, 2003: 116–21; and Charles-Edwards, 2000: 214–33.

5 For Nynia (St Ninian), MacQueen, 1990, who argues that the *Life* is based on a Latin original produced at Whithorn, c. 550–650; see also Hill et al., 1997: 1–16, on the problems of evaluating the historical Ninian.

6 Useful discussion in Snyder, 2003: 130–3; Dubricius and Illtud seem to have been operating c. 475; see Simon-Evans' introduction in Doble, 1971. St David is likely to have been active around the end of the sixth century, if his obit of 601 in the *Annales Cambriae* can be accepted.

7 The term for bishop appears to have been *sacerdos*, below which was *presbyter*, 'priest', and below that again was the *diaconus*, 'deacon'. The first two appear on memorial stones of the fifth to seventh centuries, but their appearance on memorial stones may have been a result of direct transplantation from the Continent: Thomas, 1998: 84–8.

8 E. James, 2001: 164. James outlines the growth of the myth of the 'Celtic Church' (2001: 164–70), a subject also tackled by K. Hughes, 1981, and W. Davies, 1992.

9 This view comes across very clearly in Chadwick, 1961.

10 There are many good accounts of monastic life, especially in Ireland. See particularly Hughes and Hamlin, 1997: ch. 1; Bitel, 1990, and among older sources, Bieler, 1966.

11 Bieler, 1966; Macdonald, 1984 (on Iona); Hamlin and Hughes, 1997; and Bitel, 1990.

12 Ó Kelly, 1975 – this may have been a shrine rather than a church: see Harbison, 1982: 628.

13 The calibrated date range for the mortar was between AD 980 and 1300 – R. Berger, 1995: 167.

14 Taylor and Taylor, 1965: 497–9, where some doubt was expressed that any of the fabric was in fact pre-Norman.

15 The classic study was that of Petrie, published in 1845, which has dominated later thought. For more recent appraisals Corlett, 1998; Stalley, 2000.

16 The theoretical development of these is traced in Thomas, 1971: ch. 5.

17 My thanks to the excavator Dr John Sheehan, for allowing me to mention this site in advance of publication.

18 Thomas, 1998: 7–9. This work is the clearest statement on the interpretation, but see also Howlett, 1995.

10   South-western Britain

1 For the medieval myth, Ashe, 1968.

2 The argument for the historicity of Arthur is well set out in L. Alcock, 1971, ch. 3.

3 'Whelp of the unclean Dumnonian lioness': Gildas, *De Excidio*, 28.

4 The literature on the re-interpretation of Tintagel and the subsequent investigation is extensive. See particularly Burrow, 1974; Dark, 1985; Harry and Morris, 1997; Thomas, 1993; Morris et al., 1999.

11   Wales

1 Arnold and Davies, 2000, provides a recent account. Accounts also provided in Frere, 1987; Salway, 1993; Jarrett, 1969.

2 Excavated by David Longley and the author.

3 I am indebted to David Longley for this point.

4 This is indicated by the Pillar of Eliseg at Llangollen, a Mercian style of cross erected in Powys.

5 General background, W. Davies, 1968; P. Wilson, 1966; Bowen, 1954.

6 Summary accounts of the history in Loyn, 1976; 1977: 53–4; Davies, 1982: 116–20; Redknap, 2000.

12   Ireland and the Isle of Man

1 For long it was held that the Celtic language and the use of iron was introduced to Ireland around the third century BC by La Tène immigrants, at a time when 'Celtic art' also made its appearance. Although it was recognized that the evidence for La Tène invasion was never very strong, the idea that there was a two-fold La Tène colonization of Ireland, from the Continent and from Britain (E. Rynne, 1958), won some acceptance, although there was no indication that colonization involved much more than the arrival of a leading élite, as critics of the view pointed out (Champion, 1982). An alternative view, that late Bronze Age culture continued in many parts of Ireland until the late first millennium BC, does not seem totally convincing either, however, though there is certainly some evidence for elements of late Bronze Age culture continuing (Raftery, 1994: 35–7; Cooney and Grogan, 1991). As the evidence currently stands, ironworking seems to have been acquired by native groups without any major change in population or lifestyle. The earliest find, an iron sword from the Shannon at Athlone, has been claimed to date to c. 600 BC, but the next group of iron swords span the period from the third century BC to the first century AD (Waddell, 1998: 287), and other scarce finds of ironwork suggest a similar date span. The finds of La Tène style that appear in Ireland seem to be prestige items of high status, and are concentrated in eastern Ulster and a zone stretching erratically from Meath to Galway. Elsewhere in southern Ireland there is a general absence of material displaying La Tène characteristics. See also now Raftery, 2005.

2 These are Navan (Waterman, 1997), the Emain Macha of later legend, Dun Ailinne (Knockaulin) (Wailes, 1990), Co. Kildare in Leinster, Cruachain (Rathcroghan) (Waddell, 1983), in Roscommon, the traditional capital of Connaught, as well as Tara (Newman, 1997), in Co. Meath and Uisneach, Co. Westmeath (Grogan and Donnaghy, 1997). See also now Aitchison, 1994, on later interest in these early ritual sites.

3 For this see especially Charles-Edwards, 2000; Ó Cróinín, 1995.

4 Laing, 1975a: 147–9. Later discussions on Cahercommaun: J. Raftery, 1981: 85; Caulfield, 1981: 211; Lynn, 1983: 49–50.

5 Johnson, 1999. Laing and Laing, 1990, 53, where it was suggested one brooch might be sixth-century: this view has been superseded, as this type of brooch has been found in a tenth-century context in Dublin.

6 A. O'Sullivan, E. Kelly and R. Sands, *Investigating an Early Medieval Crannog at Coolure Demesne, CoWestmeath* (2004), *http:www.ucd.ie/archdata/external/research/coolure_demesne/ 2004/COOLURE_DEMESNE_ 2004_REPORT.pdf*

7 The history of the Viking raids and settlements in Ireland is discussed in Ó Corráin, 1972; Richter, 1988: ch. 8; Ó Cróinín, 1995: ch. 9; Doherty, 1998; Larsen, 2001.

13   Southern Scotland and northern England

1 Richmond, 1958; D. Breeze, 1982: 28–32. The tribal geography has been modified slightly by Mann and Breeze, 1987: esp. 88–9, and more radically by Strang, 1998.

2 Cessford, 2001; Holmes and Hunter, 2001: 172; Holmes, 2003. Apart from some early third-century building in stone, the bath house outside the fort had furnaces

added in the late third century. A late third-century *antoninianus* was found in spoil removed from above the bath house, and stray coin finds carry the Roman activity on the site down to the early fourth century.

3 Birley argued on the evidence of his excavations in 1936–7 that the fort enjoyed some later occupation, including the provision of a water supply in the early fourth century, citing pottery of the third and fourth centuries as evidence: Birley, 1938: 321, 333, 347. Robertson said the pottery was now lost, and although coins of Severus Alexander, Maxentius and Constantine I had allegedly been found on the site, she disputed the later occupation: 1975: 4 and 286.

4 Breeze and Dobson, 2000: 224. There has been much debate about who the Attacotti were, but the most recent and most probable suggestion is that they were Irish: Rance, 2001.

5 The suggestion that Traprain was a temple site in the fourth century has been advanced primarily on the evidence of coin finds; this has convincingly been refuted.

6 The literature is extensive. Curle 1913–14 provides the original account; Laing 1973; Longley, 2001. The full report is Laing and Longley, 2006. Other directly relevant discussions in Laing, 1975b; Graham-Campbell, 1976.

7 Thomas, 1967; re-appraisal in Laing and Laing, 1990: 162–3. The sequence of shrines identified by the excavator is very dubious, as is the Irish connection discussed in the report.

8 There is evidence for an early (possibly Roman period?) cemetery of dug graves and at least one cremation, with sherds of red wheel-made pottery (Thomas, 1968b: 100–01), a pre-monastery paved road pre-dating the late fifth century (Hill et al., 1997: 26) and residual material from a stone-built structure with white calcium carbonate crust within a bank of the early monastery, which could have preceded it: perhaps the 'Candida Casa' of Bede (Hill et al., 1997: 81). There is also a Roman type of millstone from the site of the early monastery (Hill et al., 1997: 293).

14 Northern Scotland

1 There are many summary accounts of the history of the Picts. The most important are to be found in Chadwick, 1949; Wainwright, 1955a; I. Henderson, 1967; Anderson, 1973; Duncan, 1975; Smyth, 1984.

2 The main discussion of the Pictish language and its possible non-Pictish element was set out by Jackson, 1955, following late nineteenth-century commentators such as Rhys; more recent discussion of the debate in Forsyth, 1995b.

3 Okasha, 1985. In addition to her list, one has been discovered recently at Dull, Perthshire.

4 Whittington, 1974–5 for the original appraisal of *pit* names; Nicolaisen, 1996, for a more cautious view.

5 Not yet published, except as an interim from *www.headlandarchaeology.com*.

Further reading

The following is intended as a suggested starting point for further reading: full references will be found in the bibliography, which is a list of references for the book, not the subject area.

Archaeology – regional surveys

There is no book which covers the whole of the area encompassed in this study (if Laing and Laing, 1990 is discounted), but there are some good regional surveys.

For **Ireland** the best (though now somewhat outdated) is N. Edwards, 1990; Mytum, 1992, is valuable, but its processual approach may make it difficult reading for some. For Ulster, a good, simple starting point is provided by Mallory and McNeill, 1991, which covers other periods as well as the early Christian. The same may be said for Ryan, 1994, which embraces the whole of Ireland but is briefer. Of older works, De Paor and De Paor, 1958, remains a classic, though very outdated.

For **Scotland**, L. Alcock, 2003 is a very useful survey, and encompasses the whole of the north British mainland, Celtic and Saxon, without, however, including the Northern Isles or Outer Hebrides.

Wales is covered in Arnold and Davies, 2000, and the south-west peninsula of England in Todd, 1987, and Pearce, 2004.

Surveys dealing with both the history and archaeology of **Britain** in the period or part of it include Snyder, 2003 (an excellent and readable historical account of the Britons), Dark, 1994a and b and 2000 (which tend to cover the same ground as each other and which have interesting insights though are difficult to read) and Snyder, 1998 (which deals only with the fifth and sixth centuries).

There are a few regional surveys of **northern Scotland**, of which may be singled out Wainwright, 1955a, still useful despite its date, I. Henderson, 1967 (both on the Picts), Laing and Laing, 2001, and Foster, 1996 (on Picts and Scots). Harding, 2004, covers in some part the early medieval period as well as the Iron Age.

Prehistoric background

The Iron Age of Ireland is admirably covered in Raftery, 1994, and in Waddell, 1998. For Britain as a whole the classic overview is Cunliffe, 1991; Scotland is covered in Armit, 1997, and Harding, 2004. Iron Age Wales is reviewed in Lynch, Aldhouse-Green and Davies, 2000.

Documentary sources

There are now a number of general surveys of the historical evidence, again mostly regional. For Ireland the magisterial Charles-Edwards, 2000, is an invaluable reference, though sometimes difficult to read. The most recent account is provided by

D. Ó Cróinín, (ed.) 2005, which became available when this book was with the publishers. It is a considerable compilation by many hands, and reference is made to some of the chapters in it where appropriate in this book. More readily useable as an introduction is Ó Cróinín, 1995, though some of the thinking expressed is not universally held. The same may be said for the very readable Richter, 1988 (which extends its coverage to the end of the middle ages). Nor should Hughes, 1972, be overlooked despite its date; it is still a sound guide to the minefield of the sources. Of older works Ó Corráin, 1972, is still very valuable. Wales is admirably covered by W. Davies, 1982, and Scotland by Duncan, 1975, and Smyth, 1984. The last book is a highly personal but stimulating viewpoint. Mention should also be made of Byrne, 1973 (on Irish kingship), F. Kelly, 1997 (a brilliant survey of the documentary sources on farming), F. Kelly, 1988 (on law), N. Patterson, 1991, and Dillon, 1954 (both on society).

Settlement studies

For Ireland useful introductions to raths are provided by Stout, 1997, and V. Proudfoot, 1970, while crannogs are dealt with in O'Sullivan, 1998 and 2000. For Britain, Snyder, 1996, is a useful hand-list of sites. North Britain is dealt with in L. Alcock, 2003, and Pictland specifically in Ralston, 1997. For Wales, Edwards and Lane, 1988, is the best starting point; Dark, 1994b, provides a body of comparative material, even if not all would accept that his sites all belong to the period. Among key excavation reports should be listed Dunadd (Lane and Campbell, 2000), Lagore (Hencken, 1950), the Mote of Mark (Laing and Longley, 2006), Dinas Powys (Alcock, 1963), Garranes (Ó Ríordáin, 1942), Garryduff (O'Kelly, 1962), Dundurn (Alcock et al., 1989), Dumbarton Rock (Alcock and Alcock, 1990) and Cadbury Castle (L. Alcock, 1995).

Material culture

The technicalities of ironworking are discussed in Scott, 1990. The techniques of ornamental metalworking are usefully discussed in Youngs, 1989, and in Whitfield, 1987, which deals specifically with filigree work. Woodworking is discussed in Earwood, 1993, and bone and antler working in Macgregor, 1985. Imported pottery and glass have been extensively discussed: a useful starting point is to be found in Dark, 1996. Pottery alone is dealt with in Thomas, 1981b, which provides a list of finds to date and Campbell, 1996b. Campbell, 2000, is a valuable survey of imported glass.

The church

The most useful introduction to the Church in Ireland is Hughes and Hamlin, 1997; see also now Hughes 2005a and b. Of older studies Thomas, 1971, is still invaluable. A major collection of studies on the Church in Wales is to be found in Edwards and Lane, 1992. For the church in Ireland from an historical standpoint, Bieler, 1966, Hughes, 1966, and Bitel, 1990, are particularly useful. A valuable collection of studies of monastic archaeology is to be found in Herity, 1995.

General studies of key sites include those of High Island (White Marshall and Rourke, 2000a), Whithorn (Hill et al., 1997), and Iona (Ritchie, 1997). Stone buildings were discussed in Leask, 1955, though his dates are not now always acceptable. For memorial stones the key studies are Allen and Anderson, 1903, Nash-Williams, 1950, and Okasha, 1993; a new edition of Nash-Williams' classic study is in preparation.

Art

Art is well covered. General surveys are to be found in Laing and Laing, 1992 and 1995, which deal with both prehistoric and Christian art. For Ireland the classic surveys are provided by F. Henry, 1965, 1967, and 1970, and by Harbison, 1999. See also now Richardson, 2005, which though somewhat traditional is still a useful summary. Free-standing crosses are discussed in Richardson and Scarry, 1990, Harbison, 1994, and Stalley, 1996. For metalwork the starting point must be Youngs, 1989. A catalogue listing some of the major works of Irish art can be found in Ryan, 1983b. Manuscripts are discussed in Nordenfalk, 1977, and in G. Henderson, 1987. Pictish art is the subject of Henderson and Henderson, 2004. Important collections of papers are to be found in Ryan, 1987b, Spearman and Higgitt, 1993, C. Bourke, 1995, and Redknap et al., 2001.

Viking impact

For Scotland the best surveys are B. Crawford, 1987, Ritchie, 1993, and Graham-Campbell and Batey, 1998. For Ireland the starting point should be Larsen, 2001, and Clarke et al., 1998. For Wales, Redknap, 2000.

References

Adcock, G. 1978. 'The theory of interlace and interlace types in Anglian sculpture', in J. Lang (ed.), *Anglo-Saxon and Viking Age Sculpture* (= BAR Brit. Ser. 49), Oxford, 33–45

Aitchison, N. B. 1994. *Armagh and the Royal Centres in Early Medieval Ireland: Monuments, Cosmology and the Past*, Woodbridge

Aitken, W. G. 1955. 'Excavation of a chapel at St Ninian's Point, Bute', *Trans. Bute Nat. Hist. Soc.* 14: 62–76

Alcock, E. 1992. 'Burials and cemeteries in Scotland', in Edwards and Lane, 1988: 125–30

Alcock, L. 1963. *Dinas Powys: An Iron Age, Dark Age and Medieval Settlement in Glamorgan*, Cardiff

    1967. 'Excavations at Degannwy Castle, Caernarvonshire, 1961–6', *Archaeol. J.* 124: 190–201

    1970. 'Was there an Irish Sea culture-province in the Dark Ages?', in D. Moore (ed.), *The Irish Sea Province in Archaeology and History*, London, 55–65

    1971. *Arthur's Britain*, London

    1975–6. 'A multi-disciplinary chronology for Alt Clut, Castle Rock, Dumbarton', *Proc. Soc. Ant. Scot.* 107: 103–13

    1979. 'The North Britons, the Picts and the Saxons', in P. J. Casey (ed.), *The End of Roman Britain*, Oxford, 134–42

    1981. 'Early historic fortifications in Scotland', in G. Guilbert (ed.), *Hillfort Studies: Essays for A. H. A. Hogg*, Leicester, 150–80

    1983. 'Gwyr y Gogledd: an archaeological appraisal', *Arch. Cambrensis* 132: 1–18

    1987a. *Economy, Society and Warfare among the Britons and Saxons*, Cardiff

    1987b. 'Pictish studies: present and future', in Small, 1987: 80–92

    1995. *Cadbury Castle, Somerset: The Early Medieval Archaeology*, Cardiff

    1996. 'Ur-symbols in the pictographic system of the Picts', *Pictish Arts Soc. J.* 9: 10–13

    1997. 'How many Picts were there?', *Pictish Arts Soc. J.* 11: 6–8

    2003. *Kings and Warriors, Craftsmen and Priests*, Edinburgh

Alcock, L. and Alcock, E. A. 1987. 'Reconnaissance excavations 2, excavations at Dunollie Castle', *Proc. Soc. Ant. Scot.* 117: 119–47

Alcock, L. and Alcock, E. A. 1990. 'Reconnaissance excavations on Early Historic fortifications and other royal sites in Scotland, 1974–84: 4, excavations at Alt Clut, Clyde Rock, Strathclyde, 1974–75', *Proc. Soc. Ant. Scot.* 120: 95–149

Alcock, L. and Alcock, E. A. 1992. 'Reconnaisance excavations, 5: A, Forteviot; B, Urquhart Castle; C, Dunottar', *Proc. Soc. Ant. Scot.* 122: 215–87

Alcock, L., Alcock, E. A. and Driscoll, S. T. 1989. 'Reconnaisance excavations, 3: Excavations at Dundurn', *Proc. Soc. Ant. Scot.* 119: 189–226

Alexander, J. J. G. 1978. *Insular Manuscripts 6th to the 9th Century*, London

Allen, J. R. 1899. *Celtic Crosses of Wales*, Llanerch

Allen, J. R. and Anderson, J. 1903. *The Early Christian Monuments of Scotland*, Edinburgh

Anderson, A. O. and Anderson, M. (eds. and trans.) 1991. *Adomnán's Life of Columba*, rev. edn, Oxford

Anderson, M. O. 1949. 'The lists of the kings', *Scottish History Review* 28: 108–18

    1973. *Kings and Kingship in Early Scotland*, Edinburgh

    1987. 'Picts – the name and the people', in Small, 7–14

Andrews, J. H. 2005. 'The geographical element in Irish history', in Ó Cróinín (ed.), 1–31

Anon. 1977. *Folklore, Myths and Legends of Britain*, rev. edn, London

Archer, S. 1979. 'Late Roman gold and silver coin hoards in Britain: a gazetteer', in P. J. Casey (ed.), *The End of Roman Britain* (= BAR Brit. Ser. 71), Oxford, 29–64

Armit, I. (ed.) 1990. *Beyond the Brochs*, Edinburgh

    1992. *The Later Prehistory of the Western Isles of Scotland* (= BAR Brit. Ser. 221), Oxford

    1997. *Celtic Scotland*, London

Armstrong, E. C. R. 1921–2. 'Irish bronze pins of the early Christian period', *Archaeologia* 72: 71–86

Armstrong, E. C. R. and Crawford, H. S. 1922. 'The reliquary known as the Misach', *J. Royal Soc. Antiq. Ireland* 52: 105–11

Armstrong, E. C. R. and Macalister, R. A. S. 1920. 'Wooden block with leaves indented and waxed found at Springmount Bog, Co. Antrim', *J. Royal Soc. Antiq. Ireland* 1: 160–6

Arnold, B. and Gibson, D. B. (eds.) 1995. *Celtic Chiefdom, Celtic State*, Cambridge

Arnold, C. J. 1984. *Roman Britain to Saxon England*, London

Arnold, C. J. and Davies, J. L. 2000. *Roman and Early Medieval Wales*, Stroud

Ashe, G. (ed.) 1968. *The Quest for Arthur's Britain*, London

Bailey, R. 1996a. *England's Earliest Sculptors*, Toronto

Bailey, R. 1996b. *Ambiguous Birds and Beasts: Three Sculptural Puzzles in South-West Scotland*, Whithorn

Baillie, M. G. L. 1975. 'A horizontal mill of the 8th century AD at Drumard, Co. Derry', *Ulster J. Archaeol.* 38: 25–32

    1981. 'Dendrochronology: the prospects for dating throughout Ireland', in Ó Corráin, 3–22

    1986. 'A sherd of souterrain ware from a dated context', *Ulster J. Archaeol.* 49: 104–5

    1993. 'Dark Ages and dendrochronology', *Emania* 11: 3–12

Baldwin-Brown, G. 1914–15. 'Notes on a necklace of glass beads found in a cist in Dalmeny Park, South Queensferry', *Proc. Soc. Ant. Scot.* 49: 332–8

Ball, M. and Fife, J. 1993. *The Celtic Languages*, London

Ballin Smith, B. 1994. *Howe: Four Millennia of Orkney Prehistory* (= Soc. Ant. Scot. monograph 9), Edinburgh

Bammesberger, A. and Wollman, A. (eds.) 1990. *Britain 400–600: Language and History*, Heidelberg

Bannerman, J. 1974. *Studies in the History of Dalriada*, Edinburgh

Barber, J. W. 1981. 'Excavations on Iona, 1979', *Proc. Soc. Ant. Scot.* 111: 282–380

Barbour, I. 1906–7. 'Notice of a stone fort near Kirkandrews', *Proc. Soc. Ant. Scot.* 41: 68–80

Barker, P. and Higham, N. 1982. *Hen Domen, Montogomery: A Timber Castle on the English–Welsh Border*, London

Barker, P. and Lawson, J. 1971. 'A pre-Norman field-system at Hen Domen, Montgomery', *Medieval Archaeology* 15: 58–72

Barrett, G. F. and Graham, B. J. 1975. 'Some considerations concerning the dating and distribution of ring-forts in Ireland', *Ulster J. Archaeol.* 38: 33–45

Barrow, G. W. 1979. *The Round Towers of Ireland*, Dublin

  1985. *David I of Scotland 1124–1153: The Balance of Old and New*, Reading

  1989. *Kingship and Unity in Scotland, 100–1306*, Edinburgh

Barry, T. B. 1981. 'Archaeological excavations at Dunbeg promontory fort, Co. Kerry, 1977', *Proc. Royal Irish Acad.* 81c: 295–330

  1987. *The Archaeology of Medieval Ireland*, London

Bateson, J. D. 1973. 'Roman material in Ireland: a re-consideration', *Proc. Royal Irish Acad.* 73c: 21–97

  1976. 'Further finds of Roman material in Ireland', *Proc. Royal Irish Acad.* 76c: 171–80

  1981. *Enamel-working in Iron Age, Roman and Sub-Roman Britain* (= BAR Brit. Ser. 93), Oxford

Bateson, J. D. and Holmes, N. 1997. 'Roman and medieval coins found in Scotland, 1988–95', *Proc. Soc. Ant. Scot.* 127: 527–62

Batey, C. E. 1987. *Freswick Links, Caithness: A Re-appraisal of the Late Norse Site in its Context* (= BAR Brit. Ser. 179), Oxford

  1990. 'A Pictish pin from Machrihanish, Kintyre', *Glasgow Arch. J.* 16: 86–7

Batey, C. E., Jesch, J. and Morris, C. D. (eds.) 1993. *The Viking Age in Caithness, Orkney and the North Atlantic*, Edinburgh

Bayley, J. 1991. 'Archaeological evidence for Parting', in E. Pernicka and G. A. Wagner (eds.), *Archaeometry '90: Proceedings of the 27th International Symposium on Archaeometry in Heidelberg*, Basel

Bell, A. S. (ed.) 1981. *The Scottish Antiquarian Tradition*, Edinburgh

Benton, S. 1931. 'The excavation of the Sculptor's Cave, Covesea, Morayshire', *Proc. Soc. Ant. Scot.* 65: 177–216

Berger, P. 1979. 'The Ardagh Chalice, numerology and the Stowe Missal', *Eire–Ireland* 14 (3): 6–16

Berger, R. 1995. 'Radiocarbon dating of early medieval Irish monuments', *Proc. Royal Irish Acad.* 95c: 159–74

Bersu, G. 1941–6. 'Celtic homesteads in the Isle of Man', *J. Manx Museum* 5: 177–82

  1947. 'The rath at Towland, Lissue', *Ulster J. Archaeol.* 10: 30–58

  1949. 'A promontory fort on the shore of Ramsey Bay', *Antiq. J.* 29: 62–79

Bersu, G. and Wilson, D. M. 1966. *Three Viking Graves in the Isle of Man* (= Soc. Med. Arch. monograph ser. 1), London

Beveridge, E. 1930–1. 'Excavation of an earth-house at Foshigarry and a fort at Dun Thomaidh, in North Uist', *Proc. Soc. Ant. Scot.* 55: 299–356

Beveridge, E. and Callander, J. G. 1931–2. 'Earth houses at Garry Iohdrach and Bac Mhic Connain, in North Uist', *Proc. Soc. Ant. Scot.* 66: 32–66

Bibby, J. S., Heslop, R. E. F. and Hartnup, R. 1982. *Land Capability Classification for Agriculture*, Aberdeen

Bick, L. 1994. 'Tin ingots found at Praa Sands, Breague, in 1974', *Cornish Archaeology* 33: 57–70

Bidwell, P. 1999. *Hadrian's Wall 1989–1999*, Kendal

Bidwell, P. and Speak, S. 1994. *Excavations at South Shields Roman Fort*, vol. 1 (= Soc. Ant. Newcastle upon Tyne monograph 4), Newcastle

Bieler, L. (ed.) 1963. *The Irish Penitentials*, Dublin

Bieler, L. (ed.) 1966. *Ireland Harbinger of the Middle Ages*, 2nd edn, London

Bigelow, G. F. 1985. 'Sandwick, Unst and late Norse economy', in B. Smith (ed.), *Shetland Archaeology: New Work in Shetland in the 1970s*, Lerwick, 95–127

Binchy, D. A. (ed.) 1941. *Críth Gablach*, Dublin
    1962a. 'Patrick and his biographers: ancient and modern', *Studia Hibernica* 11: 7–173
    1962b. 'The passing of the old order', in B. Ó Cuív (ed.), *The Impact of the Scandinavian Invasions on the Celtic-speaking Peoples, c.800–1100* AD, Dublin, 119–32
    1970. *Celtic and Anglo-Saxon Kingship* (= O'Donnell lecture), Oxford

Birley, A. 1980. *The People of Roman Britain*, London

Birley, E. 1938. 'Excavations at Birrens 1936–1937', *Proc. Soc. Ant. Scot.* 72: 275–347

Bitel, L. M. 1990. *Isle of the Saints: Monastic Settlement and Christian Community in Early Ireland*, Ithaca
    1996. *The Land of Women: Tales of Sex and Gender from Early Christian Ireland*, Ithaca

Black, R., Gillies, W. and Ó Maolalagh, R. (eds.) 1999. *Celtic Connections: Proceedings of the 10th International Congress of Celtic Studies*, vol. 1: *Language, Literature, History, Culture*, Edinburgh

Blair, J. and Pyrah, C. (eds.) 1996. *Church Archaeology: research directions for the future* (= *Council for British Archaeology Res. Rep.* 104), London

Blair, J. and Sharpe, R. (eds.) 1992. *Pastoral Care before the Parish*, Leicester

Blindheim, M. 1984. 'A house-shaped Irish–Scots reliquary in Bologna, and its place among other reliquaries', *Acta Archaeologica* 55: 1–53

Blockley, K. (ed.) 1998. *Llawhaden, Dyfed: Excavations on a Group of Small Defended Enclosures, 1980–4*, Oxford

Böhner, K. 1958. *Die Fränkischen Altertümer des Trierer Landes*, Germanisches Denkmäler der Völkerwanderungszeit ser. B, 1, 1 and 2, Berlin

Bond, J. M. and Hunter, J. R. 1987. 'Flax growing in Orkney from the Norse period to the 18th century', *Proc. Soc. Ant. Scot.* 117: 175–81

Boon, G. C. 1962. 'A Christian monogram at Caerwent', *Bulletin Board Celtic Studies* 19: 338–44
    1992. 'The early Christian church in Gwent: the Romano-British church', *Monmouthshire Antiquary* 8: 11–24

Bourke, C. 1987. 'Irish croziers of the eighth and ninth centuries', in Ryan, 1987b: 166–73
    1991. 'The Blackwater shrine', *Dúiche Néill* 6: 103–6
    1993. 'The chronology of Irish crucifixion plaques', in Spearman and Higgitt, 1993: 175–81

Bourke, C. (ed.) 1995. *From the Isles of the North: Early Medieval Art in Ireland and Britain*, Belfast

Bourke, E. 1989. 'Stonyford: a first-century Roman burial from Ireland', *Archaeology Ireland* 4.3: 56–7
    1994. 'Glass vessels of the first to ninth centuries AD in Ireland', *J. Royal Soc. Antiq. Ireland* 124: 163–209

Bowen, E. G. 1937. 'Clawdd Mawr, Carmarthenshire', *Bulletin Board Celtic Studies* 8: 383–5
    1954. *The Settlements of the Celtic Saints in Wales*, Cardiff
    (ed.) 1975. *Wales: A Physical, Historical and Regional Geography*, London

Bowman, A. 1996. 'Post-Roman imports in Britain and Ireland: a maritime perspective', in Dark, 1996b: 97–108

Boyle, J. 2004. 'Lest the lowliest be forgotten: locating the impoverished in early medieval Ireland', *Internat. Journal of Historical Archaeology* 8.2: 85–99

Bradley, J. 1991. 'Excavations at Moynagh Lough, Co. Meath', *J. Royal Soc. Antiq. Ireland* 111: 5–26

   1993. 'Moynagh Lough: an insular workshop of the second quarter of the eighth century', in Spearman and Higgitt (eds.), 74–81

Branigan, K. 1976. *The Roman Villa in South-West England*, Bradford-on-Avon

Brassil, K. S., Owen, W. G., and Britnell, W. J. 1991. 'Prehistoric and early medieval cemeteries at Tandderwen, near Denbigh, Clwyd', *Archaeol. J.* 148: 46–97

Breeze, A. 1998. 'Pictish chains and Welsh forgeries', *Proc. Soc. Ant. Scot.* 128: 481–4

Breeze, D. 1982. *The Northern Frontiers of Roman Britain*, London

   1996. *Roman Scotland, Frontier Country*, London

Breeze, D. and Dobson, B. 2000. *Hadrian's Wall*, 4th edn, Harmondsworth

Brenan, J. 1991. *Hanging-Bowls and their Contexts* (= BAR Brit. Ser. 220), Oxford

Briggs, C. S. 1985. 'A neglected Viking burial with beads from Kilmainham, Dublin, discovered in 1847', *Medieval Archaeology* 29: 94–108

Brindley, A. L. and Lanting, J. N. 1990. 'A Roman boat in Ireland', *Archaeology Ireland* 4.3: 10–11

Britnell, W. 1990. 'Capel Maelog, Llandrindod Wells, Powys: excavatioins 1984–7', *Medieval Archaeology* 34: 27–96

Brooke, D. 1991. 'The Northumbrian settlements in Galloway and Carrick: an historical assessment', *Proc. Soc. Ant. Scot.* 121: 295–327

Brown, C. G. and Harper, A. E. T. 1984. 'Excavations on Cathedral Hill, Armagh, 1968', *Ulster J. Archaeol.* 47: 109–61

Brown, M. P. 1993. 'Patten and purpose: the Derrynaflan patten and inscriptions', in Spearman and Higgitt (eds.), 162–7

Bruce-Mitford, R. L. S. 1956. 'A Dark Age settlement at Mawgan Porth, Cornwall', in Bruce-Mitford (ed.), *Recent Archaeological Excavations in the British Isles*, London, 167–96

   (ed.) 1983. *The Sutton Hoo Ship Burial*, vol. 3: *Late Roman and Byzantine silver, hanging bowls, drinking vessels, cauldrons and other containers, textiles, lyre, pottery bottle and other items*, London

   1987. 'Ireland and the hanging-bowls: a review', in Ryan 1987a: 30–9

   1997. *Mawgan Porth: A Settlement of the Late Saxon period on the North Cornish Coast*, London

Buckley, A. 2005. 'Music in prehistoric and medieval Ireland', in Ó Cróinín (ed.), 744–813

Buckley, V. M. and Sweetman, P. D. 1991. *Archaeological Survey of County Louth*, Dublin

Bu' lock, J. D. 1960a. 'Vortigern and the pillar of Eliseg', *Antiquity* 34: 49–53

   1960b. 'The Celtic, Saxon and Scandinavian settlements at Meols in Wirral', *Trans. Historical Soc. Lancashire and Cheshire* 112: 1–28

   1972. *Pre-Conquest Cheshire, 383–1066*, Chester

Burrow, I. G. 1974. 'Tintagel – some problems', *Scottish Archaeol. Forum* 5: 99–103

   1981. *Hillfort and Hill-top Settlement in Somerset in the First to Eighth Centuries* AD (= BAR Brit. Ser. 91), Oxford

Butcher, S. A. 1977. 'Enamels from Roman Britain', in M. Apted et al. (eds.), *Ancient Monuments and their Interpretation*, London and Chichester, 41–68

Buteux, S. 1997. *Settlements at Skaill, Deerness, Orkney* (= BAR Brit. Ser. 260), Oxford

Butler, L. A. S. 1971. 'Deserted medieval settlements in Wales', in M. Bereford and J. Hurst (eds.), *Deserted Medieval Villages, Studies*, London, 249–69

  1977. 'Continuity of settlement in Wales in the central Middle Ages', in L. Laing (ed.), 61–6

Byrne, F. J. 1965. 'The Ireland of St Columba', *Historical Studies* 5: 37–58

  1973. *Irish Kings and High Kings*, London

Caldwell, D. H. 2001. 'The Monymusk Reliquary: the Brecbennoch of St Columba?', *Proc. Soc. Ant. Scot.* 131: 267–83

Cameron, K. 1968. 'Eccles in English place-names', in M. W. Barley and R. P. C. Hanson, *Christianity in Britain 300–700*, Leicester, 87–92

Cameron, N. 1996. 'The church in Scotland in the late 11th and 12th centuries', in Blair and Pyrah (eds.), 42–6

Campbell, E. 1987. 'A cross-marked quern from Dunadd and other evidence for relations between Dunadd and Iona', *Proc. Soc. Ant. Scot.* 117: 59–71

  1988. 'The post-Roman pottery', in Edwards and Lane (eds.), 124–38

  1989. 'New finds of post-Roman imported pottery and glass from South Wales', *Arch. Cambrensis* 137: 59–66

  1995. 'New evidence for glass vessels in western Britain and Ireland in the 6th/7th centuries AD', in D. Foy (ed.), *Le Verre de l'Atlantique tardive et du Haut Moyen Age*, Paris, 35–40

  1996a. 'Trade in the Dark Age west: a peripheral activity?', in Crawford (ed.), 79–91

  1996b. 'The archaeological evidence for external contacts: imports, trade and economy in Celtic Britain AD 400–800', in Dark, 1996a: 83–96

  1999. *Saints and Sea Kings*, Edinburgh

  2000. 'A review of glass vessels in western Britain and Ireland AD 400–800', in J. Price (ed.), 33–46

  2001. 'Were the Scots Irish?', *Antiquity* 75: 285–92

Campbell, E. and Lane, A. 1988. 'The pottery', in A. Haggarty, 'Iona: some results from recent work', *Proc. Soc. Ant. Scot.* 118: 208–12

  1990. 'Llangorse Crannog', *Archaeology in Wales* 30: 62–3

  1993. 'Excavations at Longbury Bank, Dyfed: an early medieval settlement in south Wales', *Medieval Archaeology* 37: 15–77

Campbell, E. and Macdonald, P. 1993. 'Excavations at Caerwent Vicarage orchard garden 1973: an extra-mural post-Roman cemetery', *Arch. Cambrensis* 142: 74–98

Carney, J. 1971. 'Three Old Irish accentual poems', *Ériu* 22: 23–80

Carrington, A. 1996. 'The horseman and the falcon: mounted falconers in Pictish sculpture', *Proc. Soc. Ant. Scot.* 126: 459–68

Carroll, J. 1995. 'Millefiori in the development of early Irish enamelling', in C. Bourke (ed.), 49–57

  2001. 'Glass bangles as a regional development in early medieval Ireland', in Redknap et al. (eds.), 101–16

Carson, R. A. G. and O'Kelly, C. 1977. 'A catalogue of Roman coins from Newgrange, Co. Meath and notes on the coins and related finds', *Proc. Royal Irish Acad.* 77C: 35–55

Carter, S. P. 1994. 'Radiocarbon dating evidence for the age of narrow cultivation ridges in Scotland', *Tools and Tillage* 7: 83–91

Carver, M. 2004. 'An Iona of the east: the early medieval monastery at Portmahomack, Tarbat Ness', *Medieval Archaeology* 48: 1–30

Cassidy, B. (ed.) 1992. *The Ruthwell Cross*, Princeton

Caulfield, S. 1981. 'Some Celtic problems in the Irish Iron Age', in D. Ó Corráin (ed.), 205–15

Cessford, C. 1994a. 'The Borgue armour and the Dumfriesshire spangenhelm', *Trans. Dumfries Galloway N.H.A.S.* 69: 73–80

    1994b. 'Early historic chains of power', *Pictish Arts Soc. J.* 6: 19–26

    1994c. 'Pictish raiders at Trusty's Hill?', *Trans. Dumfries Galloway N.H.A.S* 69: 81–8

    1999a. 'Relations between the Britons of southern Scotland and Anglo-Saxon Northumbria', in J. Hawkes and S. Mills (eds.), *Northumbria's Golden Age*, Stroud, 150–60

    1999b. 'The Tummel Bridge hoard', *Pictish Arts Soc. J.* 14: 38–47

    2001. 'Post-Severan Cramond: a late Roman and early historic British and Anglo-Saxon religious centre?', *The Heroic Age* 4 (*http://www.mun.ca/mst/heroicage/ issues/ 4/Cessford.html*)

Chadwick, H. M. 1949. *Early Scotland*, Cambridge

    1959. 'Vortigern', in N. K. Chadwick (ed.), *Studies in Early British History*, Cambridge, 21–46

Chadwick, N. K. 1961. *The Age of the Saints in the Early Celtic Church*, London

    1965. 'The colonization of Brittany from Celtic Britain', *Proc. British Academy* 51: 235–99

    1969. *Early Brittany*, Cardiff

Champion, T. 1982. 'The myth of Iron Age invasions in Ireland', in B. G. Scott (ed.), *Studies on Early Ireland: Essays in Honour of M. V. Duignan*, Dublin, 55–72

Chapman, M. 1992. *The Celts: The Construction of a Myth*, New York

Charles-Edwards, T. M. 1980. *Nau Kynywedi Teithiauc*, in D. Jenkins and M. Owen (eds.), *The Welsh Law of Women*, Cardiff, 35–9

    1989a. *The Welsh Laws*, Cardiff

    1989b. 'Early medieval kingships in the British Isles', in S. Bassett (ed.), *The Origins of Anglo-Saxon Kingdoms*, London, 28–39

    1993. *Early Irish and Welsh Kinship*, Oxford

    2000. *Early Christian Ireland*, Cambridge

Childe, V. G. and Thorneycroft, W. 1938. 'The vitrified fort at Rahoy, Morven, Argyll', *Proc. Soc. Ant. Scot.* 72: 23–43

Christison, D. and Anderson, J. 1904–5. 'Excavation of forts on the Poltalloch estates, Argyll, 1904–5', *Proc. Soc. Ant. Scot.* 39: 259–322

Clarke, D. V. 1970. 'Bone dice and the Scottish Iron Age', *Proc. Prehist. Soc.* 36: 214–32

    2002. ' "The foremost figure in all matters relating to Scottish archaeology": aspects of the work of Joseph Anderson (1832–1916)', *Proc. Soc. Ant. Scot.* 132: 1–18

Clarke, H. B., Ní Mhaonaigh, M. and Ó Floinn, R. (eds.) 1998. *Ireland and Scandinavia in the Early Viking Age*, Dublin

Clinton, M. 2001. *Souterrains of Ireland*, Dublin

Close-Brooks, J. 1974–5. 'A Pictish pin from Golspie, Sutherland', *Proc. Soc. Ant. Scot.* 106: 208–9

    1978–80. 'Excavations in the Dairy Park, Dunrobin, Sutherland, 1977', *Proc. Soc. Ant. Scot.* 110: 328–45

Close-Brooks, J. 1984. 'Some objects from peat bogs', *Proc. Soc. Ant. Scot.* 114: 578–80

1986. 'Excavations at Clatchard Craig, Fife', *Proc. Soc. Ant. Scot.* 116: 117–84

Clough, T. H. McK. and Laing, L. 1969. 'Excavations at Kirkconnel, Waterbeck, Dumfriesshire, 1968', *Trans. Dumfries Galloway N.H.A.S.* 46: 128–39

Coatsworth, E. and Pindar, M. 2002. *The Art of the Anglo-Saxon Goldsmith*, Woodbridge

Coffey, G. 1909. *Guide to the Celtic Antiquities of the Christian Period in the National Museum, Dublin*, Dublin

Coles, J. and Simpson, D. D. A. (eds.) 1968. *Studies in Ancient Europe*, Leicester

Collins, A. E. P. 1955. 'Excavations at Lough Faughan crannog, Co. Down', *Ulster J. Arch.* 18: 45–80

1966. 'Excavations at Dressogagh rath, Co. Armagh', *Ulster J. Arch.* 29: 117–29

Collins, R. 2004. 'Before "the end": Hadrian's Wall in the fourth century and after', in Collins and Gerrard (eds.), 123–32

Collins, R. and Gerrard, J. (eds.) 2004. *Debating Late Antiquity in Britain,* AD *300–700*, Oxford

Collis, J. 2003. *The Celts, Origins, Myths, Inventions*, Stroud

Comber, M. 1997. 'Lagore crannog and non-ferrous metalworking in early historic Ireland', *J. Irish Archaeology* 8: 101–14

Cool, H. E. M. 1990. 'Roman metal hair pins from southern Britain', *Archaeol. J.* 147: 148–82

2000. 'The parts left over: material culture into the fifth century', in T. Wilmott and P. Wilson (eds.), *The Late Roman Transition in the North*, Oxford (= Brit. Arch. Reps. 299): 47–65

Cooney, G. 1995. 'Theory and practice in Irish archaeology', in P. J. Ucko (ed.), *Theory in Archaeology: A World Perspective*, London, 263–77

Cooney, G. and Grogan, E. 1991. 'An archaeological solution to the "Irish" problem?', *Emania* 9: 33–43

Corlett, C. 1998. 'Interpretation of round towers – public appeal or professional opinion?', *Archaeology Ireland* 44: 24–7

Cormack, W. et al. 1995. 'Barhobble, Mochrum – excavation of a forgotten church site in Galloway', *Trans. Dumfries Galloway N.H.A.S.* 70: 5–106

Cottam, B. and Small, A. 1974. 'The distribution of settlement in southern Pictland', *Medieval Archaeology* 18: 43–65

Cotter, C. 1995. 'Western stone fort project: interim report', *Discovery Programme Reports* 2: 1–11

1996. 'Western stone fort project', *Discovery Programme Reports* 4: 1–14

Cowie, T. G. 1977–8. 'Excavations at the Catstane, Midlothian, 1977', *Proc. Soc. Ant. Scot.* 109: 166–201

Craig, D. 1991. 'Pre-Norman sculpture in Galloway: some territorial implications', in R. D. Oram and G. P. Stell (eds.), *Galloway, Land and Lordship*, Edinburgh, 45–62

1994 'The early medieval sculpture of the Glasgow area', in A. Ritchie (ed.), 73–91

Cramp, R. 1970. 'Decorated window-glass and millefiori from Monkwearmouth', *Antiq. J.* 50: 327–35

1995. *Whithorn and the Northumbrian Expansion Westwards* (= 3rd Whithorn lecture), Whithorn

Cramp, R. and Daniels, C. 1987. 'New finds from the Anglo-Saxon monastery at Hartlepool, Cleveland', *Antiquity* 61: 424–32

Craw, I. H. 1929–30. 'Excavations at Dunadd and other sites in the Poltalloch estates, Argyll', *Proc. Soc. Ant. Scot.* 64: 111–47

Crawford, B. 1987. *Scandinavian Scotland*, Leicester

  (ed.) 1994. *Scotland in Dark Age Europe*, St Andrews

  (ed.) 1996. *Scotland in Dark Age Britain*, St. Andrews

  (ed.) 2002. *The Papar in the North Atlantic: Environment and History*, St Andrews

Crawford, B. and Ballin Smith, B. 1999. *The Biggings, Papa Stour, Shetland* (= *Soc. Ant. Scot.* monograph 15), Edinburgh

Crawford, I. A. 1967. 'The divide between medieval and post-medieval in Scotland', *Post-Medieval Archaeology* 1: 84–9

  1972. 'Scot(?) Norseman and Gael', *Scottish Archaeol. Forum* 6: 1–16

Crawford, I. A. and Selkirk, A. 1996. 'The Udal', *Current Archaeology* 147: 84–94

Crawford, I. A. and Switsur, R. 1977. 'Sandscaping and C14: the Udal, North Uist', *Antiquity* 51: 124–36

Crone, B. A. 1993. 'Crannogs and chronologies', *Proc. Soc. Ant. Scot.* 123: 245–54

  2000. *The History of a Scottish Lowland Crannog: Excavations at Buiston, Ayrshire, 1989–80*, Edinburgh

Cross, T. P. and Slover, C. H. 1937. *Ancient Irish Tales*, London

Crowe, C. J. 1982. 'A note on white quartz pebbles in burials found in early Christian contexts in the Isle of Man', *Proc. I.O.M. Nat. Hist. Antiq. Soc.* 8.4: 413–15

  1984. 'Cartmel, The Earliest Christian Community', *Trans. Cumberland and Westmorland A. and A.S.* 84: 61–6

  1987. 'An excavation at Kirkmirran, Dalbeatie, 1985', *Trans. Dumfries Galloway N.H.A.S.* 61: 55–62

  1999. *Angels, Fools and Tyrants*, Edinburgh

Crowfoot, E. and Hawkes, S. C. 1967. 'Early Anglo-Saxon gold braids', *Medieval Archaeology* 11: 42–86

Crowfoot, G. M. 1945. 'The bone "gouges" of Maiden Castle and other sites', *Antiquity* 19: 157–8

Cruden, S. H. 1960a. *The Scottish Castle*, Edinburgh

  1960b. *Scottish Abbeys*, Edinburgh

  1965. 'Excavations at Birsay, Orkney', in A. Small (ed.), *Transactions of the Fourth Viking Congress*, Aberdeen, 22–31

Cruikshank, G. 1999. *The Battle of Dunnichen*, Balgavies

Cubbon, A. M. 1971. *The Art of the Manx Crosses*, Douglas

  1983. 'The archaeology of the Vikings in the Isle of Man', in Fell et al. (eds.), 13–26

Culleton, E. B. and Mitchell, G. F. 1976. 'Soil erosion following deforestation in the early Christian period in south Wexford', *J. Royal Soc. Antiq. Ireland* 106: 120–3

Cummins, W. 1999. *The Picts and their Symbols*, Stroud

Cunliffe, B. 1988. *Greeks, Romans and Barbarians: Spheres of Interaction*, London

  1991. *Iron Age Communities in Britain*, 3rd edn, London

  1997. *The Ancient Celts*, Oxford

  2001. *Facing the Ocean*, Oxford

Cuppage, J. 1986. *Archaeological Survey of the Dingle Peninsula*, Ballyferriter

Curle, A. O. 1905. 'Description of the fortifications on Ruberslaw', *Proc. Soc. Ant. Scot.* 39: 219–32

Curle, A. O. 1913–14. 'Report on the excavation of a vitrified fort at Rockcliffe, known as the Mote of Mark', *Proc. Soc. Ant. Scot.* 48: 125–68

Curle, C. L. 1939–40. 'The chronology of the early Christian monuments of Scotland', *Proc. Soc. Ant. Scot.* 74: 60–116

   1982. *Pictish and Norse Finds from the Brough of Birsay 1934–74* (= *Soc. Ant. Scot.* monograph 1), Edinburgh

Curle, J. 1923. *The Traprain Treasure*, Glasgow

   1931–2. 'An inventory of objects of Roman and provincial Roman origin found on sites in Scotland not definitely associated with Roman constructions', *Proc. Soc. Ant. Scot.* 66: 277–397

Dalland, M. 1992. 'Long cist burials at Four Winds, Longniddry, East Lothian', *Proc. Soc. Ant. Scot.* 122: 197–206

Dark, K. R. 1985. 'The plan and interpretation of Tintagel', *Cambridge Medieval Celtic Studies* 9: 1–17

   1992. 'Epigraphic, art-historical and historical approaches to the chronology of Class I inscribed stones', in Edwards and Lane (eds.), 51–61

   1994a. *Civitas to Kingdom: British Political Continuity 300–800*, Leicester

   1994b. *Discovery by Design: The Identification of Secular Elite Settlements in Western Britain AD 400–700* (= BAR Brit. Ser. 237), Oxford

   (ed.) 1996a. *External Contacts and the Economy of Late Roman and Post-Roman Britain*, Woodbridge

   1996b. 'Pottery and local production at the end of Roman Britain', in Dark 1996a: 53–66

   2000. *Britain and the End of the Roman Empire*, Stroud

Dark, K. R. and Dark, S. P. 1996. 'New archaeological and palynological evidence for a sub-Roman reoccupation of Hadrian's Wall', *Archaeologia Aeliana* 5 ser. 24: 61–9

   1997. *The Landscape of Roman Britain*, Stroud

Darvill, T. 1988. 'Excavations on the site of the early Norman castle at Gloucester, 1983–4', *Medieval Archaeology* 32: 1–49

Davey, J. 2004. 'The environs of South Cadbury in the late antique and early medieval periods', in Collins and Gerrard (eds.), 43–54

Davidson, D. A. and Carter, S. P. 1997. 'Soils and their evolution', in Edwards and Ralston (eds.), 45–62

Davies, J. 1990. *History of Wales*, London

Davies, O. 1942. 'The Twomile Stone, a prehistoric community in Co. Donegal', *J. Royal Soc. Antiq. Ireland*, 72: 98–105.

Davies, W. H. 1968. 'The church in Wales', in M. Barley and R. Hanson (eds.), *Christianity in Britain, 300–700*, Leicester, 131–50

   1982. *Wales in the Early Middle Ages*, Leicester

   1983. 'Celtic women in the early Middle Ages', in A. Cameron and E. Kuhrt (eds.), *Images of Women in Antiquity*, Detroit, 145–66

   1992. 'The myth of the Celtic church', in Edwards and Lane (eds.), 12–21

Denison, S. 2000. 'Gemstone evidence for late Roman survival', *British Archaeology* 52: 4

De Paor, L. 1955. 'A survey of Sceilg Mhichil', *J. Royal Soc. Antiq. Ireland*, 85: 174–87

   1960–1. 'Some vine scrolls and other patterns in embossed metal from Dumfriesshire', *Proc. Soc. Ant. Scot.* 94: 184–95

De Paor, L. 1987. 'The high crosses of Tech Theille (Tihilly), Kinitty and related sculpture', in Rynne (ed.), 131–58

De Paor, M. and De Paor, L. 1958. *Early Christian Ireland*, London

De Vegvar, C. N. 1987. *The Northumbrian Renaissance*, Selsingrove and London

　　1995. 'Drinking horns in Ireland and Wales: documentary sources', in C. Bourke (ed.), 81–7

Dexter, T. H. 1938. *Old Cornish Crosses*, London

Diack, F. C. 1944. *The Inscriptions of Pictland*, Aberdeen

Dickinson, T. M. 1982. 'Fowler's Type G brooches reconsidered', *Medieval Archaeology* 26: 41–68

Dillon, M. 1948. *Early Irish Literature*, Chicago

　　(ed.) 1954. *Early Irish Society*, Dublin

　　1962. *Lebor na Cert: The Book of Rights*, London

Di Martino, V. 2003. *Roman Ireland*, Cork

Dixon, P. W. 1988. 'Crickley Hill 1969–87', *Current Archaeology* 110: 73–8

　　1998. 'A rural medieval settlement in Roxburghshire: excavations at Springwood Park, Kelso, 1985–6', *Proc. Soc. Ant. Scot.* 128: 671–752

Doble, G. H. 1971. *The Lives of the Welsh Saints*, ed. D. S. Evans, Cardiff

Doherty, C. 1980. 'Exchange and trade in early medieval Ireland', *J. Royal Soc. Antiq. Ireland* 110: 67–89

　　1984. 'The basilica in early Ireland', *Peritia* 3: 303–15

　　1998. 'The Vikings in Ireland: a review', in Clarke et al. (eds.), 288–330

　　2000. 'Settlement in early Ireland: a review', in T. Barry (ed.), *A History of Settlement in Ireland*, London, 50–80

　　2001. 'The Viking impact upon Ireland', in Larsen (ed.), 29–36

Dolley, M. 1976 'Roman coins from Ireland and the date of St Patrick', *Proc. Royal Irish Acad.* 76c: 181–90

Douch, H. L. and Beard, S. W. 1970. 'Excavations at Carvossa, Probus, 1968–70', *Cornish Archaeology* 9: 93–8

Downes, J. and Ritchie, A. (eds.) 2003. *Sea Change: Orkney and Northern Europe in the Later Iron Age* AD *300–800*, Balgavies

Driscoll, S. T. 2002. *Alba: The Gaelic Kingdom of Scotland,* AD *800–1124*, Edinburgh

Driscoll, S. T. and Nieke, M. R. (eds.) 1988. *Power and Politics in Early Medieval Britain and Ireland*, Edinburgh

Driscoll, S. T. and Yeoman, P. A. 1997. *Excavations within Edinburgh Castle in 1988–91* (= *Soc. Ant. Scot.* monograph ser. 12), Edinburgh

Duignan, L. 1973. 'A hand-pin from Treanmacmurtagh Bog, Co Sligo', *J. Royal Soc. Antiq. Ireland* 103: 46–9

Duignan, M. 1944. 'Irish agriculture in early historic times', *J. Royal Soc. Antiq. Ireland* 74: 124–45

　　1951. 'The Moylough and other Irish belt shrines', *J. Galway A. and H.S.* 24: 83–94

Dumville, D. 1975–6. ' "Nennius" and the Historia Britonnum', *Studia Celtica* 10–11: 78–95

　　1977. 'Sub-Roman Britain: history and legend', *History* 62: 173–92

　　1984. 'Gildas and Maelgwn: problems of dating', in M. Lapidge and D. Dumville (eds.), *Gildas: New Approaches*, Woodbridge, 51–9

　　1985. 'The West Saxon genealogical regnal list and the chronology of early Wessex', *Peritia* 4: 21–66

Dumville, D. 1986. 'The historical value of the *Historia Britonnum*', *Arthurian Literature* 6: 1–26

1988. 'Early Welsh poetry, problems of historicity', in B. F. Roberts (ed.), *Early Welsh Poetry: Studies in the Book of Aneurin*, Aberystwyth, 1–16

1989. 'The origins of Northumbria: some aspects of the British background', in S. Bassett (ed.), *The Origins of the Anglo-Saxon Kingdoms*, Leicester, 213–22

1993. 'Saint Patrick and the Christianisation of Dál Riata', in D. Dumville (ed.), *Saint Patrick, AD 493–1993*, Woodbridge, 183–9

2000. 'The Chronicle of the Kings of Alba', in S. Taylor (ed.), *Kings, Clerics and Chronicles in Scotland, 50–1297*, Dublin, 73–86

Dunbar, J. G. and Fisher, I. 1995. *Iona: A Guide to the Monuments*, Edinburgh

Duncan, A. A. M. 1975. *Scotland: The Making of a Kingdom*, Edinburgh

Dunlevy, M. 1988. 'A classification of early Irish combs', *Proc. Royal Irish Acad.* 88c: 341–422

Earwood, C. 1990. 'Wooden artefacts from Loch Glashan crannog, mid-Argyll', *Proc. Soc. Ant. Scot.* 120: 79–94

1991–2. 'Turned wooden vessels of the early historic period from Ireland and western Scotland', *Ulster J. Archaeol.* 54–5: 154–9

1993. *Domestic Wooden Artefacts in Britain and Ireland from Neolithic to Viking Times*, Exeter

Edwards, K. and Ralston, I. B. M. 1978. 'New dating and environmental evidence from Burghead fort, Moray', *Proc. Soc. Ant. Scot.* 109: 202–10

1997. *Scotland, Environment and Archaeology, 8000 BC–AD 1000*, Chichester

Edwards, N. 1983. 'An early group of crosses from the kingdom of Ossory', *J. Royal Soc. Antiq. Ireland*, 113: 5–46

1985a. 'The origins of the free-standing stone cross in Ireland: imitation or innovation?', *Bulletin Board Celtic Studies* 32: 393–410

1985b. 'A possible Viking grave from Benllech, Anglesey', *Anglesey Antiquarian Society and Field Club Transactions* 19–24

1986. 'The South Cross, Clonmacnoise', in Higgitt (ed.), 23–36

1987. 'Abstract ornament on early medieval Irish crosses: a preliminary catalogue', in Ryan 1987b: 111–17

1990. *The Archaeology of Early Medieval Ireland*, London

1995. 'Eleventh-century Welsh illuminated manuscripts: the nature of the Irish connection', in C. Bourke (ed.), 147–55

1996. 'Identifying the archaeology of the early church in Wales and Cornwall', in Blair and Pyrah (eds.), 49–62

2001. 'Early medieval inscribed stones and stone sculpture in Wales: context and function', *Medieval Archaeology* 45: 15–40

2005. 'The archaeology of early medieval Ireland, c. 400–1169: settlement and economy', in Ó Cróinín (ed.), 235–300

Edwards, N. and Lane, A. 1988. *Early Medieval Settlements in Wales AD 400–1100*, Cardiff

1992. *The Early Church in Wales and the West* (= Oxbow monograph 16), Oxford

Eeles, F. 1933–4. 'The Monymusk reliquary or Brecbennoch of St Columba', *Proc. Soc. Ant. Scot.* 68: 433–8

Ellis Evans, D. 1990. 'Insular Celtic and the emergence of the Welsh language', in Bammesberger and Wollman (eds.), 149–78

1999. 'Linguistics and Celtic ethnogenesis', in Black et al. (eds.), 1–18

Eogan, G. 1973. 'A decade of excavations at Knowth', *Irish Univ. Rev.* spring: 66–79

1974. 'Report on the excavation of some passage graves, unprotected inhumation burials and a settlement site at Knowth', *Proc. Royal Irish Acad.* 74C: 11–112

1977. 'The Iron Age and early Christian settlement at Knowth, Co. Meath, Ireland', in V. Markotic (ed.), *Ancient Europe and the Mediterranean: Studies in Honour of Hugh Hencken*, Warminster, 69–76

Erdrich, M., Gianotta, K. M. and Hanson, W. S. 2000. 'Traprain Law: native and Roman on the northern frontier', *Proc. Soc. Ant. Scot.* 130: 441–56

Etchingham, C. and Swift, C. 2004. 'English and Pictish terms for brooch in an eighth-century Irish law text', *Medieval Archaeology* 48: 31–50

Evans, D. S. 1979. 'Irish and the languages of post-Roman Wales', *Studies* 68: 19–32

Evans, E., Dowdell, G. and Maynard, D. J. 1985. 'A third-century maritime establishment at Cold Knap, Barry, south Glamorgan', *Britannia* 16: 57–126

Evans, J. G. 1975. *The Environment of Early Man in the British Isles*, London

Evans, S. S. 1997. *Lords of Battle*, Woodbridge

Evison, V. 1975. 'Pagan Saxon whetstones', *Antiq. J.* 55: 70–85

1987. *Dover Buckland Anglo-Saxon Cemetery* (= English Heritage arch. rep. 3), London

Ewart, G. 1985. *Cruggleton Castle: Report of Excavations 1976–81*, Dumfries

Fairhurst, H. 1938–9. 'The galleried dun at Kildonan Bay, Kintyre', *Proc. Soc. Ant. Scot.* 83: 185–228

1954–6. 'The stack fort on Ugadale Point, Kintyre', *Proc. Soc. Ant. Scot.* 88: 15–22

1962. 'An Caisteal: an Iron Age fortification in Mull', *Proc. Soc. Ant. Scot.* 95: 199–207

Fanning, T. 1969. 'The ringed pins in Limerick Museum', *North Munster Antiquarian Journal* 12: 6–11

1981. 'Excavation of an early Christian cemetery and settlement at Reask, Co. Kerry', *Proc. Royal Irish Acad.* 81C: 3–172

1983. 'Some aspects of the bronze ringed pin in Scotland', in O'Connor and Clarke (eds.), 324–42

1994. *Viking Age Ringed Pins from Dublin* (= Medieval Dublin Excavations 1962–81, ser. B, 4), Dublin

Farr, C. 1997. *The Book of Kells*, London and Toronto

Faulkner, N. 2000. *Decline and Fall of Roman Britain*, Stroud

2004. 'The case for the Dark Ages', in Collins and Gerrard (eds.), 13–24

Fawcett, R. 1991. 'St Andrews, St Rule's church and the cathedral', *Proc. Royal Arch. Inst. – The St Andrews Area*, Leeds, 38–9,

Feachem, R. W. 1955. 'Fortifications', in Wainwright, 1955b: 66–86

1966. 'The hill-forts of northern Britain', in Rivet (ed.), 59–88

Fell, C., Foote, P., Graham-Campbell, J. and Thomson, R. (eds.) 1983. *The Viking Age in the Isle of Man*, London

Fellows-Jensen, G. 1983. 'Scandinavian settlement in the Isle of Man and north-west England: the place-name evidence', in Fell et al. (eds.), 37–52

2001. 'Nordic names and Loanwords in Ireland', in Larsen (ed.), 107–14

Fenton, A. and Palsson, H. (eds.) 1978. *The Northern Isles: Orkney and Shetland*, London

Ferdière, A., Rigoir, J. and Rigoir, Y. 1972. 'Céramiques Paléochrétiennes', *Revue Arch. du Centre* 43–4: 299–321

Fernie, E. 1986. 'Early church architecture in Scotland', *Proc. Soc. Ant. Scot.* 116: 393–412

Fisher, I. 1996. 'The west of Scotland', in Blair and Pyrah (eds.), 37–48

Fisher, I. 2001. *Early Medieval Sculpture in the West Highlands and Islands*, Edinburgh

Fitzpatrick, A. P. 1992. *Area Excavation on the Route of the A27 Westhamptnett Bypass, West Sussex, 2* (= Wessex arch. rep. 12)

Fitzpatrick, E. 1998. *The Early Church in Offaly*, Dublin

Fitzpatrick, E. and O'Brien, C. 1998. *The Medieval Churches of County Offaly*, Dublin.

Fleuriot, L. 1980. *Les Origines de la Bretagne*, Paris

Forsyth, C. 1995a. 'Language in Pictland, spoken and written', in Nicoll (ed.), 7–10

    1995b 'The inscriptions on the Dupplin Cross', in C. Bourke (ed.), 237–44

    1997. 'Some thoughts on Pictish symbols as a formal writing system', in Henry (ed.), 85–98

Foster, S. 1990. 'Pins, combs and the chronology of later Atlantic settlement', in Armit (ed.), 143–74

    1992. 'The state of Pictland in the age of Sutton Hoo', in M. Carver (ed.), *The Age of Sutton Hoo*, Woodbridge, 217–34

    1996. *Picts, Gaels and Scots*, London

    (ed.) 1998. *The St Andrews Sarcophagus*, Dublin

Fowler, E. 1960. 'The origin and development of the penannular brooch in Europe', *Proc. Prehist. Soc.* 26: 149–77

    1963. 'Celtic metalwork of the fifth and sixth centuries AD', *Archaeol. J.* 120: 98–160

    1968. 'Hanging bowls', in Coles and Simpson (eds.), 287–310

Fowler, P. J. 1966. 'Ridge-and-furrow cultivation at Cush, Co. Limerick', *North Munster Archaeol. J.* 10: 69–71

Fowler, P. and Thomas, C. 1962. 'Arable fields of the pre-Norman period at Gwithian', *Cornish Archaeology* 1: 61–84

Fox, A. 1952. *Roman Exeter: Excavations in War-damaged Areas*, Manchester

    1955. 'A Dark Age trading site at Bantham, S. Devon', *Antiq. J.* 35: 55–67

    1961. 'Archaeology and early history', *Transactions of the Devonshire Association*, 93: 79–80

    1964. *South-West England*, London

    1995. 'Tin ingots from Bigbury Bay', *Proc. Devon A.S.* 53: 11–23

Fox, C. 1934. 'Wat's dyke, a field survey', *Arch. Cambrensis* 89: 205–78

    1952. *Personality of Britain*, 3rd edn, Cardiff

    1955. *Offa's Dyke*, London

Fredengren, C. 2000. 'Iron Age crannogs in Lough Gara', *Archaeology Ireland* 14.2: 26–8

    2001. 'Poor people's crannogs', *Archaeology Ireland* 15.4: 24–5

    2002. *Crannogs: A Study of Peoples' Interaction with Lakes*, Bray

Freke, D. 2002. *Excavations on St Patrick's Isle, Peel, Isle of Man, 1982–88: Prehistoric, Viking, Medieval and Later*, Liverpool

Frere, S. S. 1987. *Britannia: A History of Roman Britain*, 3rd edn, London

Friell, J. G. P. and Watson, W. G. (eds.) 1984. *Pictish Studies: Settlement, Burial and Art in Dark Age Northern Britain* (= BAR Brit. Ser.), Oxford

Fulford, M. 1989. 'Byzantium and Britain: a Mediterranean perspective on post-Roman Mediterranean imports in western Britain and Ireland', *Medieval Archaeology* 33: 1–6

Fulford, M., Handley, M. and Clark, A. 2000. 'An early date for Ogham: the Silchester Ogham stone rehabilitated', *Medieval Archaeology* 44: 1–24

Fulford, M. and Peacock, D. 1984. *Excavations at Carthage: The British Mission*, vol. 1(2): *The Avenue du President Habib Bourguiba, Salammbo: The Pottery and other Ceramic Objects from the Site*, Sheffield

Fyfe, R. and Rippon, S. 2004. 'A landscape in transition? Palaeoenvironmental evidence for the end of the "Romano-British" period in southwest England', in Collins and Gerrard (eds.), 33–42

Gaillou, P. and Jones, M. 1991. *The Bretons*, Oxford

Gantz, J. 1981. *Early Irish Myths and Sagas*, Harmondsworth

Gardner, W. and Savory, H. N. 1964. *Dinorben*, Cardiff

Gaskell-Brown, C. and Harper, A. E. T. 1984. 'Excavation at Cathedral Hill, Armagh, 1968', *Ulster J. Archaeol.* 47: 109–61

Geake, H. 1999. 'When were hanging bowls deposited in Anglo-Saxon graves?', *Medieval Archaeology*, 43: 1–128.

Geddes, J. 1998. 'The art of the Book of Deer', *Proc. Soc. Ant. Scot.* 128: 537–50

Gelling, P. S. 1962–3. 'Medieval shielings in the Isle of Man', *Medieval Archaeology* 6–7: 156–72

   1957–65. 'The Braaid site', *J. Manx Museum* 6: 201–5.

   1969. 'A metalworking site at Kiondroghad, Kirk Andreas, Isle of Man', *Medieval Archaeology* 13: 67–83

   1978. 'The Iron Age', in P. Davey (ed.), *Man and Environment in the Isle of Man* (= BAR Brit. Ser. 54), Oxford, 233–43

Gerrard, J. 2004. 'How late is late? Pottery and the fifth century in south-west Britain', in Collins and Gerrard (eds.), 65–75

Gibson, D. B. 1995. 'Chiefdoms, confederacies and statehood in early Ireland', in Arnold and Gibson (eds.), 116–28

Gilchrist, R. 1988. 'A reappraisal of Dinas Powys: local exchange and specialized livestock in fifth- to seventh-century Wales', *Medieval Archaeology* 32: 50–62

Gillies, W. 1981. 'The craftsman in early Celtic Literature', *Scottish Archaeol. Forum* 11: 70–85

   1993. 'Scottish Gaelic', in Ball and Fife (eds.), 145–227

Gilmour, S. 2000. 'First millennia settlement development in the Atlantic west', in Henderson (ed.), 155–70

Gogan, L. S. 1932. *The Ardagh Chalice*, Dublin

Graham, A. 1978. 'The archaeology of Joseph Anderson', *Proc. Soc. Ant. Scot.* 107: 279–98

Graham-Campbell, J. 1972. 'Two groups of ninth-century Irish brooches', *J. Royal Soc. Antiq. Ireland* 102: 113–28

   1975. 'Bossed penannular brooches: a review of research', *Medieval Archaeology* 19: 33–47

   1976. 'The Mote of Mark and Celtic Interlace', *Antiquity* 50: 48–50

   1980. *Viking Artefacts: A Select Catalogue*, London

   1981. 'The finds', in R. Reece, *Excavations in Iona 1964 to 1974* (Inst. Arch. Lond. occ. paper 5), London, 23–6

   1983. 'Some Viking-Age penannular brooches from Scotland and the origins of the thistle brooch', in O'Connor and Clarke (eds.) 310–23

   1985. 'A lost Pictish treasure (and two Viking-age gold arm-rings) from Broch of Burgar, Orkney', *Proc. Soc. Ant. Scot.* 115: 241–61

   1991a. 'Dinas Powys Metalwork and the dating of enamelled zoomorphic penannular brooches', *Bulletin Board Celtic Studies* 38: 220–33

   1991b. 'Norrie's law, Fife: on the nature and dating of the silver hoard', *Proc. Soc. Ant. Scot.* 121: 241–59

Graham-Campbell, J. 2003. *Pictish Silver: Status and Symbol* (= Chadwick memorial lectures, 13), Cambridge

Graham-Campbell, J. and Batey, C. 1998. *Vikings in Scotland: An Archaeological Survey*, Edinburgh

Granger-Taylor, H. and Pritchard, F. 2001. 'A fine quality Insular embroidery from Llan-Gors crannog, near Brecon', in Redknap, Edwards et al. (eds.), 91–100

Green, D. 1972. 'The chariot as described in Irish literature', in A. C. Thomas (ed.), *The Iron Age in the Irish Sea Province*, London, 59–74

Green, M. A. (ed.) 1995. *The Celtic World*, London

Greene, S. 2001. 'Elusive latchets', *Archaeology Ireland* 15.4: 13–15

  2003. 'A pair of Latchets drawn by du Noyer in 1839', *Ulster J. Arch.* 62: 179–80

Grieg, C. 1971. 'Excavations at Cullykhan Castle Point, Banff', *Scottish Archaeol. Forum* 3: 15–21

Grogan, E. and Donaghy, C. 1997. 'Navel gazing at Uisneach, Co. Westmeath', *Archaeology Ireland* 11.4: 24–6

Guilbert, G. 1979. 'Dinorben 1977–8', *Current Archaeology* 65: 182–8

  1980. 'Dinorben C-14 dates', *Current Archaeology* 70: 336–7

Gunn, J. (ed.) 2000. *The Years without Summer: Tracing* AD *536 and its Aftermath* (= BAR Int. Ser. 872), Oxford

Hague, D. B. 1966. 'Burryholms', *Medieval Archaeology* 10: 184

  1974. 'Some Welsh evidence', *Scottish Archaeol. Forum* 5: 17–35

Hall, R. 1984. *The Viking Dig*, London

Hall, V. A. 2000. 'Pollen analytical investigations of the Irish landscape, AD 500–1650', *Peritia* 14: 342–71

Hallén, Y. 1994. 'The use of bone and antler at Foshigarry and Bac Mhic Connain, two Iron Age sites on North Uist, Western Isles', *Proc. Soc. Ant. Scot.* 124: 189–231

Halliday, S. P. 1982. 'Later prehistoric farming in south-west Scotland', in D. Harding (ed.), 75–91

Hamilton, J. R. C. 1956. *Excavations at Jarlshof Shetland*, Edinburgh

  1968. *Excavations at Clickhimin, Shetland*, Edinburgh

Hamlin, A. 1972. 'A chi-rho carved stone at Drumaqueran, Co. Antrim', *Ulster J. Archaeol.* 35: 22–8

  1992. 'The early Irish church: problems of identification', in Edwards and Lane (eds.), 138–45

Hamlin, A. and Foley, C. 1983. 'A women's graveyard at Carrickmore, County Tyrone, and the separate burial of women', *Ulster J. Archaeol.* 46: 41–6

Handley, M. 1998. 'The early medieval inscription of eastern Britain: function and sociology', in J. Hill and M. Swan (eds.), *The Community, the Family and the Saint: Politics and Power in Early Medieval Europe*, Turnhout, 339–61

  2001. 'The origins of Christian commemoration in late antique Britain', *Early Medieval Europe* 10.2: 177–99

Harbison, P. 1969. 'The chariot of Celtic funerary tradition', in O.-H. Frey (ed.), *Marburger Beiträge zur Archäologie der Kelten, Festschrift Dehn*, Marburg, 34–58

  1970. 'How old is Gallarus Oratory?', *Medieval Archaeology* 14: 34–59

  1971. 'The old Irish chariot', *Antiquity* 45: 34–59

  1979. 'The inscriptions on the cross of the Scriptures at Clonmacnois, Co. Offaly', *Proc. Royal Irish Acad.* 79c: 177–88

Harbison, P. 1981. 'The date of the Moylough belt-shrine', in Ó Corráin (ed.), *Irish Antiquity*, Cork, 231–9

1982. 'Early Irish churches', in H. Löwe (ed.), *Die Irland und Europa im früeren mittelalter*, vol. 2, Stuttgart, 618–29

1984. 'The bronze crucifixion plaque said to be from St John's (Rinnigan) near Athlone', *J. Irish Archaeology* 2: 1–17

1986. 'A group of early Christian carved stone monuments in Co. Donegal', in Higgitt (ed.), 49–68

1987a. 'The date of the crucifixion slabs from Duvillaun More and Inishkea North, Co. Mayo', in Rynne (ed.), 73–91

1987b. 'The Carolingian contribution to Irish sculpture', in Ryan 1987a: 105–10

1992. *The High Crosses of Ireland*, 3 vols., Bonn

1994. *Irish High Crosses, with the Figure Sculpture Explained*, Drogheda

1999. *The Golden Age of Irish Art*, London

Harden, D. B. (ed.) 1956a. *Dark Age Britain*, London

1956b. 'Glass vessels in Britain, AD 400–1000', in Harden, 1956a: 132–57

Harding, D. W. 2004. *The Iron Age in Northern Britain: Celts and Romans, Natives and Invaders*, Edinburgh

Harding, D. W. and Gilmour, S. D. M. 2000. *Iron Age Settlement at Beirgh, Risf, Isle of Lewis: Excavations 1985–95*, vol. 1, Edinburgh

Härke, H. 1997. 'Early Anglo-Saxon social structure', in J. Hines (ed.), *The Anglo-Saxons from the Migration Period to the Eighth Century: An Ethnographic Perspective*, Woodbridge, 125–70

Harper, A. E. T. 1974. 'The excavation of a rath at Crossnacreevy townland, Co. Down', *Ulster J. Archaeol.* 36–7: 32–41

Harris, A. 2003. *Byzantium, Britain and the West: The Archaeology of Cultural Identity AD 400–650*, Stroud

Harrison, S. H. 2001. 'Viking graves and grave-goods in Ireland', in Larsen (ed.), 61–76

Harry, R. and Morris, C. D. 1997. 'Excavations on the lower terrace site C, Tintagel Island, 1990–94', *Antiq. J.* 77: 1–143

Harvey, A. 1990. 'The ogham inscriptions and the Roman alphabet: two traditions or one?', *Archaeology Ireland* 4.1: 13–14

2001. 'Problems in dating the origin of the Ogham script', in Higgitt, Forsyth and Parsons (eds.), 37–50

Haseloff, G. 1987. 'Insular animal styles with special reference to Irish art in the early medieval period', in Ryan 1987a: 44–55

1991. 'Celtic enamel', in V. Kruta et al. (eds.), *The Celts*, New York, 639–42

Hayes, J. 1972. *Late Roman Pottery*, London

1980. *A Supplement to Late Roman Pottery*, London

Hedeager, L. 1988. 'The evolution of Germanic society, AD 1–400', in R. F. J. Jones, J. H F. Bloemers, S. L. Dyson and M. Biddle (eds.), *Western Europe in the First Millennium AD* (= BAR Int. Ser. 401), Oxford, 129–44.

Hemphill, S. 1911–12. 'The Gospels of Mac Regol of Birr: a study in Celtic illumination', *Proc. Royal Irish Acad.* 29c: 1–10

Hencken, H. O'N. 1932. *The Archaeology of Cornwall and Scilly*, London.

1936. 'Ballinderry 1 crannog', *Proc. Royal Irish Acad.* 43c: 103–226

1938. *Cahercommaun: A Stone Fort in Co. Clare* (= *J. Royal Soc. Antiq. Ireland* special volume)

Hencken, H. O'N 1942. 'Ballinderry 2 crannog', *Proc. Royal Irish Acad.* 47c: 1–75

    1950. 'Lagore, a royal residence of the seventh to tenth centuries AD', *Proc. Royal Irish Acad.* 53: 1–247

Henderson, G. 1987. *From Durrow to Kells, the Insular Gospel Books*, London

Henderson, G. and Henderson, I. 2004. *The Art of the Picts*, London

Henderson, I. 1957–8. 'The origin centre of the Pictish symbol stones, *Proc. Soc. Ant. Scot.* 91: 44–60

    1967. *The Picts*, London

    1971. 'The meaning of the Pictish symbol stones', in P. Meldrum (ed.), *The Dark Ages in the Highlands*, 53–68

    1979. 'The silver chain froim Whitecleugh, Shieldholm, Crawfordjohn, Lanarkshire', *Trans. Dumfries Galloway N.H.A.S.* 54: 20–8

    1982. 'Pictish art and the Book of Kells', in I. Whitelock, D. McKitterick and D. Dumville (eds.), *Ireland in Early Medieval Europe*, Cambridge, 79–105

    1987. 'The Book of Kells and the snake-boss motif on Pictish cross-slabs and the Iona crosses', in Ryan (ed.), 56–65

    1996. *Pictish Monsters: Symbol, Text and Image* (= Chadwick memorial lectures 7), Cambridge

Henderson, Jon 2000a. 'Shared traditions? The drystone settlement records of Atlantic Scotland and Ireland, 700 BC–AD 200', in Henderson, 2000b: 117–54

    (ed.) 2000b. *The Prehistory and Early History of Atlantic Europe*, Oxford

Henderson, Julian 2000. 'The production technology of Irish early Christian glass with specific reference to beads and enamels', in Price (ed.), 143–59

Henderson, Julian and Ivens, R. 1992. 'Dunmisk and glass-making in early Christian Ireland', *Antiquity* 66: 52–64

Henry, D. (ed.) 1997. *The Worm, the Germ and the Thorn, Pictish and Related Studies presented to Isabel Henderson*, Balgavies

Henry, F. 1930. 'L'inscription de Bealin', *Revue Archéologique* 5 ser. 32: 110–15

    1933. 'Emailleurs d'Occident', *Préhistoire* 2.1: 65–146

    1936. 'Hanging bowls', *J. Royal Soc. Antiq. Ireland* 66: 209–310

    1952. 'A wooden hut at Inishkea North. Co. Mayo', *J. Royal Soc. Antiq. Ireland* 82: 163–78

    1956. 'Irish enamels of the Dark Ages and their relation to the cloisonné techniques', in Harden, 1956a: 71–90

    1957. 'Early monasteries, beehive huts, and dry-stone houses in the neighbourhood of Caherciveen and Waterville (Kerry)', *Proc. Royal Irish Acad.* 57c: 45–166

    1960. 'Remarks on the decoration of three Irish psalters', *Proc. Royal Irish Acad.* 61c: 23–40

    1964. *Irish High Crosses*, Dublin

    1965. *Irish Art in the Early Christian Period*, London

    1967. *Irish Art During the Viking Invasions, 1020–1170 AD*, London

    1970. *Irish Art in the Romanesque Period, 1020–1170 AD*, London

    1974. *The Book of Kells*, London

    1980. 'Around an inscription: the cross of the scriptures at Clonmacnois', *J. Royal Soc. Antiq. Ireland* 110: 35–51

Henry, F. and Marsh-Michelli, G. L. 1962. 'A century of Irish Illumination (1070–1170)', *Proc. Royal Irish Acad.* 62c: 101–65

Henshall, A. S. 1955–6. 'The long cist cemetery at Parkburn, Midlothian', *Proc. Soc. Ant. Scot.* 89: 252–83

Herity, M. 1984. 'The layout of Irish early Christian monasteries', in Ní Chatháin and Richter (eds.), 105–16

1990. 'The hermitage on Ardoileán, County Galway', *J. Royal Soc. Antiq. Ireland* 20: 65–101

1995. *Studies in the Layout, Buildings and Art in Stone of Early Irish Monasteries*, London

Herren, M. 1982. 'Insular Latin c(h)araxare (craxare) and its derivatives', *Peritia* 3: 312–16

Hicks, C. 1980. 'A Clonmacnois workshop in stone', *J. Royal Soc. Antiq. Ireland* 110: 1–35

1993. *Animals in Early Medieval Art*, Edinburgh

Higgins, D. A. 1999. 'Survey and trial excavations at the "Ronaldsway Village" site, Ronaldsway Airport, Isle of Man', in P. Davey (ed.), *Recent Archaeological Research on the Isle of Man* (= BAR Brit. Ser. 278), Oxford, 139–52

Higgins, V. 1984. 'The animal remains', in Brown and Harper, 154–6

Higgitt, J. (ed.) 1986. *Early Medieval Sculpture in Britain and Ireland* (= BAR Brit. Ser. 152), Oxford

Higgitt, J., Forsyth, K. and Parson, N. (eds.) 2001. *Roman, Runes and Ogham*, Donnington

Higham, N. 1992. *Rome, Britain and the Anglo-Saxons*, London

Higham, N. and Jones, B. 1991. *The Carvetii*, Stroud

Hill, D. and Worthington, M. 2003. *Offa's Dyke*, Stroud

Hill, P. 2001. 'Whithorn, Latinus and the origins of Christianity in northern Britain', in H. Hamerow and A. MacGregor, *Image and Power in the Archaeology of Early Medieval Britain*, Oxford, 23–32

Hill, P. and Kucharski, K. 1990. 'Early medieval ploughing at Whithorn and the chronology of plough pebbles', *Trans. Dumfries Galloway N.H.A.S* 65: 73–83

Hill, P. et al. 1997. *Whithorn and St Ninian: The Excavation of a Monastic Town, 1984–91*, Stroud

Hillgarth, J. N. 1963. 'Visigothic Spain and early Christian Ireland', *Proc. Royal Irish Acad.* 62c: 167–94

Hines, J. 1990. 'Philology, archaeology, and the *adventus Saxonum vel Anglorum*', in Bammesberger and Wolman (eds.), 17–36

1994. 'The becoming of the English: identity, material culture and language in early Anglo-Saxon England', *Anglo-Saxon Studies in History and Archaeology* 7: 49–59

Hodkinson, B. 1987. 'A re-appraisal of the archaeological evidence for weaving in Ireland in the early Christian period', *Ulster J. Archaeol.* 50: 47–50

Hogg, A. H. A. 1960. 'Garn Boduan and Tr'er Ceiri', *Archaeol. J.* 117: 1–9

1966. 'Native settlements in Wales', in C. Thomas (ed.), *Rural Settlement in Roman Britain*, London, 28–38

Holbrook, N. 1998. *Cirencester: The Roman Town Defences, Public Buildings and Shops*, Cirencester.

Holmes, N. 2003. *Excavation of Roman Sites at Cramond, Edinburgh* (= Soc. Ant. Scot. monograph), Edinburgh

Holmes, N. and Hunter, F. 2001. 'Roman counterfeiters' moulds from Scotland', *Proc. Soc. Ant. Scot.* 131: 167–76

Holmqvist, W. 1955. 'An Irish crozier found near Stockholm', *Antiq. J.* 35: 46–51

Hooke, D. and Burnell, S. (eds.) 1995. *Landscape and Settlement in Britain* AD *400–1066*, Exeter

Hope-Taylor, B. 1977. *Yeavering: An Anglo-British Centre of Early Northumbria*, London

Hope-Taylot, B. 1980. 'Balbridie and Doon Hill', *Current Archaeology* 72:18–19

Horn, W., White Marshall, J., Rourke, D. et al. 1990. *The Forgotten Hermitage of Skellig Michael*, Berkeley and Los Angeles

Houlder, C. 1968. 'The henge monuments at Llandegai', *Antiquity* 42: 216–21

Hourihane, C. (ed.) 2001. *From Ireland Coming*, Princeton

   (ed.) 2004. *Irish Art Historical Studies in Honour of Peter Harbison*, Princeton and Dublin

Howlett, D. 1995. *The Celtic Latin Tradition in Biblical Style*, Dublin

   1998. 'Literate culture of "Dark Age" Britain', *British Archaeology* 33: 10–11

Huggett, J. W. 1988. 'Imported grave-goods and the early Anglo-Saxon economy', *Medieval Archaeology* 32: 63–96

Hughes, H. 1925. 'An ancient burial ground at Bangor', *Arch. Cambrensis* 80: 432–6

Hughes, K. 1966. *The Church in Early Irish Society*, London

   1970. *Early Christianity in Pictland*, Jarrow

   1972. *Early Christian Ireland: An Introduction to the Sources*, London

   1980. *Celtic Britain in the Early Middle Ages*, Woodbridge

   1981. 'The Celtic church: is this a valid concept?', *Cambridge Medieval Celtic Studies* 1: 1–20

   2005a. 'The church in Irish society', in Ó Cróinín (ed.), 301–370

   2005b. 'The Irish church, 800–c.1050', in Ó Cróinín (ed.), 635–55

Hughes, K. and Hamlin, A. 1997. *The Modern Traveller to the Early Irish Church*, rev. edn, Dublin

Hunt, J. 1956. 'On two D-shaped objects in the Saint-Germain Museum', *Proc. Royal Irish Acad.* 57c: 153–7

Hunter, F. 1994. 'Dowalton Loch reconsidered', *Trans. Dumfries Galloway N.H.A.S.* 69: 53–71

Hunter, J. R. 1986. *Rescue Excavations on the Brough of Birsay, 1974–82*, (= *Soc. Ant. Scot.* monograph 4), Edinburgh

   1990. 'Pool, Sanday: a case study for the late Iron Age', in Armit (ed.), 175–93

   1997. *A Persona for the Northern Picts* (= Groam House lectures), Rosemarkie

Hutchinson, G. 1979. 'The bar-lug pottery of Cornwall', *Cornish Archaeology* 18: 81–103

Isaac, G. 1990. 'Mynyddawg Mwynfawr', *Bulletin Board of Celtic Studies* 37: 111–13

Isaac, P. 1976. 'Coin hoards and history in the west', in K. Branigan and P. Fowler (eds.), *The Roman West Country*, Newton Abbot, 52–62

Ivens, R. J. 1984. 'Killyliss rath, County Tyrone', *Ulster J. Archaeol.* 47: 9–35

   1987. 'The early Christian monastic enclosure at Tullylish, Co. Down', *Ulster J. Archaeol.* 50: 55–121

   1989. 'Dunmisk fort Carrickmore, Co. Tyrone: excavations 1984–86', *Ulster J. Archaeol.* 52: 17–110

Jackson, A. 1984. *The Symbol Stones of Scotland*, Kirkwall

Jackson, K. H. 1953. *Language and History in Early Britain*, Edinburgh

   1955. 'The Pictish language', in Wainwright 1955b: 129–66

   1964. *The Oldest Irish Tradition: A Window on the Iron Age*, Cambridge

   1969. *The Gododdin Poem*, Edinburgh

   1971. *A Celtic Miscellany*, rev. edn, Harmondsworth

James, E. 1977. *Merovingian Archaeology of South-West Gaul* (= BAR Int. Ser. 27), Oxford

   1982. 'Ireland and western Gaul in the Merovingian period', in Whitelock, D., McKitterick, R. and Dumville, D (eds.), 362–86

James, E. 1992. 'Excavations in Roman Carmarthen 1978–1990', *Carmarthen Antiquary* 28: 5–36

2001. *Britain in the First Millennium*, London

James, H. 1992. 'Early medieval cemeteries in Wales', in Edwards and Lane (eds.), 90–102

James, S. 1999. *The Atlantic Celts: Ancient People or Modern Invention?*, London

Jarman, A. O. H. 1988. *Aneirin, Y Gododdin: Britain's Oldest Heroic Poem*, Llandysul

Jarrett, M. 1969. rev. edn of V. E. Nash-Williams, *The Roman Frontier in Wales*, Cardiff

Jarrett, M. and Mann, J. C. 1968–9. 'The tribes of Wales', *Welsh History Review* 4: 161–71

Jenkins, D. and Owen, M. E. 1980. *The Welsh Law of Women*, Cardiff

Jobey, G. 1959. 'Excavations at the native settlement at Huckhoe', *Archaeologia Aeliana*, 4th ser. 37: 217–78

1966. 'A field survey in Northumberland', in Rivet (ed.), 89–109

Johnson, R. 1999. 'Ballinderry crannog no. 1: a reconsideration', *Proc. Royal Irish Acad.* 99c: 23–71

2000. 'On the dating of some early medieval Irish croziers', *Medieval Archaeology* 44: 115–58

Johnstone, P. 1964. 'The Bantry boat', *Antiquity* 38: 277–84

1980. *The Sea-craft of Prehistory*, London

Jones, M. E. 1996. *The End of Roman Britain*, London and Ithaca, N.Y.

Jope, E. M. 1953. 'Report on animal remains', *Ulster J. Archaeol.* 16: 51–3

1955. 'Chariotry and paired-draught in Ireland during the early Iron Age: the evidence of some horse-bits', *Ulster J. Archaeol.* 17: 92–6

1962. 'Iron Age brooches in Ireland: a summary', *Ulster J. Archaeol.* 25: 25–38

Karkov, C., Ryan, M. and Farrell, R. (eds.) 1997. *The Insular Tradition*, New York

Keay, S. 1984. *Late Roman Amphorae in the Western Mediterranean* (= BAR S136), Oxford

Kelly, D. 1993. 'The relationship of the crosses in Argyll: the evidence of form', in Spearman and Higgitt (eds.), 219–29

1996. 'A sense of proportion: the metrical and design characteristics of some Columban high crosses', *J. Royal Soc. Antiq. Ireland* 126: 108–46

1993. 'The Lough Kinale book-shrine', in Spearman and Higgitt (eds.), 168–74

2001. 'The Hillquarter, Co. Westmeath mounts: an early medieval saddle from Ireland', in Redknap et al. (eds.), 261–74

2000. 'Tully Lough cross', *Archaeology Ireland* 17.2: 9–10

Kelly, F. 1988. *A Guide to Early Irish Law* (= Inst. of Advanced Studies monograph), Dublin

1997. *Early Irish Farming*, Dublin

Kelly, F. and Charles-Edwards, T. (eds.) 1983. *Brechbretha: An Old Irish Law-tract on Beekeeping*, Dublin

Kelly, R. S. 1990. 'Recent research on the hut group settlements of north-west Wales', in B. C. Burnham and J. L. Davies (eds.), *Conquest, Co-Existence and Change: Recent Work in Roman Wales, Trivium 25*, Lampeter, 102–11

1998. 'The wider setting', in P. J. Fasham et al. (eds.), *The Graeanog Ridge: Evolution of a Farming Landscape and its Settlements in North-West Wales*, Aberystwyth, 160–8

Kendrick, T. D. 1932. 'British hanging bowls', *Antiquity* 6: 161–84

Kendrick, T. D. and Senior, F. 1937. 'St Manchan's shrine', *Archaeologia* 86: 105–18

Kenny, J. F. 1929. *The Sources for the Early History of Ireland*, vol. 1, New York

Kermode, P. M. C. 1907. *Manx Crosses*, Douglas

1930. 'Ship burial in the Isle of Man', *Antiquaries Journal* 10: 126–33

Kilbride-Jones, H. E. 1935–6. 'Scots zoomorphic penannular brooches', *Proc. Soc. Ant. Scot.* 70: 124–38

1936–7. 'A bronze hanging bowl from Castle Tioram and a suggested absolute chronology for British hanging bowls', *Proc. Soc. Ant. Scot.* 71: 206–47

1937. 'The evolution of penannular brooches with zoomorphic terminals in Great Britain and Ireland', *Proc. Royal Irish Acad.* 43c: 379–455

1937–8. 'Glass armlets in Britain', *Proc. Soc. Ant. Scot.* 72: 366–95

1980. *Zoomorphic Penannular Brooches* (= *Soc. Ant. Lond.* res. rep. 39), London

King, H. 1992. 'Moving crosses', *Archaeology Ireland* 6.4: 22–3

Kinsella, T. (trans.) 1969. *The Tain*, Oxford

Kinvig, R. H. 1975. *The Isle of Man: A Social, Cultural and Political History*, Liverpool

Kitzinger, E. 1993. 'Interlace and icons: form and function in early Insular art', in Spearman and Higgitt (eds), 3–15

Knight, J. 1981. 'In tempore Iustini consularis: contacts between the British and Gaulish church before Augustine', in A. Detsicas (ed.), *Collectanea Historica: Essays in Memory of Stuart Rigold*, Maidstone, 54–62

1992. 'The early Christian Latin inscriptions of Britain and Gaul: chronology and context', in Edwards and Lane (eds.), 45–50

1996a. 'Seasoned with salt: Insular–Gallic contacts in the early memorial stones and cross slabs', in Dark, 1996a: 109–20

1996b. 'Late Roman and post-Roman Caerwent: some evidence of metalwork', *Arch. Cambrensis* 145: 34–66

Koch, J. T. 1987. 'A Welsh window on the Iron Age: Manawydan Mandubracios', *Cambridge Medieval Celtic Studies* 14: 17–52

1991. 'Ériu, Alba and Letha: when was a language ancestral to Gaelic first spoken in Ireland?', *Emania* 9: 17–27

1997 *The Gododdin of Aneirin: Text and Context from Dark Age North Britain*, Cardiff

(ed.) 1997. *The Celtic Heroic Age: Literary Sources for Ancient Celtic Europe and Early Ireland and Wales*, Andover, Mass.

Lacy, B. 1983. *Archaeological Survey of County Donegal*, Lifford

Laing, L. R. 1969. 'Medieval settlement archaeology in Scotland', *Scottish Archaeological Forum* 1: 69–79

1973. 'The Mote of Mark', *Current Archaeology* 4: 121–5

Laing, L. R. 1975a. 'The Angles in Scotland and the Mote of Mark', *Trans. Dumfries Galloway N.H.A.S.* 50: 37–52

1975b. *The Archaeology of Late Celtic Britain and Ireland, c. AD 400–1200*, London

(ed.) 1977. *Studies in Celtic Survival* (= BAR Brit. Ser. 37), Oxford

1988. 'The Romanization of Ireland in the fifth century AD', *Peritia* 4: 261–78

1990. 'The beginnings of "Dark Age" Celtic art', in Bammesberger and Wollmann (eds.), 37–50.

1993a. *A Catalogue of Celtic Ornamental Metalwork in the British Isles, c. AD 400–1200* (= BAR Brit. Ser. 229), Oxford

1993b. 'The Papil, Shetland stones and their significance', *Pictish Arts Soc. J.* 4: 28–36

1994. 'The hoard of Pictish silver from Norrie's Law, Fife', *Studia Celtica* 27: 11–38

1995a. 'The date and significance of the Ardchattan stone', *Pictish Arts Soc. J.* 8: 2–7

1995b. 'The provenance of the Book of Durrow', *Scottish Archaeological Review* 9–10: 115–24

Laing, L. R. 1996. 'Alternative Celtic art: early medieval non-Pictish sketches on stone in Britain', *Studia Celtica* 30: 127–46

   1997. *Later Celtic Art in Britain and Ireland*, 2nd edn, Princes Risborough

   1998. 'The early medieval sculptures from St Blane's, Bute', *Pictish Arts Soc. J.* 12: 19–23

   1999. 'The Bradwell mount and the use of millefiori in post-Roman Britain', *Studia Celtica* 33: 137–53

   2000a. 'How late were Pictish symbols employed?', *Proc. Soc. Ant. Scot.* 130: 637–50

   2000b. 'The chronology and context of Pictish relief sculpture', *Medieval Archaeology* 44: 81–114

   2001a. 'The date and context of the Glamis, Angus, carved Pictish stones', *Proc. Soc. Ant. Scot.* 131: 223–39

   2001b. 'The date of the Aberlemno churchyard stone', in Redknap et al. (eds.), 241–52

   2006. 'Romano-British metalworking and the Anglo–Saxons'

Laing, L. and Laing, J. 1984a. 'Archaeological notes on some Scottish early Christian sculptures', *Proc. Soc. Ant. Scot.* 114: 277–87

   1984ba. 'The date and origin of the Pictish Symbols', *Proc. Soc. Ant. Scot.* 114: 261–76

   1990a. *Celtic Britain and Ireland* AD *200–800: The Myth of the Dark Ages*, Dublin

   1990b. 'The early Christian period settlement at Ronaldsway, Isle of Man: a re-appraisal', *Proc. I.O.M. Nat. Hist. Antiq. Soc.* 9.3: 389–415

   1992. *Art of the Celts*, London

   1995. *Celtic Britain and Ireland, Art and Society*, London

   2001. *The Picts and the Scots*, 2nd edn, Stroud

Laing, L., Laing, J. and Longley, D. 1998. 'The early Christian and later medieval ecclesi-astical site at St Blane's, Kingarth, Bute', *Proc. Soc. Ant. Scot.* 128: 551–65

Laing, L. and Longley, D. 2006. *The Mote of Mark, a Dark Age Hillfort in South-West Scotland*, Oxford

Lamb, H. H. 1981. 'Climate from 1000 BC to 1000 AD', in M. Jones and G. Dimbleby (eds.), *The Environment of Man: The Iron Age to the Anglo-Saxon Period* (= BAR Brit. Ser.), Oxford, 53–65

Lamb, R. G. 1975–6. 'The Burri Stacks of Culswick, Shetland, and other paired-stack settlements', *Proc. Soc. Ant. Scot.* 107: 144–54

Lane, A. 1990. 'Hebridean pottery: problems of definition, chronology, presence and absence', in Armit (ed.), 108–30

   1994. 'Trade, gifts, and cultural exchange in Dark-Age western Scotland', in B. Crawford (ed.), 105–15

Lane, A. and Campbell, E. 2000. *Dunadd: An Early Dalriadic Capital*, Oxford

La Neice, S. 1983. 'Niello: an historical and technical survey', *Antiq. J.* 63: 279–97

   1990. 'Silver plating on copper, bronze and brass', *Antiq. J.* 70: 102–14

La Neice, S. and Stapleton, C. 1993. 'Niello and enamel on Irish metalwork', *Antiq. J.* 73: 148–51

Lang, J. 1972–4. 'Hogback monuments in Scotland', *Proc. Soc. Ant. Scot.* 105: 206–35

   1987. 'Eleventh-century style in decorated wood from Dublin', in Ryan, 1987a: 174–8

   1988. *Viking-Age Decorated Wood: A Study of its Ornament and Style* (= Medieval Dublin Excavations, 1962–81, ser. B.I), Dublin

   1991. 'Survival and revival in Insular art: some principles', in C. Karkov and T. Farrell (eds.), *Studies in Insular Art and Archaeology*, Oxford, Ohio, 63–77

Langdon, A. G. 1896. *Old Cornish Crosses*, Truro

Lapidge, M. and Dumville, D. (eds.) 1984. *Gildas: New Approaches*, Cambridge

Larsen, A.-C. (ed.) 2001. *The Vikings in Ireland*, Roskilde

Larsen, A.-C and Hansen, S. S. 2001. 'Viking Ireland and the Scandinavian communities in the North Atlantic', in Larsen (ed.), 115–26

Lawlor, H. C. 1925. *The Monastery of St Mochaoi at Nendrum*, Belfast

Lawson, A. J. 1976. 'Shale and jet objects from Silchester', *Archaeologia* 105: 241–75

Leask, H. G. 1955. *Early Irish Churches and Monastic Buildings*, vol. 1: *The Early Period and the Romanesque*, Dundalk

Leeds, E. T. 1936. *Early Anglo-Saxon Art and Archaeology*, Oxford

Liestol, A. 1953. 'The hanging bowl, a liturgical and domestic vessel', *Acta Archaeologica* 24: 163–70.

Limbert, D. 1996. 'Irish ringforts: a review of their origins', *Archaeol. J.* 153: 243–89

Lionard, P. 1961. 'Early Irish grave slabs', *Proc. Royal Irish Acad.* 61c: 95–169

Liversage, G. D. 1968. 'Excavations at Dalkey island, Co. Dublin, 1956–59', *Proc. Royal Irish Acad.* 66c: 53–223

Longley, D. 1991. 'The excavation of Castell, Porth Trefadog: a coastal promontory fort in north Wales', *Medieval Archaeology* 35: 64–85

   1997. 'Excavations at Bangor, Gwynedd, 1981–1989', *Archaeologia Cambrensis* 144: 52–70

   2001. 'The Mote of Mark: the archaeological context of the decorated metalwork', in Redknap et al. (eds.), 75–89

   2002. 'Orientation within early medieval cemeteries: some data from north-west Wales', *Antiq. J.* 82: 309–21

Lowe, E. A. (ed.) 1934–63. *Codices Latini Antiquiores*, Oxford

Lowe, C. 1993. 'Hoddom', *Current Archaeology* 123: 88–92

   1999. *Angels, Fools and Tyrants, Britons and Anglo-Saxons in Southern Scotland, AD 450–750*, Edinburgh

Lowry-Corry, D., Wilson, B. C. S. and Waterman, D. M. 1959. 'A newly discovered statue at the church on White Island', *Ulster J. Archaeol.* 22: 59–66

Loyn, H. R. 1976. *The Vikings in Wales* (=Dorothea Coke memorial lecture), London

   1977. *The Viking Age in Britain*, London

Lucas, A. T. 1952. 'A block wheel car from Co. Tipperary', *J. Royal Soc. Antiq. Ireland* 82: 135–44

   1953. 'The horizontal mill in Ireland', *J. Royal Soc. Antiq. Ireland* 83: 1–36

   1956. 'Footwear in Ireland', *Co. Louth Archaeol. J.* 13: 367–82

   1975. 'Souterrains: the literary evidence', *Béaloideas* 39–41, 165–91

   1989. *Cattle in Ancient Ireland*, Kilkenny

Luce, A. A. et al. (eds.) 1960. *Evangeliorum Quattuor Codex Durmachensis*, 2 vols., Olten and Lausanne

Lynch, A. 1981. *Man and Environment in South-West Ireland, 4000 BC – AD 800* (= BAR Brit. Ser. 85), Oxford

Lynch, F., Aldhouse-Green, S. and Davies, J. L. 2000. *Prehistoric Wales*, Stroud

Lynch, F. and Musson, C. 2004. 'A prehistoric and early medieval complex at Llandegai, near Bangor, North Wales', *Arch. Cambrensis* 150: 17–142

Lynn, C. J. 1975. 'The medieval ringfort – an archaeological chimera?', *Irish Archaeological Research Forum*, 2: 29–36

   1978a. 'A rath in Seacash townland, Co. Antrim', *Ulster J. Archaeol.* 41: 55–74

1978b. 'Early Christian period domestic structures: a change from round to rectangular', *Irish Archaeological Research Forum* 5: 29–45

1982. 'The excavation of Rathmullan, a raised rath and motte in County Down', *Ulster J. Archaeol.* 44–5: 65–171

Lynn, C. J. 1983. 'Some 'early ring-forts and crannogs', *J. Irish Archaeology* 1: 47–58

1985. 'Excavations on a mound at Gransha, County Down, 1972 and 1982; an interim report', *Ulster J. Archaeol.* 48: 81–90

1989. 'Deer Park farms', *Current Archaeology* 113: 193–8

1994. 'Houses in rural Ireland, AD 500–1000', *Ulster J. Archaeol.* 57: 81–94

Mac Airt, S. and MacNiocaill, G. 1983. *The Annals of Ulster (to AD 1131)*, Dublin.

McAll, C. 1980. 'The normal paradigms of a woman's life in the Irish and Welsh texts', in Jenkins and Owen (eds.), 7–22

MacArthur, W. P. 1949. 'The identification of some pestilences recorded in the Irish annals', *Irish Historical Studies* 6: 169–88

McCarthy, M. 2002. 'Rheged: an early historic kingdom near the Solway', *Proc. Soc. Ant. Scot.* 132: 357–81

Mac Canna, P. 1996. *Celtic Mythology*, London

McCarthy, M. 1998. 'Archaeozoological studies and early medieval Munster', in O'Sullivan and Monk (eds.), 62

McCone, K. 1990. *Pagan Past and Christian Present*, Maynooth

McCormick, F. 1981. 'The animal bones from ditch 1', in Barber, 313–18

1983. 'Dairying and beef production in early Christian Ireland: the faunal evidence', in Reeves-Smith and Hammond (eds.), 253–67

1993. 'Excavations at Iona, 1988', *Ulster J. Archaeol.* 56: 78–107

1995. 'Cows, ringforts and the origins of early Christian Ireland', *Emania* 13: 33–7

1997. 'Iona: the archaeology of the early monastery', in C. Bourke (ed.), *Studies in the Cult of St Columba*, Dublin, 45–68

MacDermott, M. 1955. 'The Kells crozier', *Archaeologia* 96: 59–113

1957. 'The croziers of St Dympna and St Mel and tenth-century Irish metalwork', *Proc. Royal Irish Acad.* 58c: 167–96

Macdonald, A. 1973a. 'Annat' in Scotland: a provisional review', *Scottish Studies* 17: 135–46

1973b. 'Two major early monasteries of Scottish Dalriata: Lismore and Eigg', *Scottish Archaeol. Forum* 5: 47–70

1977. 'Old Norse *Papar* names in N and W Scotland: a summary', in Laing (ed.), 107–11

1981. 'Notes on monastic archaeology and the Annals of Ulster, 650 to 1050', in Ó Corráin (ed.), 304–19

1984. 'Aspects of the monastery and monastic life in Adomnan's Life of Columba', *Peritia* 3: 271–302

2001. 'Aspects of the monastic landscape in Adomnán's Life of Columba', in J. Carey, M. Herbert and P. B. Riain (eds.), *Studies in Irish Hagiography: Saints and Scholars*, Dublin, 15–30

2002. 'The *papar* and some problems; a brief review', in B. Crawford (ed.), 13–29

Macdonald, A. and Laing, L. 1967–8. 'Early ecclesiastical sites in Scotland: a field survey, part I', *Proc. Soc. Ant. Scot.* 100: 123–34

McDonnell, H. 1994. 'Margaret Stokes and the Irish round tower: a Reappraisal', *Ulster J. Archaeol.* 57: 70–80

Mcerlean, T. 2001. 'Tidal power in the seventh and eighth centuries AD', *Archaeology Ireland* 15, no.2: 10–14

Macgregor, A. 1972–4. 'The broch of Burrian, North Ronaldsay, Orkney', *Proc. Soc. Ant. Scot.* 105: 63–118

Macgregor, A. 1976. 'Two antler crossbow bolts and some notes on the early development of the crossbow', *Proc. Soc. Ant. Scot.* 107: 317–22

   1985. *Bone, Antler, Ivory and Horn: The Technology of Skeletal Materials Since the Roman Period*, London

MacInnes, L. 1984. 'Brochs and the Roman occupation of lowland Scotland', *Proc. Soc. Ant. Scot.* 114: 235–249

McKee, H. and McKee, J. 2002. 'Counter arguments and numerical patterns in early Celtic inscriptions: a re-examination of Christian Celts: messages and images', *Medieval Archaeology* 46: 29–40

Mackie, E. 1987. 'Leckie Broch: the impact on the Scottish Iron Age', *Glasgow Arch. J.* 14: 1–18

   1994. 'Midhowe and Gurness brochs in Orkney: some problems of misinterpretation', *Archaeol. J.* 151: 98–157

Maclaren, A. 1974. 'A Norse house on Drimore Machair, S. Uist', *Glasgow Arch. J.* 3: 9–18

Maclean, D. 1995a. 'Technique and contact: carpentry-constructed Insular stone crosses', in C. Bourke (ed.), 167–76

   1995b. 'The status of the sculptor in Old Irish law and the evidence of the crosses', *Peritia* 9: 125–55

   1997. 'Maelrubai, Applecross and the late Pictish contribution west of Druimalban', in D. Henry (ed.), 173–87

MacLeod, I. 1986. *Discovering Galloway*, Edinburgh

McManus, D. 1984. 'A chronology of the Latin loan words in early Irish', *Eiru* 34: 42–3

   1991. *A Guide to Ogam*, Maynooth

Mac Neill, E. 1923. 'Ancient Irish law: the law of status or franchise', *Proc. Royal Irish Acad.* 36c: 265–316

McNeill, T. E. 1975. 'Excavations at Doonbought fort, Co. Antrim', *Ulster J. Archaeol.* 40: 63–84

Mac Niocaill, G. 1972. *Ireland before the Vikings*, Dublin

MacQueen, J. 1990. *St Nynia*, Edinburgh

McRoberts, D. 1960–1. 'The ecclesiastical significance of the St Ninian's Isle Treasure', *Proc. Soc. Ant. Scot.* 94: 301–13

Mahr, A. and Raftery, J. 1932–41. *Christian Art in Ancient Ireland*, Dublin, 2 vols. (1, ed. Mahr, 1932; 2, ed. Raftery, 1941)

Mallory, J. P. 1982. 'The sword of the Ulster Cycle', in B. Scott (ed.), 99–114

   1995. 'Haughey's Fort and the Navan complex in the late Bronze Age', in J. Waddell and E. Shee-Twohig (eds.), *Ireland in the Bronze Age*, Dublin, 73–86,

Mallory, J. P. and Hartwell, B. N. 1997. 'Down in prehistory', in L. Proudfoot and W. Nolan (eds.), *Down, History and Society*, Dublin, 1–32

Mallory, J. P. and McNeill, T. E. 1991. *The Archaeology of Ulster from Colonization to Plantation*, Belfast

Mallory, J. P. and Woodman, P. C. 1984. 'Oughtymore: an early Christian shell midden', *Ulster J. Archaeol.* 47: 51–62

Manley, J. 1994. 'Excavations at Caergwrle Castle, Clwyd, North Wales, 1988–1990', *Medieval Archaeology* 38: 83–133

Mann, J. C. and Breeze, D. J. 1987. 'Ptolemy, Tacitus and the tribes of north Britain', *Proc. Soc. Ant. Scot.* 117: 85–91

Manning, C. 1984 'The excavation of the early Christian enclosure of Killederdadrum in Lackenavenora, Co. Tipperary', *Proc. Royal Irish Acad.* 86c: 237–68

1986. 'Archaeological excavations of a succession of enclosures at Millockstown, Co. Louth', *Proc. Royal Irish Acad.* 86c: 35–81

1995. 'Clonmacnoise Cathedral – the oldest church in Ireland?', *Archaeology Ireland* 14: 30–33

Marshall, D. N. 1964. 'Report on excavations at Little Dunagoil', *Trans. Bute Nat. Hist. Soc.* 16: 1–69

Marshall, J. W. and Rourke, G. D. 2000. *High Island: An Irish Monastery in the Atlantic*, Dublin

Maryon, H. 1959. *Metalwork and Enamelling: A Practical Treatise on Gold and Silversmiths' Work and their Allied Crafts*, 4th edn, London

Maxwell, G. S. 1987. 'Settlement in southern Pictland: a new overview', in Small (ed.), 31–44

1989. *The Romans in Scotland*, Edinburgh

May, J. and Weddell, P. 2002. 'Bantham: a Dark Age puzzle', *Current Archaeology* 178: 420–2

Mayr-Harting, H. 1972. *The Coming of Christianity to Anglo-Saxon England*, London

Meaney, A. and Hawkes, S. C. 1970. *Two Anglo-Saxon Cemeteries at Winnall* (= *Soc. Medieval Archaeology* monograph 4), London

Meehan, B. 1994. *The Book of Kells*, London

1998. ' "A melody of curves across the page": art and calligraphy in the Book of Armagh', *Irish Arts Review Yearbook* 14: 90–101

Megaw, B. R. S. 1938–40. 'The ancient village of Ronaldsway', *J. Manx Museum* 4: 181–2

Megaw, R. and Megaw, J. V. S. 1989. *Celtic Art, from its Beginnings to the Book of Kells*, London

1999. 'Celtic connections past and present', in Black et al. (eds.), 19–68

Mevaert, P. 1989. 'The Book of Kells and Iona', *Art Bulletin* 71: 6–19

Meyer, K. 1895–6. 'Early relations between Gael and Brython', *Trans. Cymrodorion Soc.* 55–86

1900. 'The expulsion of the Dessi', *Y Cymmrodor* 14: 101–35

Michelli, P. 1986. 'Four Scottish croziers and their relation to the Irish tradition', *Proc. Soc. Ant. Scot.* 116: 375–92

1996. 'The inscriptions on pre-Norman Irish reliquaries', *Proc. Royal Irish Acad.* 96c: 1–48

Miles, H. 1977. 'Excavations at Killibury Hillfort, Eglosyhayle, 1975–6', *Cornish Archaeology* 16: 89–121

Miles, T. and Miles, H. 1973. 'Trethurgy', *Current Archaeology* 40: 142–7

Miller, M. 1975. 'Historicity and pedigrees of the Northcountrymen', *Bulletin Board of Celtic Studies* 26.3: 255–80

Mitchell, G. F. 1965. 'Littleton Bog, Tipperary: an Irish agricultural record', *J. Royal Soc. Antiq. Ireland* 95: 121–32

1976. *The Irish Landscape*, London

1986. *The Shell Guide to Reading the Irish Landsacape*, Dublin

Moisl, H. 1983. 'The Bernician royal dynasty and the Irish in the seventh century', *Peritia* 2: 103–26

Moloney, C. 2001. 'New evidence for the origins and evolution of Dunbar: excavations at the Captain's Cabin, Castle Park, Dunbar, East Lothian', *Proc. Soc. Ant. Scot.* 131: 283–317

Monk, M. A. 1981. 'Post-Roman drying kilns and the problem of function: a preliminary statement', in Ó Corráin (ed.), 216–30

1986. 'The evidence of macroscopic plant remains for crop husbandry in prehistoric and early historic Ireland: a review', *J. Irish Archaeology* 3: 31–6

1988. 'Excavations at Lisleagh ringfort, north Cork', *Archaeology Ireland* 2.2: 57–60

1995. 'A tale of two ringforts: Lisleagh I and II', *J. Cork Hist. Soc.* 100: 105–16

Monk, M. A. and Sheehan, J. (eds.) 1998. *Early Medieval Munster: Archaeology, History and Society*, Cork.

Moore, D. 1996. 'Ireland's oldest bridge – at Clonmacnoise', *Archaeology Ireland* 10.4: 24–7

Moore, H. and Wilson, G. 2005 'The Langskaill souterrain', *Current Archaeology*, 199: 333–5

Morris, C. D. 1983. 'The survey and excavations at Keeill Vael, Druidale, in their context', in Fell et al. (eds.), 107–31

1989. *The Birsay Bay Project*, vol. 1: *Brough Road Excavations 1976–1982* (=Durham Dept of Archaeology monographs 1), Durham

1996a. 'From Birsay to Tintagel: a personal view', in Crawford (ed.), 37–78

1996b. *The Birsay Bay Project*, vol. 2: *Sites in Birsay Village [Beachview] and on the Brough of Birsay, Orkney* (= Durham Dept of Archaeology monographs 2), Durham

Morris, C. D., Batey, C. E., Harry, R., Johnson, P. G. and Thomas, A. C. 1999. 'Recent work at Tintagel', *Medieval Archaeology* 43: 206–15

Morris, C. D. and Emery, N. 1986. 'The chapel and enclosure on the Brough of Deerness, Orkney, survey and excavations, 1975–1977', *Proc. Soc. Ant. Scot.* 116: 301–74

Morris, J. R. 1973. *The Age of Arthur*, London

(trans. and ed.) 1980. *Nennius. British History and the Welsh Annals*, Chichester

Morrison, A. 1977. 'The question of Celtic survival or continuity in some elements of rural settlement in the Scottish Highlands', in L. Laing (ed.), 67–76

Morrison, I. 1985. *Landscape with Lake Dwellings: The Crannogs of Scotland*, Edinburgh

Moscati, S. (ed.) 1991. *The Celts*, London

Moss, R. J. 1927. 'A chemical examination of the crucibles in the collection of the Royal Irish Academy', *Proc. Royal Irish Acad.* 37: 175–93

Munro, R. 1882. *Ancient Scottish Lake Dwellings*, Edinburgh

Murphy, K. 1992. 'Plas Gogerddan, Dyfed: a multi-period burial and ritual site', *Archaeol. J.* 149: 1–38

Murphy, T. F. 1961. 'A ringfort at Old Court, Co Cork', *J. Cork Archaeol. Hist. Soc.* 66: 79–92

Murray, H. 1979. 'Documentary evidence for domestic buildings in Ireland, c. 400–1200 in the light of archaeology', *Medieval Archaeology* 23: 81–97

Musson, C. and Spurgeon, C. J. 1988. 'Cwrt Llechryd, Llanelwedd: an unusual moated site in central Powys', *Medieval Archaeology* 32: 97–109

Myres, J. N. L. 1969. *Anglo-Saxon Pottery and the Settlement of England*, Oxford

Mytum, H. 1992. *The Origins of Early Christian Ireland*, London

Nash-Williams, V. E. 1950. *The Early Christian Monuments of Wales*, Cardiff

Neely, C. J. H. 1940. 'Excavations at Ronaldsway, Isle of Man', *Antiq. J.* 20: 72–86

Newman, C. 1989. 'Fowler's Type F3 early medieval penannular brooches', *Medieval Archaeology* 33: 7–20

1990. 'Further notes on Fowler's Type F3 penannular brooches', *Medieval Archaeology* 34: 147–8

Newman, C. 1997. *Tara: An Archaeological Survey* (= Discovery programme monograph 2), Dublin

Ní Chatháin, P. and Richter, M. (eds.) 1984. *Irland und Europa: Die Kirche im Frümittelalter/ Ireland and Europe: The Early Church*, Stuttgart

Nicolaisen, W. 1965 'Scottish place-names: 24, *Slew-* and *sliabh*', *Scottish Studies* 9: 91–106
1976. *Scottish Place-names*, London
1996. *The Picts and their Placenames*, Rosemarkie

Nicoll, E. (ed.) 1995. *A Pictish Panorama*, Balgavies

Nicholls, K. 1972. *Gaelic and Gaelicised Ireland in the Middle Ages*, Dublin

Nieke, M. 1993. 'Penannular and related brooches: secular ornament or symbol in action?', in Spearman and Higgitt (eds.), 128–34

Nieke, M. and Duncan, H. 1988. 'Dalriada: the establishment and maintenance of an early historic kingdom in northern Britain', in Driscoll and Nieke (eds.), 6–21

Nisbet, H. C. and Gailey, R. A. 1962: 'A survey of the antiquities of North Rona', *Archaeol. J.* 117: 88–115

Noddle, B. 1982. 'The size of red deer in Britain – past and present', in S. Limbrey and S. M. Bell (eds.), *Archaeological Aspects of Woodland Ecology*, Oxford, 315–22

Nordenfalk, C. 1947. 'Before the Book of Durrow', *Acta Archaeologica* 18: 141–74
1977. *Celtic and Anglo-Saxon Painting*, New York

Norman, E. R. and St Joseph, J. K. 1969. *Early Development of Irish Society: The Evidence of Aerial Photography*, Cambridge

North, J. J. 1963. *English Hammered Coinage*, vol. 1, London

O Brien, W. 2004. *Ross Island: Mining, Metal and Society in Early Ireland* (= Nat. Univ. of Ireland Bronze Age Studies 6), Galway

O'Brien, E. 1992. 'Pagan and Christian burial in Ireland during the first millennium AD', in Edwards and Lane (eds.), 130–7
1993. 'Contacts between Ireland and Anglo-Saxon England in the seventh century', *Anglo-Saxon Studies in Archaeology and History* 6: 93–102
1998. 'Location and Context of Viking Burials at Kilmainham and Islandbridge, Dublin', in Clarke et al. (eds.), 203–221
1999. *Post-Roman Britain to Anglo-Saxon England: Burial Practices Reviewed* (= BAR Brit. Ser. 289), Oxford
2003 'Burial practices in Ireland, first to seventh centuries AD', in Downs and Ritchie (eds.), 62–74

O'Carroll, E. 2000. 'Ireland's earliest crozier?', *Archaeology Ireland*, 14.2: 24–5

O'Connor, A. and Clarke, D. V. (eds.) 1983. *From the Stone Age to the 'Forty-Five*, Edinburgh

Ó Corráin, D. 1972. *Ireland before the Normans*, Dublin
(ed.) 1981. *Irish Antiquity: Essays and Studies presented to Professor M. J. O'Kelly*, Cork
1983. 'Some legal references to fences and fencing in early historic Ireland', in Reeves-Smith and Hammond (eds.), 247–52

Ó Corráin, D., Breatnach, L. and Breen, A. 1984. 'The laws of the Irish', *Peritia* 3: 382–438

Ó Cróinín, D. 1995. *Early Medieval Ireland, 400–1200*, London
(ed.) 2005. *A New History of Ireland*, vol. 1: *Prehistoric and Early Ireland*, Oxford

Ó Cuileanáin, C. and Murphy, T. F. 1961. 'A ringfort at Oldcourt, Co. Cork', *J. Cork Archaeol. Hist. Soc.* 66: 79–92

Oddy, W. A. 1983. 'Bronze alloys in Dark Age Europe', in Bruce-Mitford (ed.), 945–62

Oddy, W. A., Bimson, M. and La Niece, S. 1983 'The composition of niello decoration on gold, silver and bronze in the antique and medieval periods', *Studies in Conservation* 28: 29–35

O Donnabháin, B. 1986. 'The human remains', in Manning, 171–9

O'Flaherty, B. 1986. 'Loher', in C. Cotter (ed.), *Excavations 1985*, Dublin, 26–7

Ó Floinn, R. 1982. 'The Shrine of the Book of Dimma', *Éile* 1: 25–39

    1987 'Schools of metalworking in eleventh- and twelfth-century Ireland', in Ryan, 1987a: 179–87

    1994. *Irish Shrines and Reliquaries of the Middle Ages*, Dublin

    1995. 'Clonmacnoise: art and patronage in the early medieval period', in C. Bourke (ed.), 251–60

    2001a. 'Irish and Scandinavian art in the early medieval period', in Larsen (ed.), 87–98

    2001b. 'Patrons and politics: art, artefact and methodology', in M. Redknap et al. (eds.), 2–14

    2002. 'Beginnings: early medieval Ireland AD 500–850', in Wallace and Ó Floinn (eds.), 171–212.

Ogden, J. 1982. *Jewellery of the Ancient World*, London

Ó Heaildhe, P. 1992. ' "The Monk's Boat" – a Roman period relic from Lough Lene, Co Westmeath, Eire', *International Journal of Nautical Archaeology and Underwater Exploration* 21.3: 185–90

Okasha, E. 1985. 'The non-Ogam inscriptions of Pictland', *Cambridge Medieval Celtic Studies* 9: 43–67

    1993. *Corpus of Early Christian Inscribed Stones of South-west Britain*, Leicester

O'Keefe, T. 2000. *Medieval Ireland: An Archaeology*, Stroud

O'Kelly, M. J. 1956. 'An island settlement at Beginish, Co. Kerry', *Proc. Royal Irish Acad.* 57c: 159–94

    1958. 'Church Island, near Valencia, Co. Kerry', *Proc. Royal Irish Acad.* 59c: 57–136

    1962a. 'Beal Boru, Co. Clare', *J. Cork Archaeol. Hist. Soc.* 67: 1–27

    1962b. 'The excavation of two earthen ringforts at Garryduff, Co. Cork', *Proc. Royal Irish Acad.* 63c: 17–124

    1965. 'The belt shrine from Moylough, Sligo', *J. Royal Soc. Antiq. Ireland* 95: 149–88

    1967. 'Knockea, Co. Limerick', in E. Rynne (ed.), *North Munster Studies*, Limerick, 72–101

    1975. *Archaeological Survey and Excavation of St Vogue's Church Enclosure and other Monuments at Carnsore, Co. Wexford*, Dublin

O'Mahony, F. (ed.) 1994. *The Book of Kells*, Dublin

O'Meadhra, U. 1979. *Early Christian, Viking and Romanesque Art: Motif Pieces from Ireland*, Stockholm

    1987a. *Early Christian, Viking and Romanesque Art: Motif Pieces from Ireland*, vol. 2: *A Discussion*, Stockholm

    1987b. 'Irish, Insular, Saxon and Scandinavian elements in the motif-pieces from Ireland', in Ryan, 1987a: 159–65

    1993. 'Viking-age sketches and motif-pieces from the northern earldoms', in Batey et al. (eds.), 423–40

O'Neill, H. E. 1964. 'Excavation of a Celtic hermitage on St Helen's, Isles of Scilly', *Archaeol. J.* 121: 40–69

O'Rahilly, J. 1976. *Táin Bó Cuailnge*, Dublin

Organ, R. 1973. 'An examination of the Ardagh chalice – a case history', in W. J. Young (ed.), *Application of Science in the Examination of Works of Art*, Boston, 237–71

Ó Ríordáin, S. P. 1940. 'Excavations at Cush, Co.Limerick', *Proc. Royal Irish Acad.* 42c: 145–91.

    1942. 'The excavation of a large earthen ring-fort at Garranes, Co. Cork', *Proc. Royal Irish Acad.* 47c: 77–150

    1947. 'Roman material in Ireland', *Proc. Royal Irish Acad.* 51c: 35–82

    1949. 'Lough Gur excavations: Carraig Aille and the "Spectacles"', *Proc. Royal Irish Acad.* 52c: 39–111

Ó Ríordáin, S. P. and MacDermott, M. 1952. 'The excavation of a ringfort at Leterkeen, Co Mayo', *Proc. Royal Irish Acad.* 54c: 89–119

Ó Ríordáin, S. P. and Foy, J . B. 1943. 'The excavation of Leacanabuaile fort, Co. Kerry', *J. Cork Archaeol. Hist. Soc* 46: 85–98

Ó Ríordáin, B. and Rynne, E. 1961. 'A settlement in the sandhills at Dooey, Co. Donegal', *J Royal Soc. Antiq. Ireland* 91: 58–64

Orme, N. 2000. *The Saints of Cornwall*, Oxford

O'Sullivan, A. 1994. 'Harvesting the waters', *Archaeology Ireland* 8.1 (spring): 10

1998. *The Archaeology of Lake Settlement in Ireland* (= Discovery Programme monograph 4), Dublin

    2000. *Crannogs: Lake Dwellings of Early Ireland*, Dublin

O'Sullivan, A. and Boland, D. 2000. *The Clonmacnoise Bridge* (= Heritage Ireland Heritage guide no. 11), Bray

O'Sullivan, J. and Sheehan, J. 1996. *The Iveragh Peninsula: An Archaeological Survey of South Kerry*, Cork

O'Sullivan, W. 1961. *The Earliest Irish Coinage*, Dublin

    1964. *The Earliest Anglo-Irish Coinage*, Dublin

Owen, M. E. 1980. 'Shame and reparation: women's place in the kin', in Jenkins and Owen, 40–68

Padel, O. 1985. *Cornish Place-Name Elements*, Nottingham

Parker Pearson, M. and Sharples, N. 1999. *Between Land and Sea: Excavation at Dun Vulan, South Uist*, Sheffield

Parry, T. 1955. *A History of Welsh Literature*, Oxford

Patterson, C. 2001. 'Insular belt-fittings from the pagan Norse graves of Scotland: a reappraisal', in Redknap, Edwards et al. (eds.), 125–32

Patterson, N. T. 1991. *Cattle-Lords and Clansmen: Kinship and Rank in Early Ireland*, New York and London

    1995. 'Clans are not primordial: pre-Viking Irish Society and the modelling of pre-Roman societies in Europe', in Arnold and Gibson (eds.), 129–36

Pearce, S. (ed.) 1982. *The Early Church in Western Britain and Ireland: Studies presented to C. A. Ralegh Radford* (= BAR Brit. Ser. 102), Oxford

    2004. *South-western Britain in the Early Middle Ages*, Leicester

Peers, C. and Radford, C. A. R. 1943. 'The Saxon monastery of Whitby', *Archaeologia* 91: 27–88

Penhallurick, R. D. 1986. *Tin in Antiquity*, London

Penman, A. 1998. 'Botel bailey', *Current Archaeology* 156: 473–5

Perry, D. R. 2000. *Castle Park, Dunbar: Two Thousand Years on a Fortified Headland* (= Soc. Ant. Scot. monograph ser. 16), Edinburgh

Petrie, G. 1845. *The Ecclesiastical Architecture of Ireland*, 2 vols., Dublin

Petts, D. 2004. 'Burial in western Britain AD 40–80: late antique or early medieval?' in Collins and Gerrard (eds.), 77–87

Phillips, C. W. 1934. 'The excavation of a hut group at Pant-y-Saer', *Arch. Cambrensis* 89: 1–36

Phillips, J. 1984. 'The Anglo-Norman nobility', in J. Lydon (ed.), *The English in Medieval Ireland*, Dublin, 87–104

Piggott, C. M. 1947–8. 'The excavations at Hownam Rings, Roxburghshire, 1948', *Proc. Soc. Ant. Scot.* 82: 193–224

Piggott, S. 1958. 'An iron object from Dunadd', *Proc. Soc. Ant. Scot.* 86: 194

Pittock, M. G. H. 1999. *Celtic Identity and the British Image*, Manchester

Plummer, C. 1968. *Lives of Irish Saints*, 2 vols., Oxford

Pollard, S. M. 1966. 'Neolithic and Dark Age settlements on High Peak, Sidmouth, Devon', *Proc. Devon A.S.* 23: 35–59

Preston-Jones, A. 1992. 'Decoding Cornish churchyards', in Edwards and Lane (eds.), 104–24

Preston-Jones, A. and Rose, P. 1986. 'Medieval Cornwall', *Cornish Archaeology* 25: 135–85

Price, E. 2003. *Frocester: A Romano-British Settlement, its Antecedents and Successors*, Gloucester

Price, J. (ed.) 2000. *Glass in Britain and Ireland* AD *350–1100* (= Brit. Mus. occasional paper 127), London

Proudfoot, E. 1996. 'Excavation at the long cist cemetery on the Hallow Hill, St Andrews, Fife', *Proc. Soc. Ant. Scot.* 126: 385–454

Proudfoot, E. and Aliaga-Kelly, C. 1996. 'Towards an interpretation of anomalous finds and place-names of Anglo-Saxon origin in Scotland', *Anglo-Saxon Studies in Archaeology and History* 9: 1–13

Proudfoot, V. B. 1953. 'Excavation of a rath at Boho, Co. Fermanagh', *Ulster J. Archaeol.* 16: 41–57

    1958. 'Further excavations at Shaneen Park, Belfast, Ballyaghagan townland, Co. Antrim', *Ulster J. Archaeol.* 21: 18–38

    1961. 'The economy of the Irish rath', *Medieval Archaeology* 5: 4–122

    1970. 'Irish raths and cashels: some notes on origins, chronology and survivals', *Ulster J. Archaeol.* 33: 37–48

    1977. 'Economy and settlement in rural Ireland', in L. Laing (ed.), 83–106

Proudfoot, V. B. and Wilson, B. C. S. 1962. 'Further excavations at Larrybane promontory fort, Co. Antrim', *Ulster J. Archaeol.* 24–5: 91–115

Pryce, H. 1992. 'Pastoral care in early medieval Wales', in Blair and Sharpe (eds.), 41–62

Purser, J. 2002. 'Reconstructing the Lough Erne Horn', *Ulster J. Archaeol.* 61: 17–25

Quinnell, H. 2005. *Excavations at Trethurgy Round, St Austell: Insights into Roman and Post-Roman Cornwall*, Truro

Quinnell, H., Blockley, M. and Berridge, P. 1994. *Excavations at Rhuddlan, Clwyd: 1969–73, Mesolithic to Medieval*, London

Radford, C. A. R. 1935. 'Tintagel, the castle and Celtic monastery', *Antiq. J.* 15: 1–19

    1951. 'Excavations at Chapel Finnian, Mochrum', *Trans. Dumfries Galloway N.H.A.S.* 28: 28–40

    1954. 'Hoddom', *Trans. Dumfries Galloway N.H.A.S.* 31: 4–97

    1956. 'Imported pottery found at Tintagel, Cornwall', in Harden, 1956a: 59–70

    1967. 'The early Church in Strathclyde and Galloway', *Medieval Archaeology* 11: 5–26

Radford, C. A. R. 1975. *The Early Christian Inscriptions of Dumnonia*, Truro

Raftery, B. 1969. 'Freestone Hill, Co. Kilkenny: an Iron Age hillfort and Bronze Age cairn', *Proc. Royal Irish Acad.* 68c: 1–108

   1972. 'Irish hillforts', in A. C. Thomas (ed.), *The Iron Age in the Irish Sea Province*, London, 37–58

   1984. *La Tène in Ireland*, Marburg

   1994. *Pagan Celtic Ireland*, London

   1996. 'Drumanagh and Roman Ireland', *Archaeology Ireland* 35: 18

   2005. 'Iron-Age Ireland', in Ó Cróinín (ed.), 134–181

Raftery, J. 1941. 'A bronze zoomorphic brooch from Toomullin, Co. Clare', *J. Royal Soc. Antiq. Ireland* 71: 56–60

   1970. 'Bronze mount from Feltrim Hill, Co. Dublin', *J. Royal Soc. Antiq. Ireland* 100: 175–9

   1981. 'Concerning chronology', in Ó Corrain (ed.), 82–90

Rahtz, P. 1970. 'Excavations at Glastonbury Tor, Somerset', *Arch. J.* 127: 1–81.

   1974. 'Pottery in Somerset, AD 400–1066', in V. Evison, H. Hodges and J. G. Hurst (eds.), *Medieval Pottery from Excavations*, London, 95–126

   1993. *Glastonbury*, London.

Rahtz, P. and Hirst, S. 2000. *Cannington*, London

Rahtz, P., Woodward, A., Burrow, I., et al. 1992. *Cadbury Congresbury 1968–73: A Late/post-Roman Hilltop Settlement in Somerset* (= BAR Brit. Ser.), Oxford

Ralston, I. M. 1983. 'Notes on the archaeology of Kincardine and Deeside District', *The Deeside Field* 18: 73–83

   1987. 'Portknockie: promontory forts and Pictish setlement in the north-east', in Small (ed.), 15–26

   1997 'Pictish homes', in D. Henry (ed.), 17–34

Ralston, I. and Armit, I. 1997. 'The early historic period: an archaeological perspective', in Edwards and Ralston (eds.), 217–39

Ramsey, G. 2002. 'Triple pipes on Irish high crosses: identification and interpretation', *Ulster J. Archaeol.* 61: 26–36

Rance, P. 2001. 'Attacotti, Déisi and Magnus Maximus: the case for Irish federates in late Roman Britain', *Britannia* 32: 243–70

Randsborg, K. 1991. *The First Millennium in Europe and the Mediterranean*, Cambridge

Rankin, D. 1987. *Celts and the Classical World*, London

RCAHMS, 1990 = Royal Commission for Ancient and Historical Monuments of Scotland

Redknap, M. 1991. *The Christian Celts: Treasures of Late Celtic Wales*, Cardiff

   1995. 'Insular non-ferrous metalwork from Wales of the 8th to 10th centuries', in C. Bourke (ed.), 69–73

   2000. *Vikings in Wales: An Archaeological Quest*, Cardiff

Redknap, M., Campbell, E. and Lane, A. 1989. 'Llangorse crannog', *Archaeology in Wales* 29: 57–8

Redknap, M., Edwards, N., Youngs, S., Lane, A. and Knight, J. (eds.) 2001. *Pattern and Purpose in Insular Art*, Oxford

Reece, R. 1974 'Recent work on Iona', *Scottish Archaeol. Forum* 5: 36–46

Reeves-Smith, T. and Hammond, F. (eds.) 1983. *Landscape Archaeology in Ireland* (= BAR Brit. Ser. 116), Oxford

Richards, M. 1960. 'The Irish settlements in south-west Wales', *J. Royal Soc. Antiq. Ireland* 80: 133–62

Richardson, H. 1984. 'Number and symbol in early Christian Irish Art', *J. Royal Soc. Antiq. Ireland* 114: 28–47

    2005. 'Visual arts and society', in Ó Cróinín (ed.), 680–713

Richardson, H. and Scarry, J. 1990. *Irish High Crosses*, Cork

Richmond, I. A. 1958. 'Ancient geographical sources for Britain north of the Cheviot', in I. Richmond (ed.), *Roman and Native in North Britain*, London, 131–56

Richter, M. 1988. *Medieval Ireland: The Enduring Tradition*, London

Rigoir, J. 1968. 'Les sigillées paléochrétiennes grises et oranges', *Gallia* 6: 177–244

Rigoir, J., Rigoir, Y. and Meffre, J.-F. 1973. 'Les dérivées paléochrétiennes du groupe atlantique', *Gallia* 31: 364–409

Ritchie, A. 1974. 'Pict and Norseman in northern Scotland', *Scottish Archaeol. Forum* 6: 23–36

    1977. 'Excavation of Pictish and Viking age farmsteads at Buckquoy, Orkney', *Proc. Soc. Ant. Scot.* 108: 174–227

    1987. 'The Picto-Scottish interface in material culture', in Small (ed.), 59–67

    1989. *The Picts*, Edinburgh

    1993. *Viking Scotland*, London

    (ed.) 1994. *Govan and its Early Medieval Sculptures*, Stroud

    1995. 'Meigle and lay patronage in Tayside in the 9th and 10th centuries AD', *Tayside and Fife Archaeological Journal* 1: 1–10

    1997. *Iona*, London

Ritchie, A. and Breeze, D. 1991. *Invaders of Scotland*, Edinburgh

Ritchie, J. N. G. 1981. 'Excavations at Machrins, Colonsay', *Proc. Soc. Ant. Scot.* 111: 263–81

Ritchie, J. N. G. and Stevenson, J. N. 1993. 'Pictish cave art at East Wemyss, Fife', in Spearman and Higgitt (eds.), 203–8

Rivet, A. L. F. (ed.) 1966. *The Iron Age in Northern Britain*, Edinburgh

Roberts, B. F. (ed.) 1988. *Early Welsh Poetry: Studies in the Book of Aneirin*, Aberystwyth

Roberts, E. 2002, 'Great Orme Bronze Age mining and smelting site', *Current Archaeology* 181: 29–32

Roberts, T. 1992. 'Welsh ecclesiastical place-names and archaeology', in Edwards and Lane (eds.), 41–4

Robertson, A. S. 1970. 'Roman finds from non-Roman sites in Scotland', *Britannia* 1: 198–226

    1975. *Birrens (Blatobulgium)*, Edinburgh

Roe, H. 1945. 'An interpretation of certain symbolic sculptures in early Christian Ireland', *J. Royal Soc. Antiq. Ireland* 75: 1–23.

    1969. *The High Crosses of Western Ossory*, 2nd edn, Kilkenny

Rose, P. and Preston-Jones, A. 1995. 'Changes in the Cornish countryside AD 400–1100', in Hooke and Burnell (eds.), 51–67

Ross, A. 1967. *Pagan Celtic Britain*, London

Royal Commission on the Ancient and Historic Monuments of Scotland 1956. *Inventory of the County of Roxburgh*, vol. 1, Edinburgh

Royal Commission on the Ancient and Historic Monuments of Scotland 1982. *Argyll: An Inventory of the Monuments*, vol. 4: *Iona*, Edinburgh

Royal Commission on the Ancient and Historic Monuments of Scotland 1990. *North-east Perth: An Archaeological Landscape*, Edinburgh

Rutherford, A. and Ritchie, G. 1975. 'The Catstane', *Proc. Soc. Ant. Scot.* 105: 183–9

Ryan, M. 1973. 'Native pottery in early historic Ireland', *Proc. Royal Irish Acad.* 73c: 619–45

    1983a. *The Derrynaflan Hoard I, a Preliminary Account*, Dublin

    1983b. *Treasures of Ireland, Irish Art 3000 BC – 1500 AD*, Dublin

    1987a. *Ireland and Insular Art AD 500–1200*, Dublin

    1987b. 'Donore, Irish medieval metalwork from Moynalty, near Kells, Ireland', *Antiquity* 61: 57–63

    1987c. 'Some aspects of sequence and style in the metalwork of eighth- and ninth-century Ireland', in Ryan, 1987a: 66–74

    1990. 'Decorated metalwork in the Museo dell'Abbazia, Bobbio, Italy', *J. Royal Soc. Antiq. Ireland* 120: 102–11

    (ed.) 1994. *Irish Archaeology Illustrated*, Dublin

    2002. *Studies in Medieval Irish Metalwork*, London

Rynne, C. 1989. 'The introduction of the vertical watermill into Ireland: some recent archaeological evidence', *Medieval Archaeology* 33: 21–31

Rynne, E. 1956. 'Excavations at Ardcloon, Co. Mayo', *J. Royal Soc. Antiq. Ireland* 76: 203–14

    1958. 'The introduction of La Tène into Ireland', *Bericht. V. Internat. Kong. Var- und Frügesch. Hamburg*, Berlin, 705–9

    1959. 'Souterrain at Donaghmore, Co, Louth', *Co. Louth Archaeol. Hist. J.* 14.3: 148–53

    1964. 'Ringforts at Shannon airport', *Proc. Royal Irish Acad.* 63c: 245–77

    1966. 'The impact of the Vikings on Irish weapons', *Atti del VI Congresso Internazionale delle Scienze Preistorische e Protohistorische Sezioni V–VIII*, 181–6

    1982. 'A classification of pre-Viking Irish iron swords', in B. Scott (ed.), 93–7

    (ed.) 1987. *Figures from the Past: Studies on Figurative Art in Christian Ireland*, Dublin

Salway, P. 1993. *The Oxford Illustrated History of Roman Britain*, Oxford

Samson, R. 1992. 'The re-interpretation of the Pictish symbols', *J. British Archaeological Association* 145: 29–65

Saunders, A. and Harris, D. 1982. 'Excavations at Castle Gotha, St Austell', *Cornish Archaeology* 21: 109–53

Saunders, C. 1972. 'The excavation at Grambla, Wendron, 1972: interim report', *Cornish Archaeology* 11: 50–2

Savory, H. N. 1956. 'Some sub-Romano-British brooches from south Wales', in Harden, 1956a: 40–53

    1960. 'Excavations at Dinas Emrys, Beddgelert, Caernarvonshire 1954–6', *Arch. Cambrensis* 109: 13–77

Schlesinger, A. and Walls, C. 1996. 'An early church and medieval farmstead site: excavations at Llanelen, Gower', *Archaeol. J.* 153: 104–47

Scott, B. G. 1978. 'Iron "slave collars" from Lagore crannog, Co. Meath', *Proc. Royal Irish Acad.* 78c: 213–30

    (ed.) 1982. *Studies on Early Ireland: Essays in Honour of M. V. Duignan*, Belfast

    1990. *Early Irish Ironworking*, Belfast

Scott, J. G. 1961. 'Argyllshire: Loch Glashan', *Medieval Archaeology* 5: 310–11

    1989. 'The hall and motte at Courthill, Dalry, Ayrshire', *Proc. Soc. Ant. Scot.* 119: 271–8

Sellar, W. D. H. 2001. 'William Forbes Skene (1809–92): historian of Celtic Scotland', *Proc. Soc. Ant. Scot.* 131: 3–22

Sexton, R. 1998. 'Porridges, gruels and breads: the cereal foodstuffs of early medieval Ireland', in Monk and Sheehan (eds.), 76–86

Sharples, N. 1998. *Scalloway: A Broch: Late Iron Age Settlement and Medieval Cemetery in Shetland* (= Oxbow monograph 82), Oxford

Sheehan, J. 1994. 'A Merovingian background for the Ardmoneel stone?', *J. Cork Archaeol. Hist. Soc.* 99: 23–31

    1998. 'Early Viking Age silver hoards from Ireland and their Scandiavian elements', in Clarke et al. (eds.), 166–202

Sheehy, J. 1980. *The Rediscovery of Ireland's Past: The Celtic Revival 1830–1930*, London

Shepherd, I. A. G. 1983 'Pictish settlement problems in north-east Scotland', in J. C. Chapman and H. Mytum (eds.), *Settlement in North Britain 100 BC – AD 1000*, Oxford, 327–56

    1986. *Exploring Scotland's Heritage: Grampian*, Edinburgh

Sherlock, S. J. and Welch, M. G. 1992. *An Anglo-Saxon Cemetery at Norton, Cleveland* (= CBA res. rep. 82), London

Silvester, R. J. 1981. 'An excavation on the post-Roman site at Bantham, S Devon', *Proc Devon A.S.* 39: 89–118

Small, A. 1964–6. 'Excavations at Underhoull, Unst, Shetland', *Proc. Soc. Ant. Scot.* 98: 225–45

    1969. 'Burghead', *Scottish Archaeol. Forum* 1: 61–8

    (ed.) 1987. *The Picts: A New Look at Old Problems*, Aberdeen

Small, A. and Cottam, M. B. 1972. *Craig Phadrig* (= Univ. of Dundee Dept of Geography occasional papers, 1), Dundee

Small, A., Thomas, C. and Wilson, D. M. 1973. *St Ninian's Isle and its Treasure*, 2 vols., Aberdeen

Smith, A. 2000. 'Material culture and North Sea contacts in the fifth to seventh centuries AD', in Jon Henderson, 2000b: 181–8

Smith, A. N. 1993. 'Ratho quarry: enclosed cremation cemetery and sunken-featured building', *Discovery Excav. Scotland* 1993: 59–61

Smith, C. A. 1987. 'Excavations at the Ty Mawr hut circles, Holyhead: part IV – chronology and discussion', *Arch. Cambrensis* 126: 20–38

Smith, F. G. 1931–2. 'Talacre and the Viking grave', *Proceedings of the Llandudno, Colwyn Bay and District Field Club* 17: 42–50

Smith, I. 1983. 'Brito-Roman and Anglo-Saxon: the unification of the Borders', in Clack, P. and Ivy, J. (eds.), *The Borders*, Durham, 9–48

    1990. 'The archaeological background to emergent kingdoms of the Tweed basin in the early historic period', Durham, unpublished PhD thesis

    1991. 'Sprouston, Roxburghshire: an early Anglian centre of the eastern Tweed basin', *Proc. Soc. Ant. Scot.* 121: 261–94

    1996. 'The archaeology of the early Christian church in Scotland and Man, AD 400–1200', in Blair and Pyrah (eds.), 19–37

Smith, J. 1919. 'Excavations of the forts of Castlehill, Aitnock and Coalhill, Sayrs', *Proc. Soc. Ant. Scot.* 53: 137–52

Smith, R. A. 1913. 'The evolution of the handpin in Great Britain and Ireland', in *Opuscula Archaeologica Oscari Montelio Septuagenaria Dicata*, 36–289

    1913–14. 'Irish brooches through five centuries', *Archaeologia* 65: 223–50

    1917–18. 'Irish serpentine lachets', *Proc. Soc. Antiq. London* 30: 120–31

Smyth, A. 1984. *Warlords and Holy Men: Scotland* AD *80–1000*, London

Snape, M. E. 1992. 'Sub-Roman brooches from Roman sites on the northern frontier', *Archaeologia Aeliana* 20: 158–60

Snyder, C. A. 1996. *Sub-Roman Britain* (AD *400–600): A Gazetteer of Sites* (= BAR Brit. Ser. 247), Oxford

1998. *An Age of Tyrants: Britain and the Britons,* AD *400–60*, Stroud

2003. *The Britons*, Oxford

Southwick, L. 1981. *The So-called Sueno's Stone at Forres*, Moray District Library publications

Sparey-Green, C. 1982. 'The cemetery of a Romano-British Christian community at Poundbury, Dorchester, Dorset', in Pearce (ed.), 61–76

1987. *Excavations at Poundbury, Dorchester, Dorset, 1966–1982*, vol. 1: *The Settlements*, Dorchester

1996. 'Poundbury, Dorset: settlement and economy in late and post-Roman Dorchester', in Dark (ed.), 1996a: 121–52

2004. 'Living amongst the dead: Roman cemetery to post-Roman monastery at Poundbury', in Collins and Gerrard (eds.), 103–12

Spearman, R. M. 1994. 'The Govan sarcophagus – an enigmatic monument', in Ritchie (ed.), 33–46

Spearman, R. M. and Higgitt, J. (eds.) 1993. *The Age of Migrating Ideas: Early Medieval Art in Northern Britain and Ireland*, Edinburgh

Stalley, R. 1996. *Irish High Crosses*, Dublin

1997. 'The tower cross at Kells', in Karkov, Ryan and Farrell (eds.), 115–41

2000. *Irish Round Towers*, Dublin

2005. 'Ecclesiastical architecture before 1169', in Ó Cróinín (ed.), 714–43

Stallybrass, B. 1914. 'Recent discoveries at Clynnogfawr', *Arch. Cambrensis* 6th ser. 14: 271–96

Stapleton, C. P., Freestone, I. C. and Bowman, S. G. E. 1999. 'Composition and origin of early medieval opaque red enamel from Britain and Ireland', *J. Archaeological Science* 26: 913–21

Steer, K. and Keeney, G. S. 1947. 'Excavations . . . at Crock Cleugh, Roxburghshire', *Proc. Soc. Ant. Scot.* 81: 128–57

Steer, K. A. and Bannerman, J. W. M. 1977. *Late Medieval Monumental Sculpture in the West Highlands*, Edinburgh

Stell, G. 1990. *Exploring Scotland's Heritage: Dumfries and Galloway*, rev. edn, Edinburgh

Stevenson, J. B. 1991. 'Pitcarmicks and fermtouns', *Current Archaeology* 127: 288–91

Stevenson, R. B. K. 1948–9. 'Dalmahoy and other Dark Age capitals', *Proc. Soc. Ant. Scot.* 83: 186–97

1951–2. 'Celtic carved box from Orkney', *Proc. Soc. Ant. Scot.* 86: 187–90

1955a. 'Pictish art', in Wainwright, 1955b: 97–128

1955b. 'Pins and the chronology of brochs', *Proc. Prehist. Soc.* 31: 282–94

1954–6a. 'Native bangles and Roman glass', *Proc. Soc. Ant. Scot.* 88: 208–21

1954–6b. 'Pictish chain, Roman silver and bauxite beads', *Proc. Soc. Ant. Scot.* 88: 228–30

1956. 'The chronology and relationship of some Irish and Scottish crosses', *J. Royal Soc. Antiq. Ireland* 86: 84–96

1958–89. 'The lnchyra stone and other unpublished early Christian monuments', *Proc. Soc. Ant. Scot.* 92: 33–55

Stevenson, R. B. K. 1965. 'The brooch from Westness, Orkney', in B. Niclasen (ed.), *The Fifth Viking Congress*, Torshavn, 25–31

1974. 'The Hunterston brooch and its significance', *Medieval Archaeology* 18: 16–42

1976. 'The earlier metalwork of Pictland', in J. V. S. Megaw (ed.), *To Illustrate the Monuments: Essays on Archaeology presented to Stuart Piggott*, London, 246–51

1983. 'Further Notes on the Hunterston and "Tara" brooches, Monymusk reliquary and Blackness bracelet', *Proc. Soc. Ant. Scot.* 113: 469–77

1987. 'Brooches and pins: some seventh- to ninth-century problems', in Ryan, 1987a: 90–5

1989. 'The Celtic brooch from Westness, Orkney, and hinged-pins', *Proc. Soc. Ant. Scot.* 119: 239–69

Stevenson, R. B. K. and Emery, J. 1963–4. 'The Gaulcross hoard of Pictish silver', *Proc. Soc. Ant. Scot.* 97: 206–11

Stevick, R. D. 1994. *The Earliest English Bookarts: Visual and Poetic Forms before AD 1000*, Philadelphia

1998. 'The form of the "Tara" brooch', *J. Royal Soc. Antiq. Ireland* 128: 5–16

2001. 'High cross design', in Redknap et al. (eds.), 221–32

2003. 'The form of the Hunterston brooch', *Medieval Archaeology* 47: 21–40

Stewart, I. H. 1968. *The Scottish Coinage*, 2nd edn, London

Stout, M. 1997. *The Irish Ringfort*, Dublin

Strang, A. 1998. 'Recreating a possible Flavian map of Roman Britain with a detailed map for Scotland', *Proc. Soc. Ant. Scot.* 128: 425–40

Sunter, N. and Woodward, P. J. 1987. *Romano-British Industries in Purbeck*, Dorset

Sutherland, E. 1994. *In Search of the Picts, a Celtic Dark Age Nation*, London

Swan, L. 1973. 'Kilpatrick, Co. Westmeath', *Excavations 1973*: 26–7

1976. 'Excavations at Kilpatrick churchyard, Killucan, Co. Westmeath', *Riocht ma Midhe* 6, 2: 89–96

1983. 'Enclosed ecclesiastical sites and their relevance to settlement patterns of the first millennium AD', in Reeves-Smyth and Hammond (eds.), 269–80

1985. 'Monastic proto-towns in early medieval Ireland: the evidence of aerial photography, plan analysis and survey', in H. B. Clarke and A. Simms (eds.), *The Comparative History of Urban Origins in Non-Roman Europe* (= BAR S551), 2 vols., Oxford, 77–103

1994. 'Early monastic sites', in Ryan (ed.), 137–9

1995. 'Fine metalwork from the early Christian sites at Kilpatrick, Co. Westmeath', in C. Bourke (ed.), 75–80

Swanton, M. 1974. *A Corpus of Pagan Anglo-Saxon Spear Types* (= BAR Brit. Ser. 7), Oxford

Swift, C. 1995. 'Dating Irish grave slabs: the evidence of the Annals', in C. Bourke (ed.), 245–50

Tabraham, C. J. 1986. *Scottish Castles and Fortifications*, Edinburgh

Taylor, H. M. and Taylor, J. 1965. *Anglo-Saxon Architecture*, Cambridge

Thomas, A. C. 1956. 'Evidence for the post-Roman occupation of Chun Castle', *Antiq. J.* 36: 75–8

1958. *Gwithian, Ten Years' Work, 1949–58* (= West Cornwall Field Club publ.), Truro

1959. 'Dark Age imported pottery in western Britain', *Medieval Archaeology* 3: 89–111

1961a. 'Animal art of the Scottish Iron Age', *Archaeol. J.* 118: 14–64

1961b. 'Excavations at Trusty's Hill, Anwoth, 1960', *Trans. Dumfries Galloway N.H.A.S.* 38: 58–70

Thomas, A. C. 1963. 'The interpretation of the Pictish symbols', *Archaeol. J.* 120: 31–97

1966. 'The character and origin of Roman Dumnonia', in Thomas (ed.), *Rural Settlement in Roman Britain*, London, 74–98

1967. 'An early Christian cemetery and chapel at Ardwall Isle, Kirkcudbright', *Medieval Archaeology* 11: 127–88

1968a. 'Grass-marked pottery in Cornwall', in J. Coles and D. Simpson (eds.), *Studies in Ancient Europe*, Leicester, 311–32

1968b. 'The evidence from north Britain', in M. Barley and R. Hanson (eds.), *Christianity in Britain, 300–700*, Leicester, 93–122

1969. 'Lundy 1969', *Current Archaeology* 11: 138–42

1971. *The Early Christian Archaeology of North Britain*, Oxford

1972a. 'Souterrains in the Irish Sea province – a note', in A. C. Thomas (ed.), *The Iron Age in the Irish Sea Province* (= Council of British Archaeology Res. Rep. 9), London, 75–8

1972b. 'The Irish settlements in post-Roman western Britain: a survey of the evidence', *Journal of the Royal Institution of Cornwall* n.s. 6: 251–74

1973. 'Irish colonists in south-west Britain', *World Archaeology* 5: 5–12

1976. 'The end of the Roman south-west', in K. Branigan and P. Fowler (eds.), *The Roman West Country*, Newton Abbot, 198–213

1981a. *A Provisional List of Imported Pottery in Post-Roman Western Britain and Ireland* (= Inst. Cornish Studies Special Rep. 7), Redruth

1981b. *Christianity in Roman Britain to AD 500*, London

1985. *The Exploration of a Drowned Landscape*, London

1988. 'The context of Tintagel: a new model for the diffusion of post-Roman Mediterranean imports', *Cornish Archaeology* 27: 7–25

1990. '"Gallici Nautae de Galliarum Provinciis": a sixth/seventh century trade with Gaul reconsidered', *Medieval Archaeology* 34: 1–26

1992. *Whithorn's Christian Beginnings* (= First Whithorn lecture), Whithorn

1993. *Tintagel, Arthur and Archaeology*, London

1994. *And Shall these Mute Stones Speak? Post-Roman Inscriptions in Western Britain*, Cardiff

1998. *Christian Celts: Messages and Images*, Stroud

Thomas, A. C and Peacock, D. 1967. 'Class E imported pottery: a suggested origin', *Cornish Archaeology* 6: 35–46

Toal, C. 1995. *North Kerry Archaeological Survey*, Dingle

Todd, M. 1985. 'The Falkirk hoard of denarii: trade or subsidy?', *Proc. Soc. Ant. Scot.* 115: 229–32

1987. *South-West England to AD 1000*, London

Trench-Jellicoe, R. 1997. 'Pictish and related harps: their form and decoration', in D. Henry (ed.), 159–72

1999. 'A missing figure on slab fragment no. 2 from Monfeith, Angus, the A'Chill Cross, Canna, and some implications of the development of a variant form of the Virgin's hairstyle and dress in early medieval Scotland', *Proc. Soc. Ant. Scot.* 129: 597–648

Turner, S. 2004. 'Coast and countryside in "late antique" southwest England, c. AD 400–600', in Collins and Gerrard (eds.), 25–32

Turner, V. 1998. *Ancient Shetland*, London

Tylecote, R. F. 1976. *A History of Metallurgy*, London.

Tylecote, R. F. 1986. *The Prehistory of Metallurgy in the British Isles*, London

Vierck, H. 1970. 'Cortina tripodis: ein Beispiel spätantiker Traditionen der Insularen Mission', *Praehistorische Zeitschrift* 45: 236–40

Waddell, J. 1983. 'Rathcroghan – a royal site in Connacht', *J. Irish Archaeology* 1: 21–46

1998. *The Prehistoric Archaeology of Ireland*, Dublin

Wailes, B. 1970. 'Excavation at Dun Ailinne, Co. Clare', *J. Royal Soc. Antiq. Ireland* 100: 79–90

1990. 'Dun Ailinne: a summary excavation report', *Emania* 7: 10–21

Wainwright, F. T. 1955a. 'The Picts and the problem', in Wainwright 1955b: 1–53

(ed.) 1955b. *The Problem of the Picts*, London

1962. *Archaeology, Place-Names and History*, London

1963. *Souterrains of Southern Pictland*, London

1975. *Scandinavian England*, London

Wainwright, G. 1967. *Coygan Camp*, Cardiff

Wakeman, W. F. 1893. *A Survey of the Antiquarian Remains on the Island of Inismurray (Inis Muireadhaigh)*, Dublin

Walker, D. 1990. *Medieval Wales*, Cambridge

Wallace, P. 2001. 'Ireland's Viking Towns', in Larsen (ed.), 37–50

2002. 'Viking Age Ireland, AD 850–1150', in Wallace and Ó Flionn (eds.), 213–56

2005. 'The archaeology of Ireland's Viking-Age towns', in Ó Cróinín (ed.), 814–40

Wallace, P. and Ó Flionn, R. (eds.) 2002. *Treasures of the National Museum of Ireland, Irish Antiquities*, Dublin

Walsh, A. 1987. 'Excavating the Black Pig's Dyke', *Emania* 3: 5–11

1998. 'A summary classification of Viking Age swords in Ireland', in Clarke et al. (eds.), 222–35

Walsh, G. 1994. 'Preliminary report on the archaeological excavations on the summit of Croagh Patrick, 1994', *Cathair na Mart* 14: 1–10

1995. 'Iron Age settlement in Co. Mayo', *Archaeology Ireland* 32: 7–8

Walsh, P. 1983. 'The monastic settlement on Rathlin O'Birne Island, County Donegal', *J. Royal Soc. Antiq. Ireland* 113: 53–66

Waterer, J. W. 1968. 'Irish book satchels or budgets', *Medieval Archaeology* 12: 70–82

Waterman, D. M. 1956. 'The excavation of a house and souterrain at White Fort, Drumaroad', *Ulster J. Archaeol.* 19: 73–86

1958. 'Excavations at Ballyfounder rath, Co. Down', *Ulster J. Archaeol.* 21: 39–61

1963. 'Neolithic and Dark Age site at Langford Lodge', *Ulster J. Archaeol.*, 26: 43–54

1967. 'The early Christian churches and cemetery at Derry, Co. Down', *Ulster J. Archaeol.* 30: 53–75

1997. *Excavations at Navan Fort, 1961–71*, Belfast

Waterman, D. M. and Collins, A. E. P. 1966. *An Archaeological Survey of Co. Down*, Belfast

Watkins, T. 1978–80a. 'Excavation of an Iron Age open settlement at Dalladies, Kincardineshire', *Proc. Soc. Ant. Scot.* 110: 122–64

1978–80b. 'Excavation of a settlement and souterrain at Newmill, near Bankfoot, Perthshire', *Proc. Soc. Ant. Scot.* 110: 165–208

Watts, D. 1991. *Christians and Pagans in Roman Britain*, London

Warner, R. B. 1971. 'Clogher demesne', *Excavations* 2: 23–4

1972. 'Clogher demesne', *Excavations* 3: 27–8

1973. 'Clogher demesne', *Excavations* 4: 25

Warner, R. B. 1974. 'Clogher demesne', *Excavations* 5: 27

1979. 'The Irish souterrains and their background', in H. Crawford (ed.), *Subterranean Britain*, London, 100–44

1980. 'Irish souterrains: later Iron Age refuges', *Archaeologia Atlantica* 3: 81–99

1986. 'The date of the start of Lagore', *J. Irish Archaeol.* 3: 75–7

1988. 'The archaeology of early historic Irish kingship', in Driscoll and Nieke (eds.), 47–68

1994a. 'On Crannogs and kings (Part 1)', *Ulster J. Archaeol.* 57: 61–9

1994b. 'The earliest history of Ireland', in Ryan (ed.), 1994: 112–16

1995. 'Tuathal Techtmhar: a myth or ancient literary evidence for a Roman invasion?', *Emania* 13: 23–32

Webster, G. and Smith, L. 1982. 'The excavation of a Romano-British rural establishment at Barnsley Park, Gloucestershitre, 1961–79, part 2, c. 360–40+', *Trans. Bristol and Glos. Arch. Soc.* 100: 65–189

Webster, L. and Backhouse, J. 1991. *The Making of England: Anglo-Saxon Art and Culture AD 600–900*, London

Webster, P. V. 1990. 'The first Roman fort at Cardiff', in B. Burnham and J. L. Davies (eds.), *Conquest, Co-existence and Change: Recent Work in Roman Wales* (= Trivium 25), Lampeter, 35–9

Weddell, P. J. 2000. 'Excavation of a post-Roman cemetery near Kenn', *Trans. Devon A.S.* 58: 93–126

Wedderburn, L. M. M. and Grime, D. 1984. 'The cairn cemetery at Garbeg, Drumnadrochit', in Friell and Watson (eds.), 151–67

Wedlake, W. 1982. *The Excavation of the Shrine of Apollo at Nettleton, Wiltshire 1956–71* (= *Soc. Ant. Lond.* Res. Rep.), London.

Weir, D. 1993. 'A palynogical study in County Louth: interim report', *Discovery Programme Reports* 1: 104–9

1995. 'A palynological study of of landscape and agricultural development in county Louth from the second millenium BC to the Second Millennium AD', in *Discovery Programme Reports*, vol. 2: *Project Results 1993*, Dublin, 77–126

Welch, M. 1994. 'The archaeological evidence for federate settlements in Britain within the fifth century', in F. Vallet and M. Kazanski (eds.), *L'armée romaine et les barbares du IIIe au VIIe siècle*, Rouen, 269–77

Werner, M. 1981. 'The Durrow four evangelist symbols page once again', *Gesta* 20: 23–33

1990. 'The cross-carpet page in the Book of Durrow: the cult of the true cross, Adomnan and Iona', *Art Bulletin* 72: 174–223

White, R. (with Barker, P.) 1998. *Wroxeter: The Life and Death of a Roman City*, Stroud

White, R. B. 1972. 'Rescue excavations on the New Theatre site, University College Park, Bangor', *Trans. Caernarvonshire. Hist. Soc.* 33: 246–7

1982. 'Capel Eithyn', in Youngs and Clark (eds.), 226–7

White Marshall, J. and Rourke, G. D. 2000a. *High Island: An Irish Monastery in the Atlantic*, Dublin

2000b. 'The secular origin of the monastic enclosure wall of High Island, Co. Galway', *Archaeology Ireland* 14: 30–4

White Marshall, J. and Walsh, C. 1994. 'Illaunloughan: life and death on a small early monastic site', *Archaeology Ireland* 8: 24–8

White Marshall, J. and Walsh, C. 2005. *Illaunloughan Excavations 1992–1995*, Dublin

Whitelock, D., McKitterick, R. and Dumville, D. (eds.) 1982. *Ireland in Early Medieval Europe: Studies in Memory of Kathleen Hughes*, Cambridge

Whitfield, N. 1974. 'The finding of the Tara brooch', *J. Royal Soc. Antiq. Ireland* 104: 120–41

1976. 'The original appearance of the Tara brooch', *J. Royal Soc. Antiq. Ireland* 106: 5–30

1987. 'Motifs and techniques of Celtic filigree: are they original?' in Ryan, 1987a: 75–84

Whitfield, N. 1993a. 'Some new research on gold and gold filigree from early medieval Ireland and Scotland', in C. Eluère (ed.), *Outils et ateliers d'orfèvres des temps anciens*, St Germain-en-Laye, 125–36

1993b. 'The filigree of the Hunterston and "Tara" brooches', in Spearman and Higgitt, 1993: 118–27

1997. 'The Waterford kite-brooch', in M. Hurley and O. M. B. Scully, *Later Viking Age and Medieval Waterford: Excavations 1986–1992*, Waterford, 490–517

1999. 'Design and units of measure on the Hunterston brooch', in J. Hawkes and S. Mills (eds.), *Northumbria's Golden Age*, Stroud, 296–314

2001a. 'The earliest filigree from Ireland', in Redknap et al. (eds.), 141–54

2001b. 'The "Tara" brooch: an Irish emblem of status in its European context', in Hourihane (ed.), 211–47

2004. 'More thoughts on the wearing of brooches in early medieval Ireland', in Hourihane (ed.), 70–108

2005. 'A Viking Age brooch fragment from recent excavations at Temple Bar West, Dublin', in R. Bonk et al., *De Re Metallica: The Uses of Metal in the Middle Ages*, Aldershot, 63–80

Whitfield, N. and Graham-Campbell, J. 1992. 'A mount with Hiberno-Saxon animal ornament', *Trans Dumfries Galloway N.H.A.S.*, 3rd ser. 67: 9–27

Whittington, G. 1974–5. 'Placenames and the settlement pattern of dark age Scotland', *Proc. Soc. Ant. Scot.* 106: 99–110

Wilkinson, P. F. 1995. 'Excavations at Hen Gastell, Briton Ferry, West Glamorgan, 1991–92', *Medieval Archaeology* 39: 1–50

Williams, B. B. 1983. 'Early landscapes in County Antrim', in Reeves-Smith and Hammond (eds.), 233–46

1985. 'Excavations of a rath at Coolcran, Co. Fermanagh', *Ulster J. Archaeol.* 48: 69–80

Williams, B. and Yates, M. 1984. 'Excavations at Killylane, County Antrim', 47: 63–70

Williams, S. 1971. 'Tynron Doon, Dumfriesshire: a history of the site with notes on the finds, 1924–67', *Trans. Dumfries Galloway N.H.A.S.* 48: 106–20

Willmott, T. 1997. *Birdoswald: Excavations of a Roman Fort on Hadrian's Wall and its Successor Settlements, 1987–92* (= English Heritrage Arch. Rep. 14), London

2000. 'The late Roman transition at Birdoswald and on Hadrian's Wall', in T. Wilmott and P. Wilson (eds.), *The Late Roman Transition in the North* (= BAR Brit. Ser. 299), Oxford, 13–23

Wilson, D. M. 1964. *Anglo-Saxon Ornamental Metalwork 700–1100*, London

1993. *Excavation of a Romano-British villa at Wortley, Gloucestershire*, 9th Interim Rep., Keele

1995. *Excavation of a Romano-British villa at Wortley, Gloucestershire*, 11th Interim Rep., Keele

Wilson, D. M. and Blunt, C. E. 1961. 'The Trewhiddle hoard', *Archaeologia* 98: 75–122

Wilson, P. A. 1966. 'Romano-British and Welsh Christianity, continuity or discontinuity?', *Welsh History Review* 3: 5–21

Wood, I. 1987. 'The fall of the western Empire and the end of Roman Britain', *Britannia* 18: 251–62

Wood, J. 2003. 'The Orkney hood: an ancient re-cycled textile', in Downes and Ritchie (eds.), 171–5

Wooding, J. M. 1996. 'Cargoes in trade along the western seaboard', in Dark (ed.), 67–82

Woodward, A. and Leach, P. 1993. *The Uley Shrines: Excavation of a Ritual Complex on West Hill, Uley, Gloucestershire, 1977–9*, London

Woolf, A. 1998. 'Pictish matriliny reconsidered', *Innes Review* 49: 147–67

Wright, R. P. and Jackson, K. H. 1968. 'A late inscription from Wroxeter', *Antiq. J.* 48: 296–300

Yeoman, P. 1995. *Medieval Scotland*, London

Yeoman, P. and James, H. 1999. 'The Isle of May: St Ethernan revealed', *Current Archaeology* 161: 192–7

Young, A. 1955–6. 'Excavations at Dun Cuier, Isle of Barra', *Proc. Soc. Ant. Scot.* 89: 290–328

    1966. 'The sequence of Hebridean pottery', in Rivet (ed.), 45–58

Young, A. and Richardson, K. M. 1959–60. ''a Cheardach Mhor, Drimore, S. Uist', *Proc. Soc. Ant. Scot.* 93, 135–73

Youngs, S. (ed.) 1989. *The Work of Angels: Masterpieces of Celtic Metalwork, 6th – 9th Centuries AD*, London

    1993a. 'The Steeple Bumpstead boss', in Spearman and Higgit (eds.), 143–50

    1993b. 'Two medieval Celtic enamelled buckles from Leicestershire', *Trans. Leicester Arch. and Hist. Soc.* 67: 15–22

    1998. 'Medieval hanging-bowls from Wiltshire', *Wilts Arch. Mag.* 91: 35–41

Youngs, S. and Clark, J. (eds.) 1982. 'Medieval Britain in 1981', *Medieval Archaeology* 26: 164–227

Index of places

General index